Fodor's 2011

ALASKA PORTS OF CALL

Fodor's Travel Publications   New York, Toronto, London, Sydney, Auckland
www.fodors.com

D1056444

Be a Fodor's Correspondent

Your opinion matters. It matters to us. It matters to your fellow Fodor's travelers, too. And we'd like to hear it. In fact, we *need* to hear it.

When you share your experiences and opinions, you become an active member of the Fodor's community. That means we'll not only use your feedback to make our books better, but we'll publish your names and comments whenever possible. Throughout our guides, look for "Word of Mouth," excerpts of your unvarnished feedback.

Here's how you can help improve Fodor's for all of us.

Tell us when we're right. We rely on local writers to give you an insider's perspective. But our writers and staff editors—who are the best in the business—depend on you. Your positive feedback is a vote to renew our recommendations for the next edition.

Tell us when we're wrong. We're proud that we update most of our guides every year. But we're not perfect. Things change. Hotels cut services. Museums change hours. Charming cafés lose charm. If our writer didn't quite capture the essence of a place, tell us how you'd do it differently. If any of our descriptions are inaccurate or inadequate, we'll incorporate your changes in the next edition and will correct factual errors at fodors.com *immediately.*

Tell us what to include. You probably have had fantastic travel experiences that aren't yet in Fodor's. Why not share them with a community of like-minded travelers? Maybe you took an amazing shore excursion or chanced upon a fascinating Native art gallery or restaurant that you don't want to keep to yourself. Tell us why we should include it. And share your discoveries and experiences with everyone directly at fodors.com. Your input may lead us to add a new listing or highlight a place we cover with a "Highly Recommended" star or with our highest rating, "Fodor's Choice."

Give us your opinion instantly at our feedback center at www.fodors.com/feedback. You may also e-mail editors@fodors.com with the subject line "Alaska Ports of Call Editor." Or send your nominations, comments, and complaints by mail to Alaska Ports of Call Editor, Fodor's, 1745 Broadway, New York, NY 10019.

You and travelers like you are the heart of the Fodor's community. Make our community richer by sharing your experiences. Be a Fodor's correspondent.

Bon voyage!

Tim Jarrell, Publisher

FODOR'S ALASKA PORTS OF CALL 2011
Editor: Kelly Kealy

Editorial Contributors: Stephanie E. Butler, Heidi Leigh Johansen, Caroline Trefler, Eric B. Wechter
Writers: Teeka Ballas, Carissa Bluestone, Crai S. Bower, Jessica Bowman, Cedar Burnett, Linda Coffman, Carolyn B. Heller, Nick Horton, Heidi Leigh Johansen, Sue Kernaghan, Chris McBeath, Edward Readicker-Henderson, Tom Reale, Sarah Wyatt

Production Editor: Carrie Parker
Maps & Illustrations: David Lindroth, Mark Stroud, Moon Street Cartography, *cartographers;* Bob Blake, Rebecca Baer, *map editors;* William Wu, *information graphics*
Design: Fabrizio La Rocca, *creative director;* Guido Caroti, Siobhan O'Hare, *art directors;* Tina Malaney, Nora Rosansky, Chie Ushio, Jessica Walsh, Ann McBride, *designers;* Melanie Marin, *senior picture editor*
Cover Photo: (Cruise ship in College Fjord in Prince William Sound): Danny Lehman/ Corbis
Production Manager: Amanda Bullock

COPYRIGHT
Copyright © 2011 by Fodor's Travel, a division of Random House, Inc.

Fodor's is a registered trademark of Random House, Inc.

All rights reserved. Published in the United States by Fodor's Travel, a division of Random House, Inc., and in Canada by Random House of Canada, Limited, Toronto. Distributed by Random House, Inc., New York.

No maps, illustrations, or other portions of this book may be reproduced in any form without written permission from the publisher.

ISBN 978-1-4000-0495-9

ISSN 1520-0205

SPECIAL SALES
This book is available at special discounts for bulk purchases for sales promotions or premiums. Special editions, including personalized covers, excerpts of existing books, and corporate imprints, can be created in large quantities for special needs. For more information, write to Special Markets/Premium Sales, 1745 Broadway, MD 6-2, New York, New York 10019, or e-mail specialmarkets@randomhouse.com.

AN IMPORTANT TIP & AN INVITATION
Although all prices, opening times, and other details in this book are based on information supplied to us at press time, changes occur all the time in the travel world, and Fodor's cannot accept responsibility for facts that become outdated or for inadvertent errors or omissions. So **always confirm information when it matters,** especially if you're making a detour to visit a specific place. Your experiences—positive and negative— matter to us. If we have missed or misstated something, **please write to us.** We follow up on all suggestions. Contact the Alaska Ports of Call editor at editors@fodors.com or c/o Fodor's at 1745 Broadway, New York, NY 10019.

PRINTED IN SINGAPORE

10 9 8 7 6 5 4 3 2 1

CONTENTS

ABOUT
THIS BOOK

Choosing Your Cruise gives you the lowdown on the cruise lines and cruise ships that regularly ply the waters of Alaska. This section helps you sort through the various lines, ships, and itineraries available.

Ports of Embarkation gives you background on the most important ports for joining a cruise, including suggestions on where to stay and eat, and what you might want to do if you spend an extra day or two there before or after.

Ports of Call gives you our best advice on what to do in each major Alaska cruise port if you want to go your own way, as well as a run-down of our favorite shore excursions offered by most ships if you don't.

Sports and the Outdoors gives a description of each type of active excursion you can do, either with your cruise or independently. Within each section, we list the best places to go for each activity.

Disagree with any of our choices? Care to nominate a place or suggest that we rate one more highly? Visit our feedback center at www.fodors.com/feedback.

Budget Well
Hotel price categories from ¢ to $$$$ are defined in the opening pages of Chapter 2, restaurant price categories in the opening pages of chapters 2 and 3. For attractions, we always give standard adult admission fees; reductions are usually available for children, students, and senior citizens. Want to pay with plastic? **AE, D, DC, MC, V** following restaurant and hotel listings indicate whether American Express, Discover, Diners Club, MasterCard, and Visa are accepted.

Restaurants
Unless we state otherwise, restaurants are open for lunch and dinner daily. We mention dress only when there's a specific requirement and reservations only when they're essential or not accepted—it's always best to book ahead.

Hotels
Hotels have private bath, phone, TV, and air-conditioning and operate on the European Plan (aka EP, meaning without meals), unless we specify that they use the Continental Plan (CP, with a Continental breakfast), Breakfast Plan (BP, with a full breakfast), or Modified American Plan (MAP, with breakfast and dinner), or are all-inclusive (AI, including all meals

and most activities). We always list facilities but not whether you'll be charged an extra fee to use them, so when pricing accommodations, find out what's included.

Listings	
★	Fodor's Choice
★	Highly recommended
⊠	Physical address
♦	Directions or Map coordinates
⌂	Mailing address
☎	Telephone
📠	Fax
⊕	On the Web
✉	E-mail
💳	Admission fee
☉	Open/closed times
Ⓜ	Metro stations
⊟	Credit cards
Hotels & Restaurants	
🏨	Hotel
➥	Number of rooms
⟓	Facilities
⍥	Meal plans
✗	Restaurant
⟲	Reservations
🎩	Dress code
⟍	Smoking
🍷	BYOB
Outdoors	
🏌	Golf
⛺	Camping
Other	
☾	Family-friendly
⇨	See also
⊠	Branch address
☞	Take note

Experience Alaska Ports of Call

ALASKA PLANNER

What to Wear

When preparing for your Alaska cruise, remember this first rule of Alaskan thumb: be an onion. Never leave the ship without dressing in layers. Your first layer should be thin and airy so that if it gets warm your skin can breathe. Every layer over that, however, should aim to keep you warm and dry. In Alaska it is quite common for a hot and sunny day to abruptly change. For onboard dress, follow your cruise line's suggestions regarding what to bring for the evening or two you might need to wear something formal to dinner.

What to Pack

Don't forget your valid passport; American and Canadian citizens are now required to provide proof of citizenship regardless of whether their Alaska cruise is crossing international boundaries. Although disposable and small digital cameras are very handy for candid shots, they are not much good for catching wildlife from afar. A good zoom lens can be heavy, but can make all the difference. Even if you have a quality camera, pack binoculars for everyone. Be sure to take bug spray during the summer months, as the mosquitoes are large, plentiful, and fierce.

Getting to the Port

Most cruise-ship passengers fly to their port of embarkation. If you book your cruise far enough in advance, you'll be given the opportunity to purchase an air-and-sea package, which can save you money on your flight. With this option a uniformed cruise-line agent will meet you at the airport to smooth your way to the pier. Without the package you can still access the cruise's transfer service, but it might cost more than a cab or shuttle.

Boarding

The lines at check-in can be long (up to an hour of wait time), but some cruise lines provide snacks. You'll be issued a boarding card that doubles as your stateroom key and shipboard charge card. Either before you enter the check-in area or before proceeding to the ship, you and your hand luggage will pass through a security checkpoint. Once you're on board, you'll produce your boarding card once more before heading to your cabin. On a small-ship cruise, embarkation is much more relaxed and relatively line-free.

Restaurant Seating

Restaurant seating is a major consideration for most cruisers as they choose which line they'll travel with. Some cruise ships have traditional assigned dinner seatings, where you will choose between early or late seating and be assigned a table for the entire trip. Early seating is generally scheduled between 6 and 6:30 PM, while late seating can begin from 8:15 to 8:45 PM. Families with young children or older passengers often choose an early seating. Early diners are not encouraged to linger too long as the dining room needs to be prepared for the late seating, which is viewed by some passengers as more romantic and less rushed. Some lines offer open seating; you'll dine whenever you want within service hours and sit wherever you please. Still other cruise lines strike a balance of options with alternatives like à la carte restaurants and casual dinner menus in the buffet facilities.

Paying for Things on Board

Because cashless society prevails on cruise ships, during booking or check-in an imprint is made of your credit card or you place a cash deposit for use against your onboard charges. Most onboard expenditures are charged to your shipboard account (via a swipe of your key card) with your signature as verification, with the exception of casino gaming.

You'll get an itemized bill listing your purchases at the end of the voyage, and any discrepancies can be discussed at the purser's desk. To save time, check the balance of your shipboard account before the last day.

Will I Get Seasick?

Many first-time passengers are anxious about whether they'll be stricken by seasickness, but there is no way to tell until you actually sail. Modern vessels are equipped with stabilizers that eliminate much of the motion responsible for seasickness. On an Alaska cruise you will spend most of your time in calm, sheltered waters, so unless your cruise includes time out in the open sea (say, between San Francisco and Vancouver) you may not even feel the ship's movement—particularly if your ship is a megaliner. You may feel slightly more movement on a small ship, but not by much as these ships ply remote bays and coves that are even more sheltered than those traveled by regular cruise ships.

If you have a history of seasickness, don't book an inside cabin. For the terminally seasick, it will begin to resemble a moveable coffin in short order. If you do become seasick, you can use common drugs such as Dramamine and Bonine. Some people find anti-seasickness wristbands helpful; these apply gentle pressure to the wrist in lieu of drugs. Worn behind the ear, the Transderm Scop patch dispenses a continuous metered dose of medication, which is absorbed into the skin and enters the bloodstream. Apply the patch four hours before sailing and it will continue to be effective for three days.

On-Board Extras

- Cocktails: $4.50–$9
- Wine by the glass: $5.50–$9
- Beer: $5–$6
- Bottled water: $2.50–$4
- Specialty ice cream and coffee: $4–$6
- Laundry: $1–$4 per piece (where self-launder facilities are unavailable)
- Spa treatments: $100–$175
- Salon services: $30–$100
- Casino Gambling: 5 cents to $10 for slot machines; $5 and up for table games
- Bingo: $5–$10 per card for multiple games in each session

Keeping in Touch

Rates for your in-room direct-dial phone vary from $5 to as much as $15 *per minute*; most passengers reserve it for emergency use only. Some cruise ships are wired to act as cell towers, so depending on your provider and roaming charges, you might be able to somewhat-affordably use your device throughout your trip uninterrupted (though we encourage you not to—you're on vacation!). In addition to the 50¢–$1 per minute Internet fee, you might also need to pay a one-time connection charge, and the connection might be maddeningly slow. For each port, we list a less-expensive Internet option or two.

ALASKA TODAY

Politics

Alaska's politics and policies seem as wild as its hundreds of thousands of untamed acres. This is partly due to the fact that the largest state in the nation comes with a seemingly limitless supply of natural resources, and with them come conflict and controversy. Alaska's politics are thus saddled with a vast array of fiscal and environmental responsibilities, none of which are easily met. In 2008 and 2009 the state garnered national attention when former Governor Sarah Palin was nominated for vice president, Ted Stevens was convicted on corruption charges that were subsequently dismissed (but not before he lost his reelection campaign), and a slew of state legislators were convicted of bribery and corruption.

Gas and mining corporations have enormous influence on public policy in Alaska, but not without rivalry from environmentalists and subsistence advocates. An ongoing and highly publicized battle is over the proposed Pebble Mine project in Bristol Bay in Southwest Alaska. It would be the largest gold and copper mine in the world. Supporters of the mine claim it will bring much-needed jobs to the local native population. Opponents say it will irrevocably pollute the lakes, rivers, and bay, destroying the large fishing industry on which the local population relies.

Gaining national attention is the Arctic National Wildlife Refuge (ANWR), 19.2 million roadless acres supporting 45 species of land and marine mammals, 36 species of fish, and 180 species of birds. ANWR is in the northeast corner of the state and has been dubbed the Last Great Wilderness. The only way to get there is by small bush plane. Area 1002, 1.5 million acres along the refuge's coastal plain, has long been a subject of controversy, as it is thought to contain a large supply of oil.

From the Iditarod to cabin building, everything in Alaska is steeped in politics. This is inevitable, as there are more politicians per capita than police officers.

Economics

More than 75% of Alaska's revenue is derived from oil extraction. The state is also the nation's leader in commercial fishing, but ranks dead last in number of farms and farm products. There is very little manufacturing in the state. Thus, the cost of manufactured goods, produce, and other foodstuffs is considerably higher than in other states.

Because Alaska is predominantly comprised of rural villages, thousands of miles from any distribution center, the cost of living is relatively high. In Barrow, for instance, one can expect to pay $10 for a gallon of milk.

The Permanent Fund Dividend (PFD) is a sacred check that Alaskans receive once a year, and for many in the Bush it is quite literally a lifesaver. In 1977 the fund was created to receive 25% of Alaska's oil royalty income. It was designed to maintain a state income even after the reserves had been tapped out. Residents receive a check every October in amounts that vary from year to year, but are in the ballpark of $1,200. For many who live in the Bush, this annual check provides the funds they need to heat their homes in the winter.

Global Warming

Political discourse is heating up as global warming is becoming a frontline issue in Alaskan politics. Fewer and fewer people disagree that the glaciers and permafrost are melting; to Alaskans it's just a fact. It

is what to do about it that has politicians and constituents bickering.

Regardless of anyone's political persuasion, however, things are undeniably changing in Alaska. Icebergs are melting, and unfortunately for polar bears, that's where they live. In 2008 the Interior Department put polar bears on the protected species list; some environmentalists, however, believe that without addressing the causes of global warming, the designation will do little to help the bears.

As ocean temperatures rise, new migrations are starting to take effect. One unfortunate one, however, is the steady northward migration of the Humboldt giant squid. It is a voracious predator that travels in packs and is starting to be found as far north as Sitka. This could pose a serious threat to the salmon population and the fishing industry in general.

Warmer temperatures also mean new economic opportunities. As the Arctic ice melts, the region is becoming more accessible, which means there is greater possibility for more oil and gas exploration.

Many of the indigenous tribes in the Arctic region have already begun to adapt to the changes. Their hunting patterns have adjusted to the new migration times and routes of their game. Unfortunately permafrost, the frozen ground they live upon, is also melting. Centuries-old towns and villages are sinking, and the cost of possible relocation is rising into the billions of dollars.

The Arts

Visitors are often surprised to find that Alaska is filled with talented contemporary artists. For many Alaskans though, the long, dark winter is a great time to hunker down, season their craft, and prepare to sell their wares in the summer. Galleries, museums, and theaters all over the state feature local talent. During the summer months, weekend outdoor markets are also a great place to find local and native talent.

Sports

In a state of renegades, thrill seekers, and aficionados of extreme forms of entertainment, it is no wonder that the biggest sporting event occasionally requires a racer to permanently relinquish feeling in a finger or a foot. The Iditarod Trail Sled Dog Race, a 1,150-mi-long trek, is by far the most popular sporting event in Alaska. It began in 1973 in homage to the brave souls who ventured to Nome in 1925 to take medicine to villagers struck with one of the worst outbreaks of diphtheria ever recorded. Now more than 100 racers and their packs of canines converge on the ice and snow every year on the first Saturday in March to race from Anchorage to Nome. The sport is not without controversy though; mushers have come under scrutiny since several groups have made allegations of animal cruelty.

Although Alaskans from all over the state are passionate about their dog mushers, the most popular team sport is hockey. College hockey all over the state is big news, as are the Alaska Aces, the state minor-league team that feeds into the NHL's St. Louis Blues.

ALASKA PORTS OF CALL
TOP ATTRACTIONS

Skagway's Gold Rush Relics

(A) On deck at sailaway (cruise-speak for when you leave your port of embarkation), you might hear the musical theme from the John Wayne movie "North to Alaska" as a reminder that there was gold in them thar hills. Waves of fortune-seekers passed through Skagway during the gold rush of 1898, inflating the population of the small town on the northern end of Lynn Canal to more than 10,000. Today's White Pass and Yukon Railroad follows their trail from Skagway to the goldfields of the Klondike. The spirit of the gold rush lives on in town, with wooden sidewalks, horse-drawn carriages, and old-fashioned saloons that once also housed bordellos.

Glacier Bay

(B) With approximately 5,000 glaciers in Alaska it may seem peculiar that such a fuss is made about Glacier Bay, but part of its allure is the abundant wildlife,

including seals, bears, and even humpback whales. Another source of its mystique is its inaccessibility. Until 1870 it was frozen behind a wall of ice a mile high. Today, it's designated as a national park and only a limited number of permits per season are issued to the many cruise ships plying Alaska's coastal waters. If your cruise experience won't be complete without seeing Glacier Bay, choose your ship and itinerary with care.

Ketchikan's Frontier History

(C) Alaskans are a hardy breed and many still consider hunting and fishing an important part of everyday life. Ketchikan is almost a time capsule devoted to frontier living, offering the best salmon fishing possible, wilderness hikes, a hilarious lumberjack show that kids love, and the restored gold-rush-era Creek Street with buildings on pilings over a stream. Head to Creek Street for boutiques, eateries, and the infamous Dolly's House;

Dolly practiced the world's oldest profession and her home stands as a bawdy museum where period-costumed docents bid passersby to enter—for a price.

Whale-Watching

(D) Aside from an up-close encounter with a bear, humpback whale sightings are perhaps the most thrilling wildlife encounter to be had in Alaska. To spot whales, look for their blow—a waterspout that can rise 10 feet high. Whales typically blow several times before rising gently to reveal their hump backs for a few moments. Before they start a deep dive, when they might disappear for a few minutes or nearly half an hour, they may "wave" with their fluke (tail) in the air.

Flightseeing

(E) Much of the grandeur of Alaska can only be seen from the air, and flightseeing by small plane or helicopter delivers a view of otherwise inaccessible sights, such as Misty Fjords and expansive glacial ice fields. Helicopter excursions usually make a glacier landing where, depending on your tour, you might do some glacial ice-trekking or visit a dog-mushing camp to participate in a dogsled ride over the snow-covered glacier.

Denali National Park

(F) Anchored by North America's highest mountain, 20,320-foot Mt. McKinley, Denali is a must-see for cruisers who intend to visit Alaska only once and want a land-and-sea experience either before or after their north- or southbound cruise. Almost a million people a year enter the area by bus or train, making it Alaska's most visited wilderness area. Aside from the spectacular scenery, Denali is the place to see wildlife. It is home to 161 species of birds, 37 species of mammals, and at least 450 plant species. Look closely for bears, caribou, and the official state bird, the willow ptarmigan.

IF YOU LIKE

Glaciers

Every Alaska cruise includes a day of glacier viewing; it's practically a law. Tidewater glaciers—those that come right up to the water's edge—are known to rumble with a thunderous creak just before calving off icebergs with a showy splash.

Glacier Bay. Considered the best place to view glaciers, ships will most likely sidle up to Marjerie and Lamplugh glaciers during a typical nine-hour day spent in the bay; they'll only enter John Hopkins Glacier inlet in late season because sea lions are usually giving birth there the rest of the time. Cruise West is a good bet for a small-ship cruise with numerous Glacier Bay itineraries; Holland America Line and Princess Cruises are the two large ship lines with the most permits to enter.

Mendenhall Glacier. Known as "the drive-up glacier," Mendenhall glacier is one of Alaska's most accessible. Hop on the refurbished blue school bus pier-side in Juneau for an inexpensive 13-mi ride to the glacier. Park rangers are on duty at the U.S. Forest Service visitor center to answer any questions you might have after viewing the exhibits and video. To get even closer to the glacier, there is a ½-mi nature trail.

Tracy Arm, Sawyer Glacier. Waterfalls and craggy cliffs outline the long, narrow, ice-strewn Tracy Arm fjord that ships slowly creep through to reach Sawyer Glacier. Why are they creeping? Because Sawyer Glacier constantly sheds huge blocks of ice, and navigating the passage can be difficult. Depending on conditions you might not reach the glacier's face, but Tracy Arm is a good bet for iceberg photo ops.

People and Culture

Alaska's unique people and culture have been shaped by the region's history. Migrations over the Bering Land Bridge about 14,000 years ago were followed by millennia of settlement by dozens of culturally distinct Alaska Native peoples. Russian occupation followed in the 18th and 19th centuries, and that gave way to homesteaders after the eventual acquisition of the Alaska Territory by the U.S. from Russia for $7.2 million in 1867. Each wave of newcomers adds a layer of cultural identity to the region, most recently the gold fever of the early 20th century and Alaska's designation as the 49th state in 1959.

Alaska Natives. You won't find them living in igloos, though you might sail by some people tending their family's summer fish camps on remote stretches of shore. Alaska Natives share their heritage in centers such as Ketchikan's Saxman Native Village, where visitors can see the tribal house and a performance by dancers in the theater, and Totem Bight, a publicly accessible fish camp set in the rain forest with ceremonial clan house and totem poles.

Gold history. Alaska might have never made it to statehood without the Yukon Gold Rush of 1896 and the thousands of gold seekers who flooded the territory. Although there was no gold in Skagway, it became the jumping-off point for a journey on the Chilkoot Trail and possible riches. The quest for gold is illustrated here in the Klondike Gold Rush National Historical Park visitor center.

Living off the land. Many who choose to live in Alaska do so because they love being outside both for work and for play. Fishing, hunting, and logging have all played

a part in the area's commerce. You're unlikely to visit a working logging camp, but you can go salmon fishing, crab fishing, or pet sled dogs at a musher's camp.

Wildlife

Alaska really is where the wild things are. Although most creatures are abundant throughout the state, they are often elusive. To get close, consider a small-ship cruise, such as one with Lindblad, Cruise West, or American Safari. Some larger ships offer excursions that will get you close to the wildlife, too.

Bald Eagles. With a wingspan of 6 to 8 feet, these grand Alaska residents are often spotted soaring through the air in Glacier Bay and circling cruise ships docked in Juneau. When they swoop close to the water, you're likely to get a glimpse of them catching a fish for lunch.

Bears. Early in the Alaska cruising season, bears are likely to be scarce along the shoreline—they've just awakened from their annual hibernation. Late-season cruisers are more likely to spot them feeding near the water in preparation for their long winter's sleep.

Salmon. Fishermen are in luck almost any month during the Alaska cruise season. If you just want to get a look, many rivers and streams are so thick with salmon in late summer that you can almost walk across them. Just watch out for bears that might join you for lunch.

Whales. Beluga whales live along much of the coast, but you're more likely to see humpback whales in Alaska. To guarantee that you'll get more than just a glimpse of them off in the distance, take a whale-watching excursion in Juneau's Stephens Passage.

Dine and Drink

Cruise lines pride themselves on their cuisine and you'll find an abundant variety of food on hand, including regional Alaska favorites, but don't limit yourself to meals on board or you'll miss some authentic, and tasty, local dining and drinking experiences.

Salmon. Although Alaskan king crab legs may be offered only once, freshly caught Alaskan salmon will be a frequent menu item at restaurants in port and aboard every cruise ship. Holland American Line offers a different version every night.

Baked Alaska. Complete with parading waiters and flaming meringue, baked alaska has long been a festive cruise-ship tradition. Presented with a flourish, it's a staple that Holland America raises to new heights by serving sprinkled with edible gold.

Beer. Mention beer during your Alaska cruise and the Alaskan Amber brand is sure to enter the conversation. A short cab ride from downtown Juneau, Alaskan Brewing Co. offers complimentary tours and samples for guests over the age of 21 at its tasting bar.

Duck Fart. No visit to Alaska is complete without a trip to an authentic saloon to sample the state drink, a Duck Fart. Don't let the name put you off—even locals order this concoction of Kahlúa, Bailey's Irish Cream, and Crown Royal.

ALASKA'S HISTORY

The First People

No one knows when humans first began living in the northwest corner of the North American continent, and it is still a subject of great controversy and debate. One popular theory is that 12,000 years ago humans followed the eastern migration of Ice Age mammals over the Bering Land Bridge, a 1,000-mi-wide stretch of land that connected present-day Alaska to Siberia. To date, however, the oldest human remains found in Alaska are 10,300 years old, believed to be an ancestor of the Tlingit tribe.

No matter when humans first arrived, by 1750 there were 57,300 native peoples living in Russian Alaska, including Aleuts, Alutiiqs, Yup'iks, Inupiats, Athabascan, Tlingit, and Haida. Today there are more than 100,000 American Indian and Alaska Native persons living in Alaska.

Russians in Alaska

Alaska was a late bloomer on the world scene. It wasn't until 1741 that Danish navigator Vitus Bering, under Russian rule, made the Alaska region known to the world. Bering died before he could ever explore the continent or return to Russia.

Politically speaking, Russia imposed itself on Alaska in varying degrees. It was the arrival of the *promyshlenniki,* or fur hunters, that had the biggest impact on the native cultures. By most accounts, the hunters were illiterate, quarrelsome, hard-drinking, and virtually out of control. They penetrated the Aleutian Chain and made themselves masters of the islands and their inhabitants, the Aleuts. Several times the Natives revolted; their attempts were squelched, and they were brutalized.

By 1790 the small fur traders were replaced by large Russian companies. Siberian fur trader Aleksandr Andreyevich Baranov became manager of a fur-trading company and director of a settlement on Kodiak Island in 1791. He essentially governed all Russian activities in North America until 1818, when he was ordered back to Russia. Word was spreading to the Russian government that foreigners, particularly Americans, were gaining a disproportionate share of the Alaskan market. The Russian Navy was ordered to assume control of Alaska, and by 1821 it had barred all foreign ships from entering Alaskan waters. Russia created new policies forbidding any trade with non-Russians and requiring that the colonies be supplied solely by Russian ships.

The 1853 Crimean War between Imperial Russia and Britain and France put a great financial burden on Russia. It fiscally behooved the country to sell Russian Alaska. In 1867, under a treaty signed by U.S. Secretary of State William H. Seward, Alaska was sold to the United States for $7.2 million. On October 18, 1867, the territory officially changed hands. Newspapers around the nation hailed the purchase of Alaska as "Seward's Folly." Within 30 years, however, one of the biggest gold strikes in the world would bring hundreds of thousands of people to this U.S. territory.

The Gold Rush

The great Klondike gold discoveries of 1896 gained the attention of men around the nation. Due to the Depression of 1893, the need for food, money, and hope sparked a gold fever unmatched in history. Men and women alike clamored for information about Alaska, not realizing

that the Klondike was in the Yukon Territory of Canada. Perhaps if they'd known their geography Alaska would never have become the state that it is now.

The most popular route for the gold stampeders was to go entirely by water. It wasn't cheaper, but it was far easier than taking the inland route. They would start in either San Francisco or Seattle, buy passage on a steamship, and disembark more than 1,000 nautical mi later in Skagway, Alaska. No gold was in Skagway, but overnight it became a city of 20,000 miners. Gold-seekers used it as a place to negotiate and get ready for the only part of their journey that would be traversed on foot. The Chilkoot Trail was 35 challenging miles that were too rugged for pack horses. The hardest part of the journey was the climb to the summit, Chilkoot Pass. This climb was known as the Golden Staircase, a 45-degree-angle hike of nearly .75 mi. Chilkoot Pass was the gateway to Canada and the point at which the Canadian government required each person entering the territory to have at least a year's supply (approximately one ton) of food. This is partially why it took most stampeders one to three months to complete this 35-mi stretch. Once into Canada, they built boats and floated the remaining 600 mi to Dawson City, where the gold rush was taking place. By 1899 the Yukon Gold Rush was over, however, and the population of Skagway shrank dramatically.

Alaska experienced its own gold strike in Nome, on the Seward Peninsula, in 1898. The fever didn't actually hit until 1900, but because it did, gold mining all over Alaska began to get national attention.

World War II

In 1942, after the United States entered the war, the War Production Board deemed gold mining nonessential to the war effort, and forced gold mining all over the country to come to a halt. Despite the closing of mines, World War II was financially beneficial to parts of Alaska. Numerous bases and ports were strategically built around the state, and to supply them the Alaska Highway was created.

The only time Alaska had any direct involvement with the war was in June 1942, when the Japanese attacked Attu and Kiska islands in the Aleutian Chain. The attack has been recorded in history as an "incident," but it had a great impact on many lives; a few hundred casualties occurred due to friendly fire, and nearly a thousand inhabitants of the area were relocated.

Statehood

On January 3, 1959, "Seward's Folly" became the 49th state in the nation—more than 100 years after Seward first visited. Statehood gave Alaska national appeal. A mass of investors, bold entrepreneurs, tourists, and land grabbers began to arrive. It is still a new state, far from direct scrutiny by the rest of the nation. With a constantly growing, competitive industry of oil and other natural resources, Alaska has made an identity for itself that resembles that of no other state in the nation. It boasts the second-highest production of gas and oil in the country, is twice the size of the second-largest state, and has millions of lakes, minimal pollution, and endless possibilities.

FLORA AND FAUNA OF ALASKA

FAUNA

(A) Arctic Ground Squirrel (*Spermophilus parryii*): These yellowish-brown, gray-flecked rodents are among Alaska's most common and widespread mammals. Ground squirrels are known for their loud, persistent chatter. They may often be seen standing above their tundra den sites, watching for grizzlies, golden eagles, and weasels.

(B) Arctic Tern (*Sterna paradisaea*): These are the world's long-distance flying champs; some members of their species make annual migratory flights between the high Arctic and the Antarctic. Sleekly beautiful, the bird has a black cap and striking blood-red bill and feet. They often can be seen looking for small fish in ponds and coastal marshes.

(C) Bald Eagle (*Haliaeetus leucocephalus*): With a wingspan of six to eight feet, these grand Alaska residents are primarily fish eaters, but they will also take birds or small mammals when the opportunity presents itself. The world's largest gathering of bald eagles occurs in Southeast Alaska each winter, along the Chilkat River near Haines.

(D) Beluga Whale (*Dephinapterus leucas*): Belugas are gray at birth, bluish gray as adolescents, and white as adults (the word *byelukha* is Russian for "white"). Though they seem to favor fish, belugas' diet includes more than 100 different species, from crabs to squid. They live along much of the coast, from the Beaufort Sea to the Gulf of Alaska.

(E) Black-capped Chickadee (*Parus atricapillus*): This songbird is one of Alaska's most common residents. As with two close relatives, the chestnut-backed and boreal chickadees, the black-cap gets through the winters by lowering its body temperature at night and shivering through the long hours of darkness.

(F) Caribou (*Rangifer tarandus*): Sometimes called the "nomads of the north," caribou are long-distance wandering mammals. They are also the most abundant of the state's large mammals; in fact, there are more caribou in Alaska than people! The Western Arctic Caribou Herd numbers more than 400,000, while the Porcupine Caribou Herd has ranged between 110,000 and 180,000 over the past decades. Another bit of caribou trivia: they are the only members of the deer family in which both sexes grow antlers. Those of bulls may grow up to 5½ feet long with a span of up to 3 feet.

(G) Common Loon (*Gavia immer*): Some sounds seem to be the essence of wilderness: the howl of the wolf, the hooting of the owl, and the cry of the loon. The common loon is one of five *Gavia* species to inhabit Alaska (the others are the Arctic, Pacific, red-throated, and yellow-billed). Common loons are primarily fish eaters.

Excellent swimmers, they are able to stay submerged for up to three minutes.

(H) Common Raven (*Corvus corax*): A popular character in Alaska Native stories, the raven is indigenous culture is both creator and trickster. Entirely black, with a wedge-shaped tail and a heavy bill that helps distinguish it from crows, the raven is Alaska's most widespread avian resident.

(I) Common Redpoll (*Carduelis flammea*): Slightly larger than the chickadee, the common redpoll and its close cousin, the hoary redpoll (*Carduelis hornemanni*), are among the few birds to inhabit Alaska's Interior year-round. Though it looks a bit like a sparrow, this red-capped, black-bibbed songbird is a member of the finch family.

FLORA AND FAUNA OF ALASKA

Dall Sheep (*Ovis dalli dalli*): One of four wild sheep to inhabit North America, the white Dall is the only one to reside within Alaska. Residents of high alpine areas, the sheep live in mountain chains from the St. Elias Range to the Brooks Range. Though both sexes grow horns, those of females are short spikes, while males grow grand curls that are "status symbols" displayed during mating season.

Dolly Varden (*Salvelinus malma*): This sleek, flashy fish inhabits lakes and streams throughout Alaska's coastal regions. A member of the char family, it was named after a character in Charles Dickens's novel *Barnaby Rudge* because the brightly colored spots on its sides resemble Miss Dolly Varden's pink-spotted dress and hat. Some members of the species remain in freshwater all their life, while sea-run dollies may live in the ocean for two to five years before returning to spawn.

Golden Eagle (*Aquila chrysaetos*): With a wingspan of up to 7½ feet, this inland bird can often be spotted spiraling high in the sky, riding thermals. The bird usually nests on cliff faces and feeds upon small mammals and ptarmigan. The plumage of adult birds is entirely dark, except for a golden head. These migratory eagles spend their winters as far away as Kansas and New Mexico.

Great Horned Owl (*Bubo virginianus*): The best-known of Alaska's several species of owls, and one whose call is a familiar one here. It is a large owl with prominent ear tufts and a white throat with barred markings. Residing in forests from Southeast Alaska to the Interior, it preys on squirrels, hares, grouse, and other birds.

Harbor Seal (*Phoca vitulina*): Inhabiting shallow marine waters and estuaries along much of Alaska's southern coast, harbor seals may survive up to 30 years in the wild, on a diet of fish, squid, octopus, and shrimp. They, in turn, may be eaten or killed by orcas, sea lions, or humans. Solitary in the water, harbor seals love company on land, and will gather in large colonies. They weigh up to 250 pounds and range in color from black to white.

Hermit Thrush (*Catharus guttatus*): Some Alaskans argue that there is no northern song more beautiful than the flutelike warbling of the hermit thrush and its close relative, the Swainson's thrush (*Catharus ustulatus*). The two birds are difficult to tell apart, except for their songs, the hermit's reddish brown tail, and the color of their eye rings. Among the many songbird migrants to visit Alaska each spring, they begin singing in May while seeking mates and defending territories in forested regions of southern and central Alaska.

Horned Puffin (*Fratercula corniculata*): Named for the black, fleshy projections above each eye, horned puffins are favorites among birders. Included in the group of diving seabirds known as alcids, puffins spend most of their life on water, coming to land only for nesting. They are expert swimmers, using their wings to "fly" underwater and their webbed feet as rudders. Horned puffins have large orange-red and yellow bills. A close relative, the tufted puffin (*Fratercula cirrhata*) is named for its yellow ear tufts.

Lynx (*Lynx canadensis*): The lynx is the only wild cat to inhabit Alaska. It's a secretive animal that depends on stealth and quickness. It may kill birds, squirrels, and mice, but the cat's primary prey is the snowshoe hare (*Lepus americanus*), particularly in winter; its population numbers closely follow those of the

Top: Dall Sheep

hare's boom-bust cycles. Large feet and a light body help the lynx run through deep snowpack.

Moose (*Alces alces gigas*): The moose is the largest member of the deer family, the largest bulls standing 7 feet tall at the shoulders and weighing up to 1,600 pounds. The peak of breeding occurs in late September. Females give birth to calves in late May and early June; twins are the norm. Bulls enter the rut in September, the most dominant engaging in brutal fights. Though most commonly residents of woodlands, some moose live in or just outside Alaska's cities.

Mountain Goat (*Oreamnos americanus*): Sometimes confused with Dall sheep, mountain goats inhabit Alaska's coastal mountains. As adults, both males and females have sharp-pointed horns that are short and black (sheep have buff-colored horns). They also have massive chests and comparatively small hindquarters, plus bearded chins.

Musk Ox (*Ovibos moschatus*): The musk ox is considered an Ice Age relic that survived into the present at least partly because of a defensive tactic: they stand side by side and form rings to fend off predators such as grizzlies and wolves. Unfortunately for the species, that tactic didn't work very well against humans armed with guns. Alaska's last native musk oxen were killed in 1865. Musk oxen from Greenland were reintroduced here in 1930; they now reside on Nunivak Island, the North Slope of the Brooks Range, and in the Interior. The animal's most notable physical feature is its long guard hairs, which form "skirts" that nearly reach the ground. Inupiats called the musk ox *oom-ingmak*, meaning "bearded one." Beneath those coarser hairs is fine underfur called

qiviut, which can be woven into warm clothing.

Pacific Halibut (*Hippoglossus stenolepis*): The halibut is the largest of the flatfish to inhabit Alaska's coastal waters, with females weighing up to 500 pounds. Long-lived "grandmother" halibut may survive 40 years or more, producing millions of eggs each year. Bottom dwellers that feed on fish, crabs, clams, and squid, they range from the Panhandle to Norton Sound. Young halibut generally stay near shore, but older fish have been found at depths of 3,600 feet.

Pacific Salmon (*Oncorhynchus*): Five species of Pacific salmon spawn in Alaska's waters, including the king, silver, sockeye, pink, and chum. Hundreds of millions of salmon return to the state's streams and lakes each summer and fall, after spending much of their lives in saltwater. They form the backbone of Alaska's fishing industry and draw sportfishers from around the world.

Rainbow Trout (*Salmo gairdneri*): A favorite of anglers, the rainbow trout inhabits streams and lakes in Alaska's coastal regions. The Bristol Bay region is best known for large 'bows, perhaps because of its huge returns of salmon. Rainbows feed heavily on salmon eggs as well as the deteriorating flesh of spawned-out salmon. Sea-run rainbows, or steelhead, grow even larger after years spent feeding in ocean waters. The state record for steelhead/rainbow trout is 42 pounds, 3 ounces.

Top left: Lynx
Top right: Moose

FLORA AND FAUNA OF ALASKA

(A) Red fox (*Vulpes vulpes*): Though it's called the red fox, this species actually has four color phases: red, silver, black, and cross (with a cross pattern on the back and shoulders). An able hunter, the red fox preys primarily on voles and mice, but will also eat hares, squirrels, birds, insects, and berries.

(B) Sandhill crane (*Grus canadensis*): The sandhill's call has been described as "something between a French horn and a squeaky barn door." Though others may dispute that description, few would disagree that the crane's calls have a prehistoric sound. And, in fact, scientists say the species has changed little in the 9 million years since its earliest recorded fossils. Sandhills are the tallest birds to inhabit Alaska; their wingspan reaches up to 7 feet. The gray plumage of adults is set off by a bright red crown. Like geese, they fly in Vs during migratory journeys.

(C) Sea otter (*Enhydra lutris*): Sea otters don't depend on blubber to stay warm. Instead, hair trapped in their dense fur keeps their skin dry. Beneath their outer hairs, the underfur ranges in density from 170,000 to one million hairs per square inch. Not surprisingly, the otter takes good care of its coat, spending much of every day grooming. Otters also spend a lot of time eating. In one study, researchers found that adult otters consumed 14 crabs a day, equaling about one-fourth of their body weight.

(D) Sitka blacktailed deer (*Odocoileus hemionus sitkensis*): The Panhandle's rain forest is the primary home of this deer, though it has been transplanted to Prince William Sound and Kodiak. Dark gray in winter and reddish brown in summer, it's stockier than the whitetails found in the Lower 48. The deer stay at lower elevations during the snowy months of win-

ter, then move up to alpine meadows in summer.

(E) Snowy owl (*Nyctea scandiaca*): Inhabiting the open coastal tundra, the snowy owl is found from the western Aleutian Islands to the Arctic. Adults are largely white (though females have scattered light brown spots) and immature birds are heavily marked with brown. Their numbers rise and fall with swings in the population of lemmings, their primary prey. Rather than hoots, the snowy emits loud croaks and whistles.

(F) Steller sea lion (*Eumetopias jubatus*): Its ability—and tendency—to roar is what gives the sea lion its name. Because they can rotate their rear flippers and lift their bellies off the ground, sea lions can get around on land much more easily than seals can. They are also much larger, the males reaching up to 9 feet and weighing up to 1,500 pounds. They feed primarily on fish, but will also eat sea otters

and seals. They have been designated an endangered species because their populations north of the Panhandle have suffered huge declines.

(G) Walrus (*Odobenus rosmarus*): The walrus's ivory tusks can be dangerous weapons; there are stories of walruses killing polar bears when attacked. Weighing up to 2 tons, the walrus's primary food includes clams, mussels, snails, crabs, and shrimp.

(H) Willow ptarmigan (*Lagopus lagopus*): One of three species of ptarmigan (the others are the rock and the white-tailed), the willow is the most widespread. It is also Alaska's state bird. It tends to live in willow thickets, where it feeds and hides from predators. Aggressively protective parents, willow ptarmigan have been known to attack humans to defend their young.

FLORA AND FAUNA OF ALASKA

Wolf (*Canis lupus*): The largest and most majestic of the Far North's wild canines, wolves roam throughout all of mainland Alaska. They form close-knit family packs, which may range from a few animals to more than 30. Packs hunt a variety of prey, from small mammals and birds to caribou, moose, and Dall sheep. They communicate with each other through body language, barks, and howls.

Wolverine (*Gulo gulo*): Consider yourself lucky if you see a wolverine, because they are among the most secretive animals of the North. They are also fierce predators, with enormous strength and endurance. Denali biologists once reported seeing a wolverine drag a Dall sheep carcass more than 2 mi; an impressive feat, since the sheep likely weighed four times what the wolverine did. They have been known to run 40 MPH through snow when chased by hunters. Though they look a lot like bears and have the ferocity of a grizzly, wolverines are in fact the largest members of the weasel family.

Wood frog (*Rana sylvatica*): One of the few amphibians to inhabit Alaska, and the only one to live north of the Panhandle, these frogs range as far north as the Arctic, surviving winters through the help of a biochemical change that keeps them in a suspended state while frozen. Come spring, the bodies revive after thawing. Though they mate and lay eggs in water, wood frogs spend most of their lives on land.

FLORA

Balsam poplar and black cottonwood (*Populus balsamifera* and *Populus trichocarpa*): These two closely related species sometimes interbreed and are difficult, if not impossible, to tell apart. Mature trees of both species have gray bark that is rough and deeply furrowed. In midsummer they produce cottony seedpods. They also have large, shiny, arrowhead-shaped leaves.

Birch (*Betula*): Ranging from Kodiak Island to the Brooks Range, birch trees are important members of Alaska's boreal forests. Deciduous trees that prefer well-drained soils, they have white bark and green heart-to-diamond-shaped leaves with sharp points and toothed edges. One species, the paper birch (*Betula papyrifera*), is easily distinguished by its peeling, paperlike bark.

Blueberry (*Vaccinium*): A favorite of berry pickers, blueberries are found throughout Alaska, except for the farthest northern reaches of the Arctic. They come in a variety of forms, including head-high forest bushes and sprawling tundra mats. Pink, bell-shaped flowers bloom in spring, and dark blue to almost black fruits begin to ripen in July or August, depending on the locale.

Cow parsnip (*Heracleum lanatum*): Also known to some as Indian celery, cow parsnip resides in open forests and meadows. The plant may grow several feet high, with dull green leaves the size of dinner plates; thick, hairy, hollow stalks; and clusters of white flowers. Anyone who harvests—or walks among—this species must take great care. Oils on the stalks, in combination with sunlight, can produce severe skin blistering.

Devil's club (*Echinopanax horridum*): This is a prickly shrub that may grow 4 to 8 feet high and forms dense, spiny thickets in forests ranging from the Panhandle to South Central. Hikers need to be wary of this plant: its large, maple-like leaves

Top: Wood frog

(which can be a foot or more across) have spines, and needles cover its pale brown trunk. In late summer, black bears enjoy its bright red berries.

Salmonberry (*Rubus spectabilis*): The salmonberry canes, on which the leaves and fruits grow, may reach 7 feet tall; they grow in dense thickets. The juicy raspberry-like fruits may be either orange or red at maturity; the time of ripening is late June through August.

Spruce (*Picea*): Three species of spruce grow in Alaska. Sitka spruce (*Picea sitchensis*) is an important member of coastal rain-forest communities; white spruce (*Picea glauca*) prefers dry, well-drained soils in boreal forests that stretch from South Central to the Arctic; black spruce (*Picea mariana*) thrives in wet, boggy areas.

Tall fireweed (*Epilobium angustifolium*): The fireweed is among the first plants to reinhabit burn areas and, in the proper conditions, it grows well. Found throughout much of Alaska, it's a beautiful plant, with fuchsia flowers that bloom from the bottom to the top of stalks; it's said that the final opening of flowers is a sign that winter is only weeks away. Spring fireweed shoots can be eaten raw or steamed, and its blossoms can be added to salads. A related species is dwarf fireweed (*Epilobium latifolium*); also known as "river beauty," it is shorter and bushier.

Wild prickly rose (*Rosa acicularis*): Serrated leaves grow on prickly spines, and fragrant five-petal flowers begin blooming in late spring. The flowers vary from light pink to dark red. Appearing in late summer and fall, bright red rose hips rich in vitamin C can be harvested for jellies, soups, or pie.

IN THE WILD

For our suggestions for best wildlife experiences, see Enjoying Alaska's Wildlife in Chapter 5.

Willow (*Salix*): An estimated three dozen species of willow grow in Alaska. Some, like the felt-leaf willow (*Salix alaxensis*), may reach tree size; others form thickets; still others, like the Arctic willow (*Salix arctica*), hug the ground in alpine terrain. They often grow thickest in the subalpine zone between forest and tundra. Whatever the size, willows produce soft "catkins" (pussy willows), which are actually columns of densely packed flowers without petals.

—By Bill Sherwonit

Top left: Wolf
Top right: Wolverine

DID YOU KNOW?

Whether your small ship picks its way carefully through icebergs to the face of Endicott Arm's Dawes Glacier or your large ship organizes a flotilla of excursion vessels to the face of Tracy Arm's Sawyer Glacier, keep your eyes out for mama and baby harbor seals lounging on icebergs during pupping season (early summer).

SAFARI QUEST

Choosing Your Cruise

WORD OF MOUTH

"We were on the Zuiderdam 2 years ago, and thought it was great. We had a verandah and I wouldn't want to cruise otherwise. Consider the inland tour to Fairbanks."

—Aristotle

By Linda Coffman

Alaska is one of cruising's showcase destinations. Itineraries give passengers more choices than ever before—from traditional loop cruises of the Inside Passage, round-trips from Vancouver or Seattle, to one-way Inside Passage–Gulf of Alaska cruises.

Though Alaska cruises have generally attracted an older-passenger demographic, more young people and families are setting sail for the 49th state and children are a common sight aboard ship. Cruise lines have responded with youth programs and some discounted shore excursions for youngsters under 12. Shore excursions have become more active, too, often incorporating activities families can enjoy together, such as bicycling, kayaking, and hiking. Many lines also offer pre- or post-cruise land tours as an optional package trip, and onboard entertainment and learning programs are extensive. Most also hire native speakers, naturalists, or local personalities to lead discussions stimulated by the local environment.

Cruise ships may seem like floating resorts, but you can't check out and go elsewhere if you don't like your ship. The one you choose will be your home—it determines the type of accommodations you have, what kind of food you eat, what style of entertainment you see, and even the destinations you visit. If you don't enjoy your ship, you probably won't enjoy your cruise. That is why the most important choice you'll make when booking a cruise is the combined selection of cruise line and cruise ship.

CRUISING IN ALASKA

Which cruise is right for you depends on numerous factors, notably your budget, the size and style of ship you choose, and the itinerary.

ITINERARIES

Cruise ships typically follow one of two itineraries in Alaska: round-trip Inside Passage loops and one-way Inside Passage–Gulf of Alaska cruises. Itineraries are usually seven days, though some lines offer longer trips. ■ TIP➔ Keep in mind that the landscape along the Inside Passage changes dramatically over the course of the summer. In May and June, you'll see snowcapped mountains and dramatic waterfalls from snowmelt cascading down the cliff faces, but by July and August most of the snow and some waterfalls will be gone.

The most popular Alaskan ports of call are Haines, Juneau, Skagway, Ketchikan, and Sitka. Lesser-known ports in British Columbia, such as Victoria and the charming fishing port of Prince Rupert, have begun to see more cruise traffic.

Small ships typically sail within Alaska, setting sail from Juneau or other Alaskan ports, stopping at the popular ports as well as smaller, less visited villages. Some expedition vessels focus on remote beaches and fjords, with few, if any, port calls.

ROUND-TRIP INSIDE PASSAGE LOOPS

A seven-day cruise typically starts and finishes in Vancouver, British Columbia, or Seattle, Washington. The first and last days are spent at sea, traveling to and from Alaska along the mountainous coast of British Columbia. Once in Alaska, most ships call at a different port on each of four days, and reserve one day for cruising in or near Glacier Bay National Park or another glacier-rich fjord.

ONE-WAY INSIDE PASSAGE–GULF OF ALASKA ITINERARIES

These cruises depart from Vancouver, Seattle, or, occasionally, San Francisco or Los Angeles, and finish at Seward or Whittier, the seaports for Anchorage (or vice versa). They're a good choice if you want to explore Alaska by land, either before or after your cruise. For this itinerary, you'll need to fly into and out of different cities (into Vancouver and out of Anchorage, for example), which can be pricier than round-trip airfare to and from the same city.

SMALL-SHIP ALASKA-ONLY ITINERARIES

Most small ships and yachts home port in Juneau or other Alaskan ports and offer a variety of one-way and round-trip cruises entirely within Alaska. A typical small-ship cruise is a seven-day, one way or round-trip from Juneau, stopping at several Inside Passage ports—including smaller ports skipped by large cruise ships.

SMALL-SHIP INSIDE PASSAGE REPOSITIONING CRUISES

Alaska's small cruise ships and yachts are based in Juneau throughout the summer. In September they sail back to their winter homes in the Pacific Northwest; in May they return to Alaska via the Inside Passage. These trips are usually about 11 days and are often heavily discounted, because they take place during the shoulder season.

OTHER ITINERARIES

Although mainstream lines stick to the popular seven-day Alaskan itineraries, some smaller excursion lines add more exotic options. Cruise West, for example, offers voyages across the Bering Sea to Japan and Asia. You can also create your own itinerary by taking an Alaska Marine Highway System ferry to ports of your choosing.

FERRY TRAVEL

The cruise-ship season is over by October, but for independent, off-season ferry travel November is the best month. After the stormy month of October, it's still relatively warm on the Inside Passage (temperatures will average about 40°F), and it's a good month for wildlife-watching. In particular, humpback whales are abundant off Sitka, and bald eagles congregate by the thousands near Haines.

> **TIP**
>
> Although most other kinds of travel are booked over the Internet nowadays, cruises are a different story. Your best bet is still to work with a travel agent who specializes in cruises. Agents with strong relationships with the lines have a much better chance of getting you the cabin you want, and possibly even extras.

CRUISE TOURS

Most cruise lines offer the option of independent, hosted, or fully escorted land tours before or after your cruise. Independent tours give you a preplanned itinerary with confirmed hotel and transportation arrangements, but you're free to follow your interests in each town. Hosted tours are similar, but tour-company representatives are available along the route for assistance. On fully escorted tours you travel with a group, led by a tour director. Activities are preplanned (and typically prepaid), so you have a good idea of how much your trip will cost (not counting meals and incidentals) before departure. Most lines offer cruise tour itineraries that include a ride aboard the Alaska Railroad.

Running between Anchorage, Denali National Park, and Fairbanks are Holland America Line's *McKinley Explorer*, Princess Tours' *Denali Express* and *McKinley Express*, and Royal Caribbean's *Wilderness Express*, which offer unobstructed views of the passing terrain and wildlife from private glass-domed railcars. Princess Cruises and Holland America Line have the most extensive Alaska cruise tours, owning and operating their own coaches, railcars, and lodges.

In addition to rail trips to Denali, Holland America offers tours into the Yukon, as well as river cruises on the Yukon River. Princess's cruise tours include trips to the Yukon and the Kenai Peninsula. Both lines offer land excursions across the Arctic Circle to Prudhoe Bay. Several cruise lines also offer pre- and post-cruise tours of the Canadian Rockies. Of the traditional cruise-ship fleets, Carnival Cruise Lines, Norwegian Cruise Line, Disney Cruise Line, and Crystal Cruises do not currently offer cruise-tour packages in Alaska. Many cruise lines also offer pre- or post-cruise hotel and sightseeing packages in Vancouver, Seattle, or Anchorage lasting one to three days.

Cabin Cruising

INSIDE CABINS

An inside cabin is just that: a stateroom that's inside the ship with no window. These are always the least expensive cabins and are ideal for passengers who would rather spend on excursions than on upgraded accommodations. Inside cabins are generally as spacious as outside cabins, and decor and amenities are similar. Many ships locate cabins accommodating three or more passengers on the inside. ■TIP➔ For passengers who want a very dark room for sleeping, an inside cabin is ideal.

OUTSIDE CABINS

Outside cabins have either a picture window or porthole. To give the illusion of more space, these cabins might rely on the generous use of mirrors. Outside cabins are the better choice for those prone to motion sickness. ■TIP➔ Check to make sure your view of the sea is not obstructed by a lifeboat. The ship's deck plan will help you figure it out.

BALCONY CABINS

A balcony—or veranda—cabin is an outside cabin with floor-to-ceiling glass doors that open onto a private deck. Balconies are sometimes cut out of the cabin's square footage (depending on the ship). ■TIP➔ If you have small children, a veranda cabin isn't the best choice. Accidents can happen, even on balconies with solid barriers beneath the railing.

SUITES

Suites are the most lavish accommodations. Although they're always larger than regular cabins, they don't always have separate rooms for sleeping. The most expansive (and expensive) have large living rooms and separate bedrooms and may also have huge private outdoor sundecks with hot tubs and dining areas.

SMALL SHIP LINES

Most small-ship lines offer hotel add-ons, but not land tours. The exception is Cruise West, which offers fully escorted tours by rail and bus from Anchorage to Denali and Fairbanks.

DO-IT-YOURSELF LAND SEGMENTS

Independent travel by rental car or RV before or after a cruise is another option. Passengers generally begin or end their cruise in Anchorage, the most practical port city to use as a base for exploring Alaska. Almost any type of car or recreational vehicle can be rented here.

WHEN TO GO

Cruise season runs from mid-May to late September. The most popular sailing dates are from late June through August, when warm days are apt to be most plentiful. In spring, wildflowers are abundant, and you'll likely see more wildlife along the shore because the animals haven't yet migrated to higher elevations. May and June are traditionally drier than July and August. Alaska's early fall brings the splendor of autumn hues and the first snowfalls in the mountains. Animals return to low ground, and shorter days bring the possibility of seeing the northern lights.

Before You Book

If you've decided to use a travel agent, ask yourself these 10 simple questions, and you'll be better prepared to help the agent do his or her job.

1. Who will be going on the cruise?

2. What can you afford to spend for the entire trip?

3. Where would you like to go?

4. How much vacation time do you have?

5. When can you get away?

6. What are your interests?

7. Do you prefer a casual or structured vacation?

8. What kind of accommodations do you want?

9. What are your dining preferences?

10. How will you get to the embarkation port?

Daytime temperatures in May, June, and September are in the 50s and 60s. July and August averages are in the 60s and 70s, with occasional days in the 80s. Cruising in the low and shoulder seasons provides other advantages besides discounted fares: availability of ships and particular cabins is greater, and ports are almost completely free of tourists.

BOOKING YOUR CRUISE

As a rule, the majority of cruisers plan their trips four to six months ahead of time. It follows then, that a four- to six-month window should give you the pick of sailing dates, ships, itineraries, cabins, and flights to the port city. If you're looking for a standard itinerary and aren't choosy about the vessel or dates, you could wait for a last-minute discount, but they are harder to find than in the past.

If particular shore excursions are important to you, consider booking them when you book your cruise to avoid disappointment later.

CRUISE COSTS

Average fares for Alaskan itineraries vary dramatically depending on when you sail, which ship and grade of cabin you choose, and when you book. Published rates are highest during June, July, and August; you'll pay less, and have more space on ship and ashore, if you sail in May or September.

Whenever you choose to sail, remember that the brochure price is the highest fare the line can charge for a given cruise. Most lines offer early-booking discounts. Although these vary tremendously, many lines will offer at least 10% off if you book ahead of time, usually by the end of January for a summer cruise. Sometimes you can book a discounted last-minute cruise if the ship hasn't filled all its cabins, but you won't get your pick of ships, cabins, or sailing dates. However, since most cruise lines will, if asked, refund the difference in fare if it drops after you've

paid your deposit and before you
make your final payment, there's
little advantage in last-minute
booking.

SOLO TRAVELERS

Single cabins for solo travelers are
nonexistent on most ships; taking
a double cabin can cost as much
as twice the advertised per-person

rates (which are based on two people sharing a room). Some cruise lines
will find roommates of the same sex for singles so that each can travel
at the regular per-person rate.

EXTRAS

Cruise fares typically include accommodation, onboard meals and
snacks, and most onboard activities. Not normally included are airfare,
shore excursions, tips, soft drinks, alcoholic drinks, or spa treatments.
Port fees, fuel surcharges, and sales taxes are generally added to your
fare at booking.

OTHER CONSIDERATIONS

Children's programs: Virtually every line has children's programs and
Disney Cruise Line's entry into Alaska gives parents a superior option;
however, high-end lines generally only offer supervised programs when
enough children are aboard to warrant them or during school holidays.
Small ships are less likely to offer kids' programs. Check whether the
available shore excursions include activities that will appeal to kids.

Dining: Some cruise lines offer traditional assigned dining, meaning you
will dine each evening at the same table with the same companions.
Others offer open seating, allowing you to dine whenever and with
whomever you like; still others offer a choice between the two systems.
Most cruise ships have at least one restaurant in addition to the main
dining room; some have more. Most ships offer vegetarian and heart-
healthy or low-carb options.

Ports of call: You'll want to know where and when you will be stopping.
Will there be enough time in port to do what you want to do there? Will
it be the right time of day for your chosen activity? Will you tender to
shore by boat or moor up at the dock? This is important, as tendering
can take some time away from your port visit.

Onboard activities: Your cruise will likely include one or two full days
at sea. Think about how you'd like to fill the time. Do you want great
workout facilities or a spa? What about educational opportunities or
shopping? If seeing Alaska itself is your priority, choose a ship with lots
of outdoor *and* indoor viewing space.

SMALL SHIP CRUISES

We cover three of the most recognized small-ship lines sailing in Alaska, but that is by no means exhaustive. Other great small ships sailing the Inside Passage include Fantasy Cruises' *Island Spirit* (⊕ *www.smallalaskaship.com*), owned and operated by Captain Jeff Behrens. Captain Behrens is committed to rapport-building with and respect for the area's smallest communities; as a result, 32-passenger *Island Spirit* can make off-the-beaten-path port calls like Tenakee Springs (⊕ *www.tenakeespringsak.*

com), Five Finger Lighthouse (⊕ *www.5fingerlighthouse.com*), and Baranof Warm Springs, in addition to scenic anchorages like Ford's Terror that only small ships can access. Charters and photography-focused cruises are also available.

Alaska Sea Adventures (⊕ *www. yachtalaska.com*) focuses on charters and single-theme cruises on wildlife photography, birding, research, archaeology, whale migration, or fish spawning. Its two ships, *Northern Song* and *Alaska Legend*, can accommodate up to 8 passengers each.

ABOUT THE SHIPS

CRUISE SHIPS

Large cruise lines account for the majority of passengers sailing to Alaska. These typically have large cruise ships in their fleets with plentiful deck space and, often, a promenade deck that allows you to stroll the ship's perimeter. In the newest vessels, traditional meets trendy with resort-style innovations; however, they still feature cruise-ship classics, like afternoon tea and complimentary room service. The smallest cruise ships carry as few as 400 passengers, while the biggest can accommodate between 1,500 and 3,000 passengers—enough people to outnumber the residents of many Alaskan port towns. Large ships are a good choice if you're looking for nonstop activity and lots of options; they're especially appealing for groups and families with older kids. If you prefer a gentler pace and a chance to get to know your shipmates, try a smaller ship.

SMALL SHIPS

Compact expedition-type vessels bring you right up to the shoreline to skirt the face of a glacier and pull through narrow channels where big ships don't fit. These cruises focus on Alaska, and you'll see more wildlife and call into smaller ports, as well as some of the better-known towns. Talks—conducted by naturalists, native Alaskans, and other experts in the state's natural history and native cultures—are the norm. Cabins on expedition ships can be tiny, usually with no phone or TV, and bathrooms are often no bigger than cubbyholes. The dining room and lounge are usually the only public areas on these vessels; however, some are luxurious with cushy cabins, comfy lounges and libraries, and hot tubs. You won't find much nightlife aboard, but what you trade for space and onboard diversions is a unique and unforgettable glimpse of Alaska.

Many small ships are based in Juneau or another Alaska port and sail entirely within Alaska. Twice annually, some offer an Inside Passage cruise as the ships reposition to and from their winter homes elsewhere.

Small-ship cruising can be pricey, as fares tend to be inclusive (except for airfare), but with few onboard charges, and, given the size of ship and style of cruise, fewer opportunities to spend on board.

ABOUT THESE REVIEWS

For each cruise line described, ships that regularly cruise in Alaska are grouped by class or similar configuration. Some ships owned by the cruise lines listed do not include regularly scheduled Alaska cruises on their published itineraries as of this writing and are not reviewed in this book. *For a complete listing of the ships and the itineraries they are scheduled to follow in the 2011 cruising season, see the chart ⇨ Ships by Itinerary and Home Port, below.*

Many ships are designed with an eye to less-than-perfect weather. For that reason, you're likely to find indoor swimming pools featured on their deck plans. Except in rare cases, these are usually dual-purpose pools that can be covered when necessary by a sliding roof or magrodome to create an indoor-swimming environment. Our reviews indicate the total number of swimming pools found on each ship, with such permanently or temporarily covered pools included in the total and also noted as "# indoors" in parentheses.

When ships belong to the same class—or are basically similar—they're listed together in the subhead under the name of the class; the year each was introduced is also given in the same order in the statistics section. Capacity figures are based on double occupancy, but when maximum capacity numbers are available (the number of passengers a ship holds when all possible berths are filled), those are listed in parentheses. Many larger ships have three- and four-berth cabins that can substantially increase the total number of passengers on board when all berths are booked.

Unlike other cruise guides, we describe not only the features but also list the cabin dimensions for each accommodation category available on the ships reviewed. Dimensions should be considered approximate and used for comparison purposes, since they sometimes vary depending on the actual location of the cabin. For instance, while staterooms are largely prefabricated and consistent in size and configuration, those at the front of some ships may be oddly curved to conform to the shape of the bow.

Demand is high, and cruise ships are sailing at full capacity these days, so someone is satisfied by every ship. When you're armed with all the right information, we're sure you'll be able to find one that not only fits your style but that offers you the service and value you expect.

LARGE CRUISE LINES

SHIP	EMBARKATION PORT	DURATION IN NIGHTS	ITINERARY AND PORTS OF CALL
Carnival Cruise Lines			
Carnival Spirit	Seattle	7	Round-trip: Juneau, Skagway, Ketchikan, Victoria, BC, Sawyer Glacier
	Vancouver	6	One way: Ketchikan, Juneau, Skagway, disembark Seattle
	Seattle	7	One way: Ketchikan, Juneau, Skagway, Glacier Bay, disembark Vancouver
Celebrity Cruises			
Celebrity Infinity	Seattle	7	Round-trip: Ketchikan, Juneau, Skagway, Victoria, BC, Sawyer Glacier
Celebrity Century	Vancouver	7	Round-trip: Ketchikan, Juneau, Icy Strait Point, Hubbard Glacier
Celebrity Millennium	Vancouver	7	Northbound: Skagway, Ketchikan, Icy Strait Point, Hubbard Glacier
	Seward	7	Southbound: Skagway, Ketchikan, Icy Strait Point, Hubbard Glacier
Crystal Cruises			
Crystal Symphony	San Francisco	12	Round-trip: Victoria, BC, Vancouver, BC, Sitka, Skagway, Juneau, Ketchikan, Glacier Bay
Disney Cruise Line			
Disney Wonder	Vancouver	7	Round-trip: Ketchikan, Juneau, Skagway, Sawyer Glacier
Holland America Line			
Amsterdam	Seattle	14	Round-trip: Ketchikan, Skagway, Sitka, Anchorage, Homer, Kodiak, Juneau, Victoria, BC, Hubbard Glacier, Sawyer Glacier
Oosterdam	Seattle	7	Round-trip: Juneau, Sitka, Ketchikan, Victoria, BC, Glacier Bay
Statendam	Vancouver	7	Northbound: Skagway, Juneau, Ketchikan, College Fjord, Glacier Bay
	Seward	7	Southbound: Haines, Juneau, Ketchikan, College Fjord, Glacier Bay
Volendam	Vancouver	7	Round-trip: Skagway, Juneau, Ketchikan, Sawyer Glacier, Glacier Bay
Westerdam	Seattle	7	Round-trip: Juneau, Sitka, Ketchikan, Victoria, BC, Hubbard Glacier
Zaandam	Seattle	7	Round-trip: Juneau, Sitka, Ketchikan, Victoria, BC, Hubbard Glacier
Zuiderdam	Vancouver	7	Round-trip: Skagway, Juneau, Ketchikan, Sawyer Glacier, Glacier Bay
Norwegian Cruise Line			
Norwegian Pearl	Seattle	7	Round-trip: Juneau, Skagway, Ketchikan, Victoria, BC, Glacier Bay
Norwegian Star	Seattle	7	Round-trip: Juneau, Skagway, Ketchikan, Prince Rupert, BC, Sawyer Glacier
Oceania Cruises			
Regatta	San Francisco	14	Round-trip: Astoria, OR, Victoria, BC, Vancouver, BC, Sitka, Hoonah, Skagway, Juneau, Ketchikan, Hubbard Glacier, Sawyer Glacier

Ship	Port	Nights	Itinerary
Regatta cont'd.	San Francisco	12	Northbound: Astoria, OR, Victoria, BC, Wrangell, Juneau, Hoonah, Sitka, Ketchikan, Hubbard Glacier
	Vancouver	12	Southbound: Astoria, OR, Victoria, BC, Wrangell, Juneau, Hoonah, Sitka, Ketchikan, Hubbard Glacier
	Vancouver	10	Round-trip: Sitka, Hoonah, Kodiak, Wrangell, Ketchikan, Hubbard Glacier
	Vancouver	12	Northbound: Ketchikan, Wrangell, Juneau, Hoonah, Skagway, Sitka, Seward, Homer, Hubbard Glacier, College Fjord
	Vancouver	12	Southbound: Ketchikan, Wrangell, Juneau, Hoonah, Skagway, Sitka, Seward, Homer, Hubard Glacier, College Fjord
Princess Cruises			
Coral Princess	Vancouver	7	Northbound: Ketchikan, Juneau, Skagway, Glacier Bay, College Fjord
	Whittier	7	Southbound: Ketchikan, Juneau, Skagway, Glacier Bay, Hubbard Glacier
Diamond Princess	Vancouver	7	Northbound: Ketchikan, Juneau, Skagway, Glacier Bay, College Fjord
	Whittier	7	Southbound: Ketchikan, Juneau, Skagway, Glacier Bay, Hubbard Glacier
Golden Princess	Seattle	7	Round-trip: Juneau, Skagway, Ketchikan, Victoria, BC, Glacier Bay
Island Princess	Vancouver	7	Northbound: Ketchikan, Juneau, Skagway, Glacier Bay, College Fjord
	Whittier	7	Southbound: Ketchikan, Juneau, Skagway, Glacier Bay, Hubbard Glacier
Sapphire Princess	Seattle	7	Round-trip: Juneau, Skagway, Ketchikan, Victoria, BC, Sawyer Glacier
Sea Princess	San Francisco	10	Round-trip: either Icy Strait Point or Skagway, Juneau, Ketchikan, Victoria, BC, either Sawyer Glacier or Glacier Bay
Regent Seven Seas Cruises			
Seven Seas Navigator	Vancouver	7	Northbound: Sitka, Juneau, Skagway, Ketchikan, Hubbard Glacier, Sawyer Glacier
	Seward	7	Southbound: Sitka, Juneau, Skagway, Ketchikan, Hubbard Glacier, Sawyer Glacier
	San Francisco	12	Northbound: Astoria OR, Ketchikan, Juneau, Skagway, Sitka, Glacier Bay, Victoria BC, Vancouver BC
Royal Caribbean International			
Radiance of the Seas	Vancouver	7	Northbound: Ketchikan, Juneau, Skagway, Icy Strait Point, Hubbard Glacier
	Seward	7	Southbound: Ketchikan, Juneau, Skagway, Icy Strait Point, Hubbard Glacier
Rhapsody of the Seas	Seattle	7	Round-trip: Juneau, Skagway, Victoria BC, Sawyer Glacier
Silversea Cruises			
Silver Shadow	Anchorage	10	Southbound: Valdez, Skagway, Juneau, Sitka, Ketchikan, College Fjord, Hubbard Glacier, Sawyer Glacier, Vancouver
	Vancouver	7	Northbound: Ketchikan, Juneau, Skagway, Sitka, Sawyer Glacier, Hubbard Glacier
	Seward	7	Southbound: Ketchikan, Juneau, Skagway, Sitka, Sawyer Glacier, Hubbard Glacier

SMALL CRUISE-SHIP LINES

SHIP	EMBARKATION PORT	DURATION IN NIGHTS	ITINERARY AND PORTS OF CALL
American Safari Line			
Safari Explorer, Safari Quest, Safari Spirit	Juneau	7	Round-trip: Glacier Bay (2 or 3 days), Icy Strait, Admirality Island, Endicott Arm
	Seattle	14	Northbound: Prince Rupert, BC, Ketchikan, Meyer's Chuck, Petersburg, Glacier Bay, Juneau
	Juneau	14	Southbound: Glacier Bay, Tenakee Springs, Warm Springs Bay, Petersburg, Wrangell, Meyer's Chuck, Ketchikan, Misty Fiords, Friday Harbor WA, Glacier Bay, Petersburg, Meyer's Chuck, Ketchikan, Prince Rupert, BC
Cruise West			
Spirit of Columbia	Seattle	10	Northbound: Ketchikan, Petersburg, Sitka, Skagway, Haines, Sawyer Glacier, Glacier Bay, Juneau
	Juneau	10	Southbound: Ketchikan, Petersburg, Sitka, Skagway, Haines, Sawyer Glacier, Glacier Bay, Seattle
	Whittier	4	Round-trip: College Fjord, Knight Island, Chenega Glacier
Spirit of Discovery	Seattle	10	Northbound: Ketchikan, Petersburg, Sitka, Skagway, Haines, Sawyer Glacier, Glacier Bay, Juneau
	Juneau	10	Southbound: Ketchikan, Petersburg, Sitka, Skagway, Haines, Sawyer Glacier, Glacier Bay, Seattle
	Juneau	4	Round-trip: Glacier Bay (2 days)

Ship	Departure	Days	Itinerary
Spirit of Endeavour	Seattle	10	Northbound: Ketchikan, Petersburg, Sitka, Skagway, Haines, Sawyer Glacier, Glacier Bay, Juneau
	Juneau	10	Southbound: Ketchikan, Petersburg, Sitka, Skagway, Haines, Sawyer Glacier, Glacier Bay, Seattle
	Juneau	7	Round-trip: Petersburg, Sitka, Skagway, Haines, Ketchikan, Sawyer Glacier, Glacier Bay
Spirit of Yorktown	Seattle	10	Northbound: Ketchikan, Petersburg, Sitka, Skagway, Haines, Sawyer Glacier, Glacier Bay, Juneau
	Juneau	10	Southbound: Ketchikan, Petersburg, Sitka, Skagway, Haines, Sawyer Glacier, Glacier Bay, Seattle
	Juneau	7	Round-trip: Petersburg, Sitka, Skagway, Haines, Ketchikan, Sawyer Glacier, Glacier Bay

Lindblad Expeditions

Ship	Departure	Days	Itinerary
National Geographic Sea Bird and Sea Lion	Sitka	7	Northbound: Point Adolphus, Glacier Bay, Petersburg, Frederick Sound, Sawyer Glacier, Juneau
	Juneau	7	Southbound: Sawyer Glacier, Petersburg, Frederick Sound, Glacier Bay, Point Adolphus, Sitka
	Seattle	11	Northbound: San Juan Islands, Alert Bay, Misty Fiords, Frederick Island, Sitka, Glacier Bay, Point Adolphus, Juneau
	Juneau	11	Southbound: Point Adolphus, Glacier Bay, Frederick Sound, Sitka, Misty Fiords, Alert Bay, San Juan Islands, Seattle

CARNIVAL CRUISE LINES

The world's largest cruise line originated the Fun Ship concept in 1972 with the relaunch of an aging ocean liner, which got stuck on a sandbar during its maiden voyage. In true entrepreneurial spirit, founder Ted Arison shrugged off an inauspicious beginning to

Lobby Bar on board *Carnival Fantasy*

introduce superliners only a decade later. Sporting red-white-and-blue flared funnels, which are easily recognized from afar, new ships are continuously added to the fleet and rarely deviate from a successful pattern. If you find something you like on one vessel, you're likely to find something similar on another.

✉ *3655 N.W. 87 Ave., Miami, FL* ☎ *305/599–2600 or 800/227–6482* ⊕ *www.carnival.com* ☞ *Cruise Style: Mainstream.*

Each vessel features themed public rooms, ranging from ancient Egypt to futuristic motifs. More high-energy than cerebral, the entertainment consists of lavish Las Vegas–style revues presented in main show lounges by a company of singers and dancers. Other performers might include comedians, magicians, jugglers, acrobats, and even passengers taking part in the talent show or stepping up to the karaoke microphone. Live bands play a wide range of musical styles for dancing and listening in smaller lounges, and each ship has a disco.

Arrive early to get a seat for bingo and art auctions. Adult activities, particularly the competitive ones, tend to be silly and hilarious and play to full houses. Relaxing poolside can be difficult when bands crank up the volume or the cruise director selects volunteers for pool games; fortunately, it's always in fun and mostly entertaining. There's generally a quieter second pool to retreat to.

Carnival is so sure passengers will be satisfied with their cruise experience that they are the only cruise line to offer a Vacation Guarantee. Just notify them before arriving at the first port of call if you're unhappy for any reason. Should you choose to disembark at the ship's first non-U.S. port, Carnival will refund the unused portion of your cruise fare and pay for your flight back to your embarkation port. It's a generous offer for which they get very few takers.

Food

Carnival ships have both flexible dining options and casual alternative restaurants. While the tradition of two set mealtimes for dinner prevails on Carnival ships, the line's experiment with an open-seating concept—Your Time Dining—proved so successful that it has been implemented fleetwide.

While the waiters still sing and dance, the good-to-excellent dining room food appeals to American tastes. Upscale supper clubs on certain ships serve cuisine comparable to the best midrange steak houses ashore.

Carnival serves the best food of the mainstream cruise lines. In addition to the regular menu, vegetarian, low-calorie, low-carbohydrate, low-salt, and no-sugar selections are available. A children's menu includes such favorites as macaroni and cheese, chicken fingers, and peanut butter–and-jelly sandwiches. If you don't feel like dressing up for dinner, try the Lido buffet with its full meals, including sandwiches, a complete salad bar, rotisserie chicken, Asian stir-fry, and excellent pizza.

Fitness and Recreation

Manned by staff members trained to keep passengers in shipshape form, Carnival's trademark spas and fitness centers are some of the largest and best equipped at sea. Spas and salons are operated by Steiner Leisure, and treatments include a variety of massages, body wraps, and facials; salons offer hair and nail services. Tooth whitening is a recent addition to the roster. Fitness centers have state-of-the-art cardio and strength-training equipment, a jogging track, and basic exercise classes at no charge. There's a fee for personal training, body-composition analysis, and specialized classes such as yoga and Pilates.

Your Shipmates

Carnival's passengers are predominantly active Americans, mostly couples in their mid-30s to mid-50s. Many families enjoy Carnival cruises in the Caribbean year-round. Holidays and school vacation periods are very popular with families, and you'll see a lot of kids in summer. More than 650,000 children sailed on Carnival ships in 2010—a sixfold increase in just 12 years.

NOTEWORTHY

- Make yourself at home in one of the most generous standard cabins afloat—185 square feet.

- Every Carnival passenger enjoys the same service and attention, including nightly turndown service, room service, and 24-hour pizzerias.

- Watch your weight with healthy selections from the spa menu that are low in calories, cholesterol, salt, and fat.

Top: *Carnival Victory* dining room
Bottom: Enjoy the game at the bar

2

CARNIVAL CRUISE LINES

Dress Code

Two "cruise elegant" nights are standard on seven-night cruises; one is the norm on shorter sailings. Although men should feel free to wear tuxedos, dark suits (or sport coats) and ties are more prevalent. All other evenings are "cruise casual," with jeans and dress shorts permitted in the dining rooms. All ships request that no short-shorts or cutoffs be worn in public after 6 PM, but that policy is often ignored.

Junior Cruisers

Camp Carnival, run year-round by professionals, earns high marks for keeping young cruisers busy and content. Dedicated children's areas include great playrooms with separate splash pools. Toddlers from two to five years are treated to puppet shows, sponge painting, face painting, coloring, drawing, and crafts. As long as diapers and supplies are provided, staff will change toddlers. Activities for ages six to eight include arts and crafts, pizza parties, computer time, T-shirt painting, a talent show, and fitness programs. Nine- to 11-year-olds can play Ping-Pong, take dance lessons, play video games, and participate in swim parties, scavenger hunts, and sports. Tweens aged 12 to 14 appreciate the social events, parties, contests, and sports in Circle C. Every night they have access to the ships' discos, followed by late-night movies, karaoke, or pizza.

Club O2 is geared toward teens from 15 to 17. Program directors play host at the spacious teen clubs, where kicking back is the order of the day between scheduled activities. The fleetwide Y-Spa program for older teens offers a high level of pampering. Staff members also accompany teens on shore excursions designed just for them.

Top: *Carnival Triumph* walking and jogging track
Middle: *Carnival Elation* at sea
Bottom: *Carnival Destiny* penthouse suite.

Daytime group babysitting for infants two and under allows parents the freedom to explore ports of call without the kids until noon. Parents can also pursue leisurely adults-only evenings from 10 PM to 3 AM, when slumber party–style group babysitting is available for children from ages four months to 11 years. Babysitting fees are $6 an hour for one child and $4 an hour for each additional child.

CHOOSE THIS LINE IF . . .

You want an action-packed casino with a choice of table games and rows upon rows of clanging slot machines.

You don't mind standing in line—these are big ships with a lot of passengers, and lines are not uncommon.

You don't mind hearing announcements over the public-address system reminding you of what's next on the schedule.

Service

Service on Carnival ships is friendly but not polished. Stateroom attendants are not only recognized for their attention to cleanliness but also for their expertise in creating towel animals—cute critters fashioned from bath towels that appear during nightly turndown service. They've become so popular that Carnival publishes an instruction book on how to create them yourself.

Tipping

A gratuity of $10 per passenger, per day is automatically added to passenger accounts, and gratuities are distributed to stewards and waitstaff. Passengers may adjust the amount based on the level of service experienced. All beverage tabs at bars get an automatic 15% addition.

Past Passengers

After sailing on one Carnival cruise, you'll receive a complimentary two-year subscription to *Currents*, the company magazine, and access to your past sailing history on the Carnival Web site. You are recognized on subsequent cruises with color-coded key cards—Gold (starting with your second cruise) or Platinum (starting with your 10th cruise)—which serve as your entrée to a by-invitation-only cocktail reception. You're also eligible for exclusive discounts on future cruises on all the cruise lines owned by Carnival Corporation.

Platinum members are eligible for Concierge Club benefits, including priority embarkation and debarkation, guaranteed dining assignments, supper club and spa reservations, logo items, and complimentary laundry service.

GOOD TO KNOW

If you've never sailed on a Carnival ship, or haven't sailed on one in recent years, you may not understand how Carnival cruises have evolved. The shipboard atmosphere is still bright, noisy, and fun, but the beer-drinking contests and bawdy, anything-goes image are history. Unfortunately, much like Casual Friday has evolved from no tie in the office to jeans and a polo shirt, it isn't unusual to see Carnival passengers dressed very casually after dinner, even on "cruise elegant" nights. You may be surprised at how quickly some passengers can swap their fancy duds for T-shirts and shorts between the dining room and show lounge. The fun of a Carnival cruise can begin before you leave home if you log on to the Carnival Web site (⊕ *www.carnivalconnections.com*), where you will find planning tips, cruise reviews, and a message board.

DON'T CHOOSE THIS LINE IF . . .

You want an intimate, sedate atmosphere. Carnival's ships are big and bold.

You want elaborate accommodations. Carnival suites are spacious but not as feature-filled as the term *suite* may suggest.

You're turned off by men in tank tops. Casual on these ships means casual indeed.

SPIRIT CLASS
Carnival Spirit

CREW MEMBERS	930
ENTERED SERVICE	2001
700 ft. **GROSS TONS**	88,500
LENGTH	960 feet
500 ft. **NUMBER OF CABINS**	1,062
PASSENGER CAPACITY	2,124 (2,667 max)
300 ft. **WIDTH**	105.7 feet

Top: *Carnival Legend* at sea
Bottom: Spirit-class balcony
stateroom

Public Areas and Facilities
Spirit-class vessels may seem to be a throwback in size, but these sleek ships have the advantage of fitting through the Panama Canal, and, with their additional length, include all the trademark characteristics of their larger fleet mates. They're also racehorses with the speed to reach far-flung destinations.

A rosy-red skylight in the front bulkhead of the funnel—which houses the reservations-only upscale Supper Club—caps a soaring, 11-deck atrium. Lovely chapels are available for weddings, either upon embarkation or while in a port of call, and are also used for shipboard religious services.

The upper and lower interior promenade decks are unhampered by a midship restaurant or galley, which means that passenger flow throughout the ships is much improved over earlier, and even subsequent, designs.

Restaurants
One formal restaurant serves open-seating breakfast and lunch; while it serves dinner in two traditional assigned evening seatings, the line also offers an open-seating option—Your Time Dining. The casual Lido buffet with stations offers a variety of food choices (including a deli, salad bar, dessert station, and different daily regional cuisines); at night it becomes the Seaview Bistro for casual dinners. There's also an upscale supper club that requires reservations and an additional charge, a pizzeria, poolside outdoor grills for burgers, hot dogs, and the trimmings, a specialty coffee bar and patisserie, a complimentary sushi bar, and 24-hour room service with a limited menu of breakfast selections, sandwiches, and snacks.

Accommodations
Cabins: Cabins on Carnival ships are generally more spacious than industry standard, and these are no exception. Nearly 80% have an ocean view, and, of those, more than 80% have balconies. Suites and some ocean-view cabins have private balconies outfitted with chairs and tables; some cabins have balconies at least 50% larger than average. Every cabin has adequate closet and drawer/shelf storage, as well as bathroom shelves. High-thread-count linens and plush pillows and duvets

are a luxurious touch in all accommodations. Suites also have a whirlpool tub and walk-in closet.

Decor: Light-wood cabinetry, soft pastels, mirrored accents, a small refrigerator, a personal safe, a hair dryer, and a sitting area with sofa, chair, and table are typical for ocean-view cabins and suites. Inside cabins have ample room but no sitting area.

Bathrooms: Extras include shampoo and bath gel provided in shower-mounted dispensers and an array of sample toiletries, as well as fluffy towels and a wall-mounted magnifying mirror. Bathrobes for use during the cruise are provided for all.

Other Features: Decks 5, 6, and 7 each have a pair of balcony staterooms that connect to adjoining interior staterooms that are ideal for families because of their close proximity to children and teen areas. Sixteen staterooms are designed for wheelchair accessibility.

In the Know

Take a walk on the wild side. The gently curving staircase to the Supper Club is clear Plexiglas and definitely a challenge to descend if heights make you dizzy. Try it anyway—it's quite a heady experience. Wimps can use the elevator.

Pros and Cons

Pros: A quieter choice for reading than the library, which also houses the Internet center, is the delightful, enclosed, winter-garden space located forward on the exterior promenade deck. For relaxation, a soothing therapy pool sits under a skylight in the fitness center, and his-and-hers saunas and steam rooms have glass walls and sea views. Complimentary self-serve ice cream dispensers are on the Lido Deck.

Cons: These are long ships—really long ships—and you may want to consider any mobility issues and select a cabin near one of the three banks of well-placed elevators. Connecting staterooms are relatively scarce throughout the ships, but balcony dividers can be unlocked between some higher-category cabins. Avid gamers may have difficulty locating the video arcade, which is tucked away at the forward end of the ship in front of the main show lounge and accessible from the interior promenade.

Cabin Type	Size (sq. ft.)
Penthouse Suites	370 (average)
Suite	275
Ocean View	185
Interior	185

FAST FACTS

- 12 passenger decks
- Specialty restaurant, dining room, buffet, ice cream parlor, pizzeria
- Wi-Fi, safe, refrigerator
- 3 pools (1 indoor), children's pool
- Fitness classes, gym, hair salon, 4 hot tubs, sauna, spa, steam room
- 7 bars, casino, 2 dance clubs, library, showroom, video game room
- Children's programs (ages 2–17)
- Laundry facilities, laundry service
- Internet terminal

Carnival Miracle Gatsby's Garden

CELEBRITY CRUISES

The Chandris Group, owners of budget Fantasy Cruises, founded Celebrity in 1989. Initially utilizing an unlovely, refurbished former ocean liner from the Fantasy fleet, Celebrity gained a reputation for professional service and fine food despite the shabby-chic vessel

Swim-up bar under the stars

where it was elegantly served. The cruise line eventually built premium sophisticated cruise ships. Signature amenities followed, including large standard staterooms with generous storage, fully equipped spas, and butler service. Valuable art collections grace the fleet.

✉ *1050 Caribbean Way, Miami, FL*
☎ *800/647–2251*
⊕ *www.celebritycruises. com* ☞ *Cruise Style: Premium.*

Entertainment has never been a primary focus of Celebrity Cruises, although a lineup of lavish revues is presented in the main show lounges. In addition to shows featuring comedians, magicians, and jugglers, bands play a wide range of musical styles for dancing and listening in smaller lounges. You'll find guest lecturers on every Celebrity cruise. Presentations may range from financial strategies, astronomy, wine appreciation, photography tips, and politics to the food, history, and culture of ports of call. Culinary demonstrations, bingo, and art auctions are additional diversions throughout the fleet. There are plenty of activities, all outlined in the daily program of events. There are no public-address announcements for bingo or hawking of gold-by-the-inch sales. You can still play and buy, but you won't be reminded repeatedly.

While spacious accommodations in every category are a Celebrity standard, ConciergeClass, an upscale element on all ships, makes certain premium ocean-view and balcony staterooms almost the equivalent of suites in terms of service. A ConciergeClass stateroom includes numerous extras such as chilled champagne, fresh fruit, and flowers upon arrival, exclusive room-service menus, evening canapés, luxury bedding, pillows, and linens, upgraded balcony furnishings, priority boarding and luggage service, and other VIP perks. At the touch of a single telephone button, a Concierge-Class desk representative is at hand to offer assistance. Suites are still the ultimate, though, and include the services of a butler to assist with unpacking, booking spa services and dining reservations, shining shoes, and even replacing a popped button.

Food

Aside from the sophisticated ambience of its restaurants, the cuisine has always been a highlight of a Celebrity cruise. However, in early 2007, Celebrity and longtime chef Michael Roux ended their affiliation. His hands-on involvement—personally creating menus and overseeing all aspects of dining operations—was integral in helping the line achieve the reputation it enjoys today. Happily, every ship in the fleet has a highly experienced team headed by executive chefs and food and beverage managers who have developed their skills in some of the world's finest restaurants and hotels.

Alternative restaurants on the Solstice-class ships, Millennium-class ships, and *Celebrity Century* offer fine dining and table-side food preparation amid classic ocean liner and Venetian splendor. A less formal evening alternative is offered fleetwide in Lido restaurants, where you'll find a sushi bar, pizza and baked pasta, healthy spa items, and desserts. The AquaSpa Café on Solstice-class and Millennium-class ships serves light and healthy cuisine from breakfast until evening. Cafés serve a variety of coffees, teas, and pastries; some offerings carry an additional charge. Gourmet Bites, the late-night treats served by white-gloved waiters in public rooms throughout the ships, can include mini–beef Wellingtons and crispy tempura.

To further complement the food, in 2004 Celebrity introduced a proprietary Cellarmaster Selection of wines, formulated specifically for Celebrity passengers.

Fitness and Recreation

Celebrity's AquaSpa by Elemis and fitness centers are some of the most tranquil and nicely equipped at sea with thalassotherapy pools on all but Solstice-class ships and *Century* (complimentary on Millennium-class ships; a fee is assessed on *Celebrity Mercury*). Spa services are operated by Steiner Leisure, and treatments include a variety of massages, body wraps, and

Top: The *Millennium* AquaSpa
Bottom: Millennium-class cinema and conference center

2

CELEBRITY CRUISES

Top: *Century* Rendezvous
Lounge
Middle: Lounge in climate-
controlled comfort
Bottom: Lounging on deck

facials. Trendy and traditional hair and nail services are offered in the salons.

State-of-the-art exercise equipment, a jogging track, and basic fitness classes are available at no charge. There's a fee for personal training, body-composition analysis, and specialized classes such as yoga and Pilates. Golf pros offer hands-on instruction, and game simulators allow passengers to play world-famous courses. Each ship also has an Acupuncture at Sea treatment area staffed by licensed practitioners of Oriental Medicine.

Your Shipmates

Celebrity caters to American cruise passengers, primarily couples from their mid-30s to mid-50s. Many families enjoy cruising on Celebrity's fleet during summer months and holiday periods, particularly in the Caribbean. Lengthier cruises and exotic itineraries attract passengers in the over-60 age group.

Dress Code

Two formal nights are standard on seven-night cruises. Men are encouraged to wear tuxedos, but dark suits or sport coats and ties are more prevalent. Other evenings are designated "smart casual and above." Although jeans are discouraged in formal restaurants, they are appropriate for casual dining venues after 6 PM. The line requests that no shorts be worn in public areas after 6 PM, and most people observe the dress code of the evening, unlike on some other cruise lines.

Junior Cruisers

Each Celebrity vessel has a dedicated playroom and offers a four-tier program of age-appropriate games and activities designed for children ages 3 to 5, 6 to 8, and 9 to 11. Younger children must be toilet trained to participate in the programs and use the facilities; however, families are welcome to borrow toys for their non–toilet-trained kids. A fee may be assessed for participation in children's dinner parties, the Late-Night Slumber Party, and Afternoon Get-Togethers while parents are ashore in ports of call. Evening in-cabin babysitting can be arranged for a fee. All ships have

CHOOSE THIS LINE IF . . .

You want an upscale atmosphere at a really reasonable fare.

You want piping-hot late-night pizza delivered to your cabin in pizzeria fashion.

You want to dine amid elegant surroundings in some of the best restaurants at sea.

teen centers, where tweens (ages 12 to 14) and teenagers (ages 15 to 17) can hang out and attend mock-tail and pizza parties.

Service

Service on Celebrity ships is unobtrusive and polished. ConciergeClass adds an unexpected level of service and amenities that are usually reserved for luxury ships or passengers in top-category suites on other premium cruise lines.

Tipping

Gratuities (in cash) are personally distributed by passengers on the last night of the cruise. Suggested guidelines are per person per day: waiter $3.65; assistant waiter $2.10; assistant maître d' $1; cabin steward $3.50; cabin attendant in ConciergeClass $4; other service personnel $1.25; and, for suite occupants only, butler $3.50. Passengers may adjust the amount based on the level of service experienced. An automatic gratuity of 15% is added to all beverage tabs.

Past Passengers

Once you've sailed with Celebrity, you become a member of the Captain's Club and receive benefits commensurate with the number of cruises you've taken, including free upgrades, the chance to make dining reservations before sailing, and other benefits. Classic members have been on at least one Celebrity cruise. Select members have sailed at least six cruises and get more perks, including an invitation to a senior officer's cocktail party. After 10 cruises, you become an Elite member and can take advantage of a private departure lounge. Royal Caribbean International, the parent company of Celebrity Cruises, also extends the corresponding levels of their Crown & Anchor program to Celebrity Captain's Club members.

GOOD TO KNOW

Small refinements add touches of luxury to a Celebrity cruise. White-gloved stewards are present at the gangway upon embarkation to greet weary passengers with the offer of assistance.

Waiters will happily carry your trays from the buffet line to your table in the casual restaurant. Just ask the bartender for the recipe if a specialty martini or other cocktail appeals to you so you can re-create it at home.

DON'T CHOOSE THIS LINE IF . . .

You need to be reminded of when activities are scheduled. Announcements are kept to a minimum.

You look forward to boisterous pool games and wacky contests. These cruises are fairly quiet and adult-centered.

You think funky avant-garde art is weird. Abstract modernism abounds in the art collections.

MILLENNIUM CLASS
Millennium, Infinity

CREW MEMBERS	999
ENTERED SERVICE	2000, 2001
GROSS TONS	91,000
LENGTH	965 feet
NUMBER OF CABINS	975
PASSENGER CAPACITY	1,950 (2,450)
WIDTH	105 feet

700 ft.

500 ft.

300 ft.

Public Areas and Facilities

Millennium-class ships are among the largest and most feature-filled in the Celebrity fleet. Innovations include the Conservatory, a unique botanical environment, show lounges reminiscent of splendid opera houses, and an alternative restaurant where diners find themselves in the midst of authentic ocean-liner decor and memorabilia. The spas simply have to be seen to be believed—they occupy nearly as much space inside as is devoted to the adjacent outdoor Lido Deck pool area. Although the spas offer just about any treatment you can think of—and some you probably haven't—they also house a complimentary hydrotherapy pool and café. These ships have a lot to offer for families, with some of the most expansive children's facilities in the Celebrity fleet.

Rich fabrics in jewel tones mix elegantly with the abundant use of marble and wood accents throughout public areas. The atmosphere is not unlike a luxurious European hotel filled with grand spaces that flow nicely from one to the other.

Restaurants

The formal two-deck restaurant serves open-seating breakfast and lunch; evening meals are served in two traditional assigned seatings or Celebrity Select Dining, an open-seating option that allows you to be seated any time the main restaurant is open. The casual Lido buffet offers buffet-style breakfast and lunch. By night, the Lido restaurant is transformed into a sit-down restaurant with limited table service and a sushi café. Each ship features a poolside grill for burgers and other fast-food favorites, the spa café serves lighter fare, and Cova Café has specialty coffees, teas, and pastries for an extra charge. Each ship has an upscale alternative restaurant that specializes in table-side food preparation and houses a demonstration kitchen and wine cellar (and also requires reservations and a per-person cover charge). Pizza delivery and 24-hour room service augment dining choices.

Accommodations

Cabins: As on all Celebrity ships, cabins are thoughtfully designed with ample closet and drawer/shelf storage, as well as bathroom shelves in all standard inside and

Top: *Millennium* Cova Café
Bottom: *Millennium* Ocean Grill

outside categories. Some ocean-view cabins and suites have private balconies. Penthouse suites have guest powder rooms.

Amenities: Wood cabinetry, mirrored accents, a small refrigerator, a personal safe, a hair dryer, and a sitting area with sofa, chair, and table are typical standard amenities. Extras include bathroom toiletries (shampoo, soaps, and lotion) and bathrobes for use during the cruise. Suite luxuries vary, but most include a whirlpool tub, a DVD or VCR, an Internet-connected computer, and a walk-in closet, while all have butler service, personalized stationery, and a logo tote bag. For pure pleasure, Penthouse and Royal suites have outdoor whirlpool tubs on the balconies.

Worth Noting: Most staterooms and suites have convertible sofa beds, and many categories are capable of accommodating third and fourth occupants. Connecting staterooms are available in numerous categories, including Celebrity suites. Family staterooms feature huge balconies and some have not one but two sofa beds. Twenty-six staterooms are designed for wheelchair accessibility.

In the Know

Enhance your personal outdoor space by booking cabins 6035, 6030, or any of the seven cabins forward of those two on deck 6. You can't tell from the deck plan, but your balcony will be extra deep, and you won't be looking down into a lifeboat.

Pros and Cons

Pros: In lieu of atriums, Grand Foyers on these ships are stylishly appointed, multideck lobbies, with sweeping staircases crying out for grand entrances. There's no charge for use of the thalassotherapy pool in the huge AquaSpa, a facility that rivals the fanciest ashore. The AquaSpa Café serves light and healthy selections for breakfast, lunch, and dinner, as well as fresh fruit smoothies.

Cons: Crew members try extremely hard to make everyone feel special, but there are just too many passengers to expect that your every wish will be granted on a ship this size. Although you'd expect to pay far more ashore for a comparable meal in one of the extra-charge specialty restaurants, the suggested wines are overpriced. Self-service laundries are not a feature of Celebrity ships, so you'll have to pack more or use the priced-per-item laundry option.

Cabin Type	Size (sq. ft.)
Penthouse Suite	1,432
Royal Suite	538
Celebrity Suite	467
Sky Suite	251
Family Ocean View	271
ConciergeClass	191
Ocean View/ Interior	170

FAST FACTS

■ 11 passenger decks

■ Specialty restaurant, dining room, buffet, ice cream parlor, pizzeria

■ Internet (*Constellation*), Wi-Fi, safe, refrigerator, DVD (some), VCR (some)

■ 3 pools (1 indoor), children's pool

■ Fitness classes, gym, hair salon, 6 hot tubs, sauna, spa, steam room

■ 7 bars, casino, cinema, dance club, library, showroom, video game room

■ Children's programs (ages 3–17)

■ Dry cleaning, laundry service

■ Internet terminal

■ No-smoking cabins

Millennium-class conservatory

CENTURY CLASS
Century, Mercury
(only Century sails in Alaska in 2011)

	CREW MEMBERS
	858, 909
	ENTERED SERVICE
	1995, 1997
700 ft.	**GROSS TONS**
	70,606, 77,713
	LENGTH
	815, 866 feet
500 ft.	**NUMBER OF CABINS**
	875, 943
	PASSENGER CAPACITY
1,750 (2,150), 1,886 (2,681)	
300 ft.	**WIDTH**
	105 feet

Top: Formal dining on *Century*
Bottom: *Century* Shipmates
Fun Factory

Public Areas and Facilities

Although the Century Class sister ships have essentially the same layout, they differ dramatically in decor. *Century* has an eclectic air, while *Mercury* is more traditional in design and quietly elegant. Both display fine collections of modern and classical art. With an additional 50 feet in length, *Mercury* has room for a children's pool as well as a third swimming pool with a sliding roof for cover in inclement weather. A 2006 rejuvenation of *Century* added 14 suites and 10 staterooms (both inside and outside), not to mention 314 verandas—the most ever added to an existing cruise ship.

Each vessel has facilities for children and teens, but on *Mercury* they seem almost an afterthought. Adults fare better with spectacular spas and sophisticated lounges dedicated to a variety of tastes. The dining rooms are nothing short of gorgeous. Overall, the first impression is that these are fine resort hotels that just happen to float.

Restaurants

The formal two-deck restaurant serves breakfast and lunch open-seating style and evening meals in two assigned seatings or Celebrity Select Dining, an open-seating option that allows you to be seated any time the main restaurant is open. Formal dining is supplemented by a casual Lido restaurant offering buffet-style breakfast and lunch. By night, the Lido restaurant is transformed into a sit-down restaurant with table service and a sushi bar. Each ship features two poolside grills for burgers and other fast-food favorites and Cova Café, where specialty coffees, teas, and pastries are available for an additional charge. *Century* has both a complimentary spa café and an upscale, reservations-only restaurant that specializes in table-side preparation and has an extra cover charge. *Mercury*'s restaurant features windows that stretch from floor to ceiling, key for not missing a second of the scenery outside. Room service is available 24 hours and includes pizza delivered to your door.

Accommodations

Cabins: As on all Celebrity ships, cabins are thoughtfully designed with ample closet and drawer/shelf storage and bathroom shelves. Some ocean-view cabins and suites have balconies with chairs and tables. Penthouse and Royal suites have a whirlpool bathtub and separate shower as well as a walk-in closet; Penthouse suites have a guest powder room.

Amenities: Light-wood cabinetry, mirrored accents, a refrigerator, a personal safe, a hair dryer, and a sitting area with sofa, chair, and table are typical standard amenities. Extras include bathroom toiletries (shampoo, soaps, and lotion) and bathrobes for use during the cruise. Penthouse and Royal suites have an elaborate entertainment center with a large TV, while all suites include butler service, personalized stationery, VCR or DVD, and a tote bag.

Worth Noting: On *Mercury*, spacious family ocean-view staterooms have a double bed, sofa bed, and upper berth; *Century* has slightly smaller Family Veranda Staterooms. Eight staterooms are designed for wheelchair accessibility.

In the Know

While the rest of the industry was rushing to add affordable balconies to a high percentage of staterooms, Celebrity was somewhat slower to get on the bandwagon. When *Century* emerged from her drydock revitalization in June 2006 with 314 new verandas, the tide had turned.

Pros and Cons

Pros: The stogie craze has all but died, and the air has cleared in Michael's Clubs, the lounges formerly devoted to cigar smoking and now billed as piano bars. While there's a charge for the specialty coffee and Cova Café treats, complimentary croissants and pastries are available in the morning and late afternoon. Descending to dine was the tradition of great ocean liners, and these ships have stunning, descent-worthy staircases flanked by soaring columns in double-height dining rooms.

Cons: Unless you're occupying a suite or have booked a massage or other treatment from the spa menu, plan to pay a fee for relaxing in the huge saltwater therapy pool on *Mercury*. *Celebrity Century's* trendsetting thalassotherapy pool was removed during the ship's 2006 refit. *Mercury* is the only ship in the Celebrity fleet that lacks a specialty restaurant.

Cabin Type	Size (sq. ft.)
Penthouse Suite	1,101
Royal Suite	537
Sky Suite	246
Sunset Veranda	224
Century Suite*	190
Family Stateroom	192–218
Concierge, Veranda	170–175
Ocean View	172–175
Interior	171–174

*Only *Century* has Century Suites

FAST FACTS

- 10 passenger decks
- Specialty restaurant (*Century* only), dining room, buffet, ice cream parlor, pizzeria
- Wi-Fi, safe, refrigerator, DVD (some), VCR (some)
- 2 pools (*Century* only), 3 pools (1 indoor on *Mercury*), children's pool (*Mercury*)
- Fitness classes, gym, hair salon, 5 hot tubs, sauna, spa, steam room (*Mercury*)
- 7 bars (8 on *Mercury*), casino, cinema, dance club, library, showroom, video game room
- Children's programs (ages 3–17)
- Dry cleaning, laundry service
- Internet terminal
- No-smoking cabins

2

CELEBRITY CRUISES

CRYSTAL CRUISES

Winner of accolades and too many hospitality industry awards to count, Crystal Cruises offers a taste of the grandeur of the past along with all the modern touches discerning passengers demand today. Founded in 1990 and owned by Nippon Yusen Kaisha

Crystal Serenity wraparound promenade

(NYK) in Japan, Crystal ships, unlike other luxury vessels, are large, carrying upward of 900 passengers. What makes them distinctive are superior service, a variety of dining options, spacious accommodations, and some of the highest ratios of space per passenger of any cruise ship.

✉ *2049 Century Park E, Suite 1400, Los Angeles, CA* ☎ *888/799–4625 or 310/785–9300* ⊕ *www.crystalcruises. com* ☞ *Cruise Style: Luxury.*

Beginning with ship designs based on the principles of feng shui, the Eastern art of arranging your surroundings to attract positive energy, no detail is overlooked to provide passengers with the best imaginable experience. Just mention a preference for a certain food or beverage and your waiter will have it available whenever you request it.

The complete roster of entertainment and activities includes Broadway-style production shows and bingo, but where Crystal really shines is in the variety of enrichment and educational programs. Passengers can participate in the hands-on Computer University@ Sea, interactive Creative Learning Institute classes, or attend lectures featuring top experts in their fields: keyboard lessons with Yamaha, language classes by Berlitz, wellness lectures with the Cleveland Clinic, and an introduction to tai chi with the Tai Chi Cultural Center. Professional ACBL Bridge instructors are on every cruise, and dance instructors offer lessons in contemporary and social dance styles.

An added highlight for women traveling solo is the Ambassador Host Program, which brings cultured gentlemen on each cruise to dine, socialize, and dance with unaccompanied ladies.

Somewhat unique among cruise lines, Crystal Cruises' casinos observe Nevada gaming rules and offer complimentary cocktails to players at the tables and slot machines.

A delightful daily ritual is afternoon tea in the Palm Court. You're greeted by staff members in 18th-century Viennese brocade and velvet costumes for Mozart Tea, traditional scones and clotted cream are served during English Colonial Tea, and American Tea is a summertime classic created by Crystal culinary artists.

Food

The food alone is reason enough to book a Crystal cruise. Dining in the main restaurants is an event starring a Continental-inspired menu of dishes served by European-trained waiters. Off-menu item requests are honored when possible, and special dietary considerations are handled with ease. Full-course vegetarian menus are among the best at sea. Casual poolside dining beneath the stars is offered on some evenings in a relaxed, no-reservations option. A variety of hot-and-cold hors d'oeuvres are served in bars and lounges every evening before dinner and again during the wee hours.

But the specialty restaurants really shine. Jade Garden on *Crystal Symphony* serves traditional Japanese dishes as well as offerings from the menu of Wolfgang Puck's Chinois. Prego serves regional Italian cuisine by Piero Selvaggio, owner of Valentino in Los Angeles and Las Vegas.

Exclusive Wine & Champagne Makers dinners are hosted in the Vintage Room. On select evenings, casual poolside theme dinners are served under the stars.

Crystal has an extensive wine list, including its own proprietary label called C Wines, which are produced in California. Unfortunately, there are no complimentary wines with dinner, as is common on other luxury cruise lines. You won't pay extra for bottled water, soft drinks, and specialty coffees; all are included in your basic fare.

Fitness and Recreation

Large spas offer innovative pampering therapies, body wraps, and exotic Asian-inspired treatments by Steiner Leisure. Feng shui principles were scrupulously adhered to in their creation to assure the spas and salons remain havens of tranquillity.

NOTEWORTHY

■ Before sailing, each passenger receives a personal e-mail address.

■ Ambassador Hosts on Crystal cruises are cultured, well-traveled gentlemen, who are accomplished dancers and interact with female passengers.

■ Complimentary self-service laundry rooms as well as complete laundry, dry cleaning, and valet services are available.

Top: *Crystal Serenity* fitness center
Bottom: Crystal casino entrance

2

CRYSTAL CRUISES

Top: Spa treatment
Middle: Keyboard lessons
Bottom: *Crystal Symphony*
Crystal Penthouse

Fitness centers have a range of exercise and weight-training equipment and workout areas for aerobics classes, plus complimentary yoga and Pilates instruction. In addition, golfers enjoy extensive shipboard facilities, including a driving range practice cage and putting green. Passengers can leave their bags at home and rent top-quality TaylorMade clubs for use ashore. The line's resident golf pros offer complimentary lessons and group clinics.

Your Shipmates
Affluent, well-traveled couples, from their late-30s and up, are attracted to Crystal's destination-rich itineraries, shipboard enrichment programs, and elegant ambience. The average age of passengers is noticeably higher on longer itineraries.

Dress Code
Formal attire is required on at least two designated evenings, depending on the length of the cruise. Men are encouraged to wear tuxedos, and many do, although dark suits are also acceptable. Other evenings are informal or resort casual; the number of each is based on the number of sea days. The line requests that dress codes be observed in public areas after 6 PM, and few, if any, passengers disregard the suggestion. Most, in fact, dress up just a notch from guidelines.

Junior Cruisers
Although these ships are decidedly adult-oriented, Crystal welcomes children but limits the number of children under age three on any given cruise. Children under six months are not allowed without a signed waiver by parents.

Dedicated facilities for children and teens from ages 3 to 17 are staffed by counselors during holiday periods, select summer sailings, and when warranted by the number of children booked. The program is three-tiered for 3- to 7-year-olds, 8- to 12-year-olds, and 13- to 17-year-olds. Activities—including games, computer time, scavenger hunts, and arts and crafts—usually have an eye toward the educational. Teenagers can play complimentary video games to their heart's

CHOOSE THIS LINE IF . . .

You crave peace and quiet. Announcements are kept to a bare minimum, and the ambience is sedate.

You prefer to plan ahead. You can make spa, restaurant, shore excursion, and class reservations when you book your cruise.

You love sushi and other Asian delights—Crystal ships serve some of the best at sea.

content in Waves, the arcade dedicated for their use. Babysitting can be arranged with staff members for a fee. Baby food, high chairs, and booster seats are available upon request.

Service
Crystal's European-trained staff members provide gracious service in an unobtrusive manner.

Tipping
Tips may be distributed personally by passengers on the last night of the cruise or charged to shipboard accounts. Suggested gratuity guidelines per person per day are: senior waiter $5; waiter $3; cabin stewardess $5; and, for suite occupants only, butler $4. Tips for the maître d', headwaiter, assistant stewardess, and room service personnel are discretionary. Passengers may adjust the amount based on the level of service experienced. All beverage tabs include an automatic 15% gratuity. A minimum of $7 per person per dinner is suggested for the servers in specialty restaurants; a 15% gratuity is suggested for spa and salon services.

Past Passengers
You're automatically enrolled in the Crystal Society upon completion of your first Crystal cruise and are entitled to special savings and member-only events. Membership benefits increase with each completed Crystal cruise and include such perks as stateroom upgrades, shipboard spending credits, special events, gifts, air upgrades, and even free cruises. Society members also receive Crystal Cruises' complimentary quarterly magazine, which shares up-to-date information on itineraries, destinations, special offers, and society news.

GOOD TO KNOW

Two assigned dining room seatings are advertised as an advantage that offers flexibility, but the reality is that open seating is the true mark of choice and the most preferred option at this level of luxury cruising. If you haven't done so in advance, on embarkation day you can reserve a table to dine one night in each specialty restaurant, but don't dawdle until the last minute; if you wait, you may find a line has developed—one of the few lines you'll encounter on board—and all the choice dining times are already booked. You may also be able to reserve additional nights after the cruise is under way, depending on how busy the restaurants are.

DON'T CHOOSE THIS LINE IF . . .

You don't want to follow the dress code. Everyone does, and you'll stand out—and not in a good way—if you rebel.

You want total freedom. Unlike other luxury cruise lines, Crystal assigns you a seating and a table for dinner.

You want a less structured cruise. With set dining times, Crystal is a bit more regimented than other luxury lines.

CRYSTAL SYMPHONY

CREW MEMBERS	545
ENTERED SERVICE	1995
GROSS TONS	51,044
LENGTH	781 feet
NUMBER OF CABINS	470
PASSENGER CAPACITY	922 (1,010 max)
WIDTH	99 feet

700 ft.

500 ft.

300 ft.

Top: Casino gaming
Bottom: University@Sea

Public Areas and Facilities

Crystal Symphony, despite being a relatively large ship with some big-ship features, is noteworthy in the luxury market for creating intimate spaces in understated, yet sophisticated surroundings. Generous per-passenger space ratios have become a Crystal trademark, along with forward-facing observation decks, a Palm Court lounge, and a wide teak promenade encircling the ship. A complete makeover in 2006 refreshed the Bistro Café and shops, reconstructed the casino and Starlite Lounge, and added a new nightclub called Luxe. The extensive refurbishment infused all staterooms and bathrooms with a chic, boutique-style freshness.

Accented by a lovely waterfall, the focal point of the central two-deck atrium is a sculpture of two ballet dancers created especially for the space. Crystal Cove, the lobby lounge, is the spot to meet for cocktails as you make your way to the nearby dining room. Throughout the ship, public rooms shine with low-key contemporary style and flow easily from one to the next.

Restaurants

The formal restaurant serves open-seating breakfast and lunch and offers international cuisine in two traditional Main and Late assigned dinner seatings or, in a new option for 2011, Open Dining by Reservation (available between 6:15 and 9:15 PM). Although there's no additional charge for the intimate Asian- and Italian-specialty restaurants, reservations are required, and a gratuity is suggested for the servers. Exclusive Wine & Champagne Makers dinners are hosted in the Vintage Room. On select evenings, theme dinners are held poolside. Other dining choices include the Lido buffet for breakfast and lunch; a poolside grill for casual lunch throughout the afternoon; the Bistro, a specialty coffee and wine bar offering morning and afternoon snacks; and an ice cream bar. Afternoon tea is served in the Palm Court. Room service, with an extensive menu, is available 24 hours, and during dinner hours selections can be delivered from the formal restaurant menu. Suite passengers also have the option of ordering dinner from the specialty restaurants, which is served by their butlers.

Accommodations

Cabins: There are no inside cabins on *Crystal Symphony*. Still, relatively small stateroom sizes are cozy and chic with boutique-hotel-style decor. All cabins have ample closet and drawer/shelf storage, as well as bathroom shelves. Many have private balconies furnished with chairs and tables. Most suites and penthouses have a walk-in closet. Crystal Penthouse suites have guest powder rooms.

Amenities: Rich wood cabinetry, soft pastel fabrics, a small refrigerator filled with complimentary bottled water and soft drinks, a safe, two hair dryers, a flat-screen TV with a DVD player, and a sitting area with sofa, chair, and table are standard features in all cabins. Suite and penthouse extras vary, but all have a DVD/CD player, butler service, personalized stationery, and minibars with wine, beer, and choice of liquor.

Bathrooms: Every bathroom has oval glass sinks, granite counters, a full-size tub, Aveda toiletries, plush towels, and bathrobes for use during the cruise. Many suites and penthouses have a whirlpool tub and separate shower.

Worth Knowing: Five staterooms are wheelchair accessible.

In the Know

Steam rooms and saunas are complimentary, and no spa treatments or other purchases are required before using them. Simply go in anytime you please. In addition, bathrobes and disposable slippers are provided for use in the men's and women's locker rooms.

Pros and Cons

Pros: A refined and gracious atmosphere without a hint of unnecessary glitter is immediately apparent, but it's the professionalism of the staff that adds sparkle. Seating almost as many movie buffs as an average multiplex ashore and serving free popcorn, the large theater screens recent releases as well as classic favorites. If you feel the need to pack light and do laundry during your cruise or return home with clean clothing in your suitcases, passenger laundries are complimentary.

Cons: Although the wine selection is extensive, unlike other top-end luxury cruise lines, wine is not included with dinner. There are only 10 connecting staterooms and 89 staterooms with a third berth available for families. Gratuities are not included in the cost of the fare as they are on most luxury ships, but they can be pre-paid or charged to onboard accounts.

Cabin Type	Size (sq. ft.)
Crystal Penthouse	982
Penthouse Suites	491
Regular Penthouses	367
Deluxe Ocean View (w/balcony)	246
Deluxe Ocean View (regular)	202

All dimensions except for regular Deluxe staterooms (the only category that does not have a balcony) include the balcony square footage.

FAST FACTS

- 8 passenger decks
- 2 specialty restaurants, dining room, buffet, ice cream parlor
- Wi-Fi, safe, refrigerator, minibar (some), DVD
- 2 pools (1 indoor)
- Fitness classes, gym, hair salon, 2 hot tubs, sauna, spa, steam room
- 5 bars, casino, cinema, dance club, library, showroom, video game room
- Children's programs (ages 3–17)
- Dry cleaning, laundry facilities, laundry service
- Internet terminal
- No kids under 6 months

Library

DISNEY CRUISE LINE

With the launch of Disney Cruise Line in 1998, families were offered yet another reason to take a cruise. The magic of a Walt Disney resort vacation plus the romance of a sea voyage are a tempting combination, especially for adults who discovered Disney movies and the

Disney ships have a classic style

Mickey Mouse Club as children. Along with traditional shipboard activities are irresistible scheduled opportunities for the young and young-at-heart to interact with their favorite Disney characters.

✉ *210 Celebration Pl., Suite 400, Celebration, FL* ☎ *407/566–3500 or 888/325–2500* ⊕ *www.disneycruise. com* ☞ *Cruise Style: Mainstream.*

For the first time ever, Disney Cruise Line will offer Alaskan cruises during a four-month season of seven-night sailings aboard the Disney Wonder in summer 2011. To prepare for the Alaska cruises, a brand-new venue called Outlook Cafe will be added to the ship high atop deck 10. With comfortable seating and floor-to-ceiling, curved-glass windows, the 2,500-square-foot retreat is an ideal spot for relaxing with a beverage or cocktail while enjoying the bird's-eye view.

Shipboard entertainment leans heavily on popular Disney themes and characters. Parents are actively involved in the audience with their children at production shows, movies, live character meetings, deck parties, and dancing in the family nightclub. Teens have a supervised, no-adults-allowed club space in the forward fake funnel, where they gather for activities and parties. For adults, there are traditional no-kids-allowed bars and lounges with live music, dancing, theme parties, and late-night comedy, as well as daytime wine-tasting sessions, game shows, culinary arts and home entertaining demonstrations, and behind-the-scenes lectures on animation and filmmaking.

A giant LED screen has been affixed to the forward funnels where passengers can watch movies and special broadcasts while lounging in the family pool area.

Food

Don't expect top chefs and gourmet food. This is Disney, and the fare in Parrot Cay and Animator's Palate, the two casual restaurants, is all-American for the most part. Triton's restaurant is a bit fancier, with French-inspired dishes on the menus. Naturally, all have children's menus with an array of favorite sandwiches and entrées. Vegetarian and healthy selections are also available in all restaurants. A bonus is complimentary soft drinks, lemonade, and iced tea throughout the sailing. A beverage station in the buffet area is always open; however, there is a charge for soft drinks ordered from the bars and room service.

Palo, the adults-only restaurant serving northern Italian cuisine, requires reservations for a romantic evening of fine dining. Although there's a cover charge for dinner, at $15 per person it's a steal and reservations go fast. A champagne brunch on seven-night cruises also commands a $15 surcharge; high tea on seven-night cruises is $5.

Fitness and Recreation

Three swimming pools are designated for different groups: for children (Mickey's Pool, which has a waterslide and requires a parent to be present); for families (Goofy Pool); and adults (Quiet Cove). Young children who aren't potty trained can't swim in the pools but are invited to splash about in the fountain play area near Mickey's Pool. Be sure to bring their swim diapers.

The salon and spa feature a complete menu of hair- and nail-care services as well as facials and massages. The Tropical Rainforest is a soothing coed thermal suite with heated tile lounges. It's complimentary for the day if you book a spa treatment or available on a daily or cruise-long basis for a fee. Unique to Disney ships are SpaVillas, three indoor-outdoor treatment suites, each of which has a veranda with a hot tub and an open-air shower. In addition to a nicely equipped fitness center and aerobics studio are a jogging track and basketball court.

Your Shipmates

Disney Cruises appeal to kids of all ages—the young and not so young, singles, couples, and families. Multigeneration family groups are the core audience for these ships, and the facilities are ideal for family gatherings. What you might not have expected are the

Top: Dining in Palo, the adults-only restaurant
Bottom: Relax in a Mickey-approved spa

Top: Sweet treats await you on board
Middle: Enjoy a quarter-mile track for walking or jogging
Bottom: *Disney Magic* and *Disney Wonder* at sea

numerous newlywed couples celebrating their honeymoons on board.

Dress Code

Resort casual is the evening dress code for dinner in the Animator's Palate and Parrot Cay dining rooms. One-week cruises on *Disney Cruise Line* schedule a semiformal evening and a formal night, during which men are encouraged to wear tuxedos, but dark suits or sport coats and ties are acceptable for both. A sport coat is appropriate for Triton's (*Disney Wonder*) and Lumière's (*Disney Magic*) restaurant as well as Palo, the adults-only restaurant; however, you won't be turned away and could probably get by without the sport coat.

Junior Cruisers

As expected, Disney ships have extensive programs for children and teens. Parents are issued a pager for peace of mind and to alert them when their offspring need them. Complimentary age-appropriate activities are scheduled from 9 AM to midnight in the Oceaneer Club for ages 3 (toilet training required) to 7, in Oceaneer Lab for ages 8 to 12. Activities include arts projects, contests, computer games, pool parties, interactive lab stations, and opportunities for individual and group play. Ocean Quest on *Disney Magic,* designed for 10- to 14-year-olds, has video games, plasma-screen TVs, and a ship simulator where young mariners learn to steer the ship. The emphasis is on fun over education, but subtle educational themes are certainly there. Aloft is the coffeehouse-style teen club aboard *Disney Wonder*, with music, a dance floor, big-screen TV, and Internet café. Scheduled activities include challenging games, photography lessons, sporting contests, beach events, and parties, but they are also great places for teenagers 13 to 17 to just hang out with new friends in an adult-free zone.

An hourly fee is charged for child care in Flounder's Reef Nursery, which is open during select hours for infants as young as three months through three years. Supply your own diapers, and nursery attendants will change them. Private, in-cabin babysitting is not available.

CHOOSE THIS LINE IF . . .

You want to cruise with the entire family—mom, dad, the kids, and grandparents.

You enjoy having kids around. (There are adults-only areas to retreat to when the fun wears off.)

Your family enjoys Disney's theme parks and can't get enough wholesome entertainment.

Service
Friendly service is extended to all passengers with particular importance placed on treating children with the same courtesy extended to adults.

Tipping
Suggested gratuity amounts are calculated per person per cruise rather than on a per-night basis and can be added to onboard accounts or offered in cash on the last night of the cruise. Guidelines for the seven-night *Disney Wonder* cruise in Alaska recommend $84, which covers your dining room server, assistant server, head server, and stateroom host. Tips for room-service delivery, spa services, and the dining manager are at passengers' discretion. An automatic 15% gratuity is added to all bar tabs.

Past Passengers
Castaway Club membership is automatic after completing a Disney cruise. Benefits include a complimentary gift (such as a tote bag or beach towel), communication about special offers, priority check-in, invitations to shipboard cocktail parties during subsequent cruises, and a special toll-free reservation telephone number (☎ *800/449–3380*) for convenience.

2

DISNEY CRUISE LINE

GOOD TO KNOW

Silhouettes and abstract images of Mickey Mouse are cleverly hidden by Disney's creative designers throughout the ship, just as they are in the theme parks. See how many hidden Mickeys you can spot—it's a terrific family game. Other favorite pursuits are pin and autograph collecting; characters and crew members alike are happy to oblige with autographs. You can buy pins and autograph books on the ships, but the gift shops won't open until after you sail. Drop in at a Disney store before your cruise and purchase them for your kids; they'll appreciate being prepared from the get-go.

Prior to sailing, go online to reserve shore excursions, a table at the adults-only Palo restaurant, and babysitting in the nursery. Children can also be registered for youth programs, and adults can make spa appointments.

DON'T CHOOSE THIS LINE IF . . .

You want to spend a lot of quality time bonding with your kids. Your kids may not want to leave the fun activities.

You want to dine in peace and quiet. The dining rooms and buffet can be boisterous.

You want to gamble. There are no casinos, so you'll have to settle for bingo.

DISNEY MAGIC, DISNEY WONDER
(only Wonder sails in Alaska in 2011)

CREW MEMBERS	950
ENTERED SERVICE	1998, 1999
GROSS TONS	83,000
LENGTH	964 feet
NUMBER OF CABINS	877
PASSENGER CAPACITY	1,754 (2,400 max)
WIDTH	106 feet

700 ft.

500 ft.

300 ft.

Public Areas and Facilities
Reminiscent of classic ocean liners, Disney vessels have two funnels (the forward one is nonfunctional) and high-tech interiors behind their art deco and art nouveau styling. Whimsical design accents cleverly incorporate the images of Mickey Mouse and his friends without overpowering the warm and elegant decor. Artwork showcases the creativity of Disney artists and animators. The atmosphere is never stuffy.

More than 15,000 square feet—nearly an entire deck—is devoted to children's activity centers, outdoor activity areas, and swimming pools. Theaters cater to family entertainment with large-scale production shows, movies, dances, lively game shows, and even 3-D movies.

Adults-only hideaways include an avenue of theme bars and lounges tucked into the area just forward of the lobby atrium; the Promenade Lounge, near the aft elevator lobby; and Cove Café, a quiet spot adjacent to the adult pool to relax with coffee or a cocktail, surf the Internet, or read.

Restaurants
In a novel approach to dining, passengers (and their waiters) rotate through the three main dining rooms in assigned seatings. Parrot Cay and Animator's Palate are casual, while Triton's is a bit fancier. Palo is a beautifully appointed northern Italian restaurant for adults only that requires reservations for brunch, dinner, or tea and carries an extra charge. Breakfast and lunch are open seating in dining rooms. Disney characters make an appearance at a character breakfast on seven-night cruises. Breakfast, lunch, and dinner are also offered in the casual pool-deck buffet, while poolside pizzerias, snack bars, grills, and ice cream bars serve everything from pizza and hot dogs to fresh fruit, wraps, burgers, and frozen treats during the day. Specialty coffees are available in the adults-only Cove Café for an extra charge. Room service is available around the clock.

Accommodations
Cabins: Designed for families, Disney ships have some of the roomiest, most functional staterooms at sea. Natural woods, imported tiles, and a nautical flavor add to the decor, which even includes the touch of Disney-inspired artwork on the walls. Most cabins can

Top: Friendships are forged on a cruise
Bottom: *Disney Magic* at sea

accommodate at least three people and have a sitting area and unique bath-and-a-half arrangement. Three-quarters of all accommodations are outside cabins, and 44% of those include private balconies with kid-proof door handles and higher-than-usual railings for safety. All cabins have adequate closet and drawer/shelf storage, as well as bathroom shelves.

Suites: Suites are truly expansive, with master bedrooms separated from the living areas for privacy. All suites have walk-in closets, a dining table and chairs, a wet bar, a VCR, and a large balcony.

Amenities: Though not luxurious, Disney cabins are comfortably furnished. Each has a flat-screen TV, a small refrigerator, a personal safe, and a hair dryer; bathrobes are provided for use during the cruise in the top-category staterooms. All suites have concierge service.

Worth Noting: Sixteen cabins are wheelchair accessible.

In the Know
Aesthetically pleasing ship design can result in some quirky interior features. Four Navigator Verandah cabins are semiobstructed by slanting superstructure (6134, 6634, 7120, 7620); the rest have nautically furnished verandas with views through large portholes cut into the steel.

Pros and Cons
Pros: There are plenty of connecting cabins that sleep three, four, and five (two-bedroom suites sleep up to seven, one-bedroom suites sleep four or five, and deluxe family balcony staterooms sleep up to five). Soft drinks at meals and beverage stations are included in your cruise fare, so you don't have to max out your onboard account to keep everyone satisfied. Have no fear, adults aren't limited to milk and cookies—each ship has a piano bar–jazz club for easy listening and late-night cocktails.

Cons: Only potty-trained children can enter the swimming pools, so youngsters who wear swim diapers are only allowed to use the Mickey's Pool splash play area, which has a special filtration system; although a Disney cruise isn't all Disney all the time, it can get tiring for passengers who aren't really into it; there's no library on board, but limited reading materials are available in the Cove Café.

Cabin Type	Size (sq. ft.)
Walt and Roy Disney Suites	1,029
2-Bedroom Suite	945
1-Bedroom Suite	614
Deluxe Family Suite	304
Deluxe Balcony	268
Ocean View	226
Deluxe Inside	214
Standard Inside	184

FAST FACTS

- 11 passenger decks
- Specialty restaurant, 3 dining rooms, buffet, ice cream parlor, pizzeria
- Wi-Fi, safe, refrigerator
- 2 pools, children's pool
- Fitness classes, gym, hair salon, 4 hot tubs, sauna, spa
- 6 bars, cinema, dance club, 2 showrooms, video game room
- Children's programs (ages 3–17)
- Dry cleaning, laundry facilities, laundry service
- Internet terminal
- No kids under 12 weeks
- No-smoking cabins

Goofy touches up the paint on *Disney Magic*

2

HOLLAND AMERICA

Holland America Line has enjoyed a distinguished record of traditional cruises, world exploration, and transatlantic crossings since 1873—all facets of its history that are reflected in the fleet's multimillion-dollar shipboard art and antiques collections. Even the

A day on the Lido Deck

ships' names follow a pattern set long ago: all end in the suffix *dam* and are either derived from the names of various dams that cross Holland's rivers, important Dutch landmarks, or points of the compass. The names are even recycled when vessels are retired, and some are in their fifth and sixth generation of use.

✉ *300 Elliott Ave. W, Seattle, WA* ☎ *206/281–3535 or 800/577–1728* ⊕ *www. hollandamerica.com* ☞ *Cruise Style: Premium Deluxe.*

Noted for focusing on passenger comfort, Holland America Line cruises are classic in design and style, and with an infusion of younger adults and families on board, they remain refined without being stuffy or stodgy. Following a basic design theme, Holland America vessels make returning passengers feel as at home on the newest as they do on older ones.

Entertainment tends to be more Broadway-stylish than Las Vegas–brash. Colorful revues are presented in main show lounges by the ships' companies of singers and dancers. Other performances might include a range of cabaret acts: comedians, magicians, jugglers, and acrobats. Live bands play a wide range of musical styles for dancing and listening in smaller lounges and piano bars. Movies are shown daily in cinemas that double as the Culinary Arts Centers.

Holland America Line may never be considered cutting edge, but the Signature of Excellence concept introduced in 2003 sets it apart from other premium cruise lines. An interactive Culinary Arts Center offers cooking demonstrations and wine-tasting sessions; Explorations Café (powered by the *New York Times*) is a coffeehouse-style library and Internet center; and the Explorations Guest Speakers Series is supported by in-cabin televised programming on flat-screen TVs in all cabins; the traditional Crow's Nest observation lounge has a new nightclub-disco layout, video wall, and sound-and-light systems; and facilities for children and teens have been greatly expanded. Signature of Excellence upgrades were completed on the entire Holland America fleet in 2006.

Food

Holland America Line chefs, led by Master Chef Rudi Sodamin, utilize more than 500 different food items on a typical weeklong cruise to create the modern Continental cuisine and traditional favorites served to passengers. Vegetarian options as well as health-conscious cuisine are available, and special dietary requests can be handled with advance notice. Holland America's passengers used to skew older than they do now, so the sometimes bland dishes were no surprise. But the food quality, taste, and selection have greatly improved in recent years. A case in point is the reservations-required Pinnacle Grill alternative restaurants, where fresh seafood and premium cuts of Sterling Silver beef are used to prepare creative specialty dishes. The $20-per-person charge for dinner would be worth it for the Dungeness crab cakes starter and dessert alone. Other delicious traditions are afternoon tea, a Dutch Chocolate Extravaganza, and Holland America Line's signature bread pudding.

Flexible scheduling allows for early or late seatings in the two-deck, formal restaurants. Open seating from 5:15 to 9 has been introduced fleetwide.

Fitness and Recreation

Well-equipped and fully staffed fitness facilities contain state-of-the-art exercise equipment; basic fitness classes are available at no charge. There's a fee for personal training, body-composition analysis, and specialized classes such as yoga and Pilates.

Treatments in the Greenhouse Spa include a variety of massages, body wraps, and facials. Hair styling and nail services are offered in the salons. All ships have a jogging track, multiple swimming pools, and sports courts; some have hydrotherapy pools and soothing thermal suites.

Your Shipmates

No longer just your grandparents' cruise line, today's Holland America sailings attract families and discerning couples, mostly from their late-30s on up. Holidays and summer months are peak periods when you'll

NOTEWORTHY

■ Trays of mints, dried fruits, and candied ginger can be found outside the dining rooms.

■ Passengers are presented with a complimentary carryall bag imprinted with the line's logo.

■ Each ship has a wraparound promenade deck for walking, jogging, or stretching out in the shade on a padded steamer chair.

Top: Casino action
Bottom: Stay fit or stay loose

find more children in the mix. Comfortable retirees are often still in the majority, particularly on longer cruises. Families cruising together who book five or more cabins receive perks such as a fountain-soda package for each family member and a family photo for each stateroom. If the group is larger than 10 cabins or more, the Head-of-Family is recognized with an upgrade from outside stateroom to a veranda cabin. It's the best family deal at sea, and there's no extra charge.

Dress Code

Evenings on Holland America Line cruises fall into two categories: smart casual and formal. For the two formal nights standard on seven-night cruises, men are encouraged to wear tuxedos, but dark suits or sport coats and ties are acceptable, and you'll certainly see them. On smart-casual nights expect the type of attire you'd see at a country club or upscale resort. It's requested that no T-shirts, jeans, swimsuits, tank tops, or shorts be worn in public areas after 6 PM.

Junior Cruisers

Club HAL is Holland America Line's professionally staffed youth and teen program. Age-appropriate activities planned for children ages 3 to 7 include storytelling, arts and crafts, ice cream or pizza parties, and games; for children ages 8 to 12 there are arcade games, Sony PlayStations, theme parties, on-deck sports events, and scavenger hunts. Club HAL After Hours offers late-night activities from 10 PM until midnight for an hourly fee. Baby food, diapers, cribs, high chairs, and booster seats may be requested in advance of boarding. Private in-cabin babysitting is sometimes available if a staff member is willing.

Teens aged 13 to 17 have their own lounge with activities including dance contests, arcade games, sports tournaments, movies, and an exclusive sundeck on some ships. Select itineraries offer water park–type facilities and kid-friendly shore excursions to Half Moon Cay, Holland America Line's private island in the Bahamas.

Top: Soak up some sun on the outdoor deck
Middle: Production showtime
Bottom: Spa relaxation

CHOOSE THIS LINE IF . . .

You crave relaxation. Grab a padded steamer chair on the teak promenade deck and watch the sea pass by.

You like to go to the movies, especially when the popcorn is free.

You want to bring the kids. Areas designed exclusively for children and teens are hot new features on all ships.

Service

Professional, unobtrusive service by the Indonesian and Filipino staff is a fleetwide standard on Holland America Line. It isn't uncommon for a steward or server to remember the names of returning passengers from a cruise taken years before. Crew members are trained in Indonesia at a custom-built facility called the MS *Nieuw Jakarta,* where employees polish their English-language skills and learn housekeeping in mock cabins.

Tipping

Eleven dollars per passenger per day is automatically added to shipboard accounts, and gratuities are distributed to stewards and waitstaff. Passengers may adjust the amount based on the level of service experienced. Room-service tips are usually given in cash (it's at the passenger's discretion here). An automatic 15% gratuity is added to bar-service tabs.

Past Passengers

All passengers who sail with Holland America Line are automatically enrolled in the Mariner Society and receive special offers on upcoming cruises, as well as insider information concerning new ships and product enhancements. Mariner Society benefits also include preferred pricing on many cruises; Mariner baggage tags and buttons that identify you as a member during embarkation; an invitation to the Mariner Society champagne reception and awards party hosted by the captain; lapel pins and medallions acknowledging your history of Holland America sailings; a special collectible gift delivered to your cabin; and a subscription to *Mariner,* the full-color magazine featuring news and Mariner Society savings. Once you complete your first cruise, your Mariner identification number will be assigned and available for lookup online.

GOOD TO KNOW

The sound of delicate chimes still alerts Holland America Line passengers that it's mealtime. Artful flower arrangements never seem to wilt. A bowl of candied ginger is near the dining room entrance if you need a little something to settle your stomach. These simple, but nonetheless meaningful, touches are what make Holland America Line stand out from the crowd.

2

HOLLAND AMERICA

DON'T CHOOSE THIS LINE IF . . .

You want to party hard. Most of the action on these ships ends relatively early.

Dressing for dinner isn't your thing. Passengers tend to ramp up the dress code most evenings.

You have an aversion to extending tips. The line's "tipping not required" policy has been amended.

ROTTERDAM, AMSTERDAM
(only Amsterdam sails in Alaska in 2011)

CREW MEMBERS	644, 615
ENTERED SERVICE	1997, 2000
GROSS TONS	59,652, 62,735
LENGTH	780 feet
NUMBER OF CABINS	700, 690
PASSENGER CAPACITY	1,400, 1,380 (1,792 max)
WIDTH	106 feet

700 ft.

500 ft.

300 ft.

Public Areas and Facilities

Amsterdam and *Rotterdam* are sister ships, which sail on world cruises and extended voyages. The most traditional ships in the fleet, their interiors display abundant wood appointments in the public areas on promenade and lower promenade decks and priceless works of art throughout.

The Ocean Bar, Explorer's Lounge, Wajang Theater, and Crow's Nest are familiar lounges to longtime Holland American passengers. Newer additions include the spa's thermal suite, a culinary-arts demonstration center in the theater, Explorations Café, and areas for children and teens. Multimillion-dollar collections of art and artifacts are showcased throughout both vessels. In addition to works commissioned specifically for each ship, Holland America Line celebrates its heritage by featuring antiques and artworks that reflect the theme of worldwide Dutch seafaring history.

Restaurants

The formal dining room offers open-seating breakfast and lunch and a choice between two traditional assigned dinner seatings or open seating. The upscale Pinnacle Grill alternative restaurant serves lunch and dinner, requires reservations, and has a cover charge. A casual Lido restaurant serves buffet breakfast and lunch; at dinner, the Lido offers waiter service; Italian fare is served in the adjacent Canaletto Restaurant. Poolside lunch at the Terrace Grill features a variety of items ranging from nachos, grilled hamburgers, and hot dogs with all the trimmings to sandwiches and gourmet sausages. The extra-charge Explorations Café offers specialty coffees and pastries. Daily afternoon tea service is elevated to Royal Dutch High Tea once per cruise. Complimentary hors d'oeuvres are served by waiters during cocktail hour, hand-dipped chocolates are offered after dinner in the Explorer's Lounge, and a late-night buffet and chocolate extravaganza is served in the Lido Restaurant during every cruise. Room service is available 24 hours.

Accommodations

Cabins: Staterooms are spacious and comfortable, although fewer have private balconies than newer fleet mates. Every cabin has adequate closet and drawer/

Top: Pinnacle Grill dining
Bottom: *Rotterdam* at sea

shelf storage, as well as bathroom shelves. Some suites also have a whirlpool tub, powder room, and walk-in closet.

Suites: Extras include duvets on beds, a fully stocked minibar, and personalized stationery. Penthouse Verandah and Deluxe Verandah suites have exclusive use of the private Neptune Lounge, personal concierge service, canapés before dinner on request, binoculars and umbrellas for use during the cruise, an invitation to a VIP party with the captain, and complimentary laundry, pressing, and dry-cleaning services.

Amenities: All staterooms and suites are appointed with pillow-top mattresses, 250-thread-count cotton bed linens, magnifying halo-lighted mirrors, hair dryers, a fruit basket, flat-panel TVs, and DVD players. Bathrooms have Egyptian cotton towels, shampoo, body lotion, and bath gel, plus deluxe bathrobes to use during the cruise.

Worth Noting: Connecting cabins are available in a range of categories. Although there are a number of triple cabins to choose from, there are not as many that accommodate four. Twenty-one staterooms are designed for wheelchair accessibility on *Amsterdam*, 22 on *Rotterdam*.

In the Know
The creation of the expansive, floral, stained-glass ceiling that provides a focal point for *Amsterdam*'s formal dining room required the use of some state-of-the-art technology that was developed especially for the ship.

Pros and Cons
Pros: More balcony cabins, spa staterooms, and a new category of Lanai staterooms with direct access to the promenade deck, and The Retreat (a resort-style pool on the aft Lido Deck) were added to *Rotterdam* in 2009. Servers circulate throughout lounges before and after dinner with canapés and other treats. Realistic landscapes with surreal touches accent dining alcoves in the Pinnacle Grill.

Cons: Although outside cabins on the lower promenade deck are ideally situated for easy access to fresh air, occupants should heed the warning that the one-way window glass does not offer complete privacy when interior lights are on. Lounges are lively before and after dinner, but many passengers tend to call it a night early. While you'll find excellent facilities designed for kids and teens, suitable accommodations for families are sparse.

Cabin Type	Size (sq. ft.)
Penthouse Suite	1,159
Deluxe Verandah Suite	556
Verandah Suite	293
Ocean View	197
Inside	182

Dimensions include square footage for balconies.

FAST FACTS
- 9 passenger decks
- Specialty restaurant, dining room, buffet
- Wi-Fi, safe, refrigerator, minibar (some), DVD
- 2 pools (1 indoor), 2 children's pools
- Fitness classes, gym, hair salon, 2 hot tubs, sauna, spa
- 6 bars, casino, cinema, dance club, library, showroom, video game room
- Children's programs (ages 3–17)
- Dry cleaning, laundry facilities, laundry service
- Internet terminal
- No-smoking cabins (some)

A brisk walk starts the day

2

HOLLAND AMERICA

VISTA CLASS
Zuiderdam, Oosterdam, Westerdam, Noordam
(all except Noordam sail in Alaska in 2011)

CREW MEMBERS	817, 817, 817, 820
ENTERED SERVICE	2002, 2003, 2004, 2006
GROSS TONS	82,305
LENGTH	936 feet
NUMBER OF CABINS	958, 958, 958, 959
PASSENGER CAPACITY	1,916; 1,916; 1,916; 1,918
WIDTH	106 feet

700 ft.
500 ft.
300 ft.

Top: *Oosterdam* hydro pool
Bottom: Vista-class ocean-
view stateroom

Public Areas and Facilities

Ships for the 21st century, Vista-class vessels successfully integrate new, youthful, and family-friendly elements into Holland America Line's classic fleet. Exquisite Waterford crystal sculptures adorn triple-deck atriums and reflect vivid, almost daring color schemes throughout. Although all the public rooms carry the traditional Holland America names (Ocean Bar, Explorer's Lounge, Crow's Nest) and aren't much different in atmosphere, their louder decor (toned down a bit since the introduction of the *Zuiderdam*) may make them unfamiliar to returning passengers.

Only two decks are termed *promenade*, and the exterior teak promenade encircles public rooms, not cabins. As a result, numerous outside accommodations have views of the sea restricted by lifeboats on the upper promenade deck. Veterans of cruises on older Holland America ships will find the layout of public spaces somewhat different; still, everyone's favorite Crow's Nest lounges still offer those commanding views.

Restaurants

The formal dining room offers open-seating breakfast and lunch and a choice between two traditional assigned dinner seatings or open seating. The upscale Pinnacle Grill alternative restaurant serves lunch and dinner, requires reservations, and has a cover charge. A casual Lido restaurant serves buffet breakfast and lunch; at dinner the Lido offers waiter service featuring entrées from both the Lido and main dining room menus; Italian fare is served in the adjacent Canaletto Restaurant. Poolside lunch at the Terrace Grill features a variety of items ranging from nachos, grilled hamburgers, and hot dogs with all the trimmings to sandwiches and gourmet sausages. The extra-charge Explorations Café offers specialty coffees and pastries. Daily afternoon tea service is elevated to Royal Dutch High Tea once per cruise. Complimentary hors d'oeuvres are served by waiters during cocktail hour, hand-dipped chocolates are offered after dinner in the Explorer's Lounge, and a late-night buffet and chocolate extravaganza is served in the Lido Restaurant during every cruise. Room service is available 24 hours.

Accommodations

Cabins: Comfortable and roomy, 85% of all Vista-class accommodations have an ocean view, and almost 80% of those also have the luxury of a private balcony furnished with chairs, loungers, and tables. Every cabin has adequate closet and drawer/shelf storage, as well as bathroom shelves.

Suites: Suite luxuries include duvets on beds and a fully stocked minibar; some also have a whirlpool tub, powder room, and walk-in closet. Penthouse Verandah and Deluxe Verandah suites have exclusive use of the private Neptune Lounge, personal concierge service, canapés before dinner, and complimentary laundry, pressing, and dry-cleaning services.

Amenities: All staterooms and suites are appointed with pillow-top mattresses, 250-thread-count cotton bed linens, magnifying halogen-lighted makeup mirrors, hair dryers, a fruit basket, flat-panel TVs, and DVD players. Bathroom extras include Egyptian cotton towels, shampoo, body lotion, and bath gel, plus deluxe bathrobes to use during the cruise.

Worth Noting: Twenty-eight staterooms are wheelchair accessible.

In the Know

If you want complete privacy on your balcony, choose your location carefully. Take a close look at the deck plans for the ones alongside the exterior panoramic elevators. Riders have views of adjacent balconies as well as the seascape.

Pros and Cons

Pros: Adjacent to the Crow's Nest, an outdoor seating area covered in canvas is a wonderful, quiet hideaway during the day as well as when the interior is transformed into a dance club at night. Exterior panoramic elevators offer an elevated view of the seascape. Half-hour shipboard art tours are available on board the ship, loaded on iPods that you may borrow.

Cons: Missing from the Vista-class ships are self-service laundry rooms, a serious omission for families with youngsters and anyone sailing on back-to-back Caribbean itineraries or cruises of more than a week. Murals in Pinnacle Grill restaurants are strangely chintzy looking, especially considering the priceless art throughout the rest of the ships' interiors. Traditional appointments stop at the table top in the Pinnacle Grill—some chairs are silvery cast aluminum and so heavy that they don't budge without a great deal of effort.

Cabin Type	Size (sq. ft.)
Penthouse Suites	1,318
Deluxe Verandah Suite	510–700
Superior Verandah Suite	398
Deluxe Ocean View	254
Standard Ocean View	185
Inside	170–200

Dimensions include square footage for balconies.

FAST FACTS

■ 11 passenger decks

■ Specialty restaurant, dining room, buffet, pizzeria

■ Internet, Wi-Fi, safe, refrigerator, DVD

■ 2 pools (1 indoor)

■ Fitness classes, gym, hair salon, 5 hot tubs, sauna, spa, steam room

■ 9 bars, casino, cinema, 2 dance clubs, library, showroom, video game room

■ Children's programs (ages 3–17)

■ Dry cleaning, laundry service

■ Internet terminal

Westerdam at sea

2

HOLLAND AMERICA

STATENDAM CLASS
Statendam, Maasdam, Ryndam, Veendam
(only Statendam sails in Alaska in 2011)

CREW MEMBERS	580
ENTERED SERVICE	1993, 1993, 1994, 1996
GROSS TONS	55,819
LENGTH	720 feet
NUMBER OF CABINS	630
PASSENGER CAPACITY	1,260
WIDTH	101 feet

700 ft.

500 ft.

300 ft.

Public Areas and Facilities
The sister ships included in the S- or Statendam-class retain the most classic and traditional characteristics of Holland America Line vessels. Routinely updated with innovative features, including Signature of Excellence upgrades, they combine all the advantages of intimate, midsize vessels with high-tech and stylish details.

At the heart of the ships, triple-deck atriums graced by suspended glass sculptures open onto three so-called promenade decks; the lowest contains staterooms encircled by a wide, teak, outdoor deck furnished with padded steamer chairs, while interior, art-filled passageways flow past lounges and public rooms on the two decks above. It's easy to find just about any area on board, with the possible exception of the main level of the dining room. Either reach the lower dining room floor via the aft elevator, or enter one deck above and make a grand entrance down the sweeping staircase.

Restaurants
The formal dining room offers open seating breakfast and lunch and a choice between two traditional assigned dinner seatings or open seating. The upscale Pinnacle Grill alternative restaurant serves lunch and dinner, requires reservations, and has a cover charge. A casual Lido restaurant serves buffet breakfast and lunch; at dinner the Lido offers waiter service featuring entrées from both the Lido and main dining room menus; Italian fare is served in the adjacent Canaletto Restaurant. Poolside lunch at the Terrace Grill features a variety of items ranging from nachos, grilled hamburgers, and hot dogs with all the trimmings to sandwiches and gourmet sausages. The extra-charge Explorations Café offers specialty coffees and pastries. Daily afternoon tea service is elevated to Royal Dutch High Tea once per cruise. Complimentary hors d'oeuvres are served by waiters during cocktail hour, hand-dipped chocolates are offered after dinner in the Explorer's Lounge, and a late-night buffet and chocolate extravaganza is served in the Lido Restaurant during every cruise. Room service is available 24 hours.

Accommodations
Cabins: Staterooms are spacious, although fewer of them have private balconies than on newer fleet mates.

Top: Enjoy a Vegas-style show
Bottom: Deluxe veranda suite

A new cabin category—Lanai cabins, with a door that directly access the promenade deck—was added during the ship's latest upgrade. Every cabin has adequate closet and drawer/shelf storage, as well as bathroom shelves. Some suites have a whirlpool tub, powder room, and walk-in closet.

Suites: Suites have duvets on beds, a fully stocked mini-bar, and personalized stationery. Penthouse Verandah and Deluxe Verandah suites have exclusive use of the private Neptune Lounge, personal concierge service, canapés before dinner on request, binoculars and umbrellas for use during the cruise, an invitation to a VIP party with the captain, and complimentary laundry, pressing, and dry-cleaning services.

Amenities: Gone are the flowery chintz curtains and bedspreads of yesteryear—all staterooms and suites are now appointed with pillow-top mattresses, 250-thread-count cotton bed linens, magnifying lighted mirrors, hair dryers, a fruit basket, flat-panel TVs, and DVD players. Bathroom extras include Egyptian cotton towels, shampoo, body lotion, bath gel, and bathrobes.

Worth Noting: Connecting cabins are featured in a range of categories. Six staterooms are wheelchair accessible; nine are modified with ramps although doors are standard width.

In the Know
Do you recognize the portraits etched into the glass doors to the main show lounges? They are great Dutch artists for whom the spaces are named.

Pros and Cons
Pros: When the Statendam-class ships emerge from extensive dry docks scheduled over the next two years, they will feature more accommodations with balconies, Spa staterooms, a new Lanai stateroom category with direct access to the walk-around promenade deck, and the Retreat, a resort-style pool area on the aft Lido Deck. Ask for the recipe for Holland America Line's signature bread-and-butter pudding with a creamy sauce, which just might be the best in the world. Popular, yet quiet enough for conversation, the Ocean Bar hits just the right balance for late-night socializing.

Cons: Grab seats on the lower level of the main show lounges—railings on the balcony level obstruct the view. Club HAL may not be too kid-friendly if your cruise is primarily booked by older passengers. With the addition of Explorations Café, the popular—and free—Java coffee bars have been eliminated.

Cabin Type	Size (sq. ft.)
Penthouse Suite	1,159
Deluxe Verandah Suite	556
Verandah Suite	292
Lanai	197
Ocean View	196
Inside	186

Dimensions include the square footage for balconies.

FAST FACTS

- 10 passenger decks
- Specialty restaurant, dining room, buffet
- Wi-Fi, safe, minibar, refrigerator, DVD
- 2 pools (1 indoor), 2 children's pools
- Fitness classes, gym, hair salon, 2 hot tubs, sauna, spa, steam room
- 9 bars, casino, cinema, dance club, library, showroom, video game room
- Children's programs (ages 3–17)
- Dry cleaning, laundry facilities, laundry service
- Internet terminal
- No-smoking cabins (some)

Share a sunset

2

HOLLAND AMERICA

VOLENDAM, ZAANDAM

CREW MEMBERS	615
ENTERED SERVICE	1999, 2000
700 ft.	**GROSS TONS** 61, 214/61,396
	LENGTH 781 feet
500 ft.	**NUMBER OF CABINS** 716
	PASSENGER CAPACITY 1,432 (1,850 max)
300 ft.	**WIDTH** 106 feet

Public Areas and Facilities

Similar in layout to Statendam-class vessels, these slightly larger sister ships introduced playful art and interior design theme elements to Holland America Line's classic vessels. Triple-deck atriums are distinguished by a fantastic—and fiber-optic-lighted—Murano-glass sculpture on *Volendam* and, in an attempt to be hip, an almost scary towering pipe organ on *Zaandam*.

The interior decor and much of the artwork found in each vessel has a predominant theme—*Volendam* centers around flowers and *Zaandam* around music. Look for *Zaandam*'s collection of guitars autographed by famous musicians such as the Rolling Stones and a saxophone signed by former President Bill Clinton. Since the ships are larger than the original Statendam-class ships, the extra space allows for a larger specialty restaurant and a roomier feel throughout.

Restaurants

The formal dining room offers open seating breakfast and lunch and a choice between two traditional assigned dinner seatings or open seating. The upscale Pinnacle Grill alternative restaurant serves lunch and dinner, requires reservations, and has a cover charge A casual Lido restaurant serves buffet breakfast and lunch; at dinner the Lido offers waiter service featuring entrées from both the Lido and main dining room menus. Canaletto Restuaruant, adjacent to the Lido dining area, serves classic Italian fare with tableside service for dinners only. Poolside lunch at the Terrace Grill features a variety of items ranging from nachos, grilled hamburgers, and hot dogs with all the trimmings to sandwiches and gourmet sausages. The extra-charge Explorations Café offers specialty coffees and pastries. Daily afternoon tea service is elevated to Royal Dutch High Tea once per cruise. Complimentary hors d'oeuvres are served by waiters during cocktail hour, hand-dipped chocolates are offered after dinner in the Explorer's Lounge, and a late-night buffet and chocolate extravaganza is served in the Lido Restaurant during every cruise. Room service is available 24 hours.

Accommodations

Cabins: Staterooms are spacious and comfortable with a few more balconies than Statendam-class. Every cabin

Top: Celebrate a special occasion
Bottom: Deluxe veranda suite

5

has adequate closet and drawer/shelf storage, as well as bathroom shelves. Some suites have a whirlpool tub, powder room, and walk-in closet.

Suites: Suite amenities include duvets on beds, a fully stocked minibar, and personalized stationery. Penthouse Verandah and Deluxe Verandah suites have exclusive use of the private Neptune Lounge, personal concierge service, canapés before dinner on request, binoculars and umbrellas for use during the cruise, an invitation to a VIP party with the captain, and complimentary laundry, pressing, and dry-cleaning services.

Amenities: All staterooms are appointed with pillow-top mattresses, 250-thread-count cotton bed linens, magnifying halo-lighted mirrors, hair dryers, a fruit basket, flat-panel TVs, and DVD players. Bathrooms have Egyptian cotton towels, shampoo, body lotion, bath gel, and deluxe bathrobes to use during the cruise.

Worth Noting: As a nod to families, connecting cabins are featured in a range of categories. However, although the number of triple cabins is generous, there are not many that accommodate four. Twenty-two staterooms are designed for wheelchair accessibility.

In the Know
Don't be surprised if you suddenly feel you're in a ticker-tape parade during one of the high-energy production shows. Not only are the show lounges outfitted with revolving stages and hydraulic lifts, but they also feature a moving light system and confetti cannons.

Pros and Cons
Pros: The home of Holland America's new Culinary Arts Institute cooking demonstrations, the ship's theaters also continue to function as cinemas, and moviegoers still relish the complimentary freshly popped popcorn. Waiters serve made-to-order entrées in the Lido restaurant at dinner, and an evening poolside barbecue buffet is usually scheduled during each cruise. If you love cooking classes but just can't face anyone during a bad hair day, you can watch the culinary-arts demonstration on your cabin television.

Cons: Expanded spa facilities make the gym area somewhat tight. The same spa expansion also eliminated individual men's and women's steam rooms to make room for an extra-charge thermal suite. Sandwiched between the Lido pool and Lido bar, the children's wading pool area can become quite boisterous when there are a lot of families with children on board.

Cabin Type	Size (sq. ft.)
Penthouse Suite	1,126
Deluxe Verandah Suite	563
Verandah Suite	284
Ocean View	197
Inside	182

Dimensions include square footage for balconies.

FAST FACTS

- 10 passenger decks
- Specialty restaurant, dining room, buffet
- Wi-Fi, safe, minibar (some), refrigerator, DVD
- 2 pools (1 indoor), 2 children's pools
- Fitness classes, gym, hair salon, 2 hot tubs, sauna, spa
- 6 bars, casino, cinema, dance club, library, showroom, video game room
- Children's programs (ages 3–17)
- Dry cleaning, laundry facilities, laundry service
- Internet terminal

Zaandam atrium organ

NORWEGIAN CRUISE LINE

Norwegian Cruise Line (NCL) set sail in 1966 with an entirely new concept: regularly scheduled Caribbean cruises from the then-obscure port of Miami. Good food and friendly service combined with value fares established NCL as a winner for active adults

Norwegian's buffets are beautifully presented

and families. With the introduction of the now-retired SS *Norway* in 1979, NCL ushered in the era of cruises on megasize ships. Innovative and forward-looking, NCL has been a cruise-industry leader for four decades and is as much at home in Europe as it is in the Caribbean.

✉ *7665 Corporate Center Dr., Miami, FL* ☎ *305/436–4000 or 800/327–7030* ⊕ *www. ncl.com* ☞ *Cruise Style: Mainstream.*

Noted for top-quality, high-energy entertainment and emphasis on fitness facilities and programs, NCL combines action, activities, and a variety of dining options in a casual, free-flowing atmosphere. Freestyle cruising has meant an end to rigid dining schedules and dress codes. NCL ships now offer a host of flexible dining options that allow passengers to eat in the main dining rooms or any of a number of à la carte and specialty restaurants at any time and with whom they please. Now co-owned by Star Cruises and Apollo Management, a private equity company, NCL continues to be an industry innovator.

More high jinks than high-brow, entertainment after dark features extravagant Las Vegas–style revues presented in main show lounges by lavishly costumed singers and dancers. Other performers might include comedians, magicians, jugglers, and acrobats. Passengers can get into the act by taking part in talent shows or step up to the karaoke microphone. Live bands play for dancing and listening passengers in smaller lounges, and each ship has a lively disco. Some ships include shows by Chicago's world-famous Second City improvisational comedy company. With the launch of

Norwegian Epic in 2010, the Blue Man Group and Cirque Productions (a U.S.-based company somewhat similar in style to Cirque du Soleil) join NCL's talent lineup.

Casinos, bingo sessions, and art auctions are well attended. Adult games, particularly the competitive ones, are fun to participate in and provide laughs for audience members. Goofy pool games are an NCL staple, and the ships' bands crank up the volume during afternoon and evening deck parties.

From a distance, most cruise ships look so similar that it's often difficult to tell them apart, but NCL's largest, modern ships stand out with their distinctive use of hull art. Each new ship is distinguished by murals extending from bow to midship.

When others scoffed at winter cruises to the Caribbean, Bahamas, and Florida from New York City, NCL recognized the demand and has sailed with such success that others have followed in its wake. A Winter Weather Guarantee is offered should foul weather threaten to spoil your vacation plans. If departure from New York is delayed for more than 12 hours due to weather, you will receive an onboard credit of $100 per person on your current departure, or, if you decide to cancel your cruise, you will receive a cruise credit equal to the amount you paid to use on a future NCL cruise within one year and any reasonable incidental expenses you incur in rearranging your travel plans.

Food

Main dining rooms serve what is traditionally deemed Continental fare, although it's about what you would expect at a really good hotel banquet. Health-conscious menu selections are nicely prepared, and vegetarian choices are always available. Where NCL really shines is the specialty restaurants, especially the French-Mediterranean Le Bistro (on all ships), the pan-Asian restaurants, and steak houses (on the newer ships). As a rule of thumb, the newer the ship, the wider the variety, because new ships were purpose-built with as many as 10 or more places to eat. You may find Spanish tapas, an Italian trattoria, a steak house, and a pan-Asian restaurant complete with a sushi and sashimi bar and teppanyaki room. Almost all carry a cover charge or are priced à la carte and require reservations. An NCL staple, the late-night Chocoholic Buffet continues to be a favorite event.

NOTEWORTHY

■ Numerous connecting staterooms and suites can be combined to create multicabin family accommodations.

■ Freestyle cruising offers the flexibility of dining with anyone you choose and when you actually wish to eat.

■ The ships in the NCL fleet sport hull art—huge murals that make them easily recognizable from afar.

Top: Casual Freestyle dining
Bottom: Grab a front row seat at a show

2

NORWEGIAN CRUISE LINE

Fitness and Recreation

Mandara Spa offers unique and exotic spa treatments fleetwide on NCL, although facilities vary widely. Spa treatments include a long menu of massages, body wraps, and facials, and current trends in hair and nail services are offered in the salons. The latest addition on board is a medi-spa physician, who can create individualized treatment plans using nonsurgical treatments such as Botox Cosmetic. State-of-the-art exercise equipment, jogging tracks, and basic fitness classes are available at no charge. There's a fee for personal training, body-composition analysis, and specialized classes such as yoga and Pilates.

Your Shipmates

NCL's mostly American cruise passengers are active couples ranging from their mid-30s to mid-50s. Many families enjoy cruising on NCL ships during holidays and summer months. Longer cruises and more exotic itineraries attract passengers in the over-55 age group.

Dress Code

Resort casual attire is appropriate at all times; the option of one formal evening is available on all cruises of seven nights and longer. Most passengers raise the casual dress code a notch to what could be called casual chic attire.

Junior Cruisers

For children and teens, each NCL vessel offers a Kid's Crew program of supervised entertainment for young cruisers ages 2 to 17. Younger children are split into three groups, ages 2 to 5, 6 to 9, and 10 to 12; activities range from storytelling, games, and arts and crafts to dinner with counselors, pajama parties, and treasure hunts.

Group Port Play is available in the children's area to accommodate parents booked on shore excursions. Evening babysitting services are available for a fee. Parents whose children are not toilet trained are issued a beeper to alert them when diaper changing is necessary. Children under two cruise at a reduced fare, and

Top: Casino play
Middle: Windows in the dining areas mean you don't miss a minute of the scenery
Bottom: *Norwegian Dream* superior Ocean View stateroom

CHOOSE THIS LINE IF . . .

Doing your own thing is your idea of a real vacation. You could almost remove your watch and just go with the flow.

You want to leave your formal dress-up wardrobe at home.

You're competitive. There's always a pickup game in progress on the sports courts.

certain itineraries offer specials on third and fourth guests in the same stateroom. Infants under six months of age cannot travel on NCL ships.

For teens ages 13 to 17, options include sports, pool parties, teen disco, movies, and video games. Some ships have their own cool clubs where teens hang out in adult-free zones.

Service
Somewhat inconsistent, service is nonetheless congenial. Although crew members tended to be outgoing Caribbean islanders in the past; they have largely been replaced by Asians and Eastern Europeans who are well trained yet are inclined to be more reserved.

Tipping
A fixed service charge of $12 per person per day is added to shipboard accounts. An automatic 15% gratuity is added to bar tabs. Staff members may also accept cash gratuities. Passengers in suites who have access to concierge and butler services are asked to offer a cash gratuity at their own discretion.

Past Passengers
Upon completion of your first NCL cruise you're automatically enrolled in Latitudes, the club for repeat passengers. Membership benefits accrue based on the number of cruises completed: Bronze (1 through 4), Silver (5 through 8), Gold (9 through 13), and Platinum (14 or more). Everyone receives *Latitudes*, NCL's quarterly magazine, Latitudes pricing, Latitudes check-in at the pier, a ship pin, access to a special customer service desk and liaison on board, and a members-only cocktail party hosted by the captain. Higher tiers receive a welcome basket, an invitation to the captain's cocktail party, and dinner in Le Bistro, and priority for check-in, tender tickets, and disembarkation.

GOOD TO KNOW

When considering an NCL cruise, keep in mind that the ships weren't cut from a cookie-cutter mold and they differ widely in size and detail. Although all are brightly appointed and attempt to offer a comparable experience, the older ships just don't have the panache or as many Freestyle dining venues found on the newer, purpose-built ships. On the plus side, the newest vessels have many options for families, including large numbers of interconnecting staterooms that make them ideal for even supersize clans. NCL has one of the newest fleets at sea, following the introduction of two large, new vessels and retirement of some older, smaller ships.

2

NORWEGIAN CRUISE LINE

DON'T CHOOSE THIS LINE IF . . .

You don't like to pay extra for food on a ship. All the best specialty restaurants have extra charges.

You don't want to stand in line. There are lines for nearly everything.

You don't want to hear announcements. They're frequent on these ships—and loud.

JEWEL CLASS
Norwegian Jewel, Norwegian Jade, Norwegian Pearl, Norwegian Gem (only Pearl sails in Alaska in 2011)

CREW MEMBERS	1,122, 1,121, 1,124, 1,123
ENTERED SERVICE	2005, 2006, 2006, 2007
GROSS TONS	92,100, 93,500, 93,530, 93,530
LENGTH	965 feet
NUMBER OF CABINS	1,188, 1,201, 1,197, 1,197
PASSENGER CAPACITY	2,376, 2,402, 2,394, 2,394
WIDTH	105 feet

700 ft.

500 ft.

300 ft.

Public Areas and Facilities

Jewel-class ships are the next step in the continuing evolution of Freestyle ship design: the interior location of some public rooms and restaurants has been tweaked since the introduction of Freestyle cruising vessels, and new categories of deluxe accommodations have been added.

These ships have more than a dozen dining alternatives, a variety of entertainment options, enormous spas with thermal suites (for which there is a charge), and expansive areas reserved for children and teens. Pools have waterslides and a plethora of lounge chairs, although when your ship is full it can be difficult to find one in a prime location. *Norwegian Pearl* and *Norwegian Gem* introduced the line's first rock-climbing walls as well as Bliss Lounge, which has trendy South Beach decor and the first full-size 10-pin bowling alleys on modern cruise ships.

Restaurants

Two main complimentary dining rooms serve open-seating breakfast, lunch, and dinner. Specialty restaurants, including NCL's signature French restaurant Le Bistro, Cagney's Steakhouse, an Asian restaurant, sushi bar, teppanyaki room, tapas and salsa eatery, and an Italian trattoria–style restaurant carry varying cover charges and require reservations. Screens located throughout the ship illustrate the status (full, moderately busy, empty) and waiting time you can expect for each restaurant on board. Casual choices are the Lido Buffet for breakfast, lunch, and dinner; Blue Lagoon for soup, sandwiches, and snacks around the clock; and the poolside grill for lunch. Java Café serves specialty coffees and pastries for an additional charge. While the 24-hour room service menu is somewhat limited, suite occupants may order from any restaurant on the ship.

Accommodations

Cabins: NCL ships are not noted for large staterooms, but all have a small sitting area with sofa, chair, and table. Every cabin has adequate closet and drawer/shelf storage, as well as limited bathroom storage. Suites have walk-in closets.

Top: *Norwegian Jewel's* Azura restaurant
Bottom: Hydropool in the spa

Garden and Courtyard Villas: Garden Villas, with three bedrooms, a living-dining room, and private deck garden with a spa tub, are among the largest suites at sea. Courtyard Villas—not as large as Garden Villas—nevertheless have an exclusive concierge lounge and a shared private courtyard with pool, hot tub, sundeck, and small gym.

Amenities: A small refrigerator, tea/coffeemaker, personal safe, broadband Internet connection, duvets on beds, a wall-mounted hair dryer, and bathrobes are standard. Bathrooms have a shampoo–bath gel dispenser on the shower wall and a magnifying mirror. Suites have a whirlpool tub, an entertainment center with a CD/DVD player, and concierge and butler service.

Worth Noting: Some staterooms interconnect in most categories. Twenty-seven staterooms are wheelchair accessible.

In the Know
You may feel you've slipped into wonderland when you first encounter some of the fanciful furniture in the lounges aboard each ship and in Bliss Ultra Lounge on *Norwegian Pearl* and *Norwegian Gem*. Some are covered in wildly colorful velvets and are designed as thrones and even lounging beds.

Pros and Cons
Pros: Performances by Second City, Chicago's famous improvisation artists, are scheduled in the theater as well as in more intimate nightclub settings. Escape the crowds in the ship's tranquil library, which is also a good spot to gaze at the sea if your book proves to be less than compelling. With access to a private courtyard pool, hot tub, steam room, exercise area, and sundeck, Courtyard Villa accommodations are like a ship within a ship.

Cons: The thermal suites in the spa have large whirlpools, saunas, steam rooms, and a relaxation area with loungers facing the sea, but there is an additional charge to use the facility. "Freestyle" dining doesn't mean you can get a table in the main dining rooms at precisely the moment you want, but waiting times can be reduced if you time your arrival at nonpeak periods. For such a large ship, the Internet center is tiny.

Cabin Type	Size (sq. ft.)
Garden Villa	4,390
Courtyard Villa	574
Owner's Suites	823
Deluxe Owner's Suites	928
Penthouse Suite	575
Minisuite	284
Ocean View with Balcony	205–243
Ocean View	161
Inside	143

FAST FACTS

- 15 passenger decks
- 7 restaurants, 2 dining rooms, buffet, ice cream parlor, pizzeria
- Internet, Wi-Fi, safe, refrigerator, DVD (some)
- 2 pools, children's pool
- Fitness classes, gym, hair salon, 6 hot tubs, spa, steam room
- 9 bars, casino, cinema, dance club, library, showroom, video game room
- Children's programs (ages 2–17)
- Dry cleaning, laundry facilities, laundry service
- Internet terminal

The sports deck

2

NORWEGIAN CRUISE LINE

DAWN CLASS
Norwegian Star, Norwegian Dawn
(only Star sails in Alaska in 2011)

CREW MEMBERS	1,095, 1,098
ENTERED SERVICE	2001, 2002
GROSS TONS	91,740
LENGTH	935 feet
NUMBER OF CABINS	1,120, 1,126
PASSENGER CAPACITY	2,240, 2,224 (2,683 max)
WIDTH	105 feet

700 ft.

500 ft.

300 ft.

Public Areas and Facilities

Purpose-built for NCL's Freestyle cruising concept, *Norwegian Dawn* and *Norwegian Star,* the latter of which offers only Mexican Riviera and Alaska cruises, each have more than a dozen dining options, a variety of entertainment selections, expansive facilities for children and teens, and enormous spas with indoor lap pools. In what might be termed a supersize "thermal suite" on other ships, the spa areas feature indoor lap pools surrounded by lounge chairs, large whirlpools, saunas, and steam rooms, and—best of all—there's no additional charge to use any of it, unlike on other NCL ships.

These ships unveiled NCL's superdeluxe Garden Villa accommodations, English pubs, and 24-hour dining in the Blue Lagoon Restaurant. Interior spaces are bright and cheerful, especially the atrium area adjacent to the outdoor promenade, which is flooded with sunlight through expansive windows. A second, smaller garden atrium with a prominent waterfall leads the way to the spa lobby. Located near the children's splash pool is a hot tub for parents' enjoyment.

Restaurants

Two complimentary dining rooms serve open-seating meals for breakfast, lunch, or dinner. Specialty restaurants, including NCL's signature French restaurant Le Bistro, Cagney's Steakhouse, an Asian restaurant, sushi bar, teppanyaki room, Tex-Mex eatery, and Italian restaurant carry varying cover charges and require reservations. Screens located throughout the ship illustrate the status (full, moderately busy, empty) and waiting time you can expect for each restaurant on board. Casual choices are the Lido Buffet for breakfast, lunch, and dinner; Blue Lagoon for soup, sandwiches, and snacks around the clock; and the poolside grill for lunch. Java Café serves specialty coffees and pastries for an extra charge. While the 24-hour room service menu is somewhat limited, suite occupants may order from any restaurant on the ship.

Accommodations

Cabins: NCL ships are not noted for large staterooms, but all have a small sitting area with sofa, chair, and table. Most bathrooms are compartmentalized with a

Top: Cagney's Steakhouse on
Norwegian Dawn
Bottom: Minisuite

sink area, shower, and toilet separated by sliding glass doors. Every cabin has adequate closet and drawer/shelf storage, as well as limited bathroom storage. Suites have walk-in closets.

Amenities: Cherrywood cabinetry, tropical decor, mirrored accents, a small refrigerator, tea/coffeemaker, personal safe, broadband Internet connection, duvets on beds, a wall-mounted hair dryer over the dressing table, and bathrobes for use during the cruise are standard. Bathrooms have a shampoo–bath gel dispenser mounted on the shower wall as well as a magnifying mirror. Suites have a whirlpool tub, an entertainment center with a CD/DVD player, and concierge and butler service.

Worth Noting: Family-friendly staterooms interconnect in most categories, enabling families of nearly any size to find suitable accommodations. Nearly every stateroom has a third or fourth berth, and some can sleep as many as five and six. Twenty-four staterooms on *Norwegian Dawn* and 20 staterooms on *Norwegian Star* are designed for wheelchair accessibility.

In the Know

Artwork plays a major role in brightening the interiors of both vessels, but *Norwegian Dawn* has a priceless collection of original pop art, featuring original signed works by Andy Warhol, and oil paintings by impressionists Matisse, Renoir, and Monet.

Pros and Cons

Pros: Reminiscent of European opera houses, the showrooms are grand settings for the lavish production shows and have full proscenium stages. Other ships might have comedy shows, but on these you can look forward to performances by Second City, Chicago's incomparable improvisation artists, with shows in the theater as well as in more intimate nightclub settings. Three-bedroom Garden Villas are among the largest suites at sea, with private whirlpools and outdoor patios for alfresco dining.

Cons: Freestyle dining doesn't mean you can get a table in the main dining rooms at precisely the moment you want, but waiting time can be lessened by timing your arrival at nonpeak periods. Don't stop to smell the banks of flowers in the lobby—they are unabashedly fake. Overcrowding can be a problem in the buffet, popular bars, and around the Lido pools when the ships are booked to their maximum capacity.

Cabin Type	Size (sq. ft.)
Garden Villa	5,350
Owner's Suite	750
Penthouse Suite	366
Romance Suite	288
Minisuite	229
Ocean View with Balcony	166
Ocean View	158
Inside	142

FAST FACTS

- 11 passenger decks
- 7 restaurants, 2 dining rooms, buffet, ice cream parlor, pizzeria
- Internet, Wi-Fi, safe, refrigerator, DVD (some)
- 2 pools (1 indoor), children's pool
- Fitness classes, gym, hair salon, 6 hot tubs, sauna, spa, steam room
- 9 bars, casino, cinema, 2 dance clubs, library, showroom, video game room
- Children's programs (ages 2–17)
- Dry cleaning, laundry facilities (*Norwegian Dawn*), laundry service
- Internet terminal

Norwegian Dawn at sea

2

NORWEGIAN CRUISE LINE

OCEANIA CRUISES

This distinctive cruise line was founded by Frank Del Rio and Joe Watters, cruise-industry veterans with the know-how to satisfy the wants of inquisitive passengers. By offering itineraries to interesting ports of call and upscale touches—all for fares much lower

Oceania's *Regatta*

than you would expect—they are succeeding quite nicely. Oceania Cruises set sail in 2003 to carve a unique, almost boutique niche in the cruise industry by obtaining midsize R-class ships that formerly made up the popular Renaissance Cruises fleet. The line is now owned by Prestige Cruise Holdings.

✉ *8300 N.W. 33rd St., Suite 308, Miami, FL* ☎ *305/514–2300 or 800/531–5658* ⊕ *www.oceaniacruises. com* ☞ *Cruise Style: Premium.*

Intimate and cozy public spaces reflect the importance of socializing on Oceania ships. Indoor lounges feature numerous conversation areas, and even the pool deck is a social center. The Patio is a shaded slice of deck adjacent to the pool and hot tubs. Defined by billowing drapes and carpeting underfoot, it is furnished with plush sofas and chairs ideal for relaxation. Evening entertainment leans toward light cabaret, solo artists, music for dancing, and conversation with fellow passengers; however, you'll find lively karaoke sessions on the schedule as well. The sophisticated, adult atmosphere on days at sea is enhanced by a combo performing jazz or easy-listening melodies poolside.

While thickly padded single and double loungers are arranged around the pool, if more privacy appeals to you, eight private cabanas are available for rent on deck 11. Each one has a double chaise longue with a view of the sea; overhead drapery can be drawn back for sunbathing, and the side panels can be left open or closed. Waiters are on standby to offer chilled towels or serve occupants with beverages or snacks. In port, this luxury will set you back $50, but at sea it is $100

2

per day. In addition, you can request a spa service in your cabana.

Varied, destination-rich itineraries are an important characteristic of Oceania Cruises, and most sailings are in the 10- to 12-night range. Before arrival in ports of call, lectures are presented on the history, culture, tradition, and wildlife of Alaska and its people.

Culinary demonstrations by guest presenters and Oceania's own executive chefs are extremely popular. Lectures on varied topics, computer courses, hands-on arts-and-crafts classes, and wine or champagne seminars round out the popular enrichment series on board.

Food

Several top cruise-industry chefs were lured away from other cruise lines to ensure that the artistry of world-renowned master chef Jacques Pépin, who crafted five-star menus for Oceania, is properly carried out. The results are sure to please the most discriminating palate. Oceania simply serves some of the best food at sea, particularly impressive for a cruise line that charges far less than luxury rates. The main restaurant offers trendy, French-Continental cuisine with an always-on-the-menu steak, seafood, or poultry choice and a vegetarian option.

Intimate specialty restaurants require reservations, but there's no additional charge for Toscana, the Italian restaurant, or Polo Grill, the steak house. A fourth dinner option is Tapas on the Terrace, alfresco dining at the Terrace Café (the daytime Lido Deck buffet). Although service is from the buffet, outdoor seating on the aft deck is transformed into a charming Spanish courtyard with Catalonian-style candleholders and starched linens.

The Terrace Café also serves breakfast and lunch buffet-style and has a small pizzeria window that operates during the day. At an outdoor poolside grill you can order up burgers, hot dogs, and sandwiches for lunch and then take a seat; waiters are at hand to serve you either at a nearby table or your lounge chair by the pool. Afternoon tea is a decadent spread of finger foods and includes a rolling dessert cart, which has to be seen to be believed.

Fitness and Recreation

Although small, the spa, salon, and well-equipped fitness center are adequate for the number of passengers on board. In addition to individual body-toning

NOTEWORTHY

■ The Oceania signature Tranquility Bed has a firm mattress, 350-thread-count linens, goose-down pillows, and a silk-cut duvet.

■ Instead of on easels cluttering passageways, artworks for auction are displayed on stairwell landings and in lounges.

■ Pool decks are outfitted with attractive wood tables and chairs, market umbrellas, and couples' lounge chairs with cushy pads and colorful bolsters.

Top: Penthouse Suite
Bottom: Toscana Restaurant

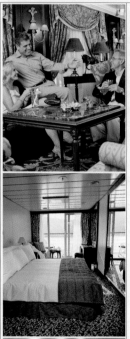

Top: Cocktails before dinner
Middle: Veranda stateroom
Bottom: Martini's Lounge

machines and complimentary exercise classes, there's a walking-jogging track circling the top of the ship. A personal trainer is available for individual instruction for an additional charge.

Your Shipmates

Oceania Cruises appeal to singles and couples from their late-30s to well-traveled retirees who have the time for and prefer longer cruises. Most are American couples attracted to the casually sophisticated atmosphere, creative cuisine, and high level of service. Many are past passengers of the now-defunct Renaissance Cruises who are loyal to their favorite ships, which now offer a variety of destination-rich itineraries.

Dress Code

Leave the formal wear at home—attire on Oceania ships is country-club casual every evening, although some guests can't help dressing up to dine in the beautifully appointed restaurants. A jacket and tie are never required for dinner, but many men wear sport jackets, as they would to dine in an upscale restaurant ashore. Jeans, shorts, T-shirts, and tennis shoes are discouraged after 6 PM in public rooms.

Junior Cruisers

Oceania Cruises are adult-oriented and not a good choice for families, particularly those traveling with infants and toddlers. No dedicated children's facilities are available, and parents are completely responsible for the behavior and entertainment. Teenagers with sophisticated tastes (and who don't mind the absence of a video arcade) might enjoy the intriguing ports of call.

Service

Highly personalized service by a mostly European staff is crisp and efficient without being intrusive. Butlers are on hand to fulfill the requests of suite guests and will even assist with packing and unpacking when asked.

Tipping

Gratuities of $12.50 per person per day are added to shipboard accounts for distribution to stewards and waitstaff; an additional $4 per person per day is added

CHOOSE THIS LINE IF . . .

Socializing is more important to you than boogying the night away.

You love to read. These ships have extensive libraries that are ideal for curling up with a good book.

You have a bad back. You're sure to love the Tranquility Beds.

for occupants of suites with butler service. Passengers may adjust the amount based on the level of service experienced. An automatic 18% gratuity is added to all bar tabs for bartenders and drink servers and to all bills for salon and spa services.

Past Passengers

After you take one Oceania cruise, you'll receive several benefits along with a free subscription to *The Oceania Club Journal*. Shipboard Club parties hosted by the captain and senior officers, complimentary amenities or exclusive privileges on select sailings, an Oceania Club membership recognition pin after 5, 10, 15, and 20 cruises, and special pricing and mailings about upcoming promotions are some of the benefits. Members further qualify for elite-level status based on the number of sailings aboard Oceania Cruises. Starting with your fifth cruise, you begin to accrue on every cruise you take, beginning with a $200 shipboard credit per stateroom on cruises five through nine. On your 10th cruise, you will receive a $400 shipboard credit per stateroom plus complimentary gratuities on cruises 10 through 14. On your 15th cruise, you will receive a $500 shipboard credit per stateroom, plus two complimentary spa treatments and complimentary gratuities on cruises 15 through 19. Once you take your 20th cruise, you get a free cruise as well as complimentary spa treatments, a shore excursion, and gratuities on all future cruises.

GOOD TO KNOW

When these ships were operated by Renaissance, they were entirely smoke-free, and many people booked cruises because of that. Now, two very small areas are set aside for smokers, one near the pool bar and the other set in a portside corner of the Horizons Lounge. Staterooms and balconies continue to be no-smoking zones, and if you light up in either spot, you could find yourself put ashore in the next port.

2

OCEANIA CRUISES

DON'T CHOOSE THIS LINE IF . . .

You like the action in a huge casino. Oceania casinos are small, and seats at a poker table can be difficult to get.

You won't take a cruise without your children. Most passengers book with Oceania anticipating a kid-free atmosphere.

Glitzy production shows are your thing. Oceania's show-rooms are decidedly low-key.

REGATTA, INSIGNIA, NAUTICA
(only Regatta sails in Alaska in 2011)

CREW MEMBERS	400
ENTERED SERVICE	1998, 1998, 2000
GROSS TONS	30,277
LENGTH	594 feet
NUMBER OF CABINS	342
PASSENGER CAPACITY	684 (824 max)
WIDTH	84 feet

700 ft.

500 ft.

300 ft.

Public Areas and Facilities

Carefully furnished to impart the atmosphere of a private English country manor, these midsize ships are casual yet elegant, with sweeping central staircases and abundant flower arrangements. Brocade and toile fabrics cover the windows, overstuffed sofas, and wing chairs to create a warm and intimate feeling throughout. The entire effect is that of a weekend retreat in the English countryside.

Authentic-looking faux fireplaces are inviting elements adjacent to cozy seating areas in the Grand Bar, near the Martini Bar's grand piano, and in the beautiful libraries—some of the best at sea with an enormous selection of best sellers, nonfiction, and travel books. The casinos are quite small and can feel cramped, and smoking is prohibited. Though there may be a wait for a seat at a poker table, there are enough slot machines to go around.

Other than decorative trompe l'oeil paintings in several public areas, the artwork is ordinary.

Restaurants

Oceania passengers enjoy the flexibility of four open-seating restaurants. The Grand Dining Room, open for breakfast, lunch, and dinner, serves Continental cuisine. Alternative, reservations-required dinner options are Toscana, which serves gourmet Italian dishes, and Polo Grill, the steak house. Terraces, the buffet restaurant, serves breakfast, lunch, and dinner and is transformed into Tapas on the Terrace after dark for a relaxed atmosphere and alfresco dining. All dining venues have nearby bars, and there's no additional cover charge for dining. In addition, a poolside grill serves hamburgers and a variety of sandwiches and salads at lunchtime, and there is a pizzeria located in the buffet area. Afternoon tea is an elaborate affair served in Horizons, the observation lounge. Room service is available 24 hours.

Accommodations

Cabins: Private balconies outfitted with chairs and tables add additional living space to nearly 75% of all outside accommodations. All cabins have a vanity-desk and a sitting area with sofa, chair, and table. Every cabin has generous closet and drawer/shelf storage and bathroom

Top: Teatime in Horizons
Bottom: Breakfast in bed

2

shelves. Owner's and Vista suites have a separate living-dining room, as well as a separate powder room.

Suites: Owner's and Vista Suites have an entertainment center with a DVD and CD player, a small refrigerator, and a second TV in the bedroom; the main bathroom has a combination shower-whirlpool tub. Penthouse suites also have refrigerators and bathtubs. Butlers are on hand to coordinate reservations and serve evening canapés and dinner ordered from any of the ship's restaurants.

Amenities: Dark-wood cabinetry, soothing blue decor, mirrored accents, personal safe, Tranquility Beds, 350-thread-count linens, goose-down pillows, and silk-cut duvets are typical stateroom features. Bathrooms have a hair dryer, shampoo, lotion, and bath gel, plus robes.

Worth Noting: Several cabins accommodate third and fourth passengers, but few have connecting doors. Three staterooms are designed for wheelchair accessibility.

In the Know

Don't plot to take the divine linens home with you—it's been tried with embarrassing consequences.

Pros and Cons

Pros: A relaxed, social atmosphere pervades all areas on board, particularly during sea days when passengers mix easily and create their own entertainment, depending very little on organized activities. Everyone has to have a photograph taken on the lobby staircase—it's practically a twin of the one in the movie *Titanic*. Choose anything chocolate from the dessert cart at teatime—Oceania ships serve some of the most lavish afternoon teas at sea.

Cons: Shipboard charges can add up fast since drink prices and even Internet services are above the average charged by most cruise lines. The one minuscule self-serve laundry room can get steamy, particularly when there's a wait for the machines. The absence of a sauna in the spa is an unfortunate oversight, although you'll be happy to find a rain shower and nifty tiled steam room in the changing areas.

Cabin Type	Size (sq. ft.)
Owner's	962
Vista Suite	786
Penthouse Suite	322
Concierge Ocean View	216
Deluxe	165
Standard Ocean View	150–165
Inside	160

FAST FACTS

■ 9 passenger decks

■ 2 specialty restaurants, dining room, buffet, pizzeria

■ Internet, Wi-Fi, safe, refrigerator, DVD (some)

■ Pool

■ Fitness classes, gym, hair salon, 3 hot tubs, spa, steam room

■ 4 bars, casino, dance club, library, showroom

■ Dry cleaning, laundry facilities, laundry service

■ Internet terminal

■ No-smoking cabins

Regatta at sea

PRINCESS CRUISES

Princess Cruises may be best known for introducing cruise travel to millions of viewers, when its flagship became the setting for *The Love Boat* television series in 1977. Since that heady time of small-screen stardom, the Princess fleet has grown both in the num-

Watch iceburgs float by from your balcony

ber and size of ships. Although most are large in scale, Princess vessels manage to create the illusion of intimacy through the use of color and decor in understated yet lovely public rooms graced by multimillion-dollar art collections.

✉ *24305 Town Center Dr., Santa Clarita, CA* ☎ *661/753–0000 or 800/774–6237* 🌐 *www. princess.com* ✆ *Cruise Style: Premium.*

Princess has also become more flexible; Personal Choice Cruising offers alternatives for open-seating dining (when you wish and with whom you please) and entertainment options as diverse as those found in resorts ashore.

The roster of adult activities still includes standbys like bingo and art auctions, but also enrichment programs featuring guest lecturers, cooking classes, wine-tasting seminars, pottery workshops, and computer and digital photography classes. Nighttime production shows tend toward Broadway-style revues presented in the main show lounge, and performers might include comedians, magicians, jugglers, and acrobats. Live bands play a wide range of musical styles for dancing and listening, and each ship has a disco.

On Pub Night the cruise director's staff leads a rollicking evening of fun with passenger participation. At the conclusion of the second formal night, champagne trickles down over a champagne waterfall, painstakingly created by the arrangement of champagne glasses in a pyramid shape. Ladies are invited to join the maître d' to assist in the pouring for a great photo op.

Lovely chapels or the wide-open decks are equally romantic settings for weddings at sea. However, the captain can officiate only on some Princess ships.

Food

Personal choices regarding where and what to eat abound, but because of the number of passengers, unless you opt for traditional assigned seating, you might have to wait for a table in one of the open-seating dining rooms. Menus are varied and extensive in the main dining rooms, and the results are good to excellent considering how much work is going on in the galleys. Vegetarian and healthy-lifestyle options are always on the menu, as well as steak, fish, or chicken. A special menu is designed especially for children.

Alternative restaurants are a staple throughout the fleet but vary by ship class. Grand-class ships have upscale steak houses and Sabatini's, an Italian restaurant; both require reservations and carry an extra cover charge. Sun-class ships offer complimentary sit-down dining in the pizzeria and a similar steak-house option, although it's in a sectioned-off area of the buffet restaurant. On *Caribbean, Crown, Emerald,* and *Ruby Princess,* a casual evening alternative to the dining rooms and usual buffet is Café Caribe—adjacent to the Lido buffet restaurant, it serves cuisine with a Caribbean flair. With a few breaks in service, Lido buffets on all ships are almost always open, and a pizzeria and grill offer casual daytime snack choices. The fleet's patisseries and ice cream bars charge for specialty coffee, some pastries, and premium ice cream. A daily British-style pub lunch served in the ships' Wheelhouse Bar is being introduced fleetwide.

Ultimate Balcony Dining—either a champagne break-fast or full-course dinner—is a full-service meal served on your cabin's balcony. The Chef's Table allows guests (for a fee) to dine on a special menu with wine pairings. After a meeting with the executive chef in the galley (and some champagne and appetizers), guests sit at a special table in the dining room. The chef joins them for dessert.

Fitness and Recreation

Spa rituals include a variety of massages, body wraps, and facials; numerous hair and nail services are offered in the salons. Both the salons and spa are operated by Steiner Leisure, and the menu of spa services includes special pampering treatments designed specifically for men and teens as well as couples. For a half-day fee, escape to the Sanctuary, which offers a relaxing

NOTEWORTHY

■ The traditional gala champagne waterfall on formal night is a not-to-be-missed event.

■ Bathrobes are provided for use during your cruise—all you have to do is ask the room steward to deliver them.

■ Wheelchair-accessible staterooms with 33-inch-wide entry and bathroom doorways, plus bathrooms fitted to ADA standards, are available in an array of categories.

Top: Place a bet in the casino
Bottom: Disco into the night

Top: Sunset at sea
Middle: Morning stretch
Bottom: Freshwater Jacuzzi

outdoor spa-inspired setting with signature beverages, light meals, massages, attentive service, and relaxing personal entertainment. All ships will feature this adults-only haven by 2010.

Modern exercise equipment, a jogging track, and basic fitness classes are available at no charge. There's a fee for personal training, body-composition analysis, and specialized classes such as yoga and Pilates. Grand-class ships have a resistance pool so you can get your laps in effortlessly.

Your Shipmates

Princess Cruises attract mostly American passengers, ranging from their mid-30s to mid-50s. Families enjoy cruising together on the Princess fleet, particularly during holiday seasons and summer months, when many children are on board. Longer cruises appeal to well-traveled retirees and couples who have the time.

Dress Code

Two formal nights are standard on seven-night cruises; an additional formal night may be scheduled on longer sailings. Men are encouraged to wear tuxedos, but dark suits are appropriate. All other evenings are casual, although jeans are discouraged, and it's requested that no shorts be worn in public areas after 6 PM.

Junior Cruisers

For young passengers ages 3 to 17, each Princess vessel (except *Ocean, Royal*, and *Pacific Princess*) has a playroom, teen center, and programs of supervised activities designed for different age groups: ages 3 to 7, 8 to 12, and 13 to 17. Activities to engage youngsters include arts and crafts, pool games, scavenger hunts, deck parties, backstage and galley tours, games, and videos. Events such as dance parties in their own disco, theme parties, athletic contests, karaoke, pizza parties, and movie fests occupy teenage passengers. With a nod toward science and educational entertainment, children also participate in learning programs focused on the environment and wildlife in areas where the ships sail.

CHOOSE THIS LINE IF . . .

You're a traveler with a disability. Princess ships are some of the most accessible at sea.

You like to gamble but hate a smoke-filled casino. Princess casinos are well ventilated and spacious.

You want a balcony. Princess ships feature them in abundance at affordable rates.

To allow parents independent time ashore, youth centers operate as usual during port days, including lunch with counselors. For an additional charge, group babysitting is available nightly from 10 PM until 1 AM. Family-friendly conveniences include self-service laundry facilities and two-way family radios that are available for rent at the Purser's Desk. Infants under six months are not permitted; private in-cabin babysitting is not available on any Princess vessel. Children under age three are welcome in the playrooms if supervised by a parent.

Service

Professional service by an international staff is efficient and friendly. It's not uncommon to be greeted in passageways by smiling stewards who know your name.

Tipping

A gratuity of $10.50 per person per day ($11 for passengers in suites and minisuites) is added to shipboard accounts for distribution to stewards and waitstaff. Passengers may adjust the amount based on the level of service experienced. An automatic 15% is added to all bar tabs for bartenders and drink servers; gratuities to other staff members may be extended at passengers' discretion.

Past Passengers

Membership in the Captain's Circle is automatic following your first Princess cruise. All members receive a free subscription to *Captain's Circle News*, a quarterly newsletter, as well as discounts on selected cruises.

Perks are determined by the number of cruises completed: Gold (2 through 5), Platinum (6 through 15), and Elite (16 and above). While Gold members receive only the magazine, an invitation to an onboard event, and the services of the Circle Host on the ship, benefits really begin to accrue once you've completed five cruises. Platinum members receive upgraded insurance (when purchasing the standard policy), expedited check-in, a debarkation lounge to wait in on the ship, and, best of all, limited free Internet access during the cruise. Elite benefits are even more lavish, with many complimentary services.

GOOD TO KNOW

Some people like the time-honored tradition of assigned seating for dinner, so they can get to know their table companions and their servers; others prefer to choose with whom they dine as well as when. Princess lets you have things your way or both ways. If you're unsure whether Personal Choice is for you, select Traditional dining when you reserve your cruise. You can easily make the switch to anytime dining once on board; however, it can be impossible to change from Personal Choice to Traditional.

PRINCESS CRUISES

2

DON'T CHOOSE THIS LINE IF . . .

You have a poor sense of direction. Most ships, especially the Grand-class ships, are very large.

You want to meet *The Love Boat* cast. That was just a TV show, and it was more than three decades ago.

You're too impatient to stand in line or wait. Debarkation from the large ships can be lengthy.

CORAL CLASS
Coral Princess, Island Princess

CREW MEMBERS	900
ENTERED SERVICE	2003, 2003
GROSS TONS	92,000
LENGTH	964
NUMBER OF CABINS	987
PASSENGER CAPACITY	1,970
WIDTH	106 feet

700 ft.

500 ft.

300 ft.

Public Areas and Facilities

Princess includes *Coral Princess* and *Island Princess* in its Sun-class category; however, they are larger ships (albeit with a similar capacity to *Sun Princess* and her two sisters), which means much more space per passenger; we feel this necessitates a separate category. All the Personal Choice features attributed to the larger Grand-class ships were incorporated into this design as well as a few unique additions, such as a demonstration kitchen and ceramics lab complete with kiln where ScholarShip@Sea programs are presented. The four-story atrium is similar to that on Sun-class ships, but public rooms are mainly spread fore and aft on two lower decks.

Although signature rooms such as the Wheelhouse Bar are more traditional, the casinos have subtle London- or Paris-like atmospheres with themed slot machines; Crooner's Bar is a retro 1960s Vegas-style martini and piano bar. In addition to the stately Princess Theater showroom, the Universe Lounge has three stages for shows and flexible seating on two levels, making it a multipurpose space.

Restaurants

Passengers may choose between traditional dinner seating times in one assigned dining room or open seating in the other formal dining room; breakfast and lunch are open seating. Alternative dinner options include reservations-only Sabatini's Italian trattoria and Bayou Café & Steakhouse (both with an extra charge). With a few breaks in service, Lido buffets on all ships are almost always open. A pub lunch is served in the Wheelhouse Bar, and a pizzeria and grill offer casual daytime snack choices. The patisseries and ice cream bars charge for specialty coffee, some pastries, and premium ice cream. Ultimate Balcony Dining and Chef's Table options are available, as is afternoon tea and 24-hour room service.

Accommodations

Cabins: Stepped out in wedding-cake fashion, more than 83% of ocean-view staterooms include Princess Cruises' trademark private balconies. Even the least expensive inside categories have plentiful storage and a small sitting area with a chair and table. Suites have two

Top: Fast-paced shows
Bottom: Plenty of locations on the ship to enjoy spectacular views

TVs, a sitting area, a wet bar, a large walk-in closet, and a separate bathtub and shower. Minisuites have a separate sitting area, two televisions, a walk-in closet, and a combination bathtub-shower.

Suites: Occupants of 16 suites receive complimentary Internet access, dry cleaning, and shoe polishing, afternoon tea and evening canapés delivered to their suites, and priority embarkation, disembarkation, and tendering privileges. An extended room service menu is also available for them, as are priority reservations for dining and shore excursions.

Amenities: Decorated in pastels and light-wood tones, typical staterooms have a personal safe, hair dryer, refrigerator, and bathrobes for use during the cruise. Bathrooms have shampoo, lotion, and bath gel.

Worth Noting: Twenty staterooms are designed for wheelchair accessibility and range in size from 217 to 374 square feet, depending upon category.

In the Know

Most midship ocean-view cabins on Emerald Deck are designated as obstructed view, and even some balcony staterooms on Emerald and Dolphin decks are considered partially obstructed. And when balconies are arranged in a stepped-out design, the lower ones aren't totally private.

Pros and Cons

Pros: As many as 20 courses in the ScholarShip@Sea Program are offered on each cruise, and you can select from ceramics, cooking fundamentals, computer, and photography classes or attend lectures on a wide range of topics. Cabins that sleep third and fourth passengers are numerous, and the best bet for families are interconnecting balcony staterooms adjacent to facilities dedicated to children and teens on Aloha Deck. The Fine Art Gallery is a dedicated spot for art-auction stock, meaning that displays don't clutter the passageways and distract from the art pieces selected to complement the decor.

Cons: Oddly, the library and card room are situated so they are often used as passageways, which results in a bit more noise than usual in areas that should be quiet. There are only 16 suites on each ship, and none are aft-facing with a view of the wake; engine pods on the funnel give the ships a futuristic space-age appearance of jet speed but function mainly as decoration—they can easily make 24 knots, but they don't fly.

Cabin Type	Size (sq. ft.)
Suite	470
Minisuite	285–302
Ocean-View Balcony	217–232
Ocean-View Standard	162
Deluxe	212
Inside	156–166

All dimensions include the square footage for balconies.

FAST FACTS

■ 11 passenger decks

■ 2 specialty restaurants, 2 dining rooms, buffet, ice cream parlor, pizzeria

■ Wi-Fi, safe, refrigerator, DVD (some)

■ 3 pools (1 indoor), children's pool

■ Fitness classes, gym, hair salon, 5 hot tubs, sauna, spa

■ 7 bars, casino, 2 dance clubs, library, 2 showrooms, video game room

■ Children's programs (ages 3–17)

■ Dry cleaning, laundry facilities, laundry service

■ Internet terminal

■ No kids under 6 months

Lavish buffets in Horizon Court

2

PRINCESS CRUISES

GRAND CLASS
Grand Princess, Golden Princess, Star Princess
(only Golden sails in Alaska in 2011)

CREW MEMBERS	1,100, 1,100, 1,200
ENTERED SERVICE	1998, 2001, 2002
GROSS TONS	109,000
LENGTH	951 feet
NUMBER OF CABINS	1,300
PASSENGER CAPACITY	2,600
WIDTH	118 feet

700 ft.

500 ft.

300 ft.

Public Areas and Facilities

When *Grand Princess* was introduced as the world's largest cruise ship in 1998, she also boasted one of the most distinctive profiles. Not only did the Skywalker's Disco appear futuristic, hovering approximately 150 feet above the waterline, but Grand-class vessels also advanced the idea of floating resort to an entirely new level with more than 700 staterooms that included private balconies.

Like their predecessors, the interiors of Grand-class ships feature soothing pastel tones with splashy glamour in the sweeping staircases and marble-floor atriums. Surprisingly intimate for such large ships, human scale in public lounges is achieved by judicious placement of furniture as unobtrusive room dividers.

The 300-square-foot Times Square–style LED screens that hover over the pools show up to seven movies or events daily.

Restaurants

Passengers may choose between two traditional dinner seating times in an assigned dining room or open seating in the ships' other two formal dining rooms; breakfast and lunch are open seating. Alternative dinner options include the reservations-only Italian and steak-house restaurants (both with an extra charge). With a few breaks in service, Lido buffets on all ships are open around the clock. A pub lunch is served in the Wheelhouse Bar, and a pizzeria and grill offer casual daytime snack choices. The patisseries and ice cream bars charge for specialty coffee, some pastries, and premium ice cream. *Star Princess* and *Golden Princess* have been outfitted with a wine bar that serves extra-charge evening snacks and artisanal cheeses; *Grand Princess* is scheduled to receive this addition as well. Ultimate Balcony Dining and Chef's Table options are available, as is afternoon tea and 24-hour room service.

Accommodations

Cabins: On these ships, 80% of the outside staterooms have balconies. The typical stateroom has a sitting area with a chair and table; even the cheapest categories have ample storage. Minisuites have a separate sitting area, a walk-in closet, a combination shower-tub, and a balcony, as well as two TVs. Grand Suites have a

Top: *Star Princess* at sea
Bottom: *Golden Princess* grand plaza atrium

separate sitting room and dining room, as well as a walk-in closet. Owner's, Penthouse, Premium, and Vista suites have a separate sitting room with a sofa bed and desk, as well as a walk-in closet.

Amenities: Decorated in attractive pastel hues, all cabins have a refrigerator, hair dryer, personal safe, and bathrobes to use during the cruise. Bathrooms have shampoo, lotion, and bath gel.

Worth Noting: Two family suites are interconnecting staterooms with a balcony that can sleep up to eight people (D105/D101 and D106/D102). Staterooms in a variety of categories will accommodate three and four people, and some adjacent cabins can be interconnected through interior doors or by unlocking doors in the balcony dividers. Twenty-eight staterooms are wheelchair accessible.

In the Know
Port and starboard balconies are stepped out from the ships' hulls in wedding-cake fashion. That means, depending on location, yours will likely be exposed a bit—or a lot—to passengers on higher decks. Exceptions are balconies on Emerald Deck, which are covered.

Pros and Cons
Pros: Skywalker's Disco has comfy semiprivate alcoves facing port and starboard and is virtually deserted during the day, when it's the ideal spot to read or just watch the sea. The convenient self-service passenger laundry rooms have ironing stations to touch up garments wrinkled from packing, and you can wash and dry a load of dirty clothing for only a few dollars. The Wheelhouse Bar, with soft lighting, comfortable leather chairs, shining brass accents, ship paintings, and nautical memorabilia, has become a Princess tradition for pre- and postdinner cocktails and dancing.

Cons: Sports bars get jam-packed and lively when important games are televised, but that also means they can become stuffy and close. Staterooms and suites located aft and above the Vista lounge can be noisy when bands crank up the volume. While there are two Grand Suites on *Grand Princess*, they aren't as large as those on *Golden Princess* and *Star Princess* and aren't aft-facing with a view of the ship's wake.

2

PRINCESS CRUISES

Cabin Type	Size (sq. ft.)
Grand Suite	730/1,314*
Other Suites	468–591
Family Suite	607
Minisuite	323
Ocean View Balcony	232–274
Standard	168
Inside	160

All dimensions include the square footage for balconies. *Grand Princess* dimensions followed by *Golden* and *Star Princess*.

FAST FACTS

- 14 passenger decks
- 2 specialty restaurants, 3 dining rooms, buffet, ice cream parlor, pizzeria
- Wi-Fi, safe, refrigerator
- 4 pools (1 indoor), children's pool
- Fitness classes, gym, hair salon, 9 hot tubs, sauna, spa, steam room
- 9 bars, casino, outdoor cinema, 2 dance clubs, library, 2 showrooms, video game room
- Children's programs (ages 3–17)
- Dry cleaning, laundry facilities, laundry service
- Internet terminal
- No kids under 6 months

Grand-class balcony stateroom

DIAMOND PRINCESS, SAPPHIRE PRINCESS

CREW MEMBERS	1,100
ENTERED SERVICE	2004, 2004
700 ft. **GROSS TONS**	116,000
LENGTH	952 feet
500 ft. **NUMBER OF CABINS**	1,337
PASSENGER CAPACITY	2,670
300 ft. **WIDTH**	123 feet

Public Areas and Facilities

Launched in the same year, these sister ships include all the features traditionally enjoyed on Princess's Grand-class vessels, but with a twist. They're larger than their Grand-class fleetmates, yet carry fewer passengers relative to their size. As a result, they have sleeker profiles, a higher ratio of space per person, and feel much roomier.

Inside, the arrangement of public rooms is a bit different, with the signature Wheelhouse Bar moved forward of its position on Grand-class ships and, in its place, an expanded Internet Café, where beverages and snacks are served. An Asian-themed full-service spa offers a relaxing thermal suite, for a fee. All the elements of a Princess ship are included, particularly the small-ship atmosphere and sparkling, yet understated, interior decoration.

Restaurants

In addition to a dining room with two traditional assigned dinner seatings, these ships have four additional dining rooms for open-seating Personal Choice cruisers. Each is smaller than those on other large Princess ships, but all offer the same menus with a few additional selections that reflect the "theme" of each dining room. Alternative dining options are the two specialty restaurants, Sabatini's and Sterling Steakhouse, which have a surcharge and require reservations. The pizzeria, grill, patisserie, and ice cream bar offer casual daytime dining and snack options. The Lido buffet and complimentary room service are available 24 hours. Ultimate Balcony Dining is offered to passengers with balcony accommodations.

Accommodations

Layout: More than 70% of accommodations feature an ocean view, and of those 78% include private balconies. Even the least expensive inside categories have ample storage and a small sitting area with chair and table. Cabins that sleep third and fourth passengers are numerous. The best for families are Family Suites on Dolphin Deck, which sleep up to six in two self-contained staterooms that connect through a living room.

Top: *Sapphire Princess* at sea
Bottom: *Diamond Princess*
Grand Plaza

Amenities: Typical stateroom features are personal safes, refrigerators, hair dryers, and bathrobes for use during the cruise. Bathroom toiletries include shampoo, lotion, and bath gel.

Suites: Suites have two televisions, a sitting area, dining area, wet bar, large walk-in closet, and separate whirlpool bathtub and shower. Minisuites have a separate sitting area, two televisions, walk-in closet, and a combination bathtub–shower.

Worth Noting: Twenty-seven staterooms are designed for wheelchair accessibility.

In the Know

Princess's trademark Skywalkers disco-lounge concept moved a step ahead on these ships with a 125-foot-wide balcony that provides commanding views over the aft end of the ship, where passengers can enjoy stargazing or a view of the wake.

Pros and Cons

Pros: With fewer passengers on board than other ships of the same size, these Princess ships feel very spacious; the swim-against-the-current pool is ideal for getting in your laps at sea; linked with Club Fusion by a spiral staircase, the tiny Wake View Bar is a romantic spot for a nightcap.

Cons: The four intimate open-seating dining rooms are smaller than on other large Princess ships and can fill up fast, so keep an alternate to your first choice in mind; there is a charge for specialty coffee drinks and premium ice cream; to walk all around the ship on Promenade Deck you'll have to negotiate a flight of stairs.

Cabin Type	Size (sq. ft.)
Suites	535–1,329
Family Suites/ Minisuites	522–354
Ocean View with Balcony	237–277
Deluxe Ocean View	197–200
Ocean View	183–194
Inside	168–182
Wheelchair Accessible	249–412

All dimensions include the square footage for balconies.

FAST FACTS

- 13 passenger decks
- 2 specialty restaurants, 5 dining rooms, buffet, ice cream parlor, pizzeria
- Wi-Fi, in-cabin safes, in-cabin refrigerators
- 5 pools
- Fitness classes, gym, hair salon, 8 hot tubs, sauna, spa, steam room
- 11 bars, casino, 2 dance clubs, library, 2 showrooms, video game room
- Children's programs (ages 3–17)
- Dry cleaning, laundry facilities, laundry service
- Computer room
- No kids under 6 months

Grand Casino on the *Diamond Princess*

SUN CLASS
Sun Princess, Dawn Princess, Sea Princess
(only Sea sails in Alaska in 2011)

CREW MEMBERS	900
ENTERED SERVICE	1995, 1997, 1998
GROSS TONS	77,000
LENGTH	856 feet
NUMBER OF CABINS	975
PASSENGER CAPACITY	1,950
WIDTH	106 feet

700 ft.
500 ft.
300 ft.

Public Areas and Facilities

Refined and graceful, Sun-class ships offer many of the choices attributed to larger Grand-class ships without sacrificing the smaller-ship atmosphere for which they're noted. The four-story atrium with a circular marble floor, stained-glass dome, and magnificent floating staircase are ideal settings for relaxation, people-watching, and making a grand entrance. Only *Sea Princess* sails Caribbean cruises; *Sun* and *Dawn Princess* are deployed in the South Pacific.

Onboard decor is a combination of neutrals and pastels, which are easy on the eyes after a sunny day ashore. The main public rooms are situated in a vertical arrangement on four lower decks, and, with the exception of promenade deck, cabins are located forward and aft. In a nice design twist, the casino is somewhat isolated, and passengers aren't forced to use it as a passageway to reach dining rooms or the art deco main show lounge. *Sea Princess* also has an outdoor Movies Under the Stars LED screen.

Restaurants

Sun-class ships have one dining room with two traditional assigned dinner seatings and one open seating dining room for Personal Choice cruisers; breakfast and lunch are open seating. Alternative dinner options are the reservations-only Sterling Steakhouse (a section of the buffet that's dressed up for the evening and for which there's a charge) and complimentary traditional Italian dishes in a trattoria-style setting in the pizzeria. With a few breaks in service, Lido buffets on all ships are almost always open. The pizzeria and a grill near the main pool offer casual daytime snack choices. The patisseries and ice cream bars charge for specialty coffee, some pastries, and premium ice cream. Ultimate Balcony Dining is available, as is afternoon tea and 24-hour room service.

Accommodations

Cabins: Princess Cruises' trademark is an abundance of staterooms with private balconies, yet even the least expensive inside categories have ample storage and a small sitting area with a chair and table. Suites have two TVs, a separate sitting area, a dining-height table with chairs, a walk-in closets, double-sink vanities, and

Top: *Sea Princess* at sea
Bottom: Sun-class ocean-view stateroom

a separate shower and whirlpool tub. Minisuites have a separate sitting area, two TVs, a walk-in closet, and a separate shower and whirlpool tub.

Amenities: Decorated in pastel tones, staterooms typically have mirrored accents, a personal safe, a refrigerator, a hair dryer, and bathrobes for use during the cruise. Bathrooms have shampoo, lotion, and bath gel.

Worth Noting: Cabins that sleep third and fourth passengers aren't as numerous as on other Princess ships, and no staterooms have interconnecting interior doors, although adjacent cabins with balconies can be connected by unlocking balcony divider doors. Nineteen staterooms are designed for wheelchair accessibility and range in size from 213 to 305 square feet, depending upon category.

In the Know

Check and double-check your bed configurations when booking an outside quad cabin for your family. There are balcony cabins with three and four berths, but some have two lower twin-size beds that cannot be pushed together to form a queen.

Pros and Cons

Pros: You can always escape the crowds by ducking into to the cozy, wood-paneled reading room, where each oversized chair faces its own bay window. No matter what flavor is on the menu, the dessert soufflés can't be beat. On Riviera Deck a dramatic, partially shaded pool with two hot tubs appears suspended between two decks with its surface between the spa and the Sun Deck above.

Cons: Horizon Court Lido buffet restaurants occupy one of the most prestigious spots on these ships—far forward, with a true view of the horizon—but that means there is no observatory lounge. There's nothing about the interior decor that'll knock your socks off—some areas still have echoes of *The Love Boat* television series sets—but the cool palette enhanced by marble accents showcases impressive original artwork and murals. These are large ships but not large enough to overcome the invasive nature of regularly scheduled art auctions.

Cabin Type	Size (sq. ft.)
Suite	538–695
Minisuite	370–536
Ocean View Balcony	179
Deluxe	173
Ocean View Standard	135–155
Interior	135–148

All dimensions include the square footage for balconies.

FAST FACTS

- 10 passenger decks
- 2 dining rooms, buffet, ice cream parlor, pizzeria
- Wi-Fi, safe, refrigerator
- 3 pools (1 indoor), children's pool
- Fitness classes, gym, hair salon, 5 hot tubs, sauna, spa, steam room
- 7 bars, casino, 2 dance clubs, library, 2 showrooms, video game room
- Children's programs (ages 3–17)
- Dry cleaning, laundry facilities, laundry service
- Internet terminal
- No kids under 6 months

Riviera pool

REGENT SEVEN SEAS CRUISES

The December 1994 merger of Radisson Diamond Cruises and Seven Seas Cruise Line launched Radisson Seven Seas Cruises with an eclectic fleet of vessels that offered a nearly all-inclusive cruise experience in sumptuous, contemporary surroundings. The

The end of a perfect day

line was rebranded as Regent Seven Seas Cruises in 2006, and ownership passed to Prestige Cruise Holdings (which also owns Oceania Cruises) in 2008.

✉ *1000 Corporate Dr., Suite 500, Ft. Lauderdale, FL* ☎ *954/776–6123 or 877/505–5370* ⊕ *www.rssc.com* ☞ *Cruise Style: Luxury.*

Even more inclusive than in the past, the line has maintained its traditional tried-and-true formula—delightful ships offering exquisite service, generous staterooms with abundant amenities, a variety of dining options, and superior lecture and enrichment programs. Guests are greeted with champagne upon boarding and find an all-inclusive beverage policy that offers not only soft drinks and bottled water, but also cocktails and select wines at all bars and restaurants throughout the ships.

The cruises are destination-focused, and most sailings host guest lecturers—historians, anthropologists, naturalists, and diplomats. Spotlight cruises center around popular pastimes and themes, such as food and wine, photography, history, archaeology, literature, performing arts, design and cultures, active exploration and wellness, antiques, jewelry and shopping, the environment, and marine life. Passengers need no urging to participate in discussions and workshops led by celebrated experts. All passengers have access to these unique experiences on board and on shore.

Activities and entertainment are tailored for each of the line's distinctive ships with the tastes of sophisticated passengers in mind. Don't expect napkin-folding demonstrations or nonstop action. Production revues, cabaret acts, concert-style piano performances, solo performers, and comedians may be featured in show lounges, with combos playing for listening and dancing in lounges and bars throughout the ships. Casinos are more akin to Monaco than Las Vegas. All ships display tasteful and varied art collections, including pieces that are for sale.

Food

Menus may appear to include the usual beef Wellington and Maine lobster, but in the hands of Regent Seven Seas chefs, the results are some of the most outstanding meals at sea. Specialty dining varies within the fleet, but the newest ships, *Seven Seas Voyager* and *Seven Seas Mariner,* have the edge with the sophisticated Signatures, featuring the cuisine of Le Cordon Bleu of Paris. Prime 7, on all three ships fleetwide, is a contemporary adaptation of the classic American steak house offering a fresh, distinctive decor and an innovative menu of the finest prime-aged steak and chops, along with fresh seafood and poultry specialties.

Held in a tranquil setting, Wine Connoisseurs Dinners are offered occasionally on longer cruises to bring together people with an interest in wine and food. Each course on the degustation menu is complemented by a wine pairing. The cost varies according to the special vintage wines that are included.

Room service menus are fairly extensive, and you can also order directly from the restaurant menus during regular serving hours.

Although special dietary requirements should be relayed to the cruise line before sailing, general considerations such as vegetarian, low-salt, or low-cholesterol food requests can be satisfied on board the ships simply by speaking with the dining room staff. Wines chosen to complement dinner menus are freely poured each evening.

Fitness and Recreation

Although gyms and exercise areas are well equipped, these are not large ships, so the facilities tend to be on the small size. Each ship has a jogging track, and the larger ones feature a variety of sports courts.

The spas and salons are operated by Canyon Ranch Spa Club, which offers an array of treatments and services that can be customized to the individual.

NOTEWORTHY

■ Passengers enjoy open-seating dining with complimentary wines of the world in the elegant restaurants.

■ Italian fare with flair is an alternate dinner option on each Regent ship.

■ Regent no longer employs ship's photographers, so you won't face a camera unless you bring your own.

Top: Sunrise jog
Bottom: *Seven Seas Navigator*

2

REGENT SEVEN SEAS CRUISES

Top: Fitness center
Middle: Pool decks are never crowded
Bottom: Pampering in the Carita of Paris spa

Your Shipmates

Regent Seven Seas Cruises are inviting to active, affluent, well-traveled couples ranging from their late-30s to retirees who enjoy the ships' chic ambience and destination-rich itineraries. Longer cruises attract veteran passengers in the over-60 age group.

Dress Code

Formal attire is required on designated evenings. Men are encouraged to wear tuxedos, and many do so; dark suits are acceptable. Cruises of 7 to 10 nights usually have one or two formal nights; longer cruises may have three. Other evenings are informal or resort casual; the number of each is based on the number of sea days. It's requested that dress codes be observed in public areas after 6 PM.

Junior Cruisers

Regent Seven Seas' vessels are adult-oriented and do not have dedicated children's facilities. However, a Club Mariner youth program for children ages 5 to 8, 9 to 12, and 13 to 17 is offered on selected sailings, both during summer months and during school holiday periods. Supervised by counselors, the organized, educational activities focus on nature and the heritage of destinations the ship will visit. Activities, including games, craft projects, movies, and food fun, are organized to ensure that every child has a memorable experience. Teens are encouraged to help counselors select the activities they prefer.

Service

The efforts of a polished, unobtrusive staff go almost unnoticed, yet special requests are handled with ease. Butlers provide an additional layer of personal service to guests in the top-category suites.

Tipping

Gratuities are included in the fare, and none are expected. To show their appreciation, passengers may elect to make a contribution to a crew welfare fund that benefits the ship's staff.

CHOOSE THIS LINE IF . . .

You want to learn the secrets of cooking like a Cordon Bleu chef (for a charge, of course).

You want to stay connected. Regent Seven Seas Internet packages are reasonably priced by the hour.

A really high-end spa experience is on your agenda.

Past Passengers

Membership in the Seven Seas Society is automatic on completion of a Regent Seven Seas cruise. Members receive 5% to 10% cruise fare savings on select sailings, exclusive shipboard and shoreside special events on select sailings, a Seven Seas Society recognition cocktail party on every sailing, and *Inspirations* newsletter highlighting special events, sailings, and destination- and travel-related information. The tiered program offers rewards based on the number of nights you have sailed with RSSC. The more you sail, the more you accrue. Bronze benefits are offered to members with 4 to 20 nights. From 21 through 74 nights, Silver members also receive complimentary Internet access on board, free pressing, and an hour of free phone time. From 75 through 199 nights, Gold members are awarded priority disembarkation at some ports, another hour of complimentary phone time, more complimentary pressing, an exclusive Gold & Platinum activity aboard or ashore on every sailing, and priority reservations at restaurants and spas. From 200 through 399, Platinum members can add complimentary air deviation services (one time per sailing), six hours of complimentary phone use, and unlimited free pressing and laundry services; Titanium members who have sailed 400 or more nights get free dry cleaning and free transfers.

GOOD TO KNOW

So why did former owners Carlson Hospitality change the name from Radisson to Regent Seven Seas back in 2006? It probably seemed logical at the time to give their new cruise line a recognizable name—Radisson. However, the name wasn't recognizable for the right reasons. Radisson Seven Seas Cruises aspired to be recognized as upscale cruise line (which it was), while the Radisson hotel chain is decidedly middle-of-the-road. The hotel name turned off some potential passengers, who didn't perceive the cruise line as being luxurious or exclusive. It just so happened that Carlson Hospitality's small, but growing, Regent chain of hotels is more in tune with today's definition of luxury and a better fit to co-brand with a top-of-the-line cruising experience. *Voilà!* A "fleet christening" accomplished the renaming and, best of all, the cruise line's initials didn't change and neither did its Web site address.

DON'T CHOOSE THIS LINE IF . . .

Connecting cabins are a must. Very few are available, and only the priciest cabins connect.

You can't imagine a cruise without lots of flashy hoopla; this line errs on the side of refinement.

You think dressing up for dinner is too much trouble. Most passengers look forward to the ritual.

SEVEN SEAS NAVIGATOR

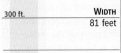

	CREW MEMBERS
	340
	ENTERED SERVICE
	1999
700 ft.	**GROSS TONS**
	33,000
	LENGTH
	560 feet
500 ft.	**NUMBER OF CABINS**
	245
	PASSENGER CAPACITY
	490
300 ft.	**WIDTH**
	81 feet

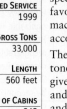

Top: Casino
Bottom: *Navigator* suite

Public Areas and Facilities

The first ship outfitted uniquely to Regent Seven Seas' specifications, the *Seven Seas Navigator* is a particular favorite of returning passengers for its small-ship intimacy, big-ship features, and comfortable, well-designed accommodations, which are all considered suites.

The generous use of wood and the addition of deep-tone accents to the predominantly blue color palette give even the larger lounges an inviting feel. Artwork and elaborate flower arrangements add a bit of sparkle and interest to the somewhat angular modern decor.

Due to the aft location of the two-deck-high main showroom, the only lounges that afford sweeping seascapes are Galileo's—typically the most popular public space, with nightly entertainment—and the Vista Lounge. Although views from the Vista Lounge are spectacular, there's no permanent bar, and it's primarily a quiet spot for reading when there are no lectures or activities scheduled there.

Restaurants

Compass Rose restaurant, the main dining room, functions on an open-seating basis for breakfast, lunch, and dinner, so there are no set dining assignments. La Veranda, the daytime buffet, serves breakfast and lunch. Prime 7, the specialty steakhouse, requires reservations for dinner, but there is no charge. Wines are chosen to complement each luncheon and dinner menu. At least once during each cruise, dinner is served alfresco on the pool deck. In addition to the buffet, a choice for casual lunch and snacks is the poolside grill. Afternoon tea is served daily, and room service is available 24 hours a day. Dinner can be ordered from the main dining room menu during restaurant hours and served en suite, course by course.

Accommodations

Cabins: Attractive textured fabrics and honeyed wood finishes add a touch of coziness to the larger-than-usual suites in all categories, 90% of which have balconies. All have a vanity-desk, walk-in closet, and sitting area with a sofa, chairs, and table. Marble bathrooms have a separate tub and shower. Master Suites have a separate sitting–dining room, a separate bedroom, and a powder room; only Grand Suites also have a powder room.

Master Suites have a second TV in the bedroom, butler service, and whirlpool tub in the master bathroom. Grand and Navigator suites are similarly outfitted. The top three suite categories feature Bose music systems. Penthouse Suites, which include butler service, are only distinguished from Deluxe Suites by location and do not have a whirlpool bathtub.

Amenities: Every suite has an entertainment center with CD/DVD player, stocked refrigerator, stocked bar, personal safe, hair dryer, and beds dressed with fine linens and duvets. Bath toiletries include shampoo, lotion, and bath gel.

Worth Noting: Very few suites have the capacity to accommodate three people, and only 10 far-forward suites adjoin with those adjacent to them. Four suites are wheelchair accessible.

In the Know

From Russia, With Love: Regent Seven Seas took over an unfinished hull that was originally destined to be a Soviet spy ship and redesigned it to create the *Seven Seas Navigator*. They did such a good job completing the interiors that even James Bond would feel at home.

Pros and Cons

Pros: The library contains hundreds of novels, best sellers, and travel books, as well as newspapers, movies for in-suite viewing, and even a selection of board games. Fellow passengers might be as wealthy as Midas, but most are unpretentious. When nothing on the menu appeals to you, don't hesitate to ask for what you'd really like to have for dinner.

Cons: Internet use can be heavy on sea days, and the lines that form in the computer area can add a bit of congestion—and inevitable noise—to the adjacent library, a space that should be a quiet haven. If you book a suite in the far-aft section of the ship, be prepared for an annoying vibration. Unless you prebook a table in Portofino online before your cruise, you could be disappointed to find it unavailable once you board.

Cabin Type	Size (sq. ft.)
Master Suite	1,067
Grand Suite	539
Navigator Suite	448
Penthouse/Balcony Suite	301
Window Suite	301*

*Except for Suite 600, which measures 516

FAST FACTS

- 8 passenger decks
- Specialty restaurant, dining room, buffet
- Wi-Fi, safe, refrigerator, DVD
- Pool
- Fitness classes, gym, hair salon, hot tub, sauna, spa, steam room
- 4 bars, casino, dance club, showroom
- Children's programs (ages 5–17)
- Dry cleaning, laundry facilities, laundry service
- Internet terminal
- No-smoking cabins

Casual poolside dining

ROYAL CARIBBEAN INTL.

Big, bigger, biggest! More than a decade ago, Royal Caribbean launched Sovereign-class ships, the first of the modern megacruise liners, which continue to be an all-around favorite of passengers who enjoy traditional cruising ambience with a touch of daring

Adventure of the Seas solarium

and whimsy tossed in. Plunging into the 21st century, each ship in the current fleet carries more passengers than the entire Royal Caribbean fleet of the 1970s and has features—such as new surfing pools—that were unheard of in the past.

✉ *1050 Royal Caribbean Way, Miami, FL* ☎ *305/539–6000 or 800/327–6700* ⊕ *www.royalcaribbean. com* ☞ *Cruise Style: Mainstream.*

All Royal Caribbean ships are topped by the company's distinctive signature Viking Crown Lounge, a place to watch the seascape by day and dance away at night. Expansive multideck atriums and the generous use of brass and floor-to-ceiling glass windows give each vessel a sense of spaciousness and style. The action is nonstop in casinos and dance clubs after dark, while daytime hours are filled with poolside games and traditional cruise activities. Port talks tend to lean heavily on shopping recommendations and the sale of shore excursions.

A variety of lounges and high-energy stage shows draws passengers of all ages out to mingle and dance the night away. Production extravaganzas showcase singers and dancers in lavish costumes. Comedians, acrobats, magicians, jugglers, and solo entertainers fill show lounges on nights when the ships' companies aren't performing. Professional ice shows are a highlight of cruises on Voyager-, Freedom-, and Oasis-class ships—the only ships at sea with ice-skating rinks.

Food

Dining is an international experience with nightly changing themes and cuisines from around the world.

Passenger preference for casual attire and a resort-like atmosphere has prompted the cruise line to add laid-back alternatives to the formal dining rooms in the Windjammer Café and, on certain ships, Johnny Rockets Diner; Seaview Café evokes the ambience of an island beachside stand. Royal Caribbean offers the choice of traditional early or late dinner seating or My Time Dining, an option that allows you to pre-reserve your preferred seating times (between the hours of 6 and 9:30 PM).

Room service is available 24 hours, but for orders between midnight and 5 AM there is a $3.95 service charge. There's a limited menu.

Royal Caribbean doesn't place emphasis on celebrity chefs or specialty alternative restaurants, although it has introduced a more upscale and intimate dinner experience in the form of an Italian specialty restaurant and/or a steak house on all but the Vision-class ships.

Fitness and Recreation

Royal Caribbean has pioneered such new and previously unheard-of features as rock-climbing walls, ice-skating rinks, bungee trampolines, and even the first self-leveling pool tables on a cruise ship. Interactive water parks, boxing rings, surfing simulators, and cantilevered whirlpools suspended 112 feet above the ocean made their debuts on the Freedom-class ships.

Facilities vary by ship class, but all Royal Caribbean ships have state-of-the-art exercise equipment, jogging tracks, and rock-climbing walls; passengers can work out independently or in classes guaranteed to sweat off extra calories. Most exercise classes are included in the fare, but there's a fee for specialized spin, yoga, and Pilates classes, as well as the services of a personal trainer. Spas and salons are top-notch, with full menus of day spa–style treatments and services for pampering and relaxation for adults and teens.

Your Shipmates

Royal Caribbean cruises have a broad appeal for active couples and singles, mostly in their 30s to 50s. Families are partial to the newer vessels that have larger staterooms, huge facilities for children and teens, and seemingly endless choices of activities and dining options.

Dress Code

Two formal nights are standard on seven-night cruises; one formal night is the norm on shorter sailings. Men are encouraged to wear tuxedos, but dark suits or sport coats and ties are more prevalent. All other evenings

NOTEWORTHY

■ Each ship's Schooner Bar features nautically inspired decor right down to a unique scent.

■ The signature Viking Crown Lounge found on every RCI ship was originally inspired by the Seattle World's Fair Space Needle.

■ Hot tubs and certain swimming pools are designated for adults only on Royal Caribbean ships.

Top: Adventure Beach for kids
Bottom: Voyager-class interior stateroom

are casual, although jeans are discouraged in restaurants. It's requested that no shorts be worn in public areas after 6 PM, although there are passengers who can't wait to change into them after dinner.

Junior Cruisers

Supervised age-appropriate activities are designed for children ages 3 through 17; babysitting services are available as well (either group or in-stateroom babysitting, but sitters will not change diapers). Children are assigned to the Adventure Ocean youth program by age. They must be at least three years old and toilet trained to participate (children who are in diapers and pull-ups or who are not toilet trained are not allowed in swimming pools or whirlpools). Youngsters who wish to join a different age group must participate in one daytime and one night activity session with their proper age group first; the manager will then make the decision based on their maturity level.

In partnership with toy maker Fisher-Price, Royal Caribbean offers interactive 45-minute Aqua Babies and Aqua Tots play sessions for children ages 6 months to 36 months. The playgroup classes, which are hosted by youth staff members, were designed by early-childhood-development experts for parents and their babies and toddlers, and teach life skills through playtime activities.

A teen center with a disco is an adult-free gathering spot that will satisfy even the pickiest teenagers.

Service

Service on Royal Caribbean ships is friendly but inconsistent. Assigned meal seatings assure that most passengers get to know the waiters and their assistants, who in turn get to know the passengers' likes and dislikes; however, that can lead to a level of familiarity that is uncomfortable to some people. Some ships have a concierge lounge for the use of suite occupants and top-level past passengers.

Tipping

Tips can be prepaid when the cruise is booked, added on to shipboard accounts, or given in cash on the last

Top: Miniature golf
Middle: *Adventure of the Seas*
Bottom: *Serenade of the Seas* rock-climbing wall

CHOOSE THIS LINE IF . . .

You want to see the sea from atop a rock wall—it's one of the few activities on these ships that's free.

You're active and adventurous. Even if your traveling companion isn't, there's an energetic staff on board to cheer you on.

You want your space. There's plenty of room to roam; quiet nooks and crannies are there if you look.

night of the cruise. Suggested gratuities per passenger per day are $3.50 for the cabin steward ($5.75 for suites), $3.50 for the waiter, $2 for the assistant waiter, and $0.75 for the headwaiter. A 15% gratuity is automatically added to all bar tabs.

Past Passengers

After one cruise, you can enroll in the Crown & Anchor Society. All members receive the *Crown & Anchor* magazine and have access to the member section on the Royal Caribbean Web site. All members receive an Ultimate Value Booklet and an invitation to a welcome-back party. Platinum members (after five cruises) also have the use of a private departure lounge and receive priority check-in (where available), the onboard use of robes during the cruise, an invitation to an exclusive onboard event, and complimentary custom air arrangements.

Diamond members (after 10 cruises) also receive consideration on a priority wait list for sold-out shore excursions and spa services, concierge service on select ships, priority departure from the ship, complimentary custom air fee, and special rates on balcony and suite accommodations. When members achieve Diamond Plus status (after 24 cruises), they're offered behind-the-scenes tours and preferred seating in main dining rooms.

2

ROYAL CARIBBEAN INTL.

DON'T CHOOSE THIS LINE IF . . .

Patience is not one of your virtues. Lines are not uncommon.

You want to do your own laundry. There are no self-service facilities on any Royal Caribbean ships.

You don't want to hear announcements, especially in your cabin. There are a lot on RCI cruises.

RADIANCE CLASS

Radiance, Brilliance, Serenade, Jewel of the Seas
(only Radiance sails in Alaska in 2011)

CREW MEMBERS	857
ENTERED SERVICE	01, 2002, 2003, 2004
GROSS TONS	90,090
LENGTH	962 feet
NUMBER OF CABINS	1,056
PASSENGER CAPACITY	2,112 (2,501 max)
WIDTH	106 feet

700 ft.

500 ft.

300 ft.

Top: pool deck
Bottom: Shared moments on
your personal balcony

Public Areas and Facilities

Considered by many people to be the most beautiful vessels in the Royal Caribbean fleet, Radiance-class ships are large but sleek and swift, with sun-filled interiors and panoramic elevators that span 10 decks along the ships' exteriors.

High-energy and glamorous spaces are abundant throughout these sister ships. From the rock-climbing wall, children's pool with waterslide, and golf area to the columned dining room, sweeping staircases, and the tropical garden of the solarium, these ships hold appeal for a wide cross section of interests and tastes.

The ships are packed with multiple dining venues, including the casual Windjammer, with its indoor and outdoor seating, and the Latte-Tudes patisserie, offering specialty coffees, pastries, and ice cream treats.

Restaurants

The double-deck-high formal dining room serves open-seating breakfast and lunch; dinner is served in two assigned seatings or open-seating My Timing Dining. For a more upscale dinner, each ship has two specialty restaurants—Portofino, serving Italian fare, and Chops Grille, a steak house. Both charge a supplement and require reservations. The casual Lido buffet offers service nearly around the clock for breakfast, lunch, dinner, and snacks. Seaview Café is open for quick lunches and dinners in a laid-back setting. A pizzeria in the Solarium serves pizza by the slice. The coffee bar features specialty coffees and pastries, for which there is a charge. Room service is available 24 hours.

Accommodations

Cabins: With the line's highest percentage of outside cabins, standard staterooms are bright and cheery as well as roomy. Nearly three-quarters of the outside cabins have private balconies. Every cabin has adequate closet and drawer/shelf storage, as well as bathroom shelves.

Suites: All full suites and family suites have private balconies and include concierge service. Top-category suites have wet bars, separate living-dining areas, multiple bathrooms, entertainment centers with flat-screen TVs, DVD players, and stereos. Some bathrooms have twin sinks, steam showers, and whirlpool tubs. Junior suites have a sitting area, vanity area, and bathroom with a tub.

Amenities: Light-wood cabinetry, a small refrigerator-minibar, broadband Internet connection, a vanity-desk, a TV, a personal safe, a hair dryer, and a sitting area with sofa, chair, and table are typical Radiance-class features in all categories. Bathroom extras include shampoo and bath gel.

Worth Noting: Fifteen staterooms are wheelchair accessible on *Radiance* and *Brilliance*; 19 on *Serenade* and *Jewel*.

In the Know

Other cruise ships may have rollicking sports bars (and these do as well), but only on the Radiance-class Royal Caribbean vessels will you find self-leveling pool tables.

Pros and Cons

Pros: Aft on deck 6, four distinct lounges and a billiard room with self-leveling pool tables form a clubby adult entertainment center furnished in rich colors and accented by warm woods. Not everyone discovers the out-of-the-way Seaview Café, making it a favored casual dining spot for those passengers who take the time to locate it. Spacious family ocean-view cabins sleep up to six people and can accommodate a roll-away bed and/or a crib; the suites also come with two twin beds (convertible into one queen size), additional bunk beds in a separate area, and a separate sitting area with a sofa bed.

Cons: With the traditional and nautical-leaning decor on these otherwise classy ships, the weird free-form atrium sculptures are a jarring throwback to earlier design elements. The location of the pizzeria in the Solarium adds a layer of confusion to an otherwise tranquil retreat. The libraries are tiny and poorly stocked for ships this size.

Cabin Type	Size (sq. ft.)
Royal Suite	1,001
Owner's Suite	512
Grand Suite	358–384
Royal Family Suite	533–586
Junior Suites	293
Superior Ocean View	204
Deluxe Ocean View	179
Large Ocean View	170
Family Ocean View	319
Interior	165

FAST FACTS

- 12 passenger decks
- 2 specialty restaurants, dining room, buffet, pizzeria
- Internet, Wi-Fi, safe, refrigerator, DVD (some)
- 2 pools (1 indoor), children's pool
- Fitness classes, gym, hair salon, 3 hot tubs, sauna, spa, steam room
- 11 bars, casino, cinema, dance club, library, showroom, video game room
- Children's programs (ages 3–17)
- Dry cleaning, laundry service
- Internet terminal
- No-smoking cabins

Sports courts

VISION CLASS
Legend, Splendour, Grandeur, Rhapsody, Vision of the Seas
(only Rhapsody sails in Alaska in 2011)

CREW MEMBERS	
720, 720, 760, 765, 765	
ENTERED SERVICE	
1995, 1996, 1996, 1997, 1998	
700 ft. **GROSS TONS**	
69,130–78,491	
LENGTH	
867, 867, 916, 915, 915 feet	
500 ft. **NUMBER OF CABINS**	
900, 900, 975, 1,000, 1,000	
PASSENGER CAPACITY	
1,800–2,000 (2,076–2,435 max)	
300 ft. **WIDTH**	
106 feet	

Top: Vision-class Owner's Suite
Bottom: *Splendour of the Seas*

Public Areas and Facilities
The first Royal Caribbean ships to offer private balconies in a number of categories, these Vision-class vessels, named for sister ship *Vision of the Seas*, have acres of glass skylights that allow sunlight to flood in and windows that offer wide sea vistas. The soaring central atrium at the heart of each ship is anchored by champagne bars and fills with music after dark.

Built in pairs, the ships follow the same general layout but are different in overall size and the total number of passengers on board. Cabin sizes also vary somewhat; as the total size of the ships increased from *Legend* and *Splendour* at 69,130 tons (1,800 passengers) to *Grandeur* at 74,140 tons (1,950 passengers), and finally, *Rhapsody* and *Vision* at 78,491 tons (2,000 passengers), so did the size of the accommodations. In some categories, it's only a matter of a few feet, so don't look for huge—or even noticeable—differences.

Restaurants
As was the norm when these ships were built, dining selections on board are pretty basic. The double-deck-high formal dining room serves evening meals in two assigned evening seatings or open-seating My Timing Dining, while breakfast and lunch in the dining room are always open seating. Windjammer, the casual Lido buffet, serves three meals a day, including a laid-back dinner. Evening meals in the formal dining room and buffet are often regionally themed and feature menus that focus on Italian, French, and American dishes. Room service is available 24 hours a day, and a poolside grill serves burgers and snacks in the solarium. A coffee bar offers specialty coffees and pastries for an additional fee. Sadly, there are no specialty restaurants on these ships.

Accommodations
Cabins: Cabins are airy and comfortable, but the smaller categories are a tight squeeze for more than two adults. Every cabin has adequate closet and drawer/ shelf storage.

Suites: All full suites and family suites have private balconies and a small minibar; full suites also include concierge service. Royal Suites have a living room; wet bar; separate dining area; entertainment center with TV, stereo, and DVD player; separate bedroom; bathroom (twin sinks, whirlpool tub, separate steam shower, bidet); and separate powder room. Owner's Suites have a separate living area; minibar; entertainment center with TV, stereo, and DVD player; dinette area; and one bathroom (twin sinks, bathtub, separate shower, bidet). Grand Suites have similar amenities on a smaller scale.

Amenities: Light woods, pastel colors, a vanity-desk, a TV, a personal safe, a hair dryer, and a sitting area with sofa, chair, and table are typical Vision-class features in all categories. Bathrooms have shampoo and bath gel.

Worth Noting: On *Legend* and *Splendour*, 17 cabins are wheelchair accessible; on *Grandeur*, *Vision*, and *Rhapsody*, 14 cabins are wheelchair accessible.

In the Know

Not all suites on Vision-class ships are created equal. A Royal Family Suite is a roomy choice for parents with younger children, but goodies that other suites receive—including bathrobes to use on board, welcome-aboard champagne, evening canapés, and concierge service—aren't included.

Pros and Cons

Pros: Open, light-filled public areas offer sea views from almost every angle on these ships. Each vessel features a double-deck-high dining room with sweeping staircases that are a huge improvement over previous ship designs. Tucked into an atrium nook, the Champagne Bar on each ship is not only an elegant spot for predinner cocktails and dancing but also for quiet after-dinner or after-the-show drinks and conversation.

Cons: Some lounges, particularly the popular Schooner Bars, serve as a thoroughfare and suffer from continuous traffic flow before and after performances in the ships' main show lounges. Accommodations lean toward the small side, unless you are willing to pay a premium for a suite. There are no specialty restaurants, and dining options are severely limited as a result.

Cabin Type	Size (sq. ft.)
Royal Suite	1,074
Owner's Suite	523
Royal Family Suite	512
Junior Suite	240
Superior Ocean View	193
Large Ocean View*	154
Interior	135–174

All cabin sizes are averages of the five ships since cabins vary in size among the Vision-class ships. *Rhapsody* has Family Ocean View cabins at 237 sq. ft.

FAST FACTS

- 11 passenger decks
- Dining room, buffet, ice cream parlor, pizzeria
- Wi-Fi, safe, refrigerator (some), DVD (some)
- 2 pools (1 indoor)
- Fitness classes, gym, hair salon, 4–6 hot tubs, sauna, spa
- 6 bars, casino, dance club, library, showroom, video game room
- Children's programs (ages 3–17)
- Dry cleaning, laundry service
- Internet terminal
- No-smoking cabins

Viking Crown lounge overlooks the pool deck

SILVERSEA CRUISES

Silversea Cruises was launched in 1994 by the former owners of Sitmar Cruises, the Lefebvre family of Rome, whose concept for the new cruise line was to build and sail the highest-quality luxury ships at sea. Intimate ships, paired with exclusive amenities and unparal-

The most captivating view on board

leled hospitality are the hallmarks of Silversea cruises. All-inclusive air-and-sea fares can be customized to include not just round-trip airfare but all transfers, porterage, and deluxe precruise accommodations as well.

✉ *110 E. Broward Blvd., Ft. Lauderdale, FL* ☎ *954/522–4477 or 800/722–9955* ⊕ *www. silversea.com* ☞ *Cruise Style: Luxury.*

Personalization is a Silversea maxim. Its ships offer more activities than other comparably sized luxury vessels. Take part in those that interest you, or opt instead for a good book and any number of quiet spots to read or snooze in the shade. Silversea's third generation of ships introduces even more luxurious features; one of the first, the 36,000-ton *Silver Spirit*, launched late in 2009.

Guest lecturers are featured on nearly every cruise; language, dance, and culinary lessons and excellent wine-appreciation sessions are always on the schedule of events. Silversea also schedules culinary arts cruises and a series of wine-focused voyages that feature award-winning authors, international wine experts, winemakers, and acclaimed chefs from the world's top restaurants. During afternoon tea, ladies gather for conversation over needlepoint, and the ranks of highly competitive trivia teams increase every successive afternoon.

After dark, the Bar is a predinner gathering spot and the late-night place for dancing to a live band. A multi-tiered show lounge is the setting for talented singers and musicians, classical concerts, magic shows, big-screen movies, and folkloric entertainers from ashore. A small casino offers slot machines and gaming tables.

Food

Dishes from the galleys of Silversea's master chefs are complemented by those of La Collection du Monde, created by Silversea's culinary partner, the world-class chefs of Relais & Châteaux. Menus include hot and cold appetizers, at least four entrée selections, a vegetarian alternative, and Cruiselite cuisine (low in cholesterol, sodium, and fat). Special off-menu orders are prepared whenever possible, provided that the ingredients are available on board. In the event that they aren't, you may find after a day in port that a trip to the market was made in order to fulfill your request.

Chef Marco Betti, the owner of Antica Pasta restaurants in Florence, Italy, and Atlanta, Georgia, has designed a new menu for La Terrazza that focuses on one of the most luxurious food trends, the "slow food" movement. The goal of the movement is to preserve the gastronomic traditions of Italy through the use of fresh, traditional foods, and it has spread throughout the world. At La Terrazza (by day, a casual buffet) the menu showcases the finest in Italian cooking, from classic favorites to Tuscan fare. The restaurant carries no surcharge. Seating is limited, so reservations are a must to ensure a table—it's one reservation you'll be glad you took the time to book.

An intimate dining experience aboard each vessel is the Wine Restaurant by Relais & Châteaux—Le Champagne. Adding a dimension to dining, the exquisite cuisine is designed to celebrate the wines served—a different celebrated vintage is served with each course. Menus and wines are chosen by Relais & Chateaux sommeliers to reflect regions of the world noted for their rich wine heritage.

An evening poolside barbecue is a weekly dinner event, weather permitting. A highlight of every cruise is the Galley Brunch, when passengers are invited into the galley to select from a feast decorated with imaginative ice and vegetable sculptures. Even when meals are served buffet-style in La Terrazza, you will seldom have to carry your own plate as waiters are at hand to assist you to your table. Wines are chosen to complement each day's luncheon and dinner menus.

Grilled foods, sandwiches, and an array of fruits and salads are served daily for lunch at the poolside Grill. Always available are extensive selections from the room-service menu. The full restaurant menu may be

NOTEWORTHY

■ Prior to departure, Silversea provides a list of port addresses, to which your mail can be forwarded throughout your voyage.

■ Gentlemen are no longer required to wear a tie with their jackets on informal evenings.

■ Silversea does not utilize the services of photographers aboard their ships.

Top: Stylish entertainment
Bottom: Terrace Café alfresco dining

Top: Table tennis
Middle: Caring personal service
Bottom: Veranda Suite

ordered from room service and can be served course by course in your suite during regular dining hours.

Fitness and Recreation

The rather small gyms are equipped with cardiovascular and weight-training equipment, and fitness classes on *Silver Whisper* and *Silver Shadow* are held in the mirror-lined, but somewhat confining, exercise room.

South Pacific–inspired Mandara Spa offers numerous treatments including exotic-sounding massages, facials, and body wraps. Hair and nail services are available in the busy salon. A plus is that appointments for spa and beauty salon treatments can be made online from 60 days until 48 hours prior to sailing.

Golfers can sign up with the pro on board for individual lessons utilizing a high-tech swing analyzer and attend complimentary golf clinics or participate in a putting contest.

Your Shipmates

Silversea Cruises appeal to sophisticated, affluent couples who enjoy the country-club-like atmosphere, exquisite cuisine, and polished service on board, not to mention the exotic ports and unique experiences ashore.

Dress Code

Two formal nights are standard on seven-night cruises and three to four nights, depending on the itinerary, on longer sailings. Men are required to wear tuxedos or dark suits after 6 PM. All other evenings are either informal, when a jacket is called for (a tie is optional, but most men wear them), or casual, when slacks with a jacket over an open-collar shirt for men and sporty dresses or skirts or pants with a sweater or blouse for women are suggested.

Junior Cruisers

Silversea Cruises is adult-oriented, does not accommodate children less than six months of age, and the cruise line limits the number of children under the age of three on board. The availability of suites for a third passenger is capacity controlled. A youth program staffed by counselors is available on holiday and select sailings.

CHOOSE THIS LINE IF . . .

Your taste leans toward learning and exploration.	You enjoy socializing as well as the option of live entertainment, just not too much of it.	You like to plan ahead. You can reserve shore tours, salon services, and spa treatments online.

No dedicated children's facilities are available, so parents are responsible for the behavior and entertainment of their children.

Service
Personalized service is exacting and hospitable yet discreet. The staff strive for perfection and often achieve it. The attitude is decidedly European and begins with a welcome-aboard flute of champagne, then continues throughout as personal preferences are remembered and satisfied. The word *no* doesn't seem to be in the staff vocabulary in any language. Guests in all suites are pampered by butlers.

Tipping
Tipping is neither required nor expected.

Past Passengers
Membership in the Venetian Society is automatic upon completion of one Silversea cruise, and members begin accruing benefits: Venetian Society cruise days and eligibility for discounts on select voyages, onboard recognition and private parties, milestone rewards; exclusive gifts, the *Venetian Society Newsletter*, ship visitation privileges, complimentary early embarkation or late debarkation at certain milestones, members-only benefits at select Leading Hotels of the World and Relais & Châteaux hotels and resorts, and select offers through Silversea's preferred partners.

Through the Friends of Society programs, members can double their accumulated cruise days and receive a shipboard spending credit by inviting friends or family members to sail on select Venetian Society sailings. Friends or family will enjoy the same Venetian Society savings as members for those cruises, a really nice perk.

GOOD TO KNOW
You might expect a bit of stodginess to creep in at this level of ultraluxury, but you wouldn't necessarily be correct. Socializing isn't quite as easygoing as on some ships, and some passengers can come off as a bit standoffish. However, you will encounter like-minded fellow passengers if you make the effort to participate in group activities, particularly the highly competitive afternoon trivia sessions. With an increasingly younger crowd on board, you are more likely to encounter partyers at late-night disco sessions than couples waltzing between courses during dinner.

2

SILVERSEA CRUISES

DON'T CHOOSE THIS LINE IF . . .
You want to dress informally at all times on your cruise. Passengers on these cruises tend to dress up.

You need highly structured activities and have to be reminded of them.

You prefer the glitter and stimulation of Las Vegas to the understated glamour of Monaco.

SILVER SHADOW, SILVER WHISPER
(only Silver Shadow sails in Alaska in 2011)

CREW MEMBERS	
	295
ENTERED SERVICE	
	2000, 2001
700 ft. **GROSS TONS**	
	28,258
LENGTH	
	610 feet
500 ft. **NUMBER OF CABINS**	
	191
PASSENGER CAPACITY	
	382
300 ft. **WIDTH**	
	82 feet

Public Areas and Facilities

The logical layout of these sister ships, with suites located in the forward two-thirds of the ship and public rooms aft, makes orientation simple. The clean, modern decor that defines public areas and lounges might seem almost stark, but it places the main emphasis on large expanses of glass for sunshine and sea views as well as passenger comfort.

Silversea ships boast unbeatable libraries stocked with best sellers, travel books, classics, and movies for in-suite viewing. Extremely wide passageways in public areas are lined with glass-front display cabinets full of interesting and unusual artifacts from the places the ships visit.

The Humidor by Davidoff is a clubby cigar smoking room with overstuffed leather seating and a ventilation system that even nonsmokers can appreciate.

Restaurants

The Restaurant, formal yet simply named, offers open-seating breakfast, lunch, and dinner during scheduled hours. Specialty dining is offered by reservation in Le Champagne, where an extra charge applies for the gourmet meal and wine pairings, and La Terrazza, which is complimentary and serves Italian cuisine. For casual meals, La Terrazza has indoor and outdoor seating for buffet-style breakfast and lunch. The outdoor Grill offers a laid-back lunch option with poolside table service. Elaborate afternoon tea is served daily. An evening poolside barbecue is a weekly dinner event as is the Galley Brunch, when passengers are invited into the galley to make their selections. Room service arrives with crystal, china, and a linen tablecloth for a complete dining room–style setup en suite. You may order at any time from the extensive room service menu or the full restaurant menu, which can be served course by course in your suite during regular dining hours.

Accommodations

Cabins: Every suite is outside with an ocean view, and more than 80% have a private teak-floor balcony. Standard suites have a sitting area that can be curtained off from the bed for more privacy. Marble bathrooms have double sinks and a separate glass-enclosed shower as well as a tub. All suites have generous walk-in closets.

Top: The casino
Bottom: A Silversea ship at sea

Top Suites: In addition to much more space, top-category suites have all the standard amenities plus dining areas, separate bedrooms, and CD players. Silver Suites and above have whirlpool tubs. The top three categories have espresso makers and separate powder rooms.

Amenities: Standard suites have an entertainment center with a TV and DVD, personalized stationery, cocktail cabinet, personal safe, and refrigerator stocked with complimentary beer, soft drinks, and bottled water. A hair dryer is provided at a vanity table, and you can request a magnifying mirror. Beds are dressed with high-quality linens, duvets, or blankets, and your choice of synthetic or down pillows. Bathrooms have huge towels and terry bathrobes for use during the cruise as well as designer shampoo, soaps, and lotion.

Worth Noting: Two suites are designed for wheelchair accessibility. All suites are served by butlers.

In the Know

Nine Terrace Suites on deck 5 have doors to the outside that access a common, semiprivate veranda area. Even though the area is not furnished, it's like having a balcony without paying a higher fare.

Pros and Cons

Pros: Champagne on ice welcomes you to your suite and continues to flow freely throughout your cruise. Sailing on a Silversea ship is like spending time as a pampered guest at a home in the Hamptons where everything is at your fingertips, and if it isn't, all you have to do is ask. Silversea is so all-inclusive that you'll find your room key–charge card is seldom used for anything but opening your suite door.

Cons: Just about the only line you're likely to encounter on a Silversea ship is the one to use a washing machine in the smallish, yet totally free laundry rooms. In an odd contrast to the contents of display cases and lovely flower arrangements, artwork on the walls is fairly ho-hum and not at all memorable. Although small, the spa's complimentary saunas and steam rooms are adequate and seldom occupied.

Cabin Type	Size (sq. ft.)
Grand Suite	1,286–1,435
Royal Suite	1,312–1,352
Owner's Suite	1,208
Silver Suite	701
Medallion Suite	521
Verandah Suite	345
Terrace Suite	287
Vista Suite	287

FAST FACTS

- 7 passenger decks
- 2 specialty restaurants, dining room, buffet
- Wi-Fi, safe, refrigerator, DVD
- Pool
- Fitness classes, gym, hair salon, 2 hot tubs, sauna, spa, steam room
- 3 bars, casino, dance club, library, showroom
- Dry cleaning, laundry facilities, laundry service
- Internet terminal

The Poolside Grille serves lunch and light snacks

AMERICAN SAFARI

"Luxury in pursuit of adventure" is the tagline for American Safari Cruises, the high-end yacht-cruise line, which operates some of the smallest vessels in Alaska. Founded in 1997 to provide upscale, luxurious yacht cruising in Alaska's Inside Passage, Ameri-

Kayak along near-deserted coasts in Southeast Alaska

can Safari Cruises' assets were acquired in February 2009 by Inner-Sea Discoveries LLC. The company continues to operate under the same well-established executive leadership and professional onboard crew, providing a seamless inclusive yacht cruise adventure. All shore excursions and activities are included in the price.

🕮 American Safari Cruises, 3826 18th Ave. W, Seattle, WA 98119 ☎ 206/284–0300 or 888/862–8881 ⊕ www.amsafari.com.

With just 12 to 21 passengers and such decadent amenities as ocean-view hot tubs, American Safari's yachts are among the most comfortable small ships cruising Alaska. Shallow drafts mean these little ships and their landing craft can reach hidden inlets and remote beaches and slip in for close-up looks at glaciers and wildlife. Itineraries are usually flexible; there's no rush to move on if the group spots a pod of whales or a family of bears. All sailing is in daylight, with nights spent at anchor in secluded coves, and the yachts stop daily to let you kayak, hike, or beachcomb. An onboard naturalist offers informal lectures and guides you on expeditions ashore. Guests on all ships have access to the bridge, so you can sip coffee and chat with the captain during the day. All three ships carry binoculars, exercise equipment, kayaks, mountain bikes, Zodiac landing crafts, and insulated suits for Zodiac excursions. There's even fishing gear, but you'll have to purchase a license to fish.

Unlike most other yachts, which have to be chartered, American Safari's vessels sail on a regular schedule and sell tickets to individuals. There's no need to charter the entire ship, although that is an option many people choose for family reunions and other group events.

Food

Chefs serve a choice of nicely presented dinner entrées, featuring fresh local ingredients and plenty of seafood. All cruises are offered as all-inclusive, so premium wines and liquors are available at every meal, and guests are welcome to help themselves to the well-provisioned bar as well as snack options set up between meals.

Fitness and Recreation

Exercise equipment and hot tubs are featured on board. Kayaks are available for a more adventurous workout.

Your Shipmates

Typical passengers tend to be discerning and well-to-do couples from mid-40s to retirees. Children are welcome, but there are no facilities designed for them.

Dress Code

Dress is always comfortably casual, and tends to be more upscale casual than jeans and a flannel shirt in the evening.

Service

Crew members tend to passenger needs discreetly, yet in a personal way—they know your name and preferences, and will even go ashore to find a particular beverage if it isn't stocked on board.

Tipping

Tips are discretionary, but a hefty 5% to 10% of the fare is suggested. A lump sum is pooled among the crew at the end of the cruise.

Choose This Line If . . .

You are curious about new places and appreciate roads less traveled.

You want to come so close to pristine waterfalls that you feel the invigorating spray.

Your plans include chartering an entire yacht for a group of friends or family to travel together.

Don't Choose This Line If . . .

You have to ask the price; these are very expensive cruises.

You can't take care of yourself and make your own good times without a rigid schedule of activities.

You have a high-maintenance wardrobe; there is an iron, but no laundry service onboard.

NOTEWORTHY

■ Umbrellas, rain slickers and pants, and mud boots are provided for your use.

■ Ports of call are close enough that ships usually anchor overnight.

■ When ships spend two full days sailing in Glacier Bay, you will not merely cruise past the scenery, but stop to go ashore or kayak with an expedition leader or park ranger.

Top: the bar on *Safari Quest*
Bottom: Get up close and personal with nature

2

AMERICAN SAFARI

SAFARI SPIRIT, SAFARI QUEST, SAFARI EXPLORER

CREW MEMBERS	6, 9, 16
ENTERED SERVICE	1999, 1998, 2008
GROSS TONS	231, 345, 698
LENGTH	105, 120, 145 feet
NUMBER OF CABINS	6, 11, 18
PASSENGER CAPACITY	12, 22, 36
WIDTH	25, 28, 36 feet

700 ft.

500 ft.

300 ft.

Top: Admiral Stateroom, *Safari Spirit*
Bottom: *Down time on Safari Quest*

Public Areas and Facilities

Safari Spirit is one of Alaska's most luxurious yachts. A forward-facing library with a 180-degree view, covered outside deck space, an on-deck hot tub, and even a sauna–steam bath are part of the pampering.

Safari Quest has warm wood trim throughout and plenty of outer deck space for spotting wildlife and taking in the passing scenery. A lounge on the top deck is a pleasant hideaway from which to enjoy the views in a relaxing setting.

American Safari's largest vessel, *Safari Explorer*, offers comfort amid casually elegant appointments. The library and cozy salons for dining and socializing are nicely balanced, with a large open viewing deck highlighted by a hot tub and nearby sauna.

Restaurants

Each ship has a dining room spacious enough to seat all passengers at once. An early-risers continental breakfast is followed by a full breakfast, lunch, predinner appetizers, and a single-seating dinner where meals are served family-style. After dinner you can retire to the Salon for cordials and chocolate truffles. Coffee, tea, and hot chocolate are available day and night, although there is no room service.

Accommodations

Layout: *Safari Spirit*'s bright, cheerful cabins—all with plush bedding, televisions and DVDs, Jacuzzi bathtubs, separate showers, and heated bathroom floors—are among the roomiest in the American Safari fleet. Three have king-size beds, and two of those feature small balconies. The other three staterooms have queen- or twin-size beds.

The four higher-end Admiral Staterooms on *Safari Quest* have sliding glass doors leading to a small balcony. Five rooms have elevated portlights rather than picture windows. One stateroom is reserved for single travelers, but also has a Pullman upper; the rest have king or queen beds. All feature televisions and DVD players; bathrooms have showers only.

Staterooms on *Safari Explorer*, the newest entry in American Safari's yachting fleet, all feature a television with DVD player, and most open directly to an outside deck. Two Admiral Staterooms have private balconies and bathrooms with whirlpool tubs and showers. Bedding configurations range from fixed king-size to twins that can be joined to form a single larger bed. Two suites and two staterooms offer triple accommodations, and there is even one stateroom with a twin bed and Pullman upper that is available for single occupancy—a rarity afloat these days.

Amenities: Accommodations on all ships feature hair dryers, terry bathrobe for use on board, slippers, and alarm clocks. Shampoo, conditioner, soap, and lotion are provided.

Worth Noting: None of American Safari's ships have wheelchair-accessible accommodations.

In the Know

With the onboard naturalist as teacher, American Safari's Kids in Nature program is offered during popular summer vacation time in Alaska's Inside Passage for children age 12 and under.

Pros and Cons

Pros: A large flat-screen TV/DVD in each ship's salon is equipped with a Hydrophone and underwater camera; in addition to fiction and nonfiction titles, educational materials highlighting destination information are available in the libraries; with the casual ambience on board and so much included—even insect repellent—you can pack light.

Cons: None of American Safari's ships has an elevator, making them a poor choice for mobility-impaired passengers; while there is exercise equipment on board, there is no fitness center or spa facility; there is no Internet access onboard, and cell-phone service is only available when the ships are near shore and within range of a cell tower.

Cabin Type	Size (sq. ft.)
Safari Spirit Staterooms	172–266
Safari Quest Staterooms	125–168
Safari Explorer Staterooms	124–263
Safari Explorer Suites	255–275

Note: American Safari literature includes specific square footage for each stateroom and suite.

FAST FACTS

- 4/4/3 passenger decks
- Dining room
- In-cabin DVD
- 1 hot tub, sauna (*Safari Spirit* and *Safari Explorer* only)
- 1 bar, library
- No-smoking cabins

Wine Library on *Safari Explorer*

AMERICAN SAFARI

2

CRUISE WEST

A big player in small ships, Seattle-based Cruise West is family-owned, which is reflected in the ships' homey atmosphere. After returning to Alaska from flying in World War II, founder Chuck West went to work as a bush pilot and dreamed of sharing Alaska's unspoiled frontier with the rest of the world. After launching and subsequently selling a tour company, he and his family founded West Travel, now known as Cruise West. Initially the company operated sightseeing tours, then expanded into cruises in the mid-1980s.

🕭 *Cruise West, 2301 5th Ave., Suite 401, Seattle, WA 98121* ☎ *206/441–8687 or 888/851–8133* ⊕ *www. cruisewest.com.*

Alaskan wilderness, wildlife, and culture take precedence over shipboard diversions on Cruise West ships. Ports of call include small fishing villages and native settlements as well as major towns. An exploration leader, who is both a naturalist and cruise coordinator, offers evening lectures and joins passengers on many of the shore activities—at least one of which is included at each port of call. At some stops local guides come on board to add their insights; schedules are flexible to make the most of wildlife sightings. Binoculars in every cabin, a library stocked with books of local interest (as well as movies on some ships), and crew members as keen to explore Alaska as the passengers all enhance the experience.

Cruise West has partnered with **PENTAX Imaging Company**, a leader in digital photography, to offer a series of Photographers' Cruises on select Alaska itineraries. There is no additional cost for the sailings co-hosted by a professional PENTAX photographer who conducts special field events and onboard workshops throughout the cruise.

Food

Wholesome meals focus on the freshest ingredients available, including an abundance of Alaska seafood. Bread is freshly baked on board every day.

Fitness and Recreation

Passengers are limited to one or two pieces of fitness equipment on board; however, the shore excursions that are included in the fare are often walking tours.

Your Shipmates

The passengers, who inevitably get to know one another during the cruise, are typically active, well-traveled over-50s. They come from all regions of the United States, as well as from Australia, Canada, and the United Kingdom. While children are certainly welcome, there are no facilities or programs designed for them.

Dress Code

Attire is always casual on board and ashore, and jeans are as formal as it gets.

Service

Provided by an all-American crew, service is friendly and personal, if not overly polished.

Tipping

Tips are included in most Cruise West fares, but gratuities for exceptional service by crew members are warmly appreciated. For shore excursions and land extensions, $2 to $3 for drivers and $5 per day for shore exploration leaders is suggested.

Choose This Line If . . .

You consider yourself more a traveler than a tourist.

Your idea of a fun evening includes board games and quiet conversation.

You want to get up close to whales and other wildlife.

Don't Choose This Line If . . .

You can't entertain yourself.

Room service is a requirement—you won't find it on these ships.

You would rather play a slot machine than attend an evening lecture.

NOTEWORTHY

■ All ships prohibit smoking indoors, and have limited smoking space outdoors.

■ The ships' shallow draft, small size, and skilled crews provide access to areas passengers on big ships can only dream about.

■ Exploration leaders share entertaining and fascinating stories from history, folklore, identification and information on the flora and fauna, and the cultural diversity of areas you will visit.

SPIRIT OF COLUMBIA, SPIRIT OF DISCOVERY

CREW MEMBERS	21, 21
ENTERED SERVICE	1979, 1976
GROSS TONS	97, 94
LENGTH	143, 166 feet
NUMBER OF CABINS	39, 43
PASSENGER CAPACITY	78, 84
WIDTH	28, 37 feet

700 ft.

500 ft.

300 ft.

Public Areas and Facilities

Smaller and older than their fleetmates, these two ships bear more resemblance to coastal packets than traditional cruise ships or megayachts. Although they have been extensively refurbished through the years, they haven't lost their cozy charm. Activities on board center around the wood-trimmed dining rooms and comfortable, if compact, lounges, each of which features a bar, some library shelving with books, and a coffee station.

The list of what you won't find aboard is longer than what you will; however, these two vessels are ideal for slipping into tight spaces and getting up close to what most passengers have come to Alaska to see—wildlife and the state's natural wonders. There's plenty of room on each ship's sundeck, and the *Spirit of Discovery*'s bow viewing area to enjoy the sights. Neither ship has an elevator.

Restaurants

Each ship has a single dining room with one seating for breakfast, lunch, and dinner. You may sit where and with whom you please, but should arrive at the beginning of the scheduled mealtime to avoid disappointment. Promptness is encouraged, and those who straggle in late will have no choice of table selection or companions. Early risers will find a continental breakfast set up in the lounge, and substantial snacks are served there in the late afternoon. A serve-yourself coffee stand is located in the lounge and you might find freshly baked cookies as well. There is no room service offered.

Accommodations

Layout: Compact is a generous description of accommodations on both vessels. The largest staterooms barely compare to an average standard cabin on modern cruise ships. Don't be surprised to find your sink located on a vanity in the sleeping area, even in the top categories. In the lowest categories the entire bathroom might be your shower. Note that "bed sizes vary from standard." What that means is that they are somewhat shorter than usual.

Amenities: *Spirit of Columbia* has deluxe and AAA categories that feature several different bedding configura-

Spirit of Discovery at sea

tions and TVs with VCR players. Deluxe cabins also have a small refrigerator. Upper Deck and Bridge Deck accommodations all open onto outside passageways. Lower Deck cabins are located "outside," but have no windows. All categories on *Spirit of Discovery* have windows for a view, but only the Deluxe accommodations have TVs with VCR players; lower categories have no TV. Neither of these Cruise West ships is equipped with hair dryers, so you should bring your own.

Worth Noting: There are no accessible accommodations for passengers who require wheelchairs or scooters for mobility. *Spirit of Discovery* has two single cabins.

In the Know

Tall people—those over six feet—may find the headroom on board both ships a bit too low for comfort. Ceilings are only about 6½ feet high, and can feel claustrophobic for even average-height passengers.

Pros and Cons

Pros: *Spirit of Columbia* is equipped for bow landing, which allows passengers to go ashore almost anywhere the ship can be beached; both ships can navigate in snug areas that larger vessels can't reach; captains of these small vessels have the authority to deviate from the scheduled itinerary if something comes up that is of more interest.

Cons: Closet and storage space in accommodations can be very tight for even two people; nightlife is virtually nonexistent, unless you are fond of games; shelving that houses books in the lounges is limited, so you will want to bring your own reading material.

Cabin Type	Size (sq. ft.)
Spirit of Columbia	80–121
Spirit of Discovery	64–126

FAST FACTS

- 4/3 passenger decks
- Dining room
- In-cabin refrigerators (some)
- In-cabin VCRs (some)
- No TV in some cabins
- 1 bar
- No-smoking cabins

2

CRUISE WEST

SPIRIT OF ENDEAVOUR, SPIRIT OF YORKTOWN

CREW MEMBERS	25, 40
ENTERED SERVICE	1980, 1988
GROSS TONS	1,425, 2,354
LENGTH	217, 257 feet
NUMBER OF CABINS	51, 69
PASSENGER CAPACITY	102, 138
WIDTH	28, 43 feet

700 ft.

500 ft.

300 ft.

Public Areas and Facilities

One of Cruise West's largest and fastest ships, *Spirit of Endeavour* has a roomy lounge with large picture windows for superb views. There's ample deck space on the stern, where everyone gathers to observe wildlife, as well as on upper decks, which are good for watching sunsets.

The *Spirit of Yorktown*'s profile is dominated by picture windows that ensure bright interior spaces. In keeping with its size, there are only two public rooms, and deck space is limited. The glass-walled observation lounge does multipurpose duty as the ship's bar, lecture room, and movie "theater."

Restaurants

Each ship has a single dining room with one seating for breakfast, lunch, and dinner. You may sit where and with whom you please, but should arrive at the beginning of the scheduled mealtime to avoid disappointment. Early risers will find a Continental breakfast set up in the lounge, and substantial snacks are served there in the late afternoon. A serve-yourself coffee stand is located in the lounge and you might find freshly baked cookies as well. There is no room service offered.

Accommodations

Layout: Most cabins aboard *Spirit of Endeavour* have picture windows, and some have connecting doors, which make them convenient for families traveling together. Most have twin beds, although a couple of cabins have queens, and all have a writing desk and TV with VCR. Bathrooms are small, but comfortable. You might want to bring your own hair dryer, as they are provided only upon request.

Amenities: Aboard *Spirit of Yorktown* most cabins have a picture window, but a few have portholes; none has a television, but all have a hair dryer. Toilets are wedged between sinks and showers, and might pose a tight squeeze for larger passengers. Although the largest staterooms are quite spacious, there are only eight of them, and only four of those have balconies. Cabins underwent refurbishment in 2007.

Worth Noting: No accommodations are designated accessible.

Spirit of Endeavor at sea

In the Know

As with all Cruise West ships, itineraries are flexible: the captain can linger to let passengers watch a group of whales and still make the next port stop on time.

Pros and Cons

Pros: Fleets of inflatable landing craft take passengers ashore for independent exploration; conversation and friendships with fellow passengers come easy on these small ships with their casual vibe; with a sundeck and bow viewing area, *Spirit of Endeavour* has plenty of outdoor space to watch for wildlife or glacier calving.

Cons: With the highest passenger concentration of Cruise West's larger ships, the *Spirit of Yorktown* can feel crowded when all passengers are inside; oddly, while the *Spirit of Endeavour* has Wi-Fi hot spots for Internet connections, none of the accommodations aboard *Spirit of Yorktown* has a TV; there are no laundry services, so pack accordingly.

Cabin Type	Size (sq. ft.)
Spirit of Endeavour	80–128
Spirit of Yorktown	121–138

FAST FACTS

- 4/4 passenger decks
- Dining room
- Wi-Fi (only *Spirit of Endeavour*)
- In-cabin safes (some)
- In-cabin refrigerators (some)
- VCRs (some, and only *Spirit of Endeavour*)
- No TV in cabins (only *Spirit of Yorktown*)
- 1 bar
- No-smoking cabins

2

CRUISE WEST

LINDBLAD EXPEDITIONS

Founded in 1979 as Special Expeditions by Sven-Olof Lindblad, the son of Lars-Eric Lindblad, the company changed its name in 1984 to Lindblad Expeditions. Every cruise is educational, focusing on soft adventure and environmentally conscientious travel through ecologically sensitive regions of Alaska. Since 2004 the line has partnered with *National Geographic* to enhance the experience by including *National Geographic* experts and photographers on board; forums to discuss current events and world issues; and participation by fellowship-funded teachers of geography and other subjects.

⌐ *Lindblad Expeditions, 96 Morton St., New York, NY 10014* ☎ *212/765–7740 or 800/397–3348* ⊕ *www.expeditions.com.*

The ships of Lindblad Expeditions spend time looking for wildlife, exploring out-of-the-way inlets, and making Zodiac landings at isolated beaches. Each ship has a fleet of kayaks as well as a video-microphone: a hydrophone (underwater microphone) is combined with an underwater camera so passengers can listen to whale songs and watch live video of what's going on beneath the waves. In the evening the ships' naturalists recap the day's sights and adventures over cocktails in the lounge. A video chronicler makes a DVD of the entire cruise that you may purchase.

Food
Lindblad prides itself on serving fresh Alaska seafood, including Dungeness crab, halibut, and Alaska king salmon, but there are also plenty of meat and vegetarian options. Breakfast is buffet-style, and lunch is served family-style. The recently launched "Seafood for Thought" program is meant to ensure that sustainable seafood is being served.

Fitness and Recreation
Both ships carry exercise equipment on deck and have a Wellness Program, with fundamentals ranging from

kayaking and hiking to yoga and Pilates, massage therapy, and body treatments.

Your Shipmates
Lindblad attracts active, adventurous, well-traveled over-40s, and quite a few singles, as the line charges one of the industry's lowest single supplements. It is making a push, however, to be more family-friendly, and staff members have undergone extensive training to tailor activities toward children. In July and August some family expeditions are offered, which follow the same itinerary as Lindblad's other trips but include a crew member dedicated to running educational programs for school-age kids. All Lindblad cruises offer substantial discounts for young people up to 21 traveling with their parents. Smoking is not permitted on board.

Dress Code
Casual and comfortable attire is always appropriate.

Service
Service is friendly and helpful, if not overly polished.

Tipping
While gratuities are at your discretion, tips of $12–$15 per person per day are suggested; these are pooled among the crew at journey's end. Tip the massage therapist individually following a treatment.

Choose This Line If . . .
You want to be an ecologically responsible traveler.

You consider travel a learning experience.

What you see from the ship is more important than the vessel itself.

Don't Choose This Line If . . .
You are mobility impaired; the ships are not accessible, and Zodiacs are used to reach shore for certain explorations.

Your happiness depends on being entertained; other than enrichment programs, there is no formal entertainment.

You consider television essential; there are none in the staterooms.

Top: Informal yet elegant dining
Bottom: kayaking

NATIONAL GEOGRAPHIC SEA BIRD/ NATIONAL GEOGRAPHIC SEA LION

CREW MEMBERS	22
ENTERED SERVICE	1982, 1981
GROSS TONS	100
LENGTH	152 feet
NUMBER OF CABINS	31
PASSENGER CAPACITY	62
WIDTH	31 feet

700 ft.
500 ft.
300 ft.

Top: *Sea Lion* at sea
Bottom: comfortable
accomodations

Public Areas and Facilities

These small, shallow-draft sister ships can tuck into nooks and crannies that bigger ships can't reach. Artwork on both includes a collection of photographs by expedition staff naturalists as well as whale and dolphin sculptures. An open-top sundeck, a forward observation lounge, and a viewing deck at the bow offer plenty of room to take in the scenery. The ships are also equipped with bowcams (underwater cameras that monitor activity), and you can navigate the camera using a joystick to observe sea life. Additional expedition equipment includes a hydrophone for eavesdropping on marine mammals, an underwater video "splash" camera to record the passing undersea scenery, and a video microscope for use during naturalists' lectures. The ship's Internet kiosk provides e-mail access. Fitness equipment is set up on the bridge deck, and the LEXspa Wellness room offers massages, body treatments, and a morning stretching program on deck.

Restaurants

All meals are served open-seating during scheduled times in a single dining room. Breakfast is a buffet with a wide selection; lunch if often served family-style. Dinner is equally informal. There is no room service.

Accommodations

Layout: These ships are comfortable, but cabins are proportionately small. All staterooms are outside, and upper-category cabins have picture windows that open; the lowest-category cabins on main deck have portholes that admit light, but do not open or afford much of a view. Most cabins have single beds that can convert to a double, and a few on the upper deck have pull-out beds to accommodate a third person.

Amenities: There are no TVs in accommodations. A functional in-cabin sink has good lighting over a square mirror and vanity that contains a hair dryer. A curtain separates the toilet and shower compartment in the "head"-style bathroom, where 100% natural, biodegradable conditioning shampoo, body wash, and body lotion are provided. It is recommended that you bring biodegradable products if you choose to use your own. There is just enough storage space to stow your belongings.

Worth Noting: No accommodations are designated accessible.

In the Know

An "open bridge" policy provides passengers the opportunity to meet the captain and his officers and learn the intricacies of navigation or simply observe.

Pros and Cons

Pros: A fleet of Zodiacs and kayaks can take you closer to the water and wildlife; a wellness specialist is onboard to lead classes in yoga and Pilates; itineraries are flexible, so as to take maximum advantage of reported wildlife sightings and weather conditions.

Cons: These ships have no elevators or accessible features for the mobility impaired; alcoholic beverages are not included in the fare, which tends to be rather steep; accommodations are basic in decor and spartan in size, with really tiny bathrooms.

Cabin Type	Size (sq. ft.)
Sea Bird	73–202
Sea Lion	73–202

FAST FACTS

- 3 passenger decks
- Dining room
- bar
- library
- Wi-Fi
- No TV in cabins
- Computer room
- No-smoking cabins

2

LINDBLAD EXPEDITIONS

Taking in the view aboard the *Sea Bird*.

ERIENCE MUSIC PROJECT

Ports of Embarkation

WORD OF MOUTH

We are in our 60's and we like HAL (www.hollandamerica.com).
Their midsize ships cruise from Vancouver and Seattle to Alaska,
and they have rail/land tours as add-ons.

—jimingso

Many northbound cruises begin in Vancouver, British Columbia, but Seattle has become an important port as well, with the opening of the Smith Cove Cruise Terminal at Terminal 91 in 2009. A few large ships sail from as far away as San Francisco and small-ship cruise lines offer sailings from Juneau, Petersburg, and Sitka, Alaska.

Anchorage is the primary starting point for cruise passengers heading south, but most ships don't actually dock there. Instead, travelers fly into and may overnight in Anchorage before being transported by bus or train to the ports of Seward or Whittier for southbound departures.

Cruise travelers frequently opt for combination packages that include a one-way north- or southbound Inside Passage cruise plus a tour by bus or train through interior Alaska (and sometimes the Yukon). Denali National Park, located too far inland to be included on round-trip Inside Passage cruises, is a particular focus of these "CruiseTour" trips.

Before or after the cruise, travelers with a more independent streak may want to rent a car and strike out on their own to places not often visited by cruise ships, such as Homer or Valdez.

PORT ESSENTIALS

RESTAURANTS AND CUISINE
Given the seaside location of the embarkation towns, it's no surprise that fresh fish and other seafood are especially popular. Fresh halibut and salmon are available throughout summer, along with specialties such as shrimp, oysters, and crab.

Seafood meals can be simply prepared fast food, like beer-battered fish-and-chips, or more elaborate dinners of halibut baked in a macadamia-nut crust with fresh mango chutney. If seafood isn't your first choice, rest assured that all the staples—including restaurants serving steaks, burgers, pizza, Mexican, or Chinese food—can also be found.

Use the coordinate (✛ B2) at the end of each listing to locate a site on the corresponding map.

WHAT IT COSTS				
¢	$	$$	$$$	$$$$
Anchorage	under $10	$10–$15	$16–$20	$21–$25	over $25
Seattle	under $8	$8–$16	$17–$24	$25–$32	over $32
Vancouver	under C$8	C$8–C$12	C$13–C$20	C$21–C$30	over C$30

Restaurant prices are for a main course at dinner, excluding tip, taxes, service charges, and liquor charges.

3

ABOUT THE HOTELS

Whether you're driving or flying into your port of embarkation, it's often more convenient to arrive the day before or to stay for a day (or longer) after your cruise. Cruise travelers often stay in one of the larger downtown hotels booked by the cruise lines in order to be closer to the ports, but you might like to make your own arrangements for a pre- or post-cruise sojourn. Therefore, we offer lodging suggestions for each port.

The hotels we list are convenient to the cruise port and the cream of the crop in each price category. Properties are assigned price categories based on the range between their least and most expensive standard double room at high season (excluding holidays).

Use the coordinate (✛ B2) at the end of each listing to locate a site on the corresponding map. Assume that hotels operate on the European Plan (EP, with no meals) unless specified that they use the All-inclusive (all meals and some drinks and activities), Continental Plan (CP, with a continental breakfast), Modified American Plan (MAP, with breakfast and dinner), or the Full American Plan (FAP, with all meals). The following price categories apply for properties in this book.

WHAT IT COSTS				
¢	$	$$	$$$	$$$$
Anchorage	under $100	$100–$150	$151–$200	$201–$250	over $250
Seattle	under $100	$100–$180	$181–$265	$266–$350	over $350
Vancouver	under C$75	C$75–C$125	C$126–C$175	C$176–C$250	over C$250

Prices are for two people in a standard double room in high season, excluding tax and service.

ANCHORAGE

Updated by
Tom Reale

By far Alaska's largest and most sophisticated city, Anchorage is in a truly spectacular location. The permanently snow-covered peaks and volcanoes of the Alaska Range lie to the west of the city, part of the craggy Chugach Range is actually within the eastern edge of the municipality, and the Talkeetna and Kenai ranges are visible to the north and south. On clear days Mt. McKinley looms on the northern horizon, and two arms of Cook Inlet embrace the town's western and southern borders.

Anchorage is Alaska's medical, financial, and banking center, and home to the executive offices of most of the Native corporations. The city has a population of roughly 290,000, approximately 40%, of the people in the state. The relative affluence of this white-collar city—with a sprinkling of olive drab from nearby military bases—fosters fine restaurants and pricey shops, first-rate entertainment, and sporting events.

Boom and bust periods followed major events: an influx of military bases during World War II; a massive buildup of Arctic missile-warning stations during the Cold War; reconstruction following the devastating Good Friday earthquake of 1964; and in the late 1960s the biggest jackpot of all—the discovery of oil at Prudhoe Bay and the construction of the Trans-Alaska Pipeline. Not surprisingly, Anchorage positioned itself as the perfect home for the pipeline administrators and support industries, and it continues to attract a large share of the state's oil-tax dollars.

Visitor Information **Anchorage Convention and Visitors Bureau** (*ACVB* ✉ *524 W. 4th Ave., Downtown* ☎ *907/276–4118, 800/478–1255 to order visitor guides* 🖷 *907/278–5559* ⊕ *www.anchorage.net*). **Log Cabin and Visitor Information Centers** (✉ *4th Ave. and F St., Downtown* ☎ *907/274–3531* ⊕ *www. anchorage.net*).

ON THE MOVE

GETTING TO THE PORT

Anchorage is the starting (or ending) point for many Alaskan cruises, but most passengers board or disembark in Seward (125 mi south on Resurrection Bay). Seward is a three-hour bus ride or four-hour train ride from Anchorage. The train station is a few blocks from downtown Anchorage. Another frequent embarkation port is Whittier (59 mi southeast of Anchorage), on the western shore of Prince William Sound. Access between Anchorage and these ports is by bus or train. Transfers are offered by the cruise lines, either as an add-on to your fare or, in the case of some luxury cruise lines or small-ship cruise lines, included in the price of your cruise. Cruise-line representatives meet airport arrivals to make the process as effortless as possible. You'll spend virtually no shore time there before you embark or after disembarkation—buses and the train also offer dock-to-airport service in both places. The few ships that do dock at Anchorage proper dock just north of downtown. There's an information booth on the pier. It's only a 15- or 20-minute walk from the town to the dock, but this is through an industrial area with heavy traffic, so it's best to take a taxi.

ARRIVING BY AIR

Ted Stevens Anchorage International Airport is 6 mi from downtown. Alaska Railroad trains have a stop both here and downtown, in addition to direct service for cruise-ship companies transporting their passengers to Seward or Whittier. Taxis queue up outside baggage-claim. A ride downtown runs about $20, not including tip.

SEWARD, WHITTIER, OR ANCHORAGE?

Here's a rundown of which cruise lines will anchor in Seward, Whittier, or Anchorage—or none of the above—in 2011:

- American Safari: none

- Carnival: none

- Celebrity: Seward

- Cruise West: Whittier

- Crystal: none

- Disney: none

- Holland America: Seward

- Lindblad Expeditions: none

- Norwegian: none

- Oceania: Anchorage

- Princess: Whittier

- Regent: Seward

- Royal Caribbean: Seward

- Silversea: Seward

Contacts Ted Stevens Anchorage International Airport (☎ *907/266–2529* ⊕ *www.anchorageairport.com*).

ARRIVING BY CAR

The Glenn Highway enters Anchorage from the north and becomes 5th Avenue near Merrill Field; this route leads directly into downtown. Gambell Street leads out of town to the south, becoming New Seward Highway at about 20th Avenue. South of town, it becomes the Seward Highway.

RENTAL CARS

Anchorage is the ideal place to rent a car for exploring sites farther afield before or after your cruise. National Car Rental has a downtown office. All the major companies (and several local operators) have airport desks and free shuttle service to the airport to pick up cars.

Contacts Arctic Rent-a-Car (☎ *907/561–2990* ✉ *1130 W. Intl. Airport Rd., Anchorage*). **Budget** (☎ *907/243–0150*). **Denali Car Rental** (☎ *907/276–1230*). **National Car Rental** (✉ *1300 E. 5th Ave., Downtown* ☎ *907/265–7553* ✉ *Ted Stevens International Airport* ☎ *907/243–3406*).

TAXIS

Downtown Anchorage is easy to navigate on foot. If you want to see some of the outlying attractions, such as Lake Hood, you'll need to hire a taxi. Taxis are on a meter system; rates start at $2 to $3 for pickup and $2.50 for each mile. Most people call for a cab, although it's possible to hail one. Alaska Cab has taxis with wheelchair lifts. In the snow-free months a network of paved trails provides good avenues for in-city travel for bicyclists and walkers.

Contacts Alaska Yellow Cab (☎ *907/222–2222*). **Alaska Cab** (☎ *907/563–5353*)

EXPLORING ANCHORAGE

DOWNTOWN ANCHORAGE

5 **Alaska Center for the Performing Arts.** The distinctive stone-and-glass building overlooks an expansive park filled with brilliant flowers all summer. Look inside for upcoming events, or relax amid the blossoms on a sunny afternoon. ⊠ *621 W. 6th Ave., at G St., Downtown* ☎ *907/263–2900, 800/478–7328 tickets* ⊕ *www.alaskapac.org* ✉ *Tours by appointment only.*

4 **Alaska Public Lands Information Center.** Stop here for information on all
☺ of Alaska's public lands, including national and state parks, national
★ forests, and wildlife refuges. You can plan a hiking, sea-kayaking, bear-viewing, or fishing trip; find out about public-use cabins; learn about Alaska's plants and animals; or head to the theater for films highlighting different parts of the state. The bookstore sells maps and nature books. Guided walks to historic downtown sights depart daily. ⊠ *605 W. 4th Ave., No. 105, at F St., Downtown* ☎ *907/271–2737* ⊕ *www.nps.gov/aplic* ☉ *Memorial Day–Labor Day, daily 9–5; Labor Day–Memorial Day, weekdays 10–5.*

6 **Anchorage Museum.** An impressive collection of historic and contem-
☺ porary Alaskan art is exhibited along with dioramas and displays on
Fodor's Choice Alaskan history and village life. You can join an informative 60-minute
★ tour (given hourly in the summer) or step into the theater to watch a film on Alaska. In the summer the first-floor atrium is the site of free daily presentations by local artists and authors. Muse restaurant, operated by the Marx Bros., serves delicious lunches, dinners, and cocktails, and the gift shop sells Alaska Native art and souvenirs. After an extensive renovation in 2008–09, the Imaginarium science museum, formerly at a separate site, was incorporated into the museum. New attractions also include a planetarium and the Smithsonian Arctic Studies Center, which features 600 Alaska Native artifacts. ⊠ *625 C St., Downtown* ☎ *907/929–9201, 907/929–9200 recorded information* ⊕ *www.anchoragemuseum.org* ✉ *$10* ☉ *Mid-May–mid-Sept., daily 9–6, until 9 Thurs. evenings; mid-Sept.–mid-May, Tues.–Sat. 10–6, Sun. noon–6.*

3 **Oscar Anderson House Museum.** City butcher Oscar Anderson built Anchorage's first permanent frame house in 1915, at a time when most of Anchorage consisted of tents. Swedish Christmas tours are held the first two weekends of December. Guided 45-minute tours are available whenever the museum is open. ⊠ *420 M St., in Elderberry Park, Downtown* ☎ *907/274–2336* ✉ *$3* ☉ *June–mid-Sept., weekdays noon–5; group tours (maximum 10 participants per group) must be arranged in advance.*

2 **Resolution Park.** This tiny park has a cantilevered viewing platform dominated by a monument to Captain Cook, whose explorations in 1778 led to the naming of Cook Inlet and many other geographic features in Alaska. Mt. Susitna, known as the Sleeping Lady, is the prominent low mountain to the northwest, and Mts. Spurr and Redoubt, active volcanoes, are just south of Mt. Susitna. Mt. McKinley, Mt. Foraker, and other peaks of the Alaska Range are often visible from more than 100 mi away. ⊠ *3rd Ave. at L St., Downtown.*

Learn about Alaska's art, history, and landscapes at the Anchorage Museum.

1 **Tony Knowles Coastal Trail.** Strollers, runners, bikers, dog walkers, and
Fodor's Choice in-line skaters cram this recreation trail on sunny summer evenings,
★ particularly around Westchester Lagoon. In winter cross-country skiers
take to it by storm. The trail begins off 2nd Avenue, west of Christensen
Drive, and curls along Cook Inlet for approximately 11 mi to Kincaid
Park, beyond the airport. In summer you might spot beluga whales
offshore in Cook Inlet. Access points are on the waterfront at the ends
of 2nd, 5th, and 9th avenues and at Westchester Lagoon.

MIDTOWN

8 **Alaska Heritage Museum at Wells Fargo.** More than 900 Alaska Native
★ artifacts are the main draw in the quiet, unassuming lobby of a large
midtown bank—it's reputed to be one of the largest private collections
of native artworks in the country. You'll also find paintings by Alaskan artists, a library of rare books, and a 46-troy-ounce gold nugget.
✉ *Wells Fargo Bank, 301 W. Northern Lights Blvd., at C St., Midtown*
☎ *907/265–2834* ⊕ *www.wellsfargohistory.com/museums/museums_
an.htm* ⬚ *Free* ⊙ *Late May–early Sept., weekdays noon–5; early Sept.–
late May, weekdays noon–4.*

EAST ANCHORAGE

10 **Alaska Botanical Garden.** The garden showcases perennials hardy enough
☺ to make it in South Central Alaska in several large display gardens, a
pergola-enclosed herb garden, and a rock garden among 110 acres of
mixed boreal forest. There's a 1-mi nature trail loop to Campbell Creek,
with views of the Chugach Range and a wildflower trail between the display gardens. Interpretive signs guide visitors and identify plants along
the trail. Children can explore the garden with an activity-filled duffel
bag Tuesday–Saturday 1–4 PM. Docent tours are available at 1 PM daily

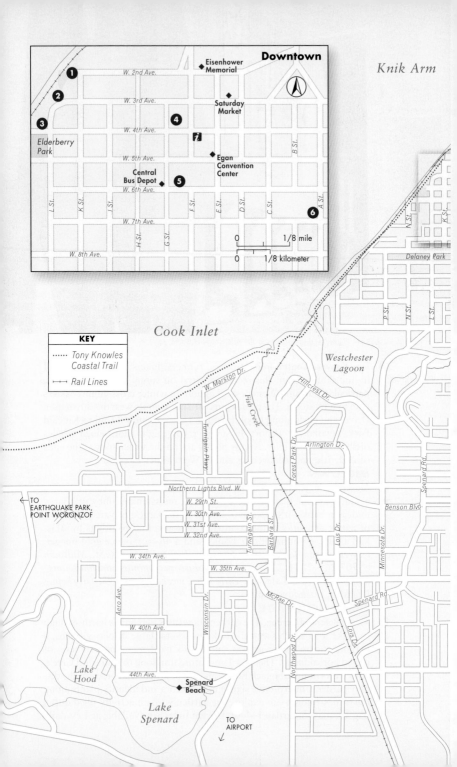

Downtown

Knik Arm

W. 2nd Ave.

Eisenhower Memorial

W. 3rd Ave.

Saturday Market

W. 4th Ave.

Elderberry Park

W. 5th Ave.

Egan Convention Center

Central Bus Depot

W. 6th Ave.

W. 7th Ave.

L St.
K St.
I St.
H St.
G St.
F St.
E St.
D St.
C St.
B St.
A St.

W. 8th Ave.

0   1/8 mile

0   1/8 kilometer

Cook Inlet

KEY

..... Tony Knowles Coastal Trail

+—+ Rail Lines

Delaney Park

P St.
N St.
L St.

Westchester Lagoon

W. Marston Dr.

Turnagain Pkwy.

Fish Creek

Hillcrest Dr.

Forest Park Dr.

Arlington Dr.

Spenard Rd.

TO EARTHQUAKE PARK, POINT WORONZOF

Northern Lights Blvd. W.

W. 29th St.

W. 30th Ave.

W. 31st Ave.

W. 32nd Ave.

Turnagain St.

Barbara St.

Benson Blvd.

Lois Dr.

Minnesota Dr.

W. 34th Ave.

W. 35th Ave.

McRae Dr.

Spenard Rd.

Aero Ave.

Wisconsin Dr.

W. 40th Ave.

Northwood Dr.

Lois Dr.

Lake Hood

44th Ave.

Spenard Beach

Lake Spenard

TO AIRPORT

Anchorage

Salmon Viewing Platform

Ship Creek

Christensen Dr.

Viking Dr.

Port Access Rd.

Post Rd.

W. 1st Ave.   E. 1st Ave.

W. 2nd Ave.

W. 3rd Ave.   E. 3rd Ave.

W. 4th Ave.   E. 4th Ave.

W. 5th Ave.   E. 5th Ave.   Glenn Hwy.

E. 6th Ave.

T St. S St. R St. Q St. P St. O St. N St. M St. L St.

Barrow St.

Gambell St.

Hyder St.

Ingra St.

City Cemetery

E. 7th Ave.

See Inset

E. 8th Ave.

W. 9th Ave.   E. 9th Ave.

W. 10th Ave.   E. 10th Ave.

W. 11th Ave.   E. 11th Ave.

W. 12th Ave.   E. 12th Ave.

W. 13th Ave.   E. 13th Ave.

W. 14th Ave.   E. 14th Ave.

W. 15th Ave.   E. 15th Ave.

B St. A St.

Cordova St.

Denali St.

Eagle St.

Fairbanks St.

Juneau St.

Karluk St.

Latouche St.

Medfra St.

Nelchina

Orca St.

E. 16th Ave.

Chester Creek Park

Sullivan Sports Arena

E. 17th Ave.

Chester Creek

Arctic Blvd.

C St.

A St.

Eagle St.

W. Fireweed La.

Redwood St.

W. 27th Ave.

Northern Lights Blvd.

Benson Blvd.

Eureka St.

Bering St.

32nd Ave.

Denali St.

E. 33rd Ave.

TO CHUGACH STATE PARK →

W. 36th Ave.   E. 36th Ave.

W. 40th Ave.

Old Seward Hwy.

Seward Hwy.

1

Credit Union Dr.

Tudor Rd.

0   1/2 mile

0   1/2 kilometer

between June 3 and September 12, or by appointment between June 1 and September 15. The gift shop and retail nursery are open Tuesday–Sunday late May to mid-September. Discovery Duffels provide activity kits for children. ⊠ *4601 Campbell Airstrip Rd., East Anchorage ✛ Off Tudor Rd. (park at Benny Benson School)* 🕿 *907/770–3692* ⊕ *www. alaskabg.org* 🖅 *$5, $10 families* ☉ *Daily during daylight hrs.*

❼ **Alaska Native Heritage Center.** On a 26-acre site facing the Chugach
☾ Mountains, this facility provides an introduction to Alaska's native
Fodor'sChoice peoples. The spacious Welcome House has interpretive displays, arti-
★ facts, photographs, demonstrations, native dances, storytelling, and films, along with a café and an upgraded gift shop selling museum-quality crafts and artwork. Step outside for a stroll around the adjacent lake, where you will pass seven village exhibits representing the 11 native cultural groups through traditional structures and exhibitions. As you enter the homes, you can visit with the culture hosts, hear their stories, and experiment with some of the tools, games, and utensils used in the past. ■ TIP➔ The Heritage Center provides a free shuttle from the downtown Log Cabin and Visitor Information Centers several times a day in summer. You can also hop a bus at the downtown transit center; Route 4 (Glenn Highway) will take you to the Heritage Center's front door. There's also a Culture Pass Joint Ticket for $26.95 that provides admission here and to the Anchorage Museum downtown; it's available at either location. ⊠ *8800 Heritage Center Dr. (Glenn Hwy. at Muldoon Rd.), East Anchorage* 🕿 *907/330–8000 or 800/315–6608* ⊕ *www.alaskanative.net* 🖅 *$24.95, $10 Alaska residents* ☉ *Mid-May (Mother's Day)–Sept., daily 9–5; Oct.–mid-May, Sat. 10–5.*

WEST ANCHORAGE

❾ **Alaska Aviation Heritage Museum.** The state's unique aviation history is pre-
☾ sented with 25 vintage aircraft—seven have been completely restored—three theaters, an observation deck along **Lake Hood,** the world's busiest seaplane base, a flight simulator, and a gift shop. Highlights include a Stearman C2B, the first plane to land on Mt. McKinley back in the early 1930s. Volunteers are working to restore a 1931 Fairchild Pilgrim aircraft and make it flyable and are eager to talk shop. A free shuttle to and from Anchorage Airport is available. ⊠ *4721 Aircraft Dr., West Anchorage* 🕿 *907/248–5325* ⊕ *www.alaskaairmuseum.org* 🖅 *$10* ☉ *May 15–Sept. 15, daily 9–5; Sept. 16–May 14, Wed.–Sun. 9–5.*

WHERE TO EAT

Smoking is banned in all Anchorage restaurants. Most local restaurants are open daily in summer, with reduced hours in winter. Only a few places require reservations, but it's always best to call ahead, especially for dinner. (⇨ *For price categories, see About the Restaurants, above.*)

DOWNTOWN

$$$ ✕ **Glacier BrewHouse.** The scent of hops permeates the cavernous, wood-
AMERICAN beam BrewHouse, where a dozen or so ales, stouts, lagers, and pil-
Fodor'sChoice sners are brewed on the premises. Locals mingle with visitors in this
★ noisy, always-busy heart-of-town restaurant, where dinner selections range from thin-crust, 10-inch pizzas to chipotle shrimp cocktail and

from barbecue pork ribs to fettuccine jambalaya and fresh seafood (in season). For dessert, don't miss the wood-oven-roasted apple-and-currant bread pudding. You can watch the hardworking chefs in the open kitchen. The brewery sits behind a glass wall, and the same owners operate the equally popular Orso, next door. ⊠ *737 W. 5th Ave., Downtown* ☎ *907/274–2739* ⊕ *www.glacierbrewhouse.com* ▭ *AE, D, MC, V* ⊹ *B2.*

$$$$
CONTINENTAL
Fodor'sChoice
★

✕ **Marx Bros. Cafe.** Inside a little frame house built in 1916, this nationally recognized 46-seat café opened in 1979 and is still going strong. The menu changes every week, and the wine list encompasses more than 700 international choices. For an appetizer, try the black-bean-and-duck soup or fresh Kachemak Bay oysters. The outstanding made-at-your-table Caesar salad is a superb opener for the baked halibut with a macadamia-nut crust served with coconut-curry sauce and fresh mango chutney. And if the sweet potato–and-pecan pie is on the menu, get it! ⊠ *627 W. 3rd Ave., Downtown* ☎ *907/278–2133* ⊕ *www.marxcafe.com* ⌕ *Reservations essential* ▭ *AE, MC, V* ☼ *Memorial Day–Labor Day, Tues.–Sat. 5:30–10; Labor Day–Memorial Day, Tues., Wed., Thurs. 6–9:30, Fri. and Sat. 5:30–10. Closed Sun. and Mon. No lunch* ⊹ *C1.*

¢–$
ECLECTIC

✕ **New Sagaya's City Market.** Stop here for quick lunches and Kaladi Brothers espresso. The in-house bakery, L'Aroma, cranks out specialty breads and pastries of all types, and the international deli and grocery serves California-style pizzas, Chinese food, lasagna, rotisserie chicken, salads, and even stuffed cabbage. You can eat inside on the sheltered patio or grab an outside table on a summer afternoon. New Sagaya's has one of the best seafood counters in town, and will even box and ship your fish. The grocery stores carry an extensive selection of Asian foodstuffs, and the produce and meat selections are excellent. ⊠ *900 W. 13th Ave., Downtown* ☎ *907/274–6173, 907/274–9797, or 800/764–1001* ⊠ *3700 Old Seward Hwy., Midtown* ☎ *907/562–9797* ⊕ *www. newsagaya.com* ▭ *AE, D, DC, MC, V* ⊹ *E3, G5.*

$$$$
ITALIAN

✕ **Orso.** One of Anchorage's culinary stars, Orso ("bear" in Italian), evokes the earthiness of a Tuscan villa. Alaskan touches flavor rustic Mediterranean dishes that include traditional pastas, fresh seafood, and locally famous desserts—most notably a delicious molten chocolate cake. Be sure to ask about the daily specials. If you can't get a table at dinner (reservations are advised), you can select from the same menu at the large bar. Upstairs you'll find a cozier, quieter space. ⊠ *737 W. 5th Ave., at G St., Downtown* ☎ *907/222–3232* ⊕ *www.orsoalaska. com* ▭ *AE, D, MC, V* ⊹ *B2.*

$$$–$$$$
AMERICAN

✕ **Sacks Café.** This colorful restaurant serves light American cuisine such as chicken and scallops over udon noodles, and local produce when available. It also features monthly wine flights, normally with three different selections of 3-ounce pours with information sheets on each wine. Be sure to ask about the daily specials, particularly the fresh king salmon and halibut. Singles congregate along a small bar, sampling wines from California, Australia, and France. The café is especially crowded during lunch, served from 11 to 2:30, and dinner begins at 5. The weekend brunch menu includes eggs Benedict, a Mexican scrambled egg dish called *migas,* and various salads and sandwiches. ⊠ *328 G*

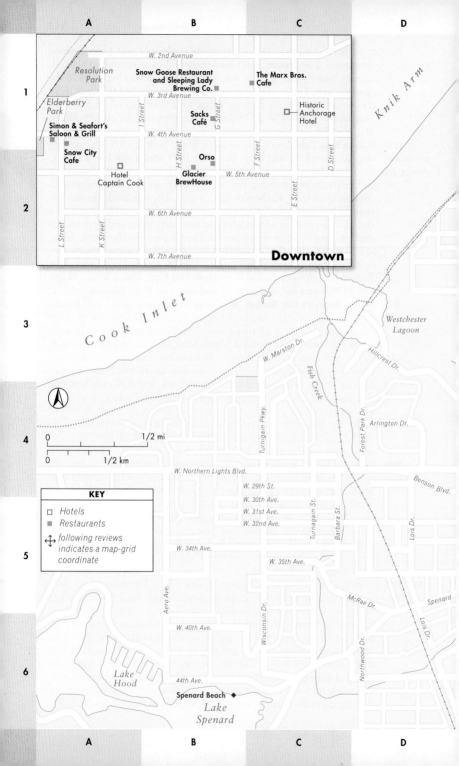

Downtown

A B C D

W. 2nd Avenue

Resolution Park

Snow Goose Restaurant and Sleeping Lady Brewing Co.

The Marx Bros. Cafe

Elderberry Park

W. 3rd Avenue

Simon & Seafort's Saloon & Grill

Sacks Café

Historic Anchorage Hotel

Snow City Cafe

W. 4th Avenue

Orso

Hotel Captain Cook

Glacier BrewHouse

W. 5th Avenue

W. 6th Avenue

W. 7th Avenue

Knik Arm

Cook Inlet

Westchester Lagoon

W. Marston Dr.

Fish Creek

Hillcrest Dr.

Forest Park Dr.

Arlington Dr.

Benson Blvd.

W. Northern Lights Blvd.

W. 29th St.
W. 30th Ave.
W. 31st Ave.
W. 32nd Ave.

Turnagain St.

Barbara St.

Lois Dr.

W. 34th Ave.

W. 35th Ave.

McRae Dr.

Spenard

Aero Ave.

W. 40th Ave.

Wisconsin Dr.

Northwood Dr.

Lois Dr.

Lake Hood

44th Ave.

Spenard Beach ◆

Lake Spenard

Turnagain Pkwy.

T Street
G Street
H Street
F Street
D Street
E Street
L Street
K Street

KEY

☐ *Hotels*
■ *Restaurants*
✛ *following reviews indicates a map-grid coordinate*

0   1/2 mi
0   1/2 km

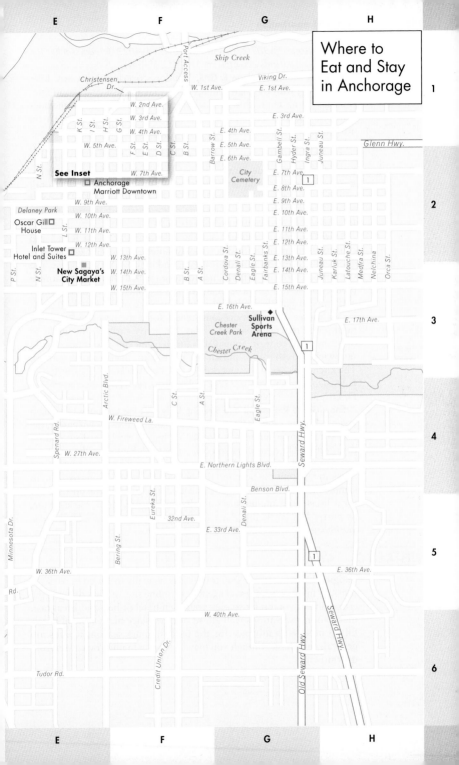

E
F
G
H

Ship Creek

Christensen Dr.

Viking Dr.

Port Access

W. 1st Ave.
E. 1st Ave.

W. 2nd Ave.
W. 3rd Ave.
E. 3rd Ave.

W. 4th Ave.

K St.
I St.
H St.
G St.
F St.
E St.
D St.
C St.
B St.

Glenn Hwy.

Barrow St.
Gambell St.
Hyder St.
Ingra St.
Juneau St.

E. 4th Ave.
W. 5th Ave.
E. 5th Ave.
E. 6th Ave.

See Inset

W. 7th Ave.

City Cemetery

E. 7th Ave.

1

□ Anchorage Marriott Downtown

E. 8th Ave.
W. 9th Ave.
E. 9th Ave.

Delaney Park

W. 10th Ave.
E. 10th Ave.

Oscar Gill □ House

W. 11th Ave.
E. 11th Ave.

L St.

Inlet Tower □ Hotel and Suites

W. 12th Ave.
E. 12th Ave.

Cordova St.
Denali St.
Eagle St.
Fairbanks St.
Juneau St.
Karluk St.
Latouche St.
Medfra St.
Nelchina
Orca St.

New Sagaya's City Market

W. 13th Ave.
E. 13th Ave.

P St.
N St.

W. 14th Ave.
E. 14th Ave.

B St.
A St.

W. 15th Ave.
E. 15th Ave.

E. 16th Ave.

Sullivan Sports Arena ◆

3

Chester Creek Park

E. 17th Ave.

Chester Creek

Arctic Blvd.

C St.
A St.

Eagle St.

W. Fireweed La.

4

Spenard Rd.

W. 27th Ave.

E. Northern Lights Blvd.

Benson Blvd.

Eureka St.

32nd Ave.

Denali St.

Minnesota Dr.

Bering St.

E. 33rd Ave.

W. 36th Ave.

1

E. 36th Ave.

5

Rd.

W. 40th Ave.

Credit Union Dr.

Old Seward Hwy.

Seward Hwy.

Seward Hwy.

Tudor Rd.

6

E
F
G
H

St., Downtown ☎ 907/276–3546 *or* 907/274–4022 ⊕ *www.sackscafe. com* ⚑ *Reservations essential* ═ *AE, MC, V* ✛ *B1.*

$$$$
SEAFOOD

✕ **Simon & Seafort's Saloon & Grill.** Windows overlooking Cook Inlet vistas, along with the high ceilings and a classic brass-and-wood interior, have long made this an Anchorage favorite. The menu includes prime rib (aged 28 days), pasta, and sesame chicken salad, but the main attraction is seafood: fish is blackened, grilled, fried, or prepared any other way you like it. Try the king crab legs or the seafood linguine, and for dessert the Brandy Ice: vanilla ice cream whipped with brandy, Kahlúa, and crème de cacao. The bar is a great spot for microbrews, single-malt scotch, and martinis; the best tables are adjacent to tall windows facing the water. ⊠ *420 L St., Downtown* ☎ 907/274–3502 ⊕ *simonandseaforts.com/page/home* ⚑ *Reservations essential* ═ *AE, DC, MC, V* ☉ *No lunch weekends* ✛ *A1.*

¢–$
ECLECTIC

✕ **Snow City Cafe.** At this unassuming café, along "Lawyer Row" and convenient to many of the downtown hotels, you'll find dependably good and reasonably priced breakfasts and lunches. Service is fast, and the setting, formerly a funky mix of mismatched chairs and Formica tables, has been upgraded, enlarged, and remodeled, but there's still a great mix of families and singles enjoying some of the best breakfasts in Anchorage. Snow City is consistently voted the best breakfast in a local poll. Breakfast is served all day, but arrive early on the weekend or be prepared to wait. Snow City's lunch menu consists of hot or cold sandwiches, fresh soups, and salads, and has lots of vegetarian options. The kitchen closes at 3 PM weekdays and 4 PM weekends. ⊠ *4th Ave. at L St., Downtown* ☎ 907/272–2489 ⊕ *www.snowcitycafe.com* ═ *AE, D, DC, MC, V* ☉ *No dinner.*

$
AMERICAN

✕ **Snow Goose Restaurant and Sleeping Lady Brewing Company.** Although you can dine indoors at this comfortable edge-of-downtown eatery, the real attraction in summer is alfresco dining on the back deck and on the rooftop. On clear days you can see Mt. McKinley on the northern horizon and the Chugach Mountains to the east. The menu emphasizes Alaskan fare, but the beer and the view are the best reasons to visit. To sample the specialty beers, gather around oak tables in the upstairs bar for a brewed-on-the-premises ale, India Pale Ale, stout, barley wine, or porter. ⊠ *717 W. 3rd Ave., Downtown* ☎ 907/277–7727 ⊕ *www. alaskabeers.com* ═ *AE, D, DC, MC, V* ✛ *B1.*

WHERE TO STAY

Lodging for most cruise-ship travelers is typically included in package tours set up through a travel agency, an online site, or directly from the cruise line. If you prefer to pick your own hotel or bed-and-breakfast, make your reservations well ahead of time, since many central hotels fill up months in advance for the peak summer season. Rooms are generally available, though you may be staying in midtown, 2 mi from downtown.

DOWNTOWN

$$$$ 🏨 **Anchorage Marriott Downtown.** One of Anchorage's biggest lodgings, the brightly decorated Marriott appeals to business travelers, tourists, and corporate clients. The hotel's Cafe Promenade serves American cuisine with an Alaskan flair. All guest rooms have huge windows; views are breathtaking from the top floors. If you stay on one of the top three levels of this 20-story hotel, you have access to a concierge lounge and are served a light breakfast as well as evening hors d'oeuvres and desserts. **Pros:** one of the newest hotels in town; modern, up-to-date facilities. **Cons:** no free Wi-Fi; cruise-ship crowds at times in summer. ⊠ *820 W. 7th Ave., Downtown* ☎ *907/279–8000 or 800/228–9290* ⊕ *www.marriott.com* ➷ *392 rooms, 3 suites* ♿ *In-room: Wi-Fi. In-hotel: restaurant, room service, bar, pool, gym, spa, bicycles, laundry service, parking (paid)* ⊟ *AE, D, DC, MC, V* ✛ *E2.*

3

$$$–$$$$ 🏨 **Historic Anchorage Hotel.** The little building has been around since
★   1916. Experienced travelers call it the only hotel in Anchorage with charm: the original sinks and tubs have been restored, and upstairs hallways are lined with Old Anchorage photos. The rooms are nicely updated with dark cherrywood furnishings and HD flat-screen TVs. The small lobby, its fireplace crackling in chilly weather, has a quaint European feel, and the staff is adept at meeting your needs. Request a corner room if possible; rooms facing the street may have traffic noise. The junior suites include sitting areas. **Pros:** excellent staff; new TVs; convenient downtown location; kids under 12 are free. **Cons:** rooms are small; no airport shuttle. ⊠ *330 E St., Downtown* ☎ *907/272–4553 or 800/544–0988* ⊕ *www.historicanchoragehotel.com* ➷ *16 rooms, 10 junior suites* ♿ *In-room: no a/c, refrigerator, Wi-Fi. In-hotel:, gym, bicycles, laundry service, no-smoking rooms, some pets allowed* ⊟ *AE, D, DC, MC, V* ⦿*CP* ✛ *C1.*

$$–$$$ 🏨 **Hotel Captain Cook.** Recalling Captain Cook's voyages to Alaska and
★   the South Pacific, dark teak paneling lines the hotel's interior, and a nautical theme continues into the guest rooms. All rooms have ceiling fans, and guests can use the separate men's and women's athletic clubs with shared indoor heated pool, business center, and other facilities, including three restaurants and a coffee, wine, and martini bar. The hotel occupies an entire city block with three towers, the tallest of which is capped by the **Crow's Nest Restaurant.** The most luxurious accommodation is found on the 19th floor of Tower III—a sprawling, 1,600-square-foot two-bedroom suite, which costs a mere $1,500 per night. **Pros:** staff very well trained and accommodating; generally considered the nicest hotel in town. **Cons:** fixtures and furnishings a bit dated; hallways can be dark. ⊠ *4th Ave. and K St., Downtown* ☎ *907/276–6000 or 800/843–1950* ⊕ *www.captaincook.com* ➷*457 rooms, including 96 suites* ♿ *In-room: Wi-Fi. In-hotel: 3 restaurants, room service, pool, gym* ⊟ *AE, D, DC, MC, V* ✛ *A2.*

$$$–$$$$ 🏨 **Inlet Tower Hotel and Suites.** Windows overlook either the Chugach
★   Mountains, the Cook Inlet, or downtown Anchorage. Built in 1952 in a residential area a few blocks south of downtown, this 14-story building was Alaska's first high-rise. A major remodeling brought spacious rooms and suites, uniquely Alaskan wallpaper, high-end linens,

large televisions, high-speed Internet lines and wireless Internet in the lobby, kitchenettes, and blackout curtains for summer mornings when the sun comes up at 3 AM. The Mixx Grill Restaurant & Bar serves fresh seafood, steaks, vegetables, and other local favorites. **Pros:** excellent restaurant on-site; the New Sagaya store and restaurant is but a stone's throw away; airport shuttle available. **Cons:** downtown attractions are a bit of a hike; hallways narrow and can be dark. ⊠ *1200 L St., Downtown* ☎ *907/276–0110 or 800/544–0786* ⊕ *www.inlettower. com* ⇆ *156 rooms, 24 suites* ⚐ *In-room: kitchen (some), refrigerator, Wi-Fi. In-hotel: restaurant, gym, laundry facilities, Internet terminal, parking (free), no-smoking rooms* ☰ *AE, D, DC, MC, V* ⊹ *E2.*

$ ⊡ **Oscar Gill House.** Gill originally built his home in the settlement of Knik (north of Anchorage) in 1913. Three years later he floated it by boat to Anchorage, where he later served as mayor for three terms and then speaker of the Territorial House. The home has been transformed into a comfortable B&B in a quiet neighborhood along Delaney Park Strip, with downtown attractions a short walk away. Two rooms share a bath with a classic claw-foot tub, and the third contains a private bath and whirlpool bath. Little touches include down comforters, free use of bicycles, and a delicious breakfast. **Pros:** great breakfast; very hospitable owners in a bit of Old Anchorage history. **Cons:** shared bath in two of the rooms; walk to downtown might be a bit of a hike for some. ⊠ *1344 W. 10th Ave., Downtown* ☎ *907/279–1344* ⊕ *www.oscargill. com* ⇆ *3 rooms, 1 with bath* ⚐ *In-room: Wi-Fi. In-hotel: no-smoking rooms* ☰ *AE, MC, V* ⊙ *BP* ⊹ *E2.*

NIGHTLIFE

BARS AND NIGHTCLUBS

Anchorage does not shut down when it gets dark. Bars here—and throughout Alaska—open early (in the morning) and close as late as 3 AM on weekends. There's a ban on smoking in bars and bingo parlors, as well as restaurants. The listings in the *Anchorage Daily News* entertainment section, published on Friday, and in the free weekly *Anchorage Press* (⊕ *www.anchoragepress.com*) range from concerts and theaters to movies and a roundup of nightspots featuring live music. You can also find concert and performance listings in the "Play" section in Friday editions of the *Anchorage Daily News* (or online at ⊕ *www.adn.com*).

Fodor'sChoice
★ **Chilkoot Charlie's** (⊠ *2435 Spenard Rd., Spenard* ☎ *907/272–1010* ⊕ *www.koots.com*), a rambling timber building with sawdust floors, 11 bars (including one made of ice), 3 dance floors, loud music (rock or swing bands and DJs) nightly, two DJs every Thursday, Friday, and Saturday, and rowdy customers, is where young Alaskans go to get crazy. This legendary bar has many unusual nooks and crannies, including a room filled with Russian artifacts and serving the finest vodka drinks, plus a reconstructed version of Alaska's infamous Birdhouse Bar. If you haven't been to 'Koots, you haven't seen Anchorage nightlife at its wildest.

Lots of old-timers favor the dark bar of **Club Paris** (⊠ *417 W. 5th Ave., Downtown* ☎ *907/277–6332* ⊕ *www.clubparisrestaurant.com*). The Paris mural and French street lamps hanging behind the bar have lost some luster, but there's still a faithful clientele. The jukebox favors swing. **Rumrunners** (⊠ *501 W. 4th Ave., Downtown* ☎ *907/278–4493* ⊕ *www.rumrunnersak.com*) is right across from Old City Hall in the center of town. A pub-grub menu brings the lunch crowd, but when evening comes the big dance floor gets packed as DJs spin the tunes. A trendy place for the dressy "in" crowd, the bar at **Simon & Seafort's Saloon & Grill** (⊠ *420 L St., Downtown* ☎ *907/274–3502* ⊕ *www.simonandseaforts.com*) has stunning views of Cook Inlet, a special single-malt scotch menu, and a wide selection of imported beers. **Snow Goose Restaurant** (⊠ *717 W. 3rd Ave., Downtown* ☎ *907/277–7727* ⊕ *www.alaskabeers.com*) is a good place to unwind with a beer inside or on the airy outside deck overlooking Cook Inlet. There's decent food, too.

Fodor'sChoice
★ **Blues Central/Chef's Inn** (⊠ *825 W. Northern Lights Blvd., Spenard* ☎ *907/272–1341*), a modest eatery, is also a blues mecca that stages bands seven nights a week.

SHOPPING

BOOKS

Easily the largest independent bookstore in Alaska, **Title Wave Books** (⊠ *1360 W. Northern Lights Blvd., Midtown* ☎ *907/278–9283 or 888/598–9283* ⊕ *www.wavebooks.com*) fills a sprawling store at one end of the REI strip mall. The shelves are filled with new and used titles and a large section of Alaska stuff, and the staff is very knowledgeable. Also here is **Kaladi Brothers Coffee Shop,** with Wi-Fi access for Web surfers.

MARKETS

In summer Anchorage's **Saturday and Sunday Markets** (☎ 907/272–5634 ⊕ *www.anchoragemarkets.com*) are open in the parking lot at 3rd Avenue and E Street. More than 300 vendors offer Alaskan-made crafts, ethnic imports, and deliciously fattening food. The open-air markets run from mid-May to mid-September, weekends 10–6. A smaller market sells local produce and crafts July through August, on Wednesday from 11 to 5, at Northway Mall in East Anchorage.

NATIVE CRAFTS

★ Several downtown shops sell quality Native Alaskan artwork, but the best buys can be found in the gift shop at the **Alaska Native Medical Center** (⊠ 4315 Diplomacy Dr., at Tudor and Bragaw Rds., East Anchorage ☎ 907/563–2662), which is open weekdays 10–2 and 11–2 on the first and third Saturday of the month. It doesn't take credit cards.

The gift shop at **Alaska Native Heritage Center** (⊠ 8800 Heritage Center Dr., Glenn Hwy. at Muldoon Rd., East Anchorage ☎ 907/330–8000 or 800/315–6608 ⊕ www.alaskanative.net) sells Native crafts. **Laura Wright Alaskan Parkys** sells distinctive Eskimo-style "parkys" (parkas) and will custom sew one for you. They're available at **Heritage Gifts** (⊠ 333 W. 4th Ave., No. 227, at D St., Downtown ☎ 907/274–4215). **Oomingmak** (⊠ 6th Ave. and H St., Downtown ☎ 907/272–9225 or 888/360–9665 ⊕ www.qiviut.com), a Native-owned cooperative, sells items made of qiviut, the warm undercoat of the musk ox. Scarves, shawls, and tunics are knitted in traditional patterns.

SEAFOOD

Get smoked reindeer meat and salmon products at **Alaska Sausage and Seafood Company** (⊠ 2914 Arctic Blvd., Midtown ☎ 907/562–3636 or 800/798–3636 ⊕ www.alaskasausage.com). **New Sagaya's City Market** (⊠ 900 W. 13th Ave., Downtown ☎ 907/274–6173 ⊕ www.newsagaya. com) sells an excellent selection of fresh seafood.

SEATTLE

Updated by Carissa Bluestone, Cedar Burnett, Nick Horton, and Heidi Leigh Johansen

Seattle has much to offer: a beautiful setting, sparkling arts and entertainment, innovative restaurants, friendly residents, green spaces galore, and Pike Place Market, which provides a wonderfully earthy focal point for downtown Seattle, with views of the ferries crossing Elliott Bay. Visitors to the city will almost certainly wish they had set aside more time to take in Seattle's charms.

Seattle, like Rome, is said to be built on seven hills. As a visitor, you're likely to spend much of your time on only two of them (Capitol Hill and Queen Anne Hill), but the city's hills are indeed the most definitive element of the city's natural and spiritual landscape. Years of largely thoughtful building practices have kept tall buildings from obscuring the lines of sight, maintaining vistas in most directions and around almost every turn. The hills are lofty, privileged perches from which residents are constantly reminded of the beauty of the forests, mountains, and waters surrounding the city—that is, when it stops raining long enough for you to enjoy those gorgeous views.

In the heart of downtown Seattle's bustling retail core, the Seattle Convention and Visitors Bureau offers ticket sales, reservation and concierge services, dining suggestions, and a handy visitor information packet and coupon book that can be e-mailed to you.

Visitor Information Seattle Convention and Visitors Bureau (✉ *7th and Pike, main floor, Washington State Convention and Trade Center* ☎ *206/461–5888* ⊕ *www.visitseattle.org*).

ON THE MOVE

3

GETTING TO THE PORT

Ships from Norwegian Cruise Line and Celebrity Cruises dock at the Bell Street Pier Cruise Terminal (Pier 66). Pier 66 is within walking distance of downtown attractions, and a city bus wrapped up in the Waterfront Streetcar logo (the real 1927 Waterfront Streetcars are out of commission until they can be upgraded) provides trolley service along the shoreline to the cruise terminal.

Holland America Line, Princess Cruises, Carnival Cruise Lines, and Royal Caribbean dock at the new Smith Cove Cruise Terminal at Terminal 91, located at the north end of the downtown waterfront Magnolia Bridge and best accessed by cruise-line motor-coach transfer, taxi, or shuttle service. Opened in spring 2009, the much-anticipated Terminal 91 replaced the old Pier 30.

Transfers to the piers between Sea-Tac Airport and designated hotels are offered by the cruise lines, either as an add-on to your fare or, in the case of some luxury cruise lines or small-ship cruise lines, included in the price of your cruise. Cruise-line representatives meet airport arrivals and are present at hotel transfer points to make the process virtually seamless.

Contacts Bell Street Pier Cruise Terminal (Pier 66) (✉ *2225 Alaskan Way* ☎ *206/615–3900* ⊕ *www.portseattle.org/seaport/cruise/*). **Smith Cove Cruise Terminal at Terminal 91** (✉ *2001 W. Garfield St.* ☎ *206/615–3900* ⊕ *www. portseattle.org/seaport/cruise/*).

ARRIVING BY AIR

The major gateway is Seattle–Tacoma International Airport (Sea-Tac).

Contacts Seattle–Tacoma International Airport (Sea-Tac) (☎ *206/433–5388* ⊕ *www.portseattle.org/seatac*).

AIRPORT TRANSFERS

Sea-Tac is about 15 mi south of downtown on I–5. It usually takes 25–40 minutes to ride between the airport and downtown. Metered cabs make the trip for about $30. Downtown Airporter has the only 24-hour door-to-door service, a flat $25 ($40 round-trip) from the airport to downtown. You can make arrangements at the Downtown Airporter counter upon arrival or online. Gray Line Downtown Airporter provides service to downtown hotels, as well, for $11–$20, depending on your destination.

If you're traveling directly to Pier 91 from the airport, contact Shuttle Express.

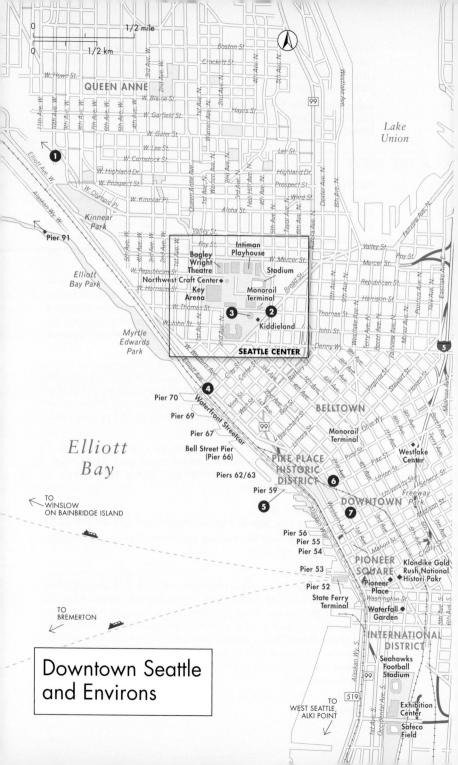

Downtown Seattle and Environs

0 —— 1/2 mile
0 —— 1/2 km

QUEEN ANNE

Boston St.
Crockett St.
W. Howe St.
W. Blaine St.
W. Garfield St.
Hayes St.
W. Galer St.
W. Lee St.
Lee St.
W. Comstock St.
W. Highland Dr.
Highland Dr.
W. Prospect St.
Prospect St.
W. Kinnear Pl.
Ward St.
W. Kinnear Pl.
Aloha St.
W. Olympic Pl.

Lake Union

99

①

Pier 91

Kinnear Park

Elliott Bay Park

Valley St.
Roy St.
Valley St.
Roy St.
Intiman Playhouse
W. Mercer St.
Mercer St.
Republican St.
Bagley Wright Theatre
Stadium
Northwest Craft Center ◆
W. Republican St.
W. Harrison St.
Harrison St.
Key Arena
Monorail Terminal
W. Thomas St.
Thomas St.
③
②
W. John St.
Kiddieland
John St.

Myrtle Edwards Park

SEATTLE CENTER

Denny Wy.

5

④
Pier 70
Waterfront Streetcar

BELLTOWN

Elliott Bay

Pier 69
Pier 67
99
Bell Street Pier
(Pier 66)
Monorail Terminal
Westlake Center
Piers 62/63
PIKE PLACE HISTORIC DISTRICT
Pike St.
Pine St.
Union St.
⑥
Pier 59
University St.
Freeway Park
⑤
DOWNTOWN
⑦

TO WINSLOW ON BAINBRIDGE ISLAND

Pier 56
Pier 55
Pier 54
Marion St.
PIONEER SQUARE
Klondike Gold Rush National Histori Pakr
Pier 53
Pioneer Place ◆
Pier 52
Washington St.
State Ferry Terminal
Waterfall Garden

TO BREMERTON

INTERNATIONAL DISTRICT

Seahawks Football Stadium

TO WEST SEATTLE, ALKI POINT

99
519
Exhibition Center
Safeco Field

Contacts **Grayline of Seattle Downtown Airporter** (☎ 206/624–5077 or 800/426–7532 ⊕ www.graylineofseattle.com). **Shuttle Express** (☎ 425/981–7000 or 800/487–7433 ⊕ www.shuttleexpress.com).

ARRIVING BY CAR

Many cruise passengers drive themselves to the port via I–90 west or toward downtown Seattle north or south on I–95. The Port of Seattle Web site has clear maps and directions to each pier.

Note that parking at both piers fills up fast. If you're driving to Pier 66, you can reserve a parking space at Bell Street Pier Garage (directly across from the pier; includes 25 handicapped parking spaces) at a discount online with Republic Parking. Fares are $16.74 plus tax per day, $15.74 plus tax if prepaid online. Note there are no facilities for oversized vehicles such as RVs.

If you're sailing with Carnival, Holland America, Princess, or Royal Caribbean from Pier 91 (Smith Cove Terminal), you can also reserve a spot ahead of time with Republic Parking. Fares are $20.92 plus tax per day for the first 7 days, $8.37 plus tax thereafter. RV and overheight vehicles for those sailing from Pier 66 can also park here at $29.29 plus tax per day. For those parking here but departing from Pier 66, a taxi voucher is available.

Contacts **Republic Parking** (⊕ www.rpnw.com). **Port of Seattle** (⊕ www.portseattle.org/seaport/cruise).

ARRIVING BY TRAIN

Amtrak provides train service north to Vancouver; south to Portland, Oakland, and Los Angeles; and east to Spokane, Chicago, and other cities. Amtrak's King Street Station is just south of downtown at 3rd Avenue South and South King Street.

Contacts **Amtrak** (☎ 800/872–7245 ⊕ www.amtrak.com).

PUBLIC TRANSPORTATION

The bus system, Metro Bus, will get you anywhere you need to go, although some routesfarther afield require a time commitment and several transfers. Within the downtown core, however, the bus is efficient—and, most of the time, it won't cost you a dime, thanks to the Ride-Free Area. The Trip Planner is a useful resource.

Built for the 1962 World's Fair, the monorail is the shortest transportation system in the city. It runs from Westlake Center (on 5th and Pine) to Seattle Center. But this is great for visitors who plan to spend a day at the Space Needle and the Seattle Center's museums. A single ride is $2.

The Seattle Streetcar, the second-shortest system in the city, was built to connect Downtown to the up-and-coming neighborhood of South Lake Union (which is directly east of Seattle Center). It runs from Westlake and Olive to the southern shore of Lake Union. A single ride is $2.25.

Contacts **Metro Bus** (☎ 206/553–3000, 206/287–8463 for automated schedule line ⊕ metro.kingcounty.gov, ⊕ tripplanner.kingcounty.gov). **Seattle Monorail** (☎ 206/905–2620 ⊕ www.seattlemonorail.com). **Seattle Streetcar** (⊕ www.seattlestreetcar.org).

Seattle is a city of many hills—and many spectacular views.

TAXIS

Seattle's taxi fleet is small, but you can sometimes hail a cab on the street, especially Downtown. Most of the time you must call for one. Except on Friday and Saturday nights, you rarely have to wait more than a few minutes for pickup. Cab rides can be pricey but useful, especially late at night when buses run infrequently. Two major cab companies are Farwest and Yellow Cab.

Contacts Farwest (☎ *206/622–1717*). **Yellow Cab** (☎ *206/622–6500*).

EXPLORING SEATTLE

The Elliott Bay waterfront is Seattle's crown jewel. Pike Place Market, the Seattle Aquarium, and the Maritime Discovery Center stretch along its densely packed shore. Just south of downtown is the historic Pioneer Square area, and a short distance north of Pike Place Market lies the Olympic Sculpture Park, a magnificent urban playground filled with gigantic works of art overlooking the ocean. North of the sculpture park is Seattle Center, a civic gathering place that's home to the Space Needle, Experience Music Project, the Science Fiction Museum, the Children's Museum, and the Pacific Science Center.

DOWNTOWN AND BELLTOWN

❹ **Olympic Sculpture Park.** This 9-acre open-air park is the spectacular out-
Fodor'sChoice door branch of the Seattle Art Museum. Since opening in 2007, the
★ Sculpture Park has become a favorite destination for picnics, strolls, and quiet contemplation. Nestled between Belltown and Elliott Bay, this gently sloping green space is planted with native shrubs and plants

Lighthouse at Alki beach, Discovery Park

and is crisscrossed with walking paths. On sunny days, the park flaunts an astounding panorama of the Olympic Mountain Range, but even the grayest afternoon casts a favorable light on the site's sculptures. The grounds are home to works by such artists as Richard Serra, Roy McMakin, Louise Bourgeois, Mark di Suvero, and Alexander Calder, whose bright-red steel "Eagle" sculpture is a local favorite—indeed, you may even see a real bald eagle passing by overhead. The PACCAR Pavilion has a gift shop, café, and more information about the park. ⊠ 2901 Western Ave., between Broad and Bay Sts., Belltown ☎ 206/654–3100 ⊕ www.seattleartmuseum.org/visit/osp ☑ Free ☉ Park open daily sunrise–sunset. PACCAR Pavilion open May–Labor Day, Tues.–Sun. 10–5; Sept.–Apr., Tues.–Sun. 10–4.

⑥ Pike Place Market. Pike Place Market, one of the nation's largest and

Fodor's Choice oldest public markets, plays host to happy, hungry crowds all year round, but summer is when things really start to heat up. Strap on some walking shoes and enjoy its many corridors: shops and stalls provide a pleasant sensory overload—stroll among the colorful flower, produce, and fish displays, plus bustling shops and lunch counters. Specialty-food items, tea, honey, jams, comic books, beads, and cookware—you'll find it all here. (⇨ For an in-depth description of Seattle's most famous landmark, see the highlighted feature in Chapter 6.) ⊠ Pike Pl. at Pike St., west of 1st Ave., Downtown ☎ 206/682–7453 ⊕ www. pikeplacemarket.org ☉ Stall hrs vary: 1st-level shops Mon.–Sat. 10–6, Sun. 11–5; underground shops daily 11–5.

❼ Seattle Art Museum. Long the pride of the city's art scene, SAM is now
better than ever after a massive expansion that connects the iconic
old building on University Street (where sculptor Jonathan Borofsky's
several-stories-high *Hammering Man* still pounds away) to a sleek,
light-filled high-rise adjacent space, on 1st Avenue and Union Street.
As you enter, you'll have the option of wandering around two floors of
free public space. The first floor includes the museum's fantastic shop,
a café that focuses on local ingredients, and drop-in workshops where
the whole family can get creative. The second floor features free exhibitions, including awesome large-scale installations. ✉ *1300 1st Ave.,
Downtown* ☎ *206/654–3100* ⊕ *www.seattleartmuseum.org* 🖃 *$15,
free 1st Thurs. of month* ☾ *Wed. and weekends 10–5, Thurs. and Fri.
10–9, 1st Thurs. until midnight.*

❺ Seattle Aquarium. The newly renovated aquarium is more popular
than ever. Among its most popular residents are the sea otters—kids,
especially, seem able to spend hours watching the delightful antics of
these creatures and their river cousins. In the Puget Sound Great Hall,
"Window on Washington Waters," a slice of Neah Bay life, is presented in a 20-foot-tall tank holding 120,000 gallons of water. The
aquarium's darkened rooms and large, lighted tanks brilliantly display
Pacific Northwest marine life. The "Life on the Edge" tide pools re-
create Washington's rocky coast and sandy beaches. Huge glass windows provide underwater views of seals and sea otters; go up top to
watch them play in their pools. Kids love the Discovery Lab, where
they can touch starfish, sea urchins, and sponges, then examine baby
barnacles and jellyfish. Nearby, cylindrical tanks hold a fascinating
octopus. ■TIP➔ Spend a few minutes in front of the octopus tank even if
you don't detect any movement. Your patience will be rewarded if you get
to see this amazing creature shimmy up the side of the tank. If you're visiting in fall or winter, dress warmly—the Marine Mammal area is on the
waterfront and catches all of those chilly Puget Sound breezes. The café
serves Ivar's chowder and kid-friendly food like burgers and chicken
fingers; a balcony has views of Elliott Bay. ✉ *1483 Alaskan Way, at Pier
59, Downtown* ☎ *206/386–4300* ⊕ *www.seattleaquarium.org* 🖃 *$17*
☾ *Daily 9:30–6 (last entry at 5).*

SEATTLE CENTER AND QUEEN ANNE

A few blocks north of downtown at the base of Queen Anne Hill, Seattle
Center is a legacy of the 1962 World's Fair. Today the 74-acre site is
home to a multitude of attractions that encompass a children's museum,
an opera hall, a science museum, a monorail, a basketball arena, and
much more. We cover the highlights below; for more information, call
☎ *206/684–7200* or check out ⊕ *www.seattlecenter.com.* Farther afield
but worth the transportation effort, Discovery Park is just outside of
the Queen Anne neighborhood.

❶ Discovery Park. Discovery Park is Seattle's largest park, and it has an
amazing variety of terrain: shaded, secluded forest trails lead to meadows, saltwater beaches, sand dunes, a lighthouse, and views that include
Puget Sound, the Cascades, and the Olympics. There are 2.8 mi of trails
through this urban wilderness, but the North Beach Trail, which takes
you along the shore to the lighthouse, is a must-see. Head to the South

Bluff Trail to get a view of Mt. Rainier and the skyline. The park has several entrances—if you want to stop at the visitor center to pick up a trail map before exploring, use the main entrance at Government Way. The North Parking Lot is much closer to the North Beach Trail and to Ballard and Fremont, if you're coming from that direction.
■TIP→ Note that the park is also easily reached from Ballard and Fremont. It's easier to combine a park day with an exploration of those neighborhoods than with a busy Downtown itinerary. (⊠ *3801 W. Government Way, Magnolia*) From Downtown, take Elliot Ave. W (which turns into 15th Ave. W), and get off at the Emerson St. exit and turn left

> ### SEATTLE CITYPASS
>
> If you're in Seattle for several days (rather than just one) before or after your cruise, look into the CityPass, which give admission to six different attractions for just $59 ($34 for kids 12 and under)—nearly half off what admission for all six would have been without a discount. The pass gives admission to the Space Needle, the Seattle Aquarium, a Seattle harbor tour, the Pacific Science Center, Woodland Park Zoo, and either the Museum of Flight or Experience Music Project/Science Fiction Museum.

onto W. Emerson. Make a right onto Gilman Ave. W (which eventually becomes W. Government Way). As you enter the park, the road becomes Washington Ave.; turn left on Utah Ave. ☎ *206/386–4236* ⊕ *www.cityofseattle.net/parks* ⊠ *Free* ☉ *Park daily 6 AM–11 PM, visitor center Tues.–Sun. 8:30–5.*

2 **Experience Music Project/Science Fiction Museum.** Seattle's most controversial architectural statement is the 140,000-square-foot complex designed by architect Frank Gehry, who drew inspiration from electric guitars to achieve the building's curvy metallic design. (Some say, however, that it looks more like robot open-heart surgery than a musical instrument.) Regardless, the building stands out among the city's cookie-cutter high-rises, and therefore it's a fitting backdrop for rock memorabilia from the likes of Bob Dylan and the grunge-scene heavies. The Science Fiction Museum (SFM) has its own wing and tackles the major themes of the genre in a way that's both smart and fun. ⊠ *325 5th Ave. N, between Broad and Thomas Sts., Seattle Center* ☎ *206/770–2700* ⊕ *www.empsfm.org* ⊠ *$15* ☉ *Sept.–May, daily 10–5; rest of yr, daily 10–8.*

3 **Space Needle.** The distinctive exterior of the 605-foot-high Space Needle is visible throughout downtown—but the view from the inside out is even better. A less-than-one-minute ride up to the observation deck yields 360-degree vistas of Downtown Seattle, the Olympic Mountains, Elliott Bay, Queen Anne Hill, Lake Union, and the Cascade Range. The Needle was built just in time for the World's Fair in 1962, but has since been refurbished with educational exhibits, interactive stations, and the glass-enclosed SpaceBase store and Pavilion spiraling around the tower's base. If you dine at the exclusive, revolving SkyCity restaurant on the top floor, admission to the observation deck is free. Or just enjoy views from the coffee bar. ⊠ *400 Broad St., at 5th Ave., Lower Queen Anne*

Fodor's Choice ★

☎ *206/905–2100* ⊕ *www.spaceneedle.com* ✉ *$16* ⊗ *Mon.–Thurs. 9:30 AM–11 PM; Fri. and Sat. 9 AM–11:30 PM, Sun. 9 AM–11 PM.*

WHERE TO EAT

Downtown is a good area for lunch; come evening, its action centers around hotel restaurants and a handful of watering holes. Pioneer Square and Belltown, on the other hand, come alive nightly with music and other entertainment. Pioneer Square features bars and restaurants that cater to baseball fans en route to Safeco Field, while Belltown's many chic restaurants and bars are packed with hipsters and urbanites.

DOWNTOWN

$$$ ╳ **Café Campagne/Campagne.** The white walls, picture windows, pressed
FRENCH linens, fresh flowers, and candles at charming French restaurant Cam-
Fodor's Choice pagne—which overlooks Pike Place Market and Elliott Bay—evoke
★ Provence. So does the robust French country fare, with starters such as grilled housemade merguez sausage, pork rillettes, and potato gnocchi with braised artichokes and black truffle butter. Main plates include pork short ribs with onion, raisin, and tomato compote; steamed mussels with expertly prepared pommes frites; and Oregon beef rib-eye with parsley-crusted marrow bones. ■TIP→ Campagne is open only for dinner, but downstairs, the equally charming (some would say even more lovely and authentic) Café Campagne serves breakfast, lunch, and dinner daily. The café is an exceptional place for a satisfying weekend brunch before hitting Pike Place Market on foot. Try the impeccable quiche du jour with green salad; poached eggs with pearl onions, bacon, and champignons; or Brioche French toast—plus a big bowl of café au lait. ⊠ *Inn at the Market, 86 Pine St., Downtown* ☎ *206/728–2800* ⊕ *www.campagnerestaurant.com* ▬ *AE, DC, MC, V* ✛ *B3.*

$ ╳ **Emmett Watson's Oyster Bar.** This unpretentious spot can be hard to
SEAFOOD find—it's in the back of Pike Place Market's Soames-Dunn Building, facing a small flower-bedecked courtyard. But for those who know their oysters, finding this place is worth the effort. Not only are the oysters very fresh and the beer icy cold, but both are inexpensive and available in any number of varieties. If you don't like oysters, try the salmon soup or the fish-and-chips—flaky pieces of fish with very little grease. ⊠ *1916 Pike Pl., Downtown* ☎ *206/448–7721* ⊛ *Reservations not accepted* ▬ *D, MC, V* ⊗ *No dinner Sun.* ✛ *B3.*

$$ ╳ **FareStart.** A project of the FareStart job-training program, this eatery
AMERICAN in a sleek, dramatic space on Virginia Street serves up an American-style lunch of sandwiches, burgers, mac-and-cheese, and fries during the week, as well as rotating specials, such as blackened-salmon sandwich, seared tuna, or goat-cheese crostini. The café is staffed by formerly homeless men and women; the spirit of community outreach runs deep. Reservations are essential for the $25 Thursday dinners, prepared by a guest chef from a constantly rotating roster of local restaurants, such as Ray's Boathouse, Volunteer Park Café, Cantinetta, or the Metropolitan Grill. The cuisine changes with the chef and therefore can be hit-or-miss. However, it's a grand experience in a lovely Downtown space. Whenever you go, you're assured a good meal for a great cause and a

real taste of Seattle's community spirit. ⊠ *700 Virginia St., Downtown* ☏ *206/443–1233* ⊕ *www.farestart.org* ▤ *AE, MC, V* ⊘ *No lunch weekends. No dinner Fri.–Wed.* ✛ *C2.*

$$$$
PACIFIC
NORTHWEST
Fodor's Choice
★

✕ **Matt's in the Market.** Your first dinner at Matt's is like a first date you hope will never end. One of the most beloved of Pike Place Market's restaurants, Matt's is now owned by Dan Bugge, who continues to value intimate dining, fresh ingredients, and superb service. An expansion nearly doubled the number of seats, all the better to enjoy old favorites—and some new dishes, as well. Perch at the bar for pints and a delicious pulled pork or hot grilled-tuna sandwich or cup of gumbo, or be seated at a table—complete with vases filled with flowers from the market—for a seasonal menu that synthesizes the best picks from the restaurant's produce vendors and an excellent wine list. At dinner, starters might include such delectable items as Manila clams steamed in beer with herbs and chilies; entrées always include at least one catch of the day—such as whole fish in saffron broth or Alaskan halibut with pea vines—as well as such delectable entrées as seafood stew, beef short ribs, or braised lamb shank with ancho chili. Locals and visitors alike keep this low-key but special spot humming. ⊠ *94 Pike St., Suite 32, Downtown* ☏ *206/467–7909* ⊕ *www.mattsinthemarket.com* ⌦ *Reservations essential* ▤ *MC, V* ⊘ *Closed Sun.* ✛ *B3.*

¢–$
COFFEEHOUSE

✕ **Monorail Espresso.** More walk-up coffee window than actual coffeehouse, this is a good spot for a surprisingly good latte when you're shopping Downtown, waiting for the bus to take you up to Capitol Hill, or have just seen one too many Starbucks and are getting thirstier and thirstier. A few blocks from the Convention Center, this casual spot frequented by bike messengers also serves up famous "Chubby" chocolate-chip cookies with a genuine smile. This place deserves its loyal following—Monorail Espresso just turned 30 years old! ⊠ *520 Pike St.,Downtown* ☏ *206/625–0449* ▤ *Cash only* ✛ *C3.*

$$$
NEW AMERICAN

✕ **Place Pigalle.** Large windows look out on Elliott Bay in this cozy spot tucked behind a meat vendor in Pike Place Market's main arcade. In nice weather, open windows let in the fresh salt breeze. Flowers brighten each table, and the staff is warm and welcoming. Despite its name, this restaurant has only a few French flourishes on an otherwise American/Pacific Northwest menu. Go for the rich oyster stew, the sea scallops with rosé champagne beurre blanc, Dungeness crab (in season), poussin with barley risotto, or the fish of the day. Local microbrews are on tap, and the wine list is thoughtfully compact. Or sip a Pastis as you gaze out the window. ⊠ *81 Pike St., Downtown* ☏ *206/624–1756* ▤ *AE, MC, V* ⊘ *No dinner Sun.* ✛ *C3.*

¢
BAKERY

✕ **Three Girls Bakery.** Smack in the center of Pike Place Market, Three Girls Bakery releases the delicious scent of fresh bread on unsuspecting pedestrians daily. These chicas also know how to make a sandwich—and they don't skimp on the fillings. Soups are satisfying, and the baked goods are outstanding. This isn't a place to enjoy a sit-down meal, and service can be a bit brusque, so plan on taking your meat-loaf sandwich, potato-cheddar soup, raspberry muffin, brownie, or macaroons elsewhere. ⊠ *1514 Pike Pl., Downtown* ☏ *206/622–1045* ▤ *No credit cards* ✛ *B3.*

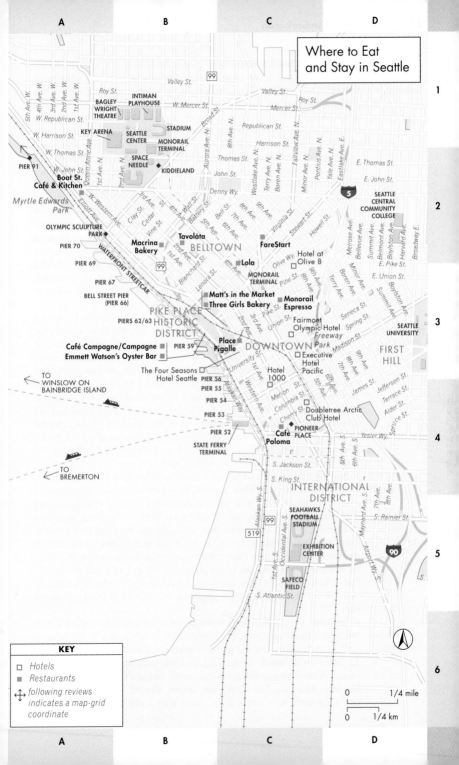

Where to Eat and Stay in Seattle

KEY

- □ Hotels
- ■ Restaurants
- ⊹ following reviews indicates a map-grid coordinate

BELLTOWN

$$$
NEW AMERICAN
Fodor'sChoice
★

✕ **Boat Street Café & Kitchen.** Two rooms decorated in a French bistro-meets–Nantucket decor have a scattering of casual tables with fresh flowers and candles. Tables often fill up with couples at night, but the lunchtime scene runs the gamut from Downtown office workers to tourists. Food is understated, fresh, and divine: start with raw oysters and a crisp glass of white wine. Next up, sautéed Medjool dates sprinkled with fleur de sel and olive oil, a radish salad with pine nuts, or a plate of the famous housemade pickles. Entrées, too, take advantage of whatever is in season, so expect anything from Oregon hanger steak with olive tapenade to spring-onion flan and Alaskan halibut with cauliflower. Though it's housed in the ground floor of an odd office building (just north of the Olympic Sculpture Park), Boat Street positively blooms in the quirky space, and the food and dining experience are memorable and uniquely Seattle. Save room for desserts: wild blackberry clafouti, honey ice cream, and vanilla bean *pot de crème* are just a few toothsome examples. Monday through Sunday, brunch and lunch is served from 10:30 to 2:30. ☒ *3131 Western Ave., Belltown* ☎ *206/632–4602* ⊕ *www.boatstreetcafe.com* ▭ *D, MC, V* ⊗ *No dinner Sun. and Mon.* ✛ *A2.*

$$$
MEDITERRANEAN
Fodor'sChoice
★

✕ **Lola.** Tom Douglas dishes out his signature Northwest style, spiked with Greek and Mediterranean touches here—another huge success for the local celebrity chef, if not his best. Mediterranean-infused cuisine takes glorious form in a tagine of goat meat with mustard and rosemary; grape leaf–wrapped trout; lamb burgers with chickpea fries; and scrumptious spreads including hummus, tzatziki, and a red-pepper concoction. Booths are usually full at this bustling, dimly lighted restaurant, which anchors the Hotel Ändra. The fabulous weekend brunches are inventive: try Tom's Big Breakfast—octopus, mustard greens, cumin-spiced yogurt, bacon, and an egg. If you still have room, there are made-to-order doughnuts, too. ☒ *2000 4th Ave., Belltown* ☎ *206/441–1430* ⊕ *www.tomdouglas.com* ▭ *D, MC, V* ✛ *C2.*

¢–$
BAKERY

✕ **Macrina Bakery.** One of Seattle's favorite bakeries is also popular for breakfast and brunch. With its perfectly executed breads and pastries—from Nutella brioche and ginger cookies to almond croissants and dark-chocolate sugar-dusted brownies—it has become a true Belltown institution, even if this small spot is usually too frenzied to invite the hours of idleness that other coffee shops may inspire. ■TIP➔ Macrina is an excellent place to take a delicious break on your way to or from the Olympic Sculpture Park. You can also wait for a table and have a larger breakfast or lunch—sandwiches, quiches, and salads are all yummy and fresh. ☒ *2408 1st Ave., Belltown* ☎ *206/448–4032* ⊕ *www.macrinabakery. com* ✛ *B2.*

$$
ITALIAN
Fodor'sChoice
★

✕ **Tavolàta.** This Belltown favorite is helmed by superstar-chef Ethan Stowell (also of Anchovies & Olives and How to Cook a Wolf). Serving up Italian goodness by the plateful in an industrial-chic bi-level space, Tavolàta is a decidedly lively, loud, and delicious night out on the town. Skinny-jeaned young things mingle with families here—and everyone has fun. The long bar serves up simple, elegant cocktails (Campari or Cynar with soda never fails). Start with a chickpea salad, buffalo mozzarella, or chilled heirloom tomato soup. Homemade pasta is the main draw here, such as fresh campanelle with mussels, squash, preserved lemon and pesto, or linguine with clams, garlic, and chili. Meat offerings are traditional with a flair: pork chop is vivified with currants and grilled radicchio; fresh halibut is poached in olive oil with escarole and mushrooms. ⊠ *2323 2nd Ave., Belltown* ☎ *206/838–8008* ⊕ *www. tavolata.com* ⊟ *D, MC, V* ✛ *B2.*

PIONEER SQUARE

¢ ✕ **Café Paloma.** The interior of this tiny café, which is close to several
CAFÉ art galleries—is filled with decorative bronze trays and rich colors. Along with coffee service, there's light lunch and dinner fare (served Thursday–Saturday in summer only) with a Mediterranean/Turkish accent: handmade dolmas, hummus, and baba ghanoush. The daily lunch specials can also feature such items as panini, salads, and pita sandwiches. ⊠ *93 Yesler Way, Pioneer Square* ☎ *206/405–1920* ⊟ *MC, V* ⊙ *Closed Sun.* ✛ *C4.*

WHERE TO STAY

$$–$$$ 🏨 **Doubletree Arctic Club Hotel.** Close to the stadiums and in the heart
Fodor'sChoice of the financial district, this early-1900s landmark hotel was lovingly
★ restored from its gentlemen's club roots in 2006 to become a classy luxury hotel. From the Alaskan-marble-sheathed foyer and the antique walrus heads on the third floor, to the Northern Lights Dome room with its leaded glass ceiling and rococo touches, the Arctic Club pays homage to a different era of Gold Rush opulence. Guest rooms are done in earthy neutrals, with buttery leather chairs, and dark-wood crown molding. Fun touches like trunks for bedside tables and walrus bottle openers continue the arctic club theme. Choose from rooms with whirlpools or deluxe showers; some standard rooms (and all the suites) also have sofa beds for those traveling with children; a few rooms have outdoor terraces. Enjoy cocktails in their Polar Bar or sit for serious noshing at the Northwest-influenced, urban-casual JUNO restaurant. **Pros:** cool, unique property; great staff; right on the bus line. **Cons:** fitness center is small; not in the absolute heart of Downtown; rooms are a bit dark. ⊠ *700 3rd Ave., Downtown,* ☎ *206/340–0340* ⊕ *www. doubletree1.hilton.com* ⇥ *120 rooms* ⚏ *In-room: a/c, safe, refrigerator (some), DVD, Wi-Fi. In-hotel: restaurant, room service, 2 bars, gym, laundry service, Internet terminal, Wi-Fi hotspot, parking (paid), some pets allowed* ⊟ *AE, D, DC, MC, V* ✛ *C3.*

$ 🏨 **Executive Hotel Pacific.** Price and location are the selling points for this low-profile, 1929 property tucked into a neighborhood filled with fancy hotels. Often populated with word-of-mouth travelers, the hotel's 4th Avenue entrance is through a coffee shop, and its Spring Street entrance is marked only by a small awning. Guest rooms are done up in tan and beige, with white bed linens and burgundy throw blankets. All rooms have flat-screen TVs, free Wi-Fi, and iPod-dock alarm clocks. Note that because this is an older building, rooms are small, but most have city views. A Seattle's Best Coffee greets guests on the first floor and sells breakfast items, but restaurants around the hotel offer better options.

Pros: great value and location; friendly staff. **Cons:** readers complain of traffic noise; shabby rooms; spotty housekeeping. ⊠ *400 Spring St., Downtown* ☎ *206/623–3900 or 800/426–1165* ⊕ *www.executivehotels. net/seattle* ⇗ *154 rooms* ☐ *In-room: Wi-Fi. In-hotel: restaurant, gym, public Internet, parking (fee), some pets allowed* ☐ *AE, D, DC, MC, V* ⷤ*EP* ⊹ *C3.*

$$$$ ⬚ **The Fairmont Olympic Hotel.** Grand and stately, the Fairmont Olympic
ↂ transports travelers to another time. Between the marble floors, bro-
Fodor'sChoice cade chairs, silk wallpaper, Corinthian columns, massive chandeliers,
★ and sweeping staircases worthy of Rhett Butler, this old-world hotel personifies class and elegance. It's no wonder that so many Seattleites get married in this Renaissance Revival hotel—it's as close to a princess palace as most of us will ever get to experience. Guest rooms are lovely and light, with French Country touches like pale yellow wallpaper and traditional floral patterns. The suites are a popular option for parents with kids—sofa beds are separated from the bedroom, and rollaway beds are available. **Pros:** elegant and spacious lobby; great location; excellent service; fabulous on-site dining. **Cons:** rooms are a bit small for the price; may be a little too old-school for trendy travelers. ⊠ *411 University St., Downtown* ☎ *206/621–1700 or 800/441–1414* ⊕ *www. fairmont.com/seattle* ⇗ *232 rooms, 218 suites* ☐ *In-room: safe, DVD (some), Wi-Fi. In-hotel: 2 restaurants, room service, bar, pool, gym, children's programs, laundry service, Wi-Fi hotspot, parking (fee), some pets allowed* ☐ *AE, D, DC, MC, V* ⊹ *C3.*

$$$$ ⬚ **Four Seasons Hotel Seattle.** The newest hotel jewel (or mega-diamond)
Fodor'sChoice in downtown Seattle gazes out over Elliott Bay and the Olympic Moun-
★ tains from Union Street and 1st Avenue, just south of the Pike Place Market. Steps from Benaroya Hall and the Seattle Art Museum, the hotel is polished and elegant, with Eastern accents and plush furnishings set against a definite modern-Northwest backdrop, in which materials, such as stone and fine hardwoods, take center stage, as seen in the sleek reception area. An extensive day spa and an infinity-pool terrace over- looking Puget Sound will help you relax after a long day of exploring Seattle's hilly terrain. Floor-to-ceiling windows in the guest rooms are unforgettable; lovely linens, comfortable living spaces, and sleek marble bathrooms with deep soaking tubs, luxurious rain showers, and TVs embedded in the mirrors are added bonuses. The vibe here isn't preten- tious, but it's certainly not laid-back Northwest either. **Pros:** amazing views; wonderful aesthetics; large rooms with luxurious bathrooms; lovely spa. **Cons:** Four Seasons regulars might not click with this mod- ern take on the brand; some guests say service kinks need to be ironed out. ⊠ *99 Union St., Downtown* ☎ *206/749–7000* ⊕ *www.fourseasons. com* ⇗ *134 rooms,13 suites* ☐ *In-room: safe, refrigerator (some), DVD, Wi-Fi. In-hotel: restaurant, room service, bar, pool, gym, spa, children's programs, laundry service, parking (paid), some pets allowed* ☐ *AE, D, DC, MC, V* ⊹ *C3.*

$$ ⬚ **Hotel 1000.** Chic and cosmopolitan, Hotel 1000 is luxe and decid-
Fodor'sChoice edly art-forward and modern—the centerpiece of the small lobby is a
★ dramatically lighted glass staircase (don't worry, there's an elevator) and original artwork by Pacific Northwest artist J.P. Canlis. Studio 1000,

Matt's in the Market

the small sitting room off the lobby, pairs an elegant fire pit with mid-century modern swiveling leather chairs—making guests feel not unlike cocktail-toting extras in a James Bond feature. The designers wanted the hotel to have a distinctly Pacific Northwest feel, and they've succeeded without being campy. The whole hotel is done in dark woods and deep earth tones with an occasional blue accent to represent the water. Elegant raw-silk throws and fabrics aren't local per se, but they could be seen as a nod to the city's sizable Thai community. Rooms are full of surprising touches, including large tubs that fill from the ceiling. Hotel 1000 is without a doubt the most high-tech hotel in the city. Your phone will do everything from check the weather and airline schedules to give you restaurant suggestions; MP3 players and iPod docking stations are standard amenities. If you ever get tired of fiddling with the gadgets in your room, there's a state-of-the-art virtual golf club, programmed with some of the world's most challenging courses. **Pros:** lots of high-tech perks; guests feel pampered; hotel is hip without being alienating. **Cons:** rooms can be dark; rooms without views look out on a cement wall; restaurant can be overpriced. ⊠ *1000 1st Ave., Downtown* ☎ *206/957–1000* ⊕ *www.hotel1000seattle.com* ⮲ *101 rooms, 19 suites* ♿ *In-room: safe, refrigerator, DVD, Wi-Fi. In-hotel: restaurant, room service, bar, gym, spa, laundry service, Wi-Fi hotspot, parking (paid), some pets allowed* ⊟ *AE, MC, V* ✛ *C4.*

\$\$
Fodor's Choice
★

🖬 **Hyatt at Olive 8.** In a city that's known for environmental responsibility, being the greenest hotel in Seattle is no small feat, but the Hyatt at Olive 8 has achieved the honor by becoming the first LEED-certified hotel in the city. Design enthusiasts take note: you won't find any mud-hut aesthetics here—environmentally friendly has rarely been this chic.

The hotel manages to be modern and minimalist without being austere, with a warm blue-and-brown palette, tasteful metal accents, and dark- and light-wood interplay. Maybe it's the floor-to-ceiling windows flooding the place with light or extensive Elaia Spa, but the guests seem remarkably relaxed here. Middle-aged globe-trotters with sensible Euro shoes mix seamlessly with Tokyo hipsters and businessmen in the coffee and wine bar with (gasp) reasonable prices and cushy furniture. Visitors also enjoy the on-site restaurant's extensive list of local wines and beer while seated around a reclaimed tree-turned-table that was downed by the 2007 windstorm. Standard rooms are well appointed with the same color scheme in a long, narrow layout and offer fun enviro touches like dual-flush toilets, fresh-air vents, built-in benches, and low-flow showerheads. Allergy and asthma sufferers will also be happy with the complete lack of smell in the hotel—low VOC paint, wool carpeting, and natural materials were used throughout, so the off-gassing typical with newer hotels is nowhere to be found. From the green roof to the serene indoor pool and huge fitness center with yoga studio, this Hyatt proves that what's good for the planet can also be good for you—not to mention luxurious. **Pros:** central location; superb amenities; environmental responsibility; wonderful spa. **Cons:** standard rooms have showers only; fee for Wi-Fi use. ⊠ *1635 8th Ave., Downtown* ☎ *206/ 695–1234* ⊕ *www.olive8.hyatt.com* ⤲ *333 rooms, 13 suites* ⌂ *In-room: safe, refrigerator, Wi-Fi. In-hotel: restaurant, room service, bar, pool, gym, spa, laundry service, Internet terminal, Wi-Fi hotspot, parking (paid)* ⊟ *AE, D, DC, MC, V* ✛ *C3.*

NIGHTLIFE

The grunge-rock legacy of Nirvana, Soundgarden, and Pearl Jam still reverberates in local music venues, which showcase up-and-coming pop, punk, heavy metal, and alternative bands, along with healthy doses of other genres.

Two free papers, the *Stranger* and *Seattle Weekly* (distributed on Thursday; see ⊕ *www.thestranger.com* or ⊕ *www.seattleweekly.com*), provide detailed music, art, and nightlife listings. Friday editions of the *Seattle Times* have pullout sections detailing weekend events.

Bars and clubs stay open until 2 AM. Cabs are easy to find, and some buses run until the early morning hours (see ⊕ *www.transit.metrokc. gov*). After the witching hour, cabs are the best option for those not willing to hoof it. Pioneer Square—home to a plethora of rock, jazz, and electronic music clubs—features a joint cover charge of $10 that covers admission to six bars; simply pay the cover at the first club you visit, get a hand stamp, and roam at will.

BARS AND CLUBS

★ **Oliver's** (⊠ *405 Olive Way, Downtown* ☎ *206/382–6995*), in the Mayflower Park Hotel, is famous for its martinis. In fact, having a cocktail here is like having afternoon tea in some parts of the world. Wing chairs, low tables, and lots of natural light make it easy to relax after a hectic day of sightseeing.

Spur Gastropub (✉ *113 Blanchard St., Belltown* ☎ *206/728–6706* ⊕ *www.spurseattle.com*) is a favorite among foodies. The inventive small plates and carefully curated drink menu (Spur is owned by the same folks who run Tavern Law on Capitol Hill), and stylish "pioneer-lite" space also make this a very popular nightspot. Spur can be a bit spendy, so it may make sense to save your visit for happy hour (Sunday–Thursday 5–7) or for a late-night snack (it serves a special pairing menu from 11 to 1:30).

★ **Vessel** (✉ *1312 5th Ave., Downtown* ☎ *206/652–5222* ⊕ *www. vesselseattle.com*) is the place to go Downtown for intricate and inventive cocktails. The specialty drinks are outstanding here, and you're bound to find a few concoctions that you won't find anywhere else. Service can be a bit slow on crowded weekends, but just spend the time people-watching in the attractive, supermodern bi-level space. This is a sophisticated place (leave the sport sandals at home) that knows it doesn't have to trade on pretension—it's all about the drinks, such as the Frick, with bourbon, Cinzano Rosso, peach bitters, and dried fig, or the Blueberry Flip, with brandy, crème de mûre, egg, and bitters.

Fodor's Choice **Zig Zag Café** (✉ *1501 Western Ave., Downtown* ☎ *206/625–1146*
★ ⊕ *zigzagseattle.com*) gives Oliver's at the Mayflower Hotel a run for its money when it comes to pouring perfect martinis—plus, it's much more eclectic and laid-back here. A mixed crowd of mostly locals hunts out this unique spot at Pike Place Market's Hillclimb (a nearly hidden stairwell leading down to the piers). A simple, ho-hum food menu includes cheese and meat plates, bruschetta, soup, salad, olives, and nuts. A small patio is the place to be on a summery happy-hour evening. Zig Zag is friendly; retro without being obnoxiously ironic; and very Seattle—with the occasional live music show, to boot.

SHOPPING

Seattle's retail core might feel business-crisp by day, but it's casual and arts-centered by night, and the shopping scene reflects both these moods. Within a few square blocks—between 1st Avenue on the west and Boren Avenue on the east, and from University Street to Olive Way—you can find department-store flagships, several high-gloss vertical malls, dozens of upper-echelon boutiques, and elite retail chains. One block closer to Elliott Bay, on Western Avenue, several high-end home-furnishings showrooms make up an informal "Furniture Row." The Waterfront, with its small, kitschy stores and open-air restaurants, is a great place to dawdle. ■ TIP→ Seattle's best shopping is found in the small neighborhood made up of 4th, 5th, and 6th avenues between Pine and Spring streets, and 1st Avenue between Virginia and Madison streets.

BOOKS

Fodor's Choice **Peter Miller Architectural & Design Books and Supplies.** Aesthetes and archi-
★ tects regularly haunt this floor-to-ceiling stocked shop for all things design. This is a great shop for quirky, unforgettable gifts, like a Black Dot sketchbook, and Arne Jacobsen wall clock, or an aerodynamic umbrella. ✉ *1930 1st Ave., Downtown* ☎ *206/441–4114* ⊕ *www. petermiller.com*.

GIFTS AND HOME DECOR

Schmancy. Weird and wonderful, this toy store is more surreal art fun-house than FAO Schwarz. Pick up a crocheted zombie (with a cute little bow), a felted Ishmael's whale, your very own Hugh Hefner figurine—or how about a pork-chop pillow? ⊠ *1932 2nd Ave., Downtown* ☎ *206/728–8008* ⊕ *www.schmancytoys.com.*

Fodor's Choice ★

★ **Sur La Table.** Culinary artists and foodies have flocked to this popular Pike Place Market destination since 1972. Sur La Table's flagship shop is packed to the rafters with many thousands of kitchen items. ⊠ *84 Pine St., Downtown* ☎ *206/448–2244* ⊕ *www.surlatable.com.*

WINE AND SPECIALTY FOODS

DeLaurenti Specialty Food and Wine. Attention foodies: clear out your hotel minibars and make room for delectable treats from DeLaurenti. If you're planning any picnics, swing by here first. Imported meats and cheeses crowd the deli cases, and packaged delicacies pack the aisles. ⊠ *1435 1st Ave., Downtown* ☎ *206/622–0141* ⊕ *www.delaurenti.com.*

Fodor's Choice ★

★ **Pike and Western Wine Shop.** The folks at Pike and Western have spent the last 35 years carving out the shop's reputation as one of the best wine shops in the city. With well over 1,000 wines personally selected from the Pacific Northwest and around the world—and expert advice from friendly salespeople to guide your choice—this shop offers taste-driven picks in a welcoming environment. ⊠ *1934 Pike Pl., Downtown* ☎ *206/441–1307* ⊕ *www.pikeandwestern.com.*

OUTDOOR CLOTHING AND EQUIPMENT

REI. Recreational Equipment, Inc. (REI) is Seattle's sports-equipment mega-mecca. The enormous flagship store in South Lake Union has an incredible selection of outdoor gear—from polar-fleece jackets and wool socks to down vests, hiking boots, raingear, and much more—as well as its own 65-foot climbing wall. You can test things out on the mountain-bike test trail or in the simulated rain booth. ⊠ *222 Yale Ave. N, South Lake Union* ☎ *206/223–1944* ⊕ *www.rei.com.*

Fodor's Choice ★

VANCOUVER, BRITISH COLUMBIA

Updated by
Crai S. Bower,
Carolyn B.
Heller, and
Chris McBeath

Cosmopolitan Vancouver has a spectacular setting. Tall fir trees stand practically downtown, the Coast Mountains tower close by, the ocean laps at the doorstep, and people from every corner of the earth create a youthful and vibrant atmosphere.

Vancouver is a young city, even by North American standards. It was not yet a town in 1871, when British Columbia became part of the Canadian confederation. The city's history, such as it is, remains visible to the naked eye: eras are stacked east to west along the waterfront like some century-old archaeological dig—from cobblestone, late-Victorian Gastown to shiny postmodern glass cathedrals of commerce grazing the sunset.

Long a port city in a resource-based province, Vancouver is relatively new to tourism and, for that matter, to its famous laid-back West Coast lifestyle. Most locals mark Expo '86, when the city cleaned up old industrial sites and generated new tourism infrastructure, as the turning point. Another makeover is in the works now, as Vancouver, with Whistler, prepares to host the 2010 Winter Olympics. The mild climate, exquisite natural scenery, and relaxed outdoor lifestyle continually attract new residents, and the number of visitors is increasing for the same reasons.

There is much to see and do in Vancouver, but when time is limited (as it usually is for cruise-ship passengers), the most popular options are a stroll through Gastown and Chinatown, a visit to Granville Island, or a driving or biking tour of Stanley Park. If you have more time, head to the Museum of Anthropology, on the University of British Columbia campus; it's worth a trip.

For maps and information, stop at the Vancouver Visitor Centre. It's across the street from Canada Place and next door to the Fairmont Waterfront Hotel.

Visitor Information Vancouver Visitor Centre (⊠ *200 Burrard St.* ☎ *604/683–2000*).

ON THE MOVE

GETTING TO THE PORT

Embarkation or disembarkation in Vancouver makes a scenic start or finish to an Alaska cruise. Sailing through Burrard Inlet, ships pass the forested shores of Stanley Park and sail beneath the graceful sweep of the Lions Gate Bridge. Most ships calling at Vancouver dock at the Canada Place cruise-ship terminal on the downtown waterfront, a few minutes' walk from the city center. Its rooftop of dramatic white sails makes it instantly recognizable.

A few vessels depart from the Ballantyne cruise-ship terminal, which is a 10- to 15-minute, C$15 cab ride from downtown.

Transfers between the airport and the piers are offered by the cruise lines, either as a fare add-on or, in the case of some luxury cruise lines or small-ship cruise lines, included in the price of your cruise. Cruise-line representatives meet airport arrivals or are present at hotel transfer points to make the process stress-free.

Contacts Ballantyne cruise ship terminal (⊠ *655 Centennial Rd.* ☎ *604/665–9000 or 888/767–8826* ⊕ *www.portvancouver.com*). **Canada Place cruise ship terminal** (⊠ *999 Canada Place Way* ☎ *604/665–9000 or 888/767–8826* ⊕ *www.portvancouver.com*).

ARRIVING BY AIR

Vancouver International Airport is 16 km (10 mi) south of downtown in the suburb of Richmond. It takes 30 to 45 minutes to get downtown from the airport.

Contacts Vancouver International Airport (☎ *604/207–7077* ⊕ *www.yvr.ca*).

AIRPORT TRANSFERS

The Vancouver Airporter Service bus leaves the domestic and international terminals approximately every 30 minutes, stopping at major downtown hotels and at the Canada Place cruise-ship terminal. It's

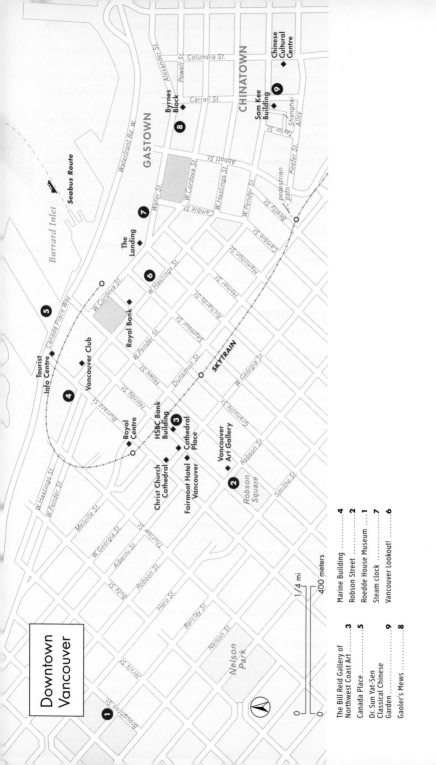

Downtown Vancouver

Burrard Inlet

Seabus Route

GASTOWN

CHINATOWN

Nelson Park

Robson Square

SKYTRAIN

Tourist
Info Centre

Vancouver Club

Royal Bank

The Landing

Byrnes
Block

Sam Kee
Building

Chinese
Cultural
Centre

Shanghai
Alley

pedestrian
path

Royal
Centre

HSBC Bank
Building

Cathedral
Place

Christ Church
Cathedral

Fairmont Hotel
Vancouver

Vancouver
Art Gallery

Canada Place Way

Waterfront Rd. W.

W. Cordova St.
W. Cordova St.
Water St.
W. Hastings St.
W. Hastings St.
W. Pender St.
W. Pender St.
W. Georgia St.
Dunsmuir St.
Robson St.
Smithe St.

Cambie St.
Abbott St.
Carrall St.
Columbia St.
Powell St.
Alexander St.
Taylor St.
Keefer St.
Beatty St.
Homer St.
Hamilton St.
Richards St.
Seymour St.
Granville St.
Howe St.
Hornby St.
Burrard St.

W. Hastings St.
W. Pender St.
W. Georgia St.
Melville St.
Alberni St.
Robson St.
Haro St.
Barclay St.
Nelson St.
Broughton St.
Jervis St.
Bute St.
Thurlow St.

1/4 mi

400 meters

The Bill Reid Gallery of
Northwest Coast Art **3**
Canada Place **5**
Dr. Sun Yat-Sen
Classical Chinese
Garden **9**
Gaoler's Mews **8**

Marine Building **4**
Robson Street **2**
Roedde House Museum ... **1**
Steam clock **7**
Vancouver Lookout! **6**

C$14 one-way and C$22 round-trip. Taxi stands are in front of the terminal building; the fare downtown is about C$35 (about C$40 to Ballantyne Pier). Local cab companies include Black Top Cabs and Yellow Cabs, both of which serve the whole Vancouver area. Limousine service from LimoJet Gold costs about C$70 to C$80 one-way.

The Canada Line, the newest addition to Vancouver's rapid transit system, runs passengers directly from the Vancouver International Airport to the Canada Place cruise-ship terminal (and stops en route) in just 25 minutes. The station is inside the airport, on Level 4 between the domestic and international terminals. The trains, which are fully wheelchair accessible and allow plenty of room for luggage, begin running before 5 AM and leave every four to six minutes during peak hours, and every 10 minutes from 11 PM until end of service (between 12:30 and 1:15 AM). Fares are C$5 plus the cost of a fare for the time of day you're traveling. Passes such as DayPasses or FareSavers are exempt from the extra $5 charge. Visit TransLink's Web site for more fare details.

Contacts Black Top Cabs (☎ *604/681–2181*). **LimoJet Gold** (☎ *604/273–1331 or 800/278–8742* ⊕ *www.limojetgold.com*). **TransLink** (☎ *604/953–3333* ⊕ *www.translink.ca*). **Vancouver Airporter Service** (☎ *604/946–8866 or 800/668–3141* ⊕ *www.yvrairporter.com*). **Yellow Cab** (☎ *604/681–1111*).

ARRIVING BY CAR

From the south, I–5 from Seattle becomes Highway 99 at the U.S.–Canada border. Vancouver is a three-hour drive (226 km [140 mi]) from Seattle. It's best to avoid border crossings during peak times such as holidays and weekends. Highway 1, the Trans-Canada Highway, enters Vancouver from the east. To avoid traffic, arrive after rush hour (8:30 AM).

Vancouver's evening rush-hour traffic starts early—about 3 PM on weekdays. The worst bottlenecks outside the city center are the North Shore bridges, the George Massey Tunnel on Highway 99 south of Vancouver, and Highway 1 through Coquitlam and Surrey. The BC Ministry of Transportation (☎ *800/550–4997* ⊕ *www.drivebc.ca*) has updates.

Vincipark offers secure underground parking in a two-level garage at Canada Place. Rates are C$23 per day for cruise passengers if reserved in advance. The entrance is at the foot of Howe Street. Cruisepark has a secured uncovered lot five minutes away from Canada Place. Reservations via Web or phone are recommended. Rates start at C$120 per seven-day period.

Contacts Vincipark (✉ *999 Canada Place Way* ☎ *604/684–2251 or 866/856–8080* ⊕ *www.vinciparkcanadaplace.ca*). **Cruisepark** (✉ *455 Waterfront Rd.* ☎ *800/665–0050* ⊕ *www.cruisepark.com*).

EXPLORING VANCOUVER

Vancouver is easy to navigate. The heart of the city—which includes the downtown area, the Canada Place cruise-ship terminal, Gastown, Chinatown, Stanley Park, and the West End high-rise residential neighborhood—sits on a peninsula hemmed in by English Bay and the Pacific Ocean to the west; by False Creek, the inlet home to Granville Island,

Beaches might not be the first thing you think of in Vancouver, but in summer Kits beach is quite a hot spot.

to the south; and by Burrard Inlet, the working port of the city, to the north, past which loom the North Shore mountains.

DOWNTOWN AND THE WEST END

❸ **The Bill Reid Gallery of Northwest Coast Art.** Vancouver's newest aboriginal art gallery, named after one of B.C.'s preeminent artists, Bill Reid (1920–98), is as much a legacy of his works as it is a showcase of current artists. Displays include wood carvings, jewelry, print, and sculpture. The gallery may be small but its expansive offerings often include artist talks and noon-hour presentations. Bill Reid is best known for his bronze statue, "The Spirit of Haida Gwaii, The Jade Canoe"—measuring 12 feet x 20 feet, the original is an iconic meeting place at the Vancouver International Airport and its image is on the back of the Canadian $20 bill. ⌧ *639 Hornby St., Downtown* ☎ *604/682-3455* ⊕ *www.billreidgallery.ca.* ⌧ *C$10* ⊗ *Wed.–Sun. 11–5.*

Fodor's Choice
★

❺ **Canada Place.** Extending four city blocks (about a mile and a half) north into Burrard Inlet, this complex (once a cargo pier) mimics the style and size of a luxury ocean liner, with exterior esplanades. The Teflon-coated fiberglass roof, shaped like five sails (the material was invented by NASA and once used in astronaut space suits), has become a Vancouver skyline landmark. Home to Vancouver's main cruise-ship terminal, Canada Place can accommodate up to four luxury liners at once. It's also home to the luxurious **Pan Pacific Hotel** and the **Vancouver Convention and Exhibition Centre** (☎ 604/647-7390), which links to an even-more-impressive expansion via outdoor plazas and an underground art gallery–themed tunnel. The promenades, which wind all the way to Stanley Park, present spectacular vantage points to view
★

Burrard Inlet and the North Shore Mountains; plaques posted at intervals offer historical information about the city and its waterfront. At the north end of the complex, at the **Port Authority Interpretive Centre** (☎ 604/665–9179 ⚇ Free ☉ Weekdays 9–4), you can catch a video about the workings of the port, see some historic images of Vancouver's waterfront, or try your hand at a virtual container-loading game. Also at the north end, the **CN IMAX Theatre** (☎ 604/682–4629 ⚇ C$14, higher prices for some films) shows films on a five-story-high screen. ⊠ 999 Canada Place Way, Downtown ☎ 604/775–7200 ⊕ www.canadaplace.ca.

NIGHT MARKET

If you're in the area in summer on a Friday, Saturday, or Sunday, check out Chinatown's bustling Night Market for food and tchotchkes: the 200 block of East Pender and Keefer are closed to traffic from 6:30–11 PM (until midnight on Saturday).

3

❹ ★ **Marine Building.** Inspired by New York's Chrysler Building, the terra-cotta bas-reliefs on this 21-story, 1930s art deco structure depict the history of transportation—airships, steamships, locomotives, and submarines—as well as Mayan and Egyptian motifs and images of marine life. Step inside for a look at the beautifully restored interior, then walk to the corner of Hastings and Hornby streets for the best view of the building. It serves as the headquarters of the Daily Planet in the TV show, Smallville. ⊠ 355 Burrard St., Downtown.

❷ **Robson Street.** Robson, Vancouver's busiest shopping street, is lined with see-and-be-seen sidewalk cafés, chain stores, and high-end boutiques. The street, which links downtown to the West End, is particularly lively between Jervis and Burrard streets and stays that way into the evening with buskers and entertainers.

OFF THE BEATEN PATH ❶ **Roedde House Museum.** Two blocks south of Robson Street, on Barclay, is the Roedde (pronounced roh-dee) House Museum, an 1893 house in the Queen Anne Revival style, set among Victorian-style gardens. Tours of the restored, antiques-furnished interior take about an hour. On Sunday, tours are followed by tea and cookies. The gardens (free) can be visited anytime. ⊠ 1415 Barclay St., between Broughton and Nicola, West End ☎ 604/684–7040 ⊕ www.roeddehouse.org ⚇ C$5; Sun. C$6, including tea ☉ Tues.– Sun. 2–4.

❻ ☾ **Vancouver Lookout!** The lookout looks like a flying saucer stuck atop a high-rise and at 553 feet high, it affords one of the best views of Vancouver. A glass elevator whizzes you up 50 stories to the circular observation deck, where knowledgeable guides point out the sights and give a tour every hour on the hour. On a clear day you can see Vancouver Island and Mt. Baker in Washington State. The top-floor restaurant makes one complete revolution per hour; the elevator ride up is free for diners. ■TIP➜ Tickets are good all day, so you can visit in daytime and return for another look after dark. ⊠ 555 W. Hastings St., Downtown ☎ 604/689–0421 ⊕ www.vancouverlookout.com ⚇ C$13 ☉ May–mid-Oct., daily 8:30 AM–10:30 PM; mid-Oct.–Apr., daily 9–9.

GASTOWN AND CHINATOWN

Be aware that you might come across one or two seedy corners: it's all pretty safe by day, but you might prefer to cab it at night.

9 **★** **Dr. Sun Yat-Sen Classical Chinese Garden.** The first authentic Ming Dynasty–style garden outside China, this small garden was built in 1986 by 52 artisans from Suzhou, China. It incorporates design elements and traditional materials from several of Suzhou's centuries-old private gardens. No power tools, screws, or nails were used in the construction. Guided tours (45 minutes long), included in the ticket price, are conducted on the hour between mid-June and the end of August (call ahead for off-season tour times); they are valuable for understanding the philosophy and symbolism that are central to the garden's design. A concert series, including classical, Asian, world, jazz, and sacred music, plays on Friday evenings in July, August, and September. The free public park next door is also designed as a traditional Chinese garden. ■TIP→ Covered walkways make this a good rainy-day choice. ⊠ *578 Carrall St., Chinatown* ☎ *604/662–3207* ⊕ *www.vancouverchinesegarden.com* ☞ *C$10* ☽ *May–mid-June and Sept., daily 10–6; mid-June–Aug., daily 9:30–7; Oct., daily 10–4; Nov.–Apr., Tues.–Sun. 10–4.*

8 **Gaoler's Mews.** Once the site of the city's first civic buildings—the constable's cabin and customs house, and a two-cell log jail—this atmospheric brick-paved courtyard is home to cafés, an Irish pub, and architectural offices. ⊠ *Behind 12 Water St., Gastown.*

7 **Steam Clock.** An underground steam system, which also heats many local buildings, supplies the world's first steam clock—possibly Vancouver's most-photographed attraction. On the quarter hour a steam whistle rings out the Westminster chimes, and on the hour a huge cloud of steam spews from the apparatus. The ingenious design, based on an 1875 mechanism, was built in 1977 by Ray Saunders of Landmark Clocks (at 123 Cambie Street) to commemorate the community effort that saved Gastown from demolition. ⊠ *Water St., Gastown.*

STANLEY PARK

Fodor'sChoice **★** A 1,000-acre wilderness park, only blocks from the downtown section of a major city, is a rare treasure. Vancouverites use it, protect it, and love it with such zeal that when it was proposed that the 120-year-old Hollow Tree be axed due to safety concerns, citizens rallied, raised funds, and literally engineered its salvation.

Stanley Park is, perhaps, the single most prized possession of Vancouverites, who make use of it fervently to cycle, walk, jog, Rollerblade, play cricket and tennis, and enjoy outdoor art shows and theater performances alongside attractions such as the renowned aquarium.

When a storm swept across the park's shores in December 2006, it destroyed close to 10,000 trees as well as parts of the perimeter seawall. Locals contributed thousands of dollars to the clean-up and replanting effort in addition to the monies set aside by local authorities. The storm's silver lining was that it cleared some dead-wood areas, making room for the reintroduction of many of the park's original species of trees. It also gave rise to an unusual ecological arts program in which ephemeral sculptures have been placed in various outdoor locations.

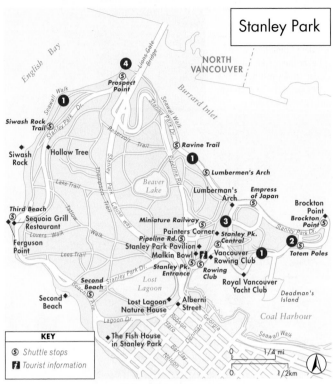

Stanley Park

KEY

ⓢ *Shuttle stops*

🛈 *Tourist information*

Made of natural and organic materials, the elements are constantly changing the look of each piece which, over the course of its 24-month "display period," will decay and return to the earth.

GETTING THERE AND AROUND

To get to the park by public transit, take Stanley Park Bus 19 from the corner of Pender and Howe, downtown. It's possible to see the park by car, entering at the foot of Georgia Street and driving counterclockwise around the one-way Stanley Park Drive.

The **Stanley Park Shuttle** (☎ *604/257–8400* ⊕ *www.vancouver.ca/parks/*) operates mid-June to mid-September between 10 AM and 6:30 PM, providing frequent (every 15 minutes) transportation to 15 major park sights. Pick it up on Pipeline Road, near the Georgia Street park entrance, or at any of the stops in the park. The fare is C$2.

For information about guided nature walks in the park, contact the **Lost Lagoon Nature House** (☎ *604/257–8544* ⊕ *www.stanleyparkecology.ca*) on the south shore of Lost Lagoon, at the foot of Alberni Street. They operate May to September, Tuesday through Sunday, 9–4:30.

❹ **Prospect Point.** At 211 feet, Prospect Point is the highest point in the park and provides striking views of the Lions Gate Bridge (watch for cruise ships passing below), the North Shore, and Burrard Inlet. There's also a year-round souvenir shop, a snack bar with terrific ice cream, and a

restaurant (May–September only). From the seawall, you can see where cormorants build their seaweed nests along the cliff ledges.

① Seawall. The seawall path, a 9-km (5½-mi) paved shoreline route popu-
Fodor's Choice lar with walkers, cyclists, and in-line skaters, is one of several car-free
★ zones within the park. If you have the time (about a half day) and the energy, strolling the entire seawall is an exhilarating experience. It extends an additional mile east past the marinas, cafés, and waterfront condominiums of Coal Harbour to Canada Place downtown, so you could start your walk or ride from there. From the south side of the park, the seawall continues for another 28 km (17 mi) along Vancouver's waterfront, to the University of British Columbia, allowing for a pleasant, if ambitious, day's bike ride. Along the seawall, cyclists must wear helmets and stay on their side of the path. Within Stanley Park, cyclists must ride in a counterclockwise direction.

The seawall can get crowded on summer weekends, but inside the park is a 28-km (17-mi) network of peaceful walking and cycling paths through old- and second-growth forest. The wheelchair-accessible Beaver Lake Interpretive Trail is a good choice if you're interested in park ecology. Take a map—they're available at the park-information booth and many of the concession stands—and don't go into the woods alone or after dusk.

② Totem poles. Totem poles are an important art form among native peoples along British Columbia's coast. These eight poles, all carved in the latter half of the 20th century, include replicas of poles originally brought to the park from the north coast in the 1920s, as well as poles carved specifically for the park by First Nations artists. The several styles of poles represent a cross section of B.C. native groups, including the Kwakwaka'wakw, Haida, and Nisga'a. The combination of carved animals, fish, birds, and mythological creatures represents clan history. An information center near the site has a snack bar, a gift shop, and information about B.C.'s First Nations.

③ Vancouver Aquarium Marine Science Centre. Massive pools with windows
☾ below water level let you come face to face with beluga whales, sea
★ otters, sea lions, dolphins, and harbor seals at this research and educational facility. In the Amazon rain-forest gallery you can walk through a jungle populated with piranhas, caimans, and tropical birds, and in summer, you'll be surrounded by hundreds of free-flying butterflies. Other displays, many with hands-on features for kids, show the underwater life of coastal British Columbia and the Canadian Arctic. A Tropic Zone is home to exotic freshwater and saltwater life, including clown fish, moray eels, and black-tip reef sharks. Beluga whale, sea lion, and dolphin shows, as well as dive shows (where divers swim with aquatic life, including sharks) are held daily. Make sure to check out the 4-D film experience; it's a multisensory show that puts mist, smell, and wind into the 3-D equation. For an extra fee, you can help the trainers feed and train otters, belugas, and sea lions. There's also a café and a gift shop. Be prepared for lines on weekends and school holidays. ■TIP→ The quietest time to visit is before 11 AM or after 3 PM. ✉ *841 Avison Way, Stanley Park* ☎ *604/659–3474* ⊕ *www.vanaqua.*

org ✉ *C$22* ☉ *July–Labor Day, daily 9:30–7; Labor Day–June, daily 9:30–5:30.*

Fodor'sChoice ## GRANVILLE ISLAND
★

This 35-acre peninsula in False Creek, just south of downtown Vancouver, is home to one of North America's most successful urban-redevelopment schemes. Once a derelict industrial site, Granville Island is now a vibrant urban park, with a bustling public market, several theaters, galleries, crafts shops, and artisans' studios.

GETTING THERE AND AROUND

The mini Aquabus ferries are a favorite way to get to Granville Island (it's about a two-minute ride); they depart from the south end of Hornby Street, a 15-minute walk from downtown Vancouver. The Aquabus delivers passengers across False Creek to the Granville Island Public Market *(see below)*. The larger False Creek ferries leave every five minutes for Granville Island from a dock behind the Vancouver Aquatic Centre, on Beach Avenue. Still another option is to take a 20-minute ride on a TransLink bus: from Waterfront Station or stops on Granville Street, take False Creek South Bus 50 to the edge of the island. Buses 4 UBC and 7 Dunbar will also take you within a few minutes' walk of the island. The market is a short walk from the bus, ferry, or tram stop. If you drive, parking is free for up to three hours, and paid parking is available in four garages on the island. If your schedule is tight, you can tour Granville Island in two to three hours. If you like to shop you could spend a full day.

Look out for the **Downtown Historic Railway** (☎ *604/665–3903* ⊕ *www. trams.bc.ca*), two early-20th-century electric trams scheduled to run on summer weekends and holiday afternoons from Science World to Granville Island. Olympics-related construction forced the railway to cease operation for a few years but it's scheduled to resume in 2010.

Fodor'sChoice **Granville Island Public Market.** Because no chain stores are allowed in this
★ 50,000-square-foot building, each shop here is unique. Dozens of stalls sell locally grown produce direct from the farm; others sell crafts, chocolates, cheese, fish, meat, flowers, and exotic foods. On Thursdays in summer, market gardeners sell fruit and vegetables from trucks outside. At the north end of the market you can pick up a snack, lunch, or coffee at one of the many food stalls. The Market Courtyard, on the waterside, is a good place to catch street entertainers—be prepared to get roped into the action, if only to check the padlocks of an escape artist's gear. Weekends can get madly busy. ✉ *1689 Johnston St., Granville Island* ☎ *604/666–5784* ⊕ *www.granvilleisland.com* ☉ *Daily 9–7.*

OUTSIDE DOWNTOWN

Fodor'sChoice **Museum of Anthropology.** Part of the University of British Columbia, the
★ MOA has one of the world's leading collections of Northwest Coast First Nations art. The Great Hall displays dramatic cedar poles, bentwood boxes, and canoes adorned with traditional Northwest Coast–painted designs. On clear days, the gallery's 50-foot-tall windows reveal a striking backdrop of mountains and sea. Another highlight is the work of the late Bill Reid, one of Canada's most respected Haida artists. In *The Raven and the First Men* (1980), carved in yellow cedar, he tells

a Haida story of creation. Reid's gold-and-silver jewelry work is also on display, as are exquisite carvings of gold, silver, and argillite (a black shale found on Haida Gwaii, also known as the Queen Charlotte Islands) by other First Nations artists. Arthur Erickson designed the cliff-top structure that houses the MOA, which also has a book and fine-art shop and a summertime café. To reach the museum by tran-

> ### CHINATOWN NIGHT MARKET
>
> For interesting eats, check out the stalls at the Chinatown night market, open from mid-May to early September, 6:30 PM to 11 PM, Friday through Sunday. The market is on Keefer Street, between Columbia and Main streets.

sit, take UBC bus 4 from Granville Street or bus 44 from Burrard Street downtown to the university loop, a 10-minute walk from the museum. ■ TIP➔ Pay parking is available in the Rose Garden parking lot, across Marine Drive from the museum. ⊠ *University of British Columbia, 6393 N.W. Marine Dr., Point Grey* ☎ *604/822–5087* ⊕ *www.moa.ubc.ca* ✑ *C$11, Tues. 5–9 C$6* ⊙ *Memorial Day–Labor Day, Tues. 10–9, Wed.–Mon. 10–5; Labor Day–Memorial Day, Tues. 11–9, Wed.–Sun. 11–5.*

WHERE TO EAT

A diverse gastronomic experience awaits you in cosmopolitan Vancouver. A wave of Asian immigration and tourism has brought a proliferation of upscale Asian eateries. Cutting-edge restaurants currently perfecting and defining Pacific Northwest fare—including such home-grown regional favorites as salmon and oysters, accompanied by British Columbia wines—have become some of the city's leading attractions.

You're also spoiled for choice when it comes to casual and budget dining. Good choices include Asian cafés or any of the pubs listed in the Nightlife section; many have both an adults-only pub and a separate restaurant section where kids are welcome. A bylaw bans smoking indoors in all Vancouver restaurants, bars, and pubs.

Vancouver dining is fairly informal. Casual but neat dress is appropriate everywhere. A 15% tip is expected. A 5% Goods and Services Tax (GST) is added to the food portion of the bill and a 10% liquor tax is charged on wine, beer, and spirits. Some restaurants build the liquor tax into the price of the beverage, but others add it to the bill.

DOWNTOWN AND THE WEST END

$$ ✕ **Bin 941.** Part tapas restaurant, part up-tempo bar, this bustling, often
ECLECTIC noisy hole-in-the-wall claims to have launched Vancouver's small-plates trend. Among the adventurous snack-size dishes, you might find bison satay, crab cakes topped with burnt-orange chipotle sauce, or grilled lamb sirloin served with tomato salad and feta vinaigrette. Snack on one or two, or order a bunch and have a feast. The Bin is open until 2 AM (midnight on Sunday). Bin 942, a sister spot in Kitsilano, is a touch more subdued. ⊠ *941 Davie St., Downtown* ☎ *604/683–1246* ⊕ *www.bin941. com* ⚴ *Reservations not accepted* ☰ *MC, V* ⊙ *No lunch* ✛ *D4.*

$$$$
SEAFOOD
*Fodor's*Choice
★

✕ **C Restaurant.** Save your pennies, fish fans—dishes such as crispy trout served with oven-dried tomato and braised fennel, spice-rubbed tuna grilled ultrarare, or lingcod paired with smoked-ham-hock broth have established this spot as Vancouver's most innovative seafood restaurant. Start with shucked oysters from the raw bar or perhaps the seared scallops wrapped in octopus "bacon," and finish with an assortment of handmade chocolate truffles and petits fours. The elaborate 6- or 14-course tasting menus with optional wine pairings highlight regional seafood. Both the ultramodern interior and the waterside patio overlook False Creek, but dine before dark to enjoy the view. ⊠ *2–1600 Howe St., Downtown* 🕾 *604/681–1164* ⊕ *www.crestaurant.com* ⊟ *AE, DC, MC, V* ☾ *No lunch weekends or Nov.–Feb.* ⊹ *C5.*

¢–$$
CHINESE

✕ **Hon's Wun-Tun House.** This Vancouver minichain has been keeping residents and tourists in Chinese comfort food since the 1970s. You can find better Chinese food elsewhere, but Hon's locations are convenient and the prices are reasonable. The best bets on the 300-item menu are the dumplings and noodle dishes, any of the Chinese vegetables, and anything with barbecued meat. The Robson Street outlet has a separate kitchen for vegetarians and an army of fast-moving waitresses. The original Keefer Street location is in the heart of Chinatown. ⊠ *1339 Robson St., West End* 🕾 *604/685–0871* ⊕ *www.hons.ca* ⌂ *Reservations not accepted* ⊟ *MC, V* ⊹ *D2* ⊠ *268 Keefer St., Chinatown* 🕾 *604/688– 0871* ⌂ *Reservations not accepted* ⊟ *MC, V* ⊹ *H4.*

GASTOWN AND CHINATOWN

$–$$
ECLECTIC

✕ **Salt Tasting Room.** If your idea of a perfect lunch or light supper revolves around fine cured meats, artisanal cheeses, and a glass of wine from a wide-ranging list, find your way to this sleek spare space in a decidedly unsleek Gastown lane. The restaurant has no kitchen and simply assembles its first-quality provisions, perhaps meaty *bunderfleisch* (cured beef), smoked pork chops, or B.C.-made Camembert, with accompanying condiments, into artfully composed grazers' delights— more like an upscale picnic than a full meal. There's no sign out front, so look for the salt-shaker flag in Blood Alley, which is off Abbott Street, half a block south of Water Street. ⊠ *45 Blood Alley, Gastown* 🕾 *604/633–1912* ⊕ *www.salttastingroom.com* ⊟ *AE, MC, V* ⊹ *G3.*

YALETOWN AND FALSE CREEK

$$$–$$$$
SEAFOOD
*Fodor's*Choice
★

✕ **Blue Water Cafe.** Executive chef Frank Pabst features both popular and lesser-known local seafood (including frequently overlooked varieties like mackerel or herring) at this fashionable restaurant. You might start with B.C. sardines stuffed with pine-nut *gremolata*, a pairing of Dungeness crab and flying squid, or a selection of raw oysters. Main dishes are seafood centric, too—perhaps white sturgeon grilled with wheat berries, capers, and peppery greens, or a Japanese-style seafood stew. Ask the staff to recommend wine pairings from the B.C.-focused list. You can dine in the warmly lit interior or outside on the former loading dock that's now a lovely terrace. ■ TIP➜ **The sushi chef turns out both classic and new creations—they're pricey but rank among the city's best.** ⊠ *1095 Hamilton St., Yaletown* 🕾 *604/688–8078* ⊕ *www.bluewatercafe.net* ⊟ *AE, DC, MC, V* ☾ *No lunch* ⊹ *E5.*

3

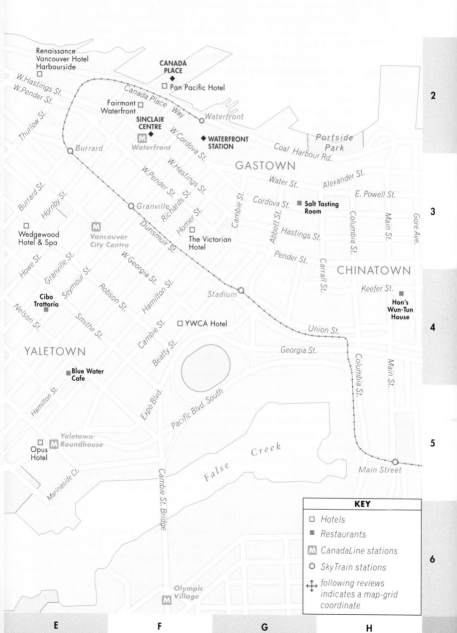

E   F   G   H

1

Burrard Inlet

Renaissance
Vancouver Hotel
Harbourside

W.Hastings St.

W.Pender St.

CANADA PLACE
◆
☐ Pan Pacific Hotel

Canada Place Way

2

Fairmont ☐
Waterfront

Thurlow St.

SINCLAIR CENTRE
Ⓜ
Waterfront

W.Cordova St.

◆ **WATERFRONT STATION**

Ⓦ Waterfront

Ⓦ Burrard

Coal Harbour Rd.

Portside Park

GASTOWN

Water St.

Alexander St.

Burrard St.

Hornby St.

W.Pender St.

W.Hastings St.

Richards St.

Cambie St.

Cordova St.

■ **Salt Tasting Room**

E. Powell St.

Columbia St.

Main St.

Gore Ave.

3

Ⓦ Granville

Dunsmuir St.

Homer St.

Abbott St.

Hastings St.

Carrall St.

CHINATOWN

☐
Wedgewood
Hotel & Spa

Ⓜ
Vancouver City Centre

Howe St.

Granville St.

Seymour St.

W.Georgia St.

Hamilton St.

☐ The Victorian Hotel

Pender St.

Keefer St. ■
Hon's Wun-Tun House

Robson St.

Ⓦ Stadium

Union St.

■
Cibo Trattoria

Nelson St.

Smithe St.

Cambie St.

Beatty St.

☐ YWCA Hotel

Georgia St.

4

YALETOWN

■ **Blue Water Cafe**

Hamilton St.

Expo Blvd.

Pacific Blvd. South

Columbia St.

Main St.

False Creek

☐
Opus
Hotel

Ⓜ *Yaletown-Roundhouse*

Marinaside Ct.

Cambie St. Bridge

Ⓦ Main Street

5

Olympic Village
Ⓜ

6

E   F   G   H

STANLEY PARK

$$$–$$$$ ✕ **The Fish House in Stanley Park.** This 1930s former sports pavilion with
SEAFOOD two verandas and a fireplace is surrounded by gardens, tucked between
Stanley Park's tennis courts and putting green. Chef Karen Barnaby's
food, including fresh oysters, grilled ahi tuna steak with a green-
peppercorn sauce, and corn-husk-wrapped salmon with a maple glaze,
is flavorful and unpretentious. Check the fresh sheet for the current day's
catch. Traditional English afternoon tea is served between 2 and 4 daily.
⊠ *8901 Stanley Park Dr., Stanley Park* ☎ *604/681–7275 or 877/681–
7275* ⊕ *www.fishhousestanleypark.com* ▱ *AE, DC, MC, V* ✛ *A1.*

$$$–$$$$ ✕ **The Teahouse in Stanley Park.** The former officers' mess in Stanley Park is
MODERN perfectly poised for watching sunsets over the water. The Pacific North-
CANADIAN west menu is not especially innovative, but it includes such specialties as
beet-and-endive salad topped with warm goat cheese, and mushrooms
stuffed with crab and mascarpone cheese, as well as seasonally chang-
ing treatments of B.C. salmon, halibut, and steak. In summer you can
dine on the patio. ⊠ *7501 Stanley Park Dr., Ferguson Point, Stanley
Park* ☎ *604/669–3281 or 800/280–9893* ⊕ *www.vancouverdine.com*
▱ *AE, MC, V* ✛ *A1.*

GRANVILLE ISLAND

$–$$ ✕ **Go Fish.** If the weather's fine, head for this seafood stand on the docks
SEAFOOD near Granville Island. It's owned by Gord Martin, of Bin 941/942 fame,
so it's not your ordinary chippie. The menu is short—highlights include
fish-and-chips, grilled salmon or tuna sandwiches, and fish tacos—but
the quality is first-rate. It's hugely popular, and on sunny summer days,
the waits can be maddening, so try to avoid the busiest times: noon to
2 PM and 5 PM to closing (which is at dusk). Since there are just a few
(outdoor) tables, be prepared to take your food to go. To get here, walk
along the waterfront path from Granville Island; by car, drive east from
Burrard Street on 1st Avenue until it ends at the docks. ⊠ *1505 W. 1st
Ave., Fisherman's Wharf, Kitsilano* ☎ *604/730–5039* ⊕ *www.bin941.
com* ▱ *MC, V* ☺ *Closed Mon. No dinner* ✛ *A3.*

WHERE TO STAY

Accommodations in Vancouver range from luxurious waterfront hotels
to neighborhood B&Bs and basic European-style pensions. Many of
the best choices are in the downtown core, either in the central business district or in the West End near Stanley Park. The chart in the
Port Essentials section shows high-season prices, but from mid-October
through May rates throughout the city can drop as much as 50%.
Most Vancouver hotels are completely no-smoking in both rooms and
public areas.

DOWNTOWN AND THE WEST END

$$$$ ▦ **Fairmont Waterfront.** This luxuriously modern 23-story hotel is across
the street from the Convention and Exhibition Centre and the Canada
Place cruise-ship terminal, but it's the floor-to-ceiling windows with
ocean, park, and mountain views in most guest rooms that really make
this hotel special. Adorned with blond-wood furniture and contemporary
Canadian artwork, each room also has a window that opens. Elevator

Take a walk and explore the outdoor totem poles at Vancouver's Museum of Anthropology.

waits can be frustrating so consider asking for a room on a lower floor, though you'll be sacrificing a view for this minor convenience. Next to the mountain-view pool is a rooftop herb garden—an aromatic retreat open to guests that includes a number of beehives, which are harvested on Friday afternoons (the honey is used in ganache truffles and honey-basil cocktails). The hotel's canine ambassador, Holly, is usually available for petting, pampering, and taking for strolls. **Pros:** harbor views; proximity to cruise-ship terminal; the lovely terraced pool near the patio herb garden; fresh honey products. **Cons:** long elevator queues; the seemingly always-busy lobby lounge; the garden patio if you're at all bee phobic. ⊠ *900 Canada Pl. Way, Downtown* ☎ *604/691–1991* ⊕ *www.fairmont.com/waterfront* ⌇ *489 rooms, 29 suites* ⊱ *In-room: safe (some), kitchen (some), refrigerator, Internet. In-hotel: restaurant, room service, bar, pool, gym, laundry service, Wi-Fi hotspot, parking (paid), some pets allowed* ⊟ *AE, D, DC, MC, V* ✦ *F2.*

$$$$ ☗ **Pan Pacific Hotel.** A centerpiece of waterfront Canada Place, the luxurious Pan Pacific shares a complex with the Vancouver Convention and Exhibition Centre and Vancouver's main cruise-ship terminal. Rooms are large and modern with maple wood throughout, Italian linens, and stunning ocean, mountain, or skyline views, all of which have been enjoyed by a star-studded list of royals, celebs, and well-heeled newsmakers. High-end suites, some with private steam room, sauna, or baby-grand piano, are popular with visiting VIPs. If you're staying over a Friday or Saturday night, Puccini and pasta were never as good as at the Italian Opera Buffet in the main dining room. The Five Sails Restaurant is quieter and more exclusive. **Pros:** the harbor views; it's only an elevator ride to the cruise-ship terminal; the "go the extra mile" service attitude. **Cons:** the atrium is open to the convention center's main lobby, so the hotel foyer, lounge, and entrance fill with delegates bearing conference badges talking shop, nabbing the best seats in the house, and vying for taxis. ✉ *999 Canada Pl., Downtown* ☎ *604/662–8111, 800/663–1515 in Canada, 800/937–1515 in U.S.* ⊕ *www.panpacific. com* ⊂ *465 rooms, 39 suites* ♿ *In-room: safe, kitchen (some), refrigerator, Wi-Fi. In-hotel: 2 restaurants, room service, bar, pool, gym, spa, laundry service, Wi-Fi hotspot, parking (paid), some pets allowed* ⊟ *AE, DC, MC, V* ⊹ *F2.*

$$$–$$$$ 🏨 **Renaissance Vancouver Hotel Harbourside.** With a lobby of glass walls this business-district hotel takes full advantage of its view-filled waterfront location. And the op-art decor in lime, orange, and black adds even greater drama. Rooms are larger than average and have either step-out or full-size glassed-in balconies with city or (in the more expensive rooms) partial water and mountain views. There's an indoor pool, a health club, and direct access to a waterside park—take all this and combine it with the "kids under 12 eat free" policy, and you have a good choice for families in an ocean-side high-rise. **Pros:** at the outer edge of the financial district; waterfront views. **Cons:** it's a five-block walk to major shopping and within a half block of the convention center expansion and a waterfront walkway leading to Stanley Park. ✉ *1133 W. Hastings St., Downtown* ☎ *604/689–9211 or 800/905–8582* ⊕ *www.renaissancevancouver.com* ⊂ *434 rooms, 8 suites* ♿ *In-room: safe (some), Wi-Fi. In-hotel: restaurant, bar, pool, gym, laundry service, Wi-Fi hotspot, parking (paid), some pets allowed* ⊟ *AE, D, DC, MC, V* ⊹ *E2.*

$$–$$$ 🏨 **Sylvia Hotel.** To stay at the Sylvia in June through August, you must
Fodor's Choice book six months to a year ahead: this Virginia-creeper-covered 1912
★ building is popular because of its low rates and near-perfect location: about 25 feet from the beach on scenic English Bay, 200 feet from Stanley Park, and a 20-minute walk from Robson Street. The rooms and apartment-style suites vary from tiny to spacious. Many of the basic but comfortable rooms are large enough to sleep four and all have windows that open. The restaurant and bar are popular and its tenure on English Bay has made it a nostalgic haunt for Vancouverites. **Pros:** beachfront location; close to restaurants; a good place to mingle with the locals. **Cons:** older building; parking can be difficult if the lot is full; the 15-minute walk to the downtown core is slightly uphill. ✉ *1154 Gilford St., West End* ☎ *604/681–9321* ⊕ *www.sylviahotel.com* ⊂ *97 rooms, 22 suites* ♿ *In-room: kitchen (some), Wi-Fi. In-hotel: restaurant, room service, bar, laundry service, Internet terminal, parking (paid), some pets allowed* ⊟ *AE, DC, MC, V* ⊹ *B2.*

$$–$$$ 🏨 **The Victorian Hotel.** Budget hotels can be handsome, as in the gleaming hardwood floors, high ceilings, and chandeliers at this prettily restored 1898 European-style pension. This is one of Vancouver's best-value accommodations—guest rooms in the two connecting three-story buildings have down duvets, Oriental rugs atop hardwood floors, lush draperies, and period furniture; a few have bay windows or mountain views. Some of the private bathrooms are outfitted with marble tiles

and granite countertops (though some have a shower and no tub). Even the shared baths are spotlessly clean and nicely appointed. With three queen beds, room #15 is a good choice for families. **Pros:** great location for the price; helpful staff; clean; comfortable. **Cons:** location near the "rummy part of town" a few blocks east. It's relatively safe (honest), but common sense says you would probably take a cab to the door after midnight rather than walk. ⊠ *514 Homer St., Downtown* ☎ *604/681–6369 or 877/681–6369* ⊕ *www.victorianhotel.ca* ⤶ *39 rooms, 18 with bath* ♿ *In-room: Internet, refrigerator (some). In-hotel: laundry service, Wi-Fi hotspot, parking (paid)* ▭ *MC, V* ❄ *CP* ⊹ *E3.*

$$$$
Fodor's Choice
★

🏨 **Wedgewood Hotel & Spa.** The small lavish Wedgewood is a member of the exclusive Relais & Châteaux Group, and is run by an owner who cares fervently about her guests. The lobby and guest rooms display a flair for old-world Italian luster with original artwork and antiques selected by the proprietor on her European travels. Guest rooms are capacious and each has a balcony. The four penthouse suites have fireplaces, luxury spa bathrooms, and private garden terraces. All the extra touches are here, too: afternoon ice delivery, dark-out drapes, robes, and a morning newspaper. The turndown service includes homemade cookies and bottled water. The sophisticated Bacchus restaurant and lounge ($$$–$$$$) is in the lobby; it's also a terrific stop for afternoon tea after shopping along Robson Street. The tiny but posh on-site spa is incredibly popular—book ahead for an appointment. **Pros:** personalized and attentive service; afternoon tea with finesse; great location close to top shops. **Cons:** small size means it books quickly. ⊠ *845 Hornby St., Downtown* ☎ *604/689–7777 or 800/663–0666* ⊕ *www.wedgewoodhotel.com* ⤶ *41 rooms, 43 suites* ♿ *In-room: safe, refrigerator, Wi-Fi. In-hotel: restaurant, room service, bar, gym, spa, laundry facilities, laundry service, Wi-Fi hotspot, parking (paid)* ▭ *AE, D, DC, MC, V* ⊹ *E3.*

$–$$

🏨 **YWCA Hotel.** A secure, modern high-rise in the heart of the entertainment district and steps from Yaletown, the YWCA has bright, comfortable rooms—a few big enough to sleep five. Some share a bath down the hall, some share a bath between two rooms, and others have private baths. TV lounges and shared kitchens are available for all guests, and rates include use of the YWCA adults-only pool and fitness facility, a 15-minute walk away at 535 Hornby Street. **Pros:** clean and friendly; access to high-quality fitness center; a terrific alternative to hostel accommodation. **Cons:** shared facilities. ⊠ *733 Beatty St., Downtown* ☎ *604/895–5830 or 800/663–1424* ⊕ *www.ywcahotel.com* ⤶ *155 rooms, 40 with bath* ♿ *In-room: refrigerator, no TV (some), Wi-Fi. In-hotel: laundry facilities, Internet terminal, Wi-Fi hotspot, parking (paid)* ▭ *AE, MC, V* ⊹ *F4.*

YALETOWN AND FALSE CREEK

$$$$
Fodor's Choice
★

🏨 **Opus Hotel.** The design team had a good time with this boutique hotel, creating fictitious characters and designing rooms for each. Billy's room is fun and offbeat, with pop art and lime-green accents. Dede's room has leopard skin, velveteen, and faux-fur accents, while Bob and Carol's place has softer edges and golden tones. Amenities are fun, too: look for mini-oxygen canisters in the bathrooms—a whiff'll clear your head if

An underwater view of a beluga whale at the Vancouver Aquarium.

you have a hangover, and it'll stimulate blood flow for other pursuits. Most rooms have a full wall of windows, lots of natural light, and views of the city or the Japanese garden in the courtyard. Two rooms have private access to the garden; seventh-floor rooms have balconies. The brand-new Canada Line from the airport is steps away. **Pros:** central Yaletown location right by a rapid transit station; lobby bar is a fashionable meeting spot. **Cons:** renovated heritage building has no views; surrounding neighborhood is mostly high-rises; trendy nightspots nearby can be noisy at night. ⊠ *322 Davie St., Yaletown* ☎ *604/642–6787 or 866/642–6787* ⊕ *www.opushotel.com* ↝ *85 rooms, 11 suites* ⌂ *In-room: safe, refrigerator, DVD (some), Wi-Fi. In-hotel: restaurant, room service, bar, gym, bicycles, laundry service, Wi-Fi hotspot, parking (paid), some pets allowed* ⊟ *AE, DC, MC, V* ⊕ *E5.*

NIGHTLIFE

For information on events, pick up a free copy of the *Georgia Straight*, available at cafés and bookstores around town, or look in the entertainment section of the *Vancouver Sun* (Thursday's paper has listings). For tickets, book through **Ticketmaster** (☎ *604/280–4444* ⊕ *www. ticketmaster.ca*). You can pick up half-price tickets on the day of the event, as well as full-price advance tickets, at **Tickets Tonight** (⊠ *200 Burrard St., Downtown* ☎ *604/684–2787* ⊕ *www.ticketstonight.ca*), at the Vancouver Tourist Info Centre.

BARS, PUBS, AND LOUNGES

Chambar. This restaurant-cum-lounge has great bartenders and character. The back dining room has views of False Creek while the bar is all exposed-brick walls, vibrant art, and soft lighting. Try the Luini's Madonna: Amaretto, rose water, and fresh citrus served over ice. ✉ *562 Beatty St., Gastown* ☎ *604/879–7119.*

★ **The Diamond.** At the top of a narrow staircase above Maple Tree Square, in one of the city's oldest buildings, the Diamond merges speakeasy simplicity with lounge cool. The large windows open completely providing an ideal vantage point to observe the Square's impromptu street theater as you sip something special. You can choose among "boozy," "proper," or "delicate" options on the drinks menu. ✉ *6 Powell St., Gastown* ☎ *604/408–2891.*

Fodor'sChoice **Pourhouse.** Paying homage to the Klondike Gold Rush and Pioneer ★ Square spirit, Pourhouse has quickly appeared on numerous local top 10 lists. Gold Fashioned, Centennial, and Prospector take libation lovers on a historical tour of the city's highlights, while Pork and Beans, Welsh Rarebit, and Carpet Bag Steak show what a little imagination and fresh ingredients can do to transform tried-and-true dining options. ✉ *162 Water St., Gastown* ☎ *604/568–7022.*

Watermark on Kits Beach. No summer visit to Vancouver is complete without an afternoon spent sipping lovely B.C. whites at the Watermark patio as the sun sets over the beach volleyball matches and bathing beauties at Kits Beach. ✉ *1305 Arbutus St., Kitsilano* ☎ *604/738–5487.*

BREWPUBS

Dockside Brewing Company. This popular local hangout has a seaside patio, casual Pacific Northwest restaurant, and house-brewed German-style beer. ✉ *Granville Island Hotel, 1253 Johnston St., Granville Island* ☎ *604/685–7070.*

Steamworks. Home to a pub, restaurant, and coffee bar, this hipster and urban-professional hangout has great harbor views, delish food, and beer that's brewed traditionally, in small batches. ✉ *375 Water St., Gastown* ☎ *604/689–2739.*

SHOPPING

Store hours are generally 10–6 Monday, Tuesday, Wednesday, and Saturday; 10–9 Thursday and Friday; and 11–6 Sunday. A new tax replacing the 7% Provincial Sales Tax (PST) and 5% Goods and Services Tax (GST) has been proposed: the HST (Harmonized Sales Tax) of 12% at this writing is due to be in effect for the 2011 cruising season, but either way it's the same 12%.

SHOPPING DISTRICTS

Alberni Street. One block north of Robson, Alberni Street at Burrard is geared to higher-income shoppers, with names such as Tiffany & Co., Louis Vuitton, Gucci, Coach, Hermès, and Betsey Johnson.

Gastown and Chinatown. A hip crowd—restaurateurs, advertising gurus, photographers, and other creative types—have settled into Gastown, so the boutiques have gotten cooler. Look for locally designed and one-of-a-kind clothing and accessories, First Nations art, as well as souvenirs—both kitschy and expensive. Bustling Chinatown—centered on Pender and Main streets—is full of Chinese bakeries, restaurants, herbalists, tea merchants, and import shops.

Granville Island. On the south side of False Creek, Granville Island has a lively food market and a wealth of galleries, crafts shops, and artisans' studios. It gets so busy, especially on summer weekends, that the crowds can detract from the pleasure of the place; you're best off getting there before 11 AM.

Robson Street. Particularly the blocks between Burrard and Bute streets, this is the city's main fashion-shopping and people-watching artery. The Gap and Banana Republic have their flagship stores here, as do Canadian fashion outlets Club Monaco and Roots. Souvenir shops, shoe stores, and cafés fill the gaps. West of Bute, the shops cater to the thousands of Japanese and Korean students in town to study English: Asian food shops, video outlets, and cheap noodle bars abound.

Yaletown. Frequently described as Vancouver's SoHo, this neighborhood on the north bank of False Creek is home to boutiques, home furnishings stores, and restaurants—many in converted warehouses—that cater to a trendy, moneyed crowd.

NATIVE CRAFTS

★ **Coastal Peoples Fine Arts Gallery.** The gorgeous books and postcards make affordable souvenirs though you could well be tempted by the impressive collection of First Nations jewelry, ceremonial masks, prints, and carvings. ⊠ *1024 Mainland St., Yaletown* ☎ *604/685–9298* ⊠ *312 Water St., Gastown* ☎ *604/684–9222.*

Fodor's Choice **Hill's Native Art.** This highly respected store has Vancouver's largest selec-
★ tion of First Nations art. If you think the main level is impressive, go upstairs where the collector-quality stuff is. ⊠ *165 Water St., Gastown* ☎ *604/685–4249.*

Ports of Call

WORD OF MOUTH

"We did many tours on our own, booked well in advance of leaving home. Whale watching in Juneau; helicopter to a glacier in Juneau ($$$ but worth it) and seaplane to Anan Creek to see the bears feed on Salmon. Oh, took the train in Skagway as well."

—rncheryl

Updated by Teeka Ballas, Edward Readicker-Henderson, Sue Kernaghan, and Sarah Wyatt

There's never a dull day on an Alaskan cruise, and whether your ship is scheduled to make a port call, cruise by glaciers, or glide through majestic fjords, you'll have constant opportunities to explore the culture, wildlife, history, and amazing scenery that make Alaska so unique. Most port cities are small and easily explored on foot, but if you prefer to be shown the sights, your ship will offer organized shore excursions at each stop along the way.

Popular activities include city tours, flightseeing, charter fishing, river rafting, and visits to Native communities. You can also, for the sake of shorter trips or more active excursions, readily organize your own tour through a local vendor.

The ports visited and the amount of time spent in each vary depending on the cruise line and itinerary, but most ships stop in Ketchikan, Juneau, and Skagway—the three big draws in Southeast Alaska. Some ports, such as Homer and Metlakatla, are visited by only a couple of the small-ship cruise lines, while other adventure ships head out to explore the wild places in the Bering Sea.

Each town has its highlights. For example, Ketchikan has a wealth of native artifacts, Skagway has lots of gold-rush history, Sitka has a rich Russian and native heritage, and Juneau has glacier trips. There are also ample shopping opportunities in most ports, but beware of tacky tourist traps. Nearly all Southeast towns, but especially Haines, Sitka, and Ketchikan, have great art galleries.

To help you plan your trip, we've compiled a list of the most worthwhile excursions available in each port of call. Also look out for "Best Bets" boxes; these highlight a port's top experiences so you don't shell out for a flightseeing trip in one place, for example, when the experience would be better elsewhere. ⇨ *For in-depth information on outdoor activities all around Alaska, see Chapter 5, Sports and Wilderness Adventures.*

PORT ESSENTIALS

RESTAURANTS AND CUISINE
Not surprisingly, seafood dominates most menus. In summer, salmon, halibut, crab, cod, and prawns are usually fresh. Restaurants are informal and casual clothes are the norm; you'll never be sent away for wearing jeans in an Alaskan restaurant.

WHAT IT COSTS					
	¢	$	$$	$$$	$$$$
Alaskan Ports	under $9	$9–$15	$16–$20	$21–$25	over $25
Canadian Ports	under C$15	C$15–C$20	C$21–C$30	C$31–C$40	over C$40

*Prices are per person for a main course at dinner.

OUTDOOR ACTIVITIES
There are hikes and walks in or near every Alaska port town. Well-maintained trails are easily accessible from even the largest cities; lush forests and wilderness areas, port and glacier views, and mountaintop panoramas are often within a few hours' walk of downtown areas. More adventurous travelers will enjoy paddling sea kayaks in the protected waters of Southeast and South Central Alaska; companies in most ports rent kayaks and give lessons and tours. Fishing enthusiasts from all over the world come to Alaska for a chance to land a trophy salmon or halibut. Cycling, glacier hikes, flightseeing, or bear-viewing shore excursions in some ports also offer cruise passengers an opportunity to engage with Alaska's endless landscape.

BARS AND SALOONS
Shooting the breeze at a bar or saloon can be a delightfully colorful contrast to barstool-surfing the cruise-ship lounge areas. There isn't really a difference between saloons and bars; some saloons offer a setting that lets travelers pretend they've stepped back in time to the gold rush, but other places that call themselves bars can be equally historic and interesting. High-volume watering holes in the busiest ports (such as the Red Dog in Juneau and the Red Onion in Skagway) serve food in addition to drinks. Pubs in Canadian ports often have an Irish or British rather than gold-rush theme; all serve food, and many even brew their own beer.

SHOPPING
Alaskan native handicrafts range from Tlingit totem poles—a few inches high to more than 30 feet tall—to Athabascan beaded slippers and fur garments. Traditional pieces of art (or imitations thereof) are found in gift shops up and down the coast: Inupiat spirit masks, Yupik dolls and dance fans, Tlingit button blankets and silver jewelry, and Aleut grass baskets and carved wooden items. Salmon, halibut, crab, and other frozen fish are very popular souvenirs (shipped home to meet you, of course) and make great gifts. Most towns have at least one local company that packs and ships fresh, smoked, or frozen seafood.

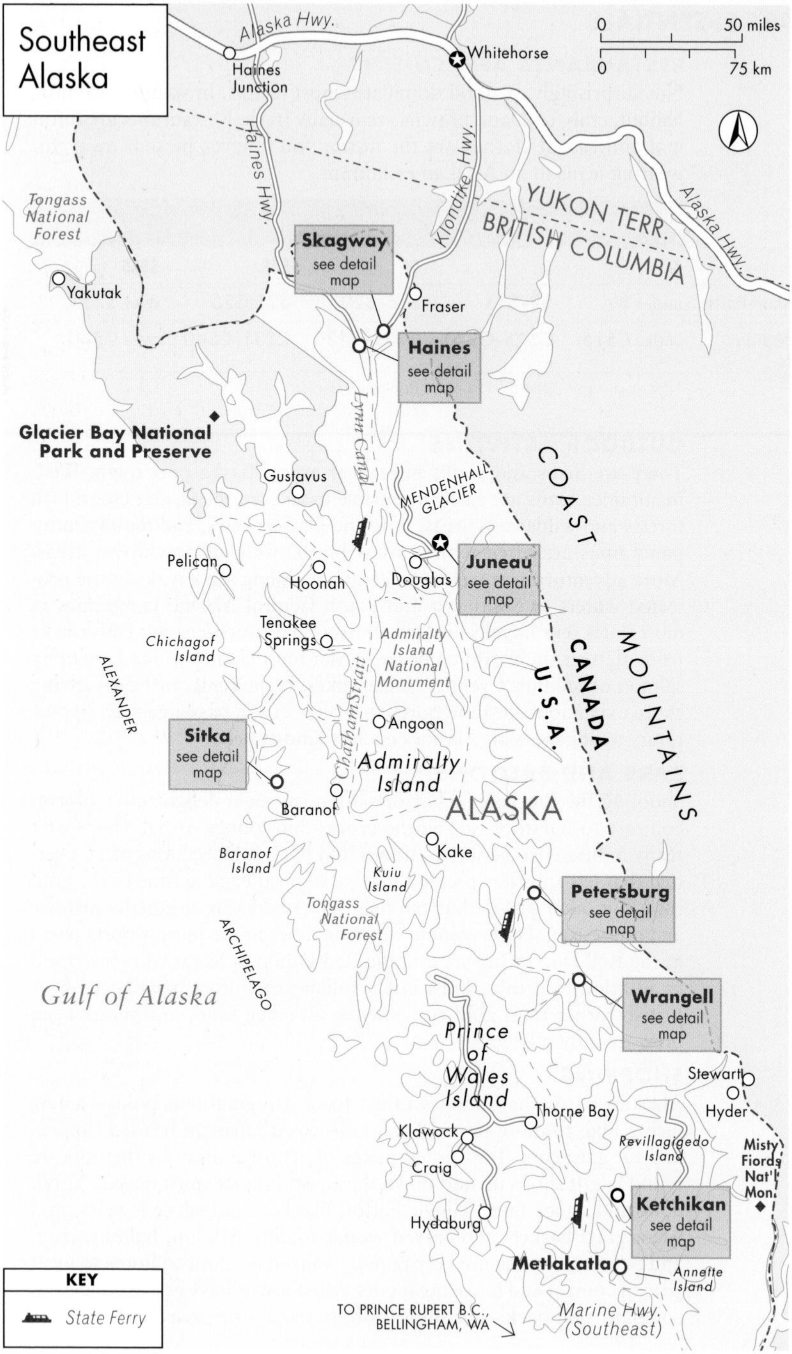
Southeast Alaska
Alaska Hwy.
Haines Junction
Whitehorse
0 50 miles
0 75 km
Haines Hwy.
Klondike Hwy.
YUKON TERR.
BRITISH COLUMBIA
Alaska Hwy.
Tongass National Forest
Yakutak
Skagway see detail map
Fraser
Haines see detail map
Lynn Canal
Glacier Bay National Park and Preserve
Gustavus
MENDENHALL GLACIER
COAST MOUNTAINS
Pelican
Hoonah
Douglas
Juneau see detail map
Tenakee Springs
Chichagof Island
Admiralty Island National Monument
CANADA
U.S.A.
ALEXANDER
Chatham Strait
Angoon
Sitka see detail map
Admiralty Island
Baranof
ALASKA
Kake
Baranof Island
Kuiu Island
Tongass National Forest
Petersburg see detail map
ARCHIPELAGO
Gulf of Alaska
Wrangell see detail map
Prince of Wales Island
Stewart
Hyder
Thorne Bay
Klawock
Revillagigedo Island
Craig
Misty Fiords Nat'l Mon.
Hydaburg
Ketchikan see detail map
Metlakatla
Annette Island
TO PRINCE RUPERT B.C., BELLINGHAM, WA
Marine Hwy. (Southeast)
KEY
State Ferry

To ensure authenticity, buy items tagged with the state-approved AUTHEN-TIC NATIVE HANDCRAFT FROM ALASKA "Silverhand" label, or look for the polar-bear symbol indicating products made in Alaska. Although these symbols are designed to ensure authentic Alaskan and native-made products, not all items lacking them are inauthentic. Better pricestend to be found in the more remote villages, in museum shops, or in crafts fairs such as Anchorage's downtown Saturday Market. ⇨ *For more on buying native crafts, see Made in Alaska in this chapter.*

SHORE EXCURSIONS

Shore excursions arranged by the cruise line are a convenient way to see the sights, but you'll pay extra for this convenience. Before your cruise, you'll receive a booklet describing the shore excursions your cruise line offers. Most cruise lines let you book excursions in advance online, where you'll find descriptions and sometimes pricing; all sell them on board during the cruise. If you cancel your excursion, you may incur penalties, the amount varying with the number of days remaining until the tour. Because these trips are specialized, many have limited capacity and are sold on a first-come, first-served basis.

CORDOVA

A small town with the spectacular backdrop of snowy Mt. Eccles, Cordova is the gateway to the Copper River delta—one of the great birding areas of North America. Perched on Orca Inlet in eastern Prince William Sound, Cordova began life early in the 20th century as the port city for the Copper River and Northwestern Railway, which was built to serve the Kennicott Copper mines 191 mi away in the Wrangell Mountains.

Since the mines and the railroad shut down in 1938, Cordova's economy has depended heavily on fishing. Attempts to develop a road along the abandoned railroad line connecting to the state highway system were dashed by the 1964 earthquake, so Cordova remains isolated. Access is limited to airplane, ferry, or cruise ship.

COMING ASHORE

SHORE EXCURSIONS

Ilanka Cultural Center. Visit the Ilanka Cultural Center, where you will meet members of the Eyak Native Corporation, who will share their culture and the history of their people and present-day life experiences. ✉ *110 Nicholoff Way* ☎ *907/424–7903* ⊕ *www.ilankacenter.org* ✉ *This tour is offered to Cruise West passengers at no charge.*

Sea Kayaking in Orca Inlet. Don the gear provided by your naturalist guide and, after a beachside lesson, board two-person sea kayaks to paddle the shoreline while you watch for sea otters, harbor seals, and seabirds. A hearty snack of famous Copper River salmon is served. ⊙ *4–7 hrs* ✉ *$75–$115.*

TRANSPORTATION AND TOURS

FROM THE PIER

Cruise ships dock at the boat harbor, and Cordova is a short walk uphill from here.

Tour buses meet ships, or you can catch a cab. A cab ride within the downtown area will run about $3.50.

CITY TOURS

Wild Hare Taxi Service (☎ 907/424–3939) provides tours for $60 an hour for up to seven people.

VISITOR INFORMATION

Pick up maps and tour brochures from the **Cordova Chamber of Commerce Visitor Center** (✉ *404 1st St.* ☎ *907/424–7260* ⊕ *www.cordovachamber. com*). The Center can also suggest short self-led walking tours through this small, easily navigated town.

INTERNET Check your e-mail at the **Cordova Public Library** (✉ *622 1st St.* ☎ *907/424– 6667* ⊕ *www.cordovalibrary.org*). Or try the **Orca Book & Sound Co.** (✉ *507 1st St.* ☎ *907/424–5305*), with rates at $9 an hour (but you're only charged for the minutes used).

EXPLORING CORDOVA

Drive out of town along the Copper River Highway and visit the **Copper River delta.** This 700,000-acre wetland is one of North America's most spectacular vistas. The two-lane highway crosses marshes, forests, streams, lakes, and ponds that are home to countless shorebirds, waterfowl, and other bird species. Numerous terrestrial mammals including moose, wolves, lynx, mink, and beavers live here, too, and the Copper River salmon runs are world famous.

The **Million Dollar Bridge,** at Mile 48, was a railroad project completed in 1910 for the Copper River and Northwestern Railway to carry copper ore to market from the mines at Kennicott. Soon after construction was completed, the nearby Childs and Miles glaciers threatened to overrun the railroad and bridge. Although the glaciers stopped short of the railroad, the copper market collapsed in 1938, making the route economically obsolete. The far span of the bridge was toppled by the Good Friday earthquake in 1964 and was not rebuilt until 2005.

From the end of the road you can view the **Childs Glacier.** Although there is no visitor center, there is a covered viewing area next to the bridge, where you can see the face of the glacier and wait for a huge chunk of ice to topple into the river.

CORDOVA BEST BETS

Copper River delta sightseeing. Rent a car and drive the 50-mi road across the delta. Stop to watch birds and scan for wildlife at the roadside viewing areas, and end the trip at the Million Dollar Bridge and the Childs Glacier Recreation Area.

Take in a festival. Cordova has some great festivals that take place during the cruising season. The Shorebird Festival is in May, the Copper River Wild! Salmon Festival takes place in July.

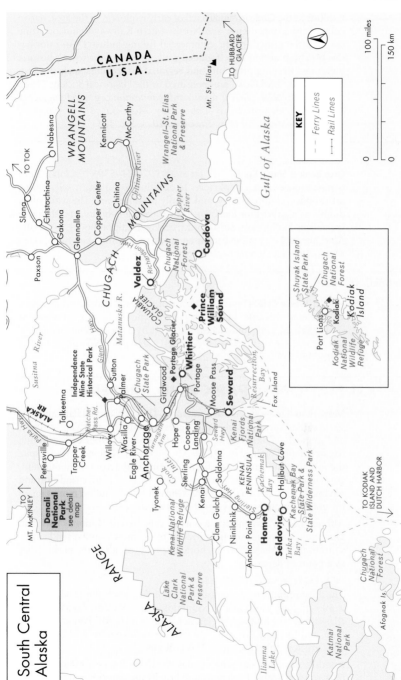

Exhibits at the **Cordova Museum** tell of early explorers to the area, native culture, the Copper River and Northwestern Railway/Kennicott Mine era, and the growth of the commercial fishing industry. An informative brochure outlines a self-guided walking tour of the town's historic buildings. Evening programs and regional art exhibits such as "Fish Follies" and "Bird Flew" are sponsored by the Historical Society. ⊠ 622 *1st St.* ☎ *907/424–6665* ⊕ *www.cordovamuseum.org* 🖅 *$1 suggested donation* ⊙ *Memorial Day–Labor Day, Mon.–Sat. 10–6, Sun. 2–4; Labor Day–Memorial Day, Tues.–Fri. 10–5, Sat. 1–5.*

SHOPPING

Orca Book & Sound Co. (⊠ *507 1st St.* ☎ *907/424–5305* ⊙ *Closed Sun.*) is much more than a bookstore. In addition to books, it sells music, art supplies, children's toys, and locally produced art. The walls often double as a gallery for local works or traveling exhibits, and the store specializes in old, rare, out-of-print, and first-edition books, especially Alaskana. ■TIP➔ In the back is an espresso-smoothie bar; the upstairs area has wireless Internet access for a small fee.

WHERE TO EAT

¢–$ ✕ **Killer Whale Café.** Have a breakfast of espresso and baked goods or
CAFÉ an omelet at this café. For lunch you can choose from a deli menu of soups, salads, and sandwiches, followed by a fresh, homemade dessert. ⊠ *507 1st St.* ☎ *907/424–7733* ▭ *Cash only* ⊙ *No dinner. Closed Oct.–May 1.*

DENALI NATIONAL PARK AND PRESERVE

More than 6 million acres of wilderness, Denali National Park and Preserve is the heart of Alaska: the biggest mountains, the wildest rivers, and so much wildlife you'll probably end up frying your camera trying to catch it all. Founded in 1917 as Mt. McKinley National Park (despite the fact that the park's then borders went right across the mountain), government caught up with thousands of years of Native tradition and renamed the park Denali in 1980. One road in, the tallest mountain on the continent, and endless possibilities await you.

Although it isn't technically a port of call, Denali National Park and Preserve is, quite understandably, one of the most popular land extensions to an Alaska cruise. Anchorage, 240 mi south of the park, serves as a point of departure.

GEOLOGY AND TERRAIN

The most prominent geological feature of the park is the Alaska Range, a 600-mi-long crescent of mountains that separates South Central Alaska from the Interior. Mt. Hunter (14,573 feet), Mt. Foraker (17,400 feet), and Mt. McKinley (20,320 feet) are the mammoths of the group. Glaciers flow from the entire Alaska Range.

Another, smaller group of mountains, the Outer Range north of Denali's park road, is a mix of volcanics and heavily metamorphosed sediments.

Though not as breathtaking as the Alaska Range, the Outer Range is popular with hikers and backpackers because its summits and ridges are not as technically difficult to reach.

Several of Denali's most spectacular landforms are deep in the park, but are still visible from the park road. The multicolor volcanic rocks at Cathedral Mountain and Polychrome Pass reflect the vivid hues of the American Southwest. The braided channels of glacially fed streams such as the Teklanika, Toklat, and McKinley rivers serve as highway routes for both animals and hikers. The debris- and tundra-covered ice of the Muldrow Glacier, one of the largest glaciers to flow out of Denali National Park's high mountains, is visible from Eielson Visitor Center, at Mile 66 of the park road. Wonder Lake, a dark and narrow kettle pond that's a remnant from Alaska's ice ages, lies at Mile 85, just a few miles from the former gold-boom camp of Kantishna.

WILDLIFE

Thirty-seven species of mammals reside in the park, from wolves and bears to little brown bats and pygmy shrews that weigh a fraction of an ounce. The park also has a surprisingly large avian population in summer, with 167 identified species. Most of the birds migrate in fall, leaving only two dozen year-round resident species, including ravens, boreal chickadees, and hawk owls. Some of the summer birds travel thousands of miles to nest and breed in subarctic valleys, hills, and ponds. The northern wheatear migrates from southern Asia, warblers arrive from Central and South America, and the arctic tern annually travels 24,000 mi while commuting between the arctic and Antarctica.

The most sought-after species among visitors are the large mammals: grizzlies, wolves, Dall sheep, moose, and caribou. All inhabit the forest or tundra landscape that surrounds Denali Park Road. You can expect to see Dall sheep finding their way across high meadows, grizzlies and caribou frequenting stream bottoms and tundra, moose in the forested areas both near the park entrance and deep in the park, and the occasional wolf or fox that may dart across the road.

EXPLORING DENALI

You can take a tour bus or the Alaska Railroad from Anchorage to the Denali National Park entrance. Princess, Holland America, and Royal Caribbean attach their own railcars behind these trains for a more luxurious experience. Most cruise passengers stay one or two nights in hotels at a riverside settlement called Denali Park, just outside the park entrance. Shuttle buses provide transportation from your hotel to the park's busy visitor center, where you can watch slide shows on the park, purchase maps and books, or check the schedule for naturalist presentations and sled-dog demonstrations. Access to the park itself is by bus on day tours. If you aren't visiting Denali as part of your cruise package, make reservations for a tour or outdoor adventure that fits your style (*see Outdoor Activities for Denali National Park, below*). All the major hotels in the Denali Park area have good restaurants on the premises, and most travelers choose to dine there.

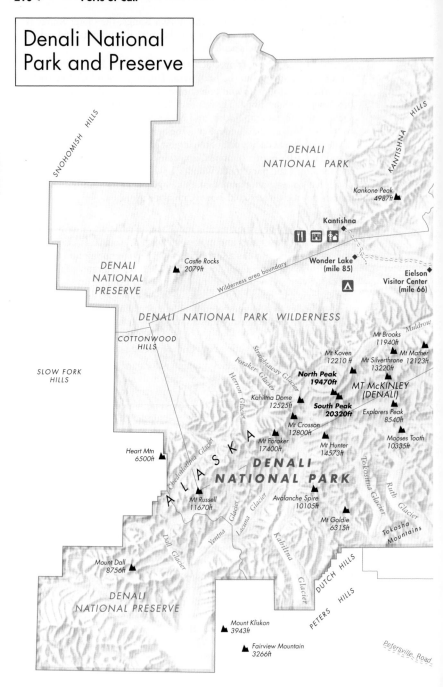

Denali National Park and Preserve

SNOHOMISH HILLS

DENALI NATIONAL PARK

KANTISHNA HILLS

Kankone Peak
4987ft ▲

Kantishna
🍴 🏛 🚻 ◆

DENALI NATIONAL PRESERVE

Castle Rocks
2079ft ▲

Wilderness area boundary

Wonder Lake
(mile 85)

Eielson
Visitor Center
(mile 66)

🔺

DENALI NATIONAL PARK WILDERNESS

COTTONWOOD HILLS

SLOW FORK HILLS

Muldrow

Mt Brooks
11940ft ▲

Straightaway Glacier

Mt Koven
12210 ft ▲

Mt Mather 12123ft ▲
Mt Silverthrone
13220ft ▲

Foraker Glacier

North Peak
19470ft ▲

MT McKINLEY
(DENALI)

Herron Glacier

Kahiltna Dome
12525ft ▲

South Peak
20320ft ▲

Explorers Peak
8540ft ▲

Mt Crosson
12800ft ▲

Mooses Tooth
10335ft ▲

Heart Mtn
6500ft ▲

Chedolothna Glacier

Mt Foraker
17400ft ▲

Mt Hunter
14573ft ▲

A L A S K A

Tokositna Glacier

Ruth Glacier

DENALI NATIONAL PARK

Mt Russell
11670ft ▲

Yentna Glacier

Lacuna Glacier

Avalanche Spire
10105ft ▲

Mt Goldie
6315ft ▲

Tokosha Mountains

Mount Dall
8756ft ▲

Dall Glacier

Kahiltna Glacier

DUTCH HILLS

DENALI NATIONAL PRESERVE

PETERS HILLS

Mount Kliskon
3943ft ▲

Fairview Mountain
3266ft ▲

Petersville Road

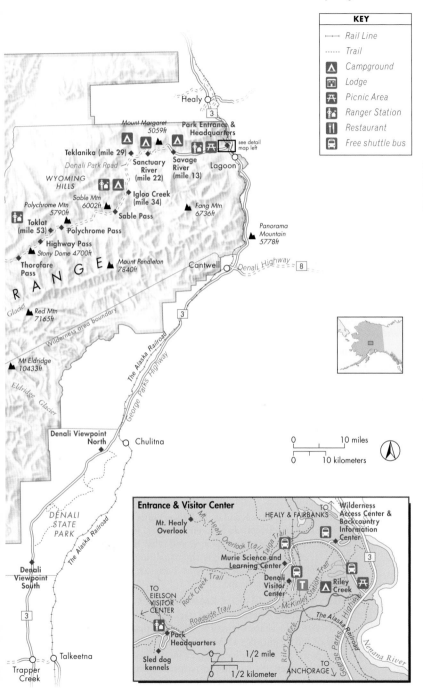

KEY

- ⊢——⊣ Rail Line
- .... Trail
- 🏕 Campground
- 🏨 Lodge
- 🏞 Picnic Area
- 🛖 Ranger Station
- 🍴 Restaurant
- 🚌 Free shuttle bus

4

Healy

3

Park Entrance & Headquarters

Mount Margaret 5059ft

see detail map left

Teklanika (mile 29)

Denali Park Road

Sanctuary River (mile 22)

Savage River (mile 13)

Lagoon

WYOMING HILLS

Sable Mtn 6002ft

Igloo Creek (mile 34)

Polychrome Mtn 5790ft

Fang Mtn 6736ft

Toklat (mile 53)

Sable Pass

Polychrome Pass

Panorama Mountain 5778ft

Highway Pass

Stony Dome 4700ft

Thorofare Pass

Mount Pendleton 7840ft

Cantwell

Denali Highway

8

R A N G E

Glacier

Red Mtn 7165ft

3

Wilderness area boundary

The Alaska Railroad

Mt Eldridge 10433ft

George Parks Highway

Eldridge Glacier

Denali Viewpoint North

Chulitna

0 ⊢——⊣ 10 miles

0 ⊢——⊣ 10 kilometers

DENALI STATE PARK

The Alaska Railroad

Denali Viewpoint South

3

Talkeetna

Trapper Creek

Entrance & Visitor Center

TO HEALY & FAIRBANKS

Wilderness Access Center & Backcountry Information Center

Mt. Healy Overlook

Mt. Healy Overlook Trail

Taiga Trail

3

Murie Science and Learning Center

Rock Creek Trail

Denali Visitor Center

McKinley Station Trail

Riley Creek

TO EIELSON VISITOR CENTER

Roadside Trail

Riley Creek

The Alaska Railroad

Park Headquarters

Sled dog kennels

1/2 mile

0 ⊢——⊣ 1/2 kilometer

TO ANCHORAGE

George Parks Highway

Nenana River

The 90-mi Denali Park Road winds from the park entrance to Wonder Lake and Kantishna, the historic mining community in the heart of the park. Public access along this road is limited to tour and shuttle buses that depart from the Wilderness Access Center. The Park Road is paved for the first 15 mi and gravel the rest of the way.

The Wilderness Access Center near the park's entrance (at Mile 237 of the Parks Highway, or Mile 1 of the Park Road) is the transportation hub, with bus and campsite reservations. The adjacent Backcountry Information building has hiking details for those heading into the wilderness, including current data on animal sightings, river-crossing conditions, weather, and closed areas.

PARK BASICS

Admission to Denali is $10 per person or $20 per vehicle. The **Wilderness Access Center** (⌧ *Mile 1, Park Rd.* ☎ *907/683–9274*) near the park's entrance at Mile 237.3, George Parks Highway, is where you can handle reservations for roadside camping and bus trips into the park. A smaller building nearby is the **Backcountry Information Center,** for those visitors who want to travel and stay overnight in the wilderness. The Backcountry Information Center has backcountry permits and hiking information, including current data on animal sightings (remember the whole park is bear territory), river-crossing conditions, weather, and closed areas. The center is closed in winter (mid-September through mid-May). ■TIP➔ Free permits are required for overnight backpacking trips, but you won't need one for day hiking.

Open from mid-May to mid-September, the **Denali Visitor Center** (⌧ *Mi 1.5, Park Rd. 99755* ☎ *907/683–2294* ⊕ *www.nps.gov/dena*) exhibits beautiful displays about the park's natural and cultural history, and holds regular showings of *Heartbeats of Denali* in the Karstens Theater. In addition, the center offers a wide variety of interpretive programs and a chance to browse the nearby Denali Bookstore, a great source for wildlife guides, birding guides, and picture books; send some to relatives to make them jealous of your trip.

Next to the Denali Visitor Center, **Murie Science and Learning Center** (⌧ *Mi 1.5, Park Rd.* ☎ *907/683–1269* ⊕ *www.murieslc.com*) is the foundation of the park's science-based education programs, and also serves as the winter visitor center when the Denali Visitor Center is closed.

At Mile 66 on the Park Road is the **Eielson Visitor Center,** the park's pride and joy. LEED-certified as a green building, Eielson offers amazing views of the mountain, the glaciers, and what happens to a landscape when glaciers go away. Inside is the usual interpretive material. The center offers a daily guided walk at 1 PM, an easy 45-minute or so exploration of the landscape.

TOUR, SHUTTLE, AND CAMPER BUSES

Don't be alarmed by the crowded park entrance; that gets left behind quickly. After the chaos of private businesses that line the George Parks Highway and the throngs at the visitor center, there's pretty much nothing else in the park but wilderness. From the bus you'll have the opportunity to see Denali's wildlife in natural settings, as the animals are habituated to the road and vehicles, and go about their daily routine

Mt. McKinley. Alaskans call Mt. McKinley by its original name, Denali, which means "the High One."

with little bother. In fact, the animals really like the road: it's easier for them to walk along it than to work through the tundra and tussocks.

Bus trips take time. The maximum speed limit is 35 MPH. Add in rest stops, wildlife sightings, and slowdowns for passing, and it's an 8- to 11-hour day to reach the heart of the park and the best Denali views from Miles 62–85. *All prices listed below are for adults, and include the $10 park admission fee, unless otherwise noted.* ■ TIP➔ If you decide to tour the park by bus, you have two choices: a sightseeing bus tour offered by a park concessionaire or a ride on the shuttle bus. The differences between the two are significant.

Tour buses (☎ *800/622–7275, 907/272–7275 in Alaska or outside U.S.* ⊕ *www.reservedenali.com*) offer a guided introduction to the park. Advance reservations are required for the tour buses and are recommended for the park shuttles. Reservations for the following season become available on December 1, so if you're not booking your extension through the cruise line, you'll want to make your independent reservation as soon as you can after firmnig up your cruise dates. You can usually get on the bus of your choice with less than a week's notice—and you can almost always get on a shuttle bus within a day or two—but try not to count on that.

Rides through the park include a five-hour Natural History Tour ($60.75) a six- to eight-hour Tundra Wilderness Tour ($103), and an 11- to 12-hour Kantishna Experience ($155). These prices do not include the park entrance fee. Trips are fully narrated by the driver-guides and include a snack or box lunch and hot drinks. Although the Natural History Tour lasts five hours, it only goes 17 mi into the park (2 mi beyond the private-vehicle turnaround), emphasizing Denali's human and natural history. Do not take this tour if you want the best wildlife or Mt. McKinley viewing opportunities. You might see a moose or two, but not much else. The Tundra Wilderness Tour is a great way to go for a fun, thorough introduction to the park, but if it leaves you wanting more, the Kantishna Experience travels the entire length of the road, features an interpretive guide and ranger, lunch, and some walking. Note, though, that none of the tours allows you to leave the bus without the group or travel independently through the park.

MT. MCKINLEY

Also commonly known by its Athabascan Indian name, Denali—"The High One"—North America's highest mountain is the world's tallest when measured from base to top: the great mountain rises more than 18,000 feet above surrounding lowlands. Unfortunately for visitors with little time to spend in the area, McKinley is wreathed in clouds on average two days of every three in summer, so cross your fingers and hope for a clear day when you visit.

The park's **shuttle buses** (☎ 800/622–7275 or 907/272–7275 ⊕ *www.reservedenali.com*) don't include a formal interpretive program or food and drink. ■ TIP→ They're less expensive, and you can get off the bus and take a hike or just stop and sightsee, then catch another bus along the road. Most of the drivers are well versed in the park's features and will point out plant, animal, and geologic sights. The shuttles are less formal than the tour buses, and generally less comfortable. They do stop to watch and photograph wildlife, but with a schedule to keep, time is sometimes limited. Shuttle-bus round-trip fares are $24 to the Toklat River at Mile 53; $30.75 to Eielson Visitor Center at Mile 66; and $42.25 to Wonder Lake at Mile 85. They also run a shuttle to Kantishna, for $46; the trip takes about 13 hours. Kids 14 and under ride free on the shuttles; 15- to 17-year-olds pay ½ adult fare on all shuttle buses.

Camper buses (☎ 800/622–7275 or 907/272–7275 ⊕ *www.reservedenali.com*) serve permitted backpackers and those staying in campgrounds along the road. Seats in the back of the bus are removed for gear storage and there is no formal narration, although the bus drivers aren't likely to let you miss anything important. The $30.75 pass includes transportation anywhere down the road as far as Wonder Lake for the length of the backpacker's stay. Get off and on in the same manner as with the shuttle buses.

OUTDOOR ACTIVITIES

FLIGHTSEEING

A flightseeing tour of the park is one of the best ways to get a sense of the Alaska Range's size and scope. Flightseeing is also the best way to get close-up views of Mt. McKinley and its neighboring giants, and maybe even stand on a glacier, all without the hassle of days of hiking and lugging food and gear. Most Denali flightseeing is done out of Talkeetna, a small end-of-the-road town between Anchorage and Denali, and the operators will offer several tours, including a quick fly-by, a summit tour, a glacier landing. Something for everybody, although we suggest you take the longest, most detailed tour you can afford, so you don't go back home wishing you'd had a chance to see more.

GUIDED TOURS

If you're travelling here as an extension of your cruise, your cruise line will likely have a ranger-led tour planned. If not, you can take free ranger-guided discovery hikes and learn more about the park's natural and human history. Rangers lead daily hikes throughout summer. Inquire at the visitor center.

Privately operated, narrated bus tours are available through **Denali Park Resorts** (☎ 907/276–7234 or 800/276–7234 ⊕ www.denaliparkresorts. com).

HIKING TERRAIN AND BACKCOUNTRY TRAVEL

You can have one of North America's premier hiking and wilderness experiences in Denali with the proper planning: know your goals; consult park staff before setting out to learn Leave No Trace and bear etiquette; carry proper clothing, food, and water; and don't try to cover too much ground in too short a time. You won't walk through the park at the speed you're used to hiking most places in the Lower 48. Besides the distractions of drop-dead gorgeous landscape, the territory is simply rougher and more varied here than most places down South. Plus it's a good idea to plan for animal delays here.

NATURE TRAILS AND SHORT WALKS

You don't need to go off-trail to have a great experience. The entrance area has more than a half-dozen forest and tundra trails. These range from easy to challenging, so there's something suitable for all ages and hiking abilities. Some, like the **Taiga Loop Trail** and **McKinley Station Loop Trail,** are less than 1.5 mi; others, like the **Rock Creek Trail** and **Triple Lakes Trail,** are several miles round-trip, with an altitude gain of hundreds of feet. Along these paths you may see beavers working on their lodges in Horseshoe Lake; red squirrels chattering in trees; red foxes hunting for rodents; sheep grazing on tundra; golden eagles gliding over alpine ridges; and moose feeding on willow.

The **Savage River Trail,** farthest from the park entrance and as far as private vehicles are allowed, offers a 1.75-mi round-trip hike along a raging river and under rocky cliffs. Be on the lookout for caribou, Dall sheep, foxes, and marmots.

The only relatively long, marked trail for hiking in the park, **Mt. Healy Overlook Trail,** is accessible from the entrance area; it gains 1,700 feet in 2.5 mi and takes about four hours round-trip, with outstanding views of the Nenana River below and the Alaska Range, including the upper slopes of Mt. McKinley.

KAYAKING AND RAFTING

Several privately owned raft and tour companies operate along the Parks Highway near the entrance to Denali, and they schedule daily rafting, both in the fairly placid areas on the Nenana and through the 10-mi-long Nenana River canyon, which has stretches of Class IV–V rapids—enough to make you think you're on a very wet roller coaster. The Nenana is Alaska's most accessible white water, and if you don't mind getting a little chilly, a river trip is not just a lot of fun, it's a fantastic way to see a different side of the landscape.

Alaska Raft Adventures books 1½- to 2-hour-long white-water and scenic raft trips along Nenana River through **Denali Park Resorts** (☎ 907/276–7234 or 800/276–7234 ⊕ *www.denaliparkresorts.com*). **Whitewater trips give you two options: do the work and paddle yourself, or sit back and let a guide do the work.**

GLACIER BAY NATIONAL PARK AND PRESERVE

Fodor's Choice ★ **Glacier Bay National Park and Preserve.** Cruising Glacier Bay is like revisiting the Little Ice Age—it's one of the few places in the world where you can approach such a variety of massive tidewater glaciers. You can witness a spectacular process called "calving," foreshadowed by a cannon-blast-like sound, in which bergs the size of 10-story office buildings come crashing down from the side of a glacier. Each cannon blast signifies another step in the glacier's steady retreat. The calving iceberg sends tons of water and spray skyward, propelling mini–tidal waves outward from the point of impact. Johns Hopkins Glacier calves so often and with such volume that large cruise ships can seldom come within 2 mi of its face.

Although the Tlingit have lived in the area for 10,000 years, the bay was first popularized by naturalist John Muir, who visited in 1879. Just 100 years before, the bay had been completely choked with ice. By 1916, though, the ice had retreated 65 mi—the most rapid glacial retreat ever recorded. To preserve its clues to the world's geological history, Glacier Bay was declared a national monument in 1925, and became a national park in 1980. Today Muir's namesake glacier, like others in the park, continues to retreat dramatically. Its terminus is now scores of miles farther up the bay from the small cabin he built at its face during his time there.

Your experience in Glacier Bay will depend partly on the size of your ship. Large cruise ships tend to stay midchannel, while small yachtlike ships spend more time closer to shore. Smaller ships give you a better view of the calving ice and wildlife, but on a big ship you can get a loftier perspective. Both come within ¼ mi of the glaciers themselves.

For more info, check out: ⊕ *www.nps.gov/glba*.

GLACIER RUNDOWN

The most frequently viewed glaciers are in the west arm of Glacier Bay. Ships linger in front of five glaciers, giving you ample time to admire their stunning and ever-changing faces. First, most ships stop briefly at Reid Glacier, which flows down from the Brady Icefield, before

Glacier Bay National Park and Preserve

KEY

〜 *Historical extent*
1794 *of glaciation*

ALASKA

BRITISH
COLUMBIA

CANADA
UNITED STATES

Muir Glacier

Riggs Glacier

Casement Glacier

TO MT. FAIRWEATHER
1907

Tarr Inlet

Reid Glacier

Carroll Glacier

Reid Inlet

1976
1972
1948

1960

1966

1966
1892

Russell Island

1892

1880

Wachusett

1966

1929

1949

1929

1907

East Arm Muir Inlet

Adams Inlet

West Arm

Queen Inlet

1892

1907

Tidal Inlet

1892

1907

Beartrack River

TO JOHNS HOPKINS
GLACIER

Lamplugh Glacier

1907

1892

1879

1907

1892

1907

1919

1860

1860

1857

1845

Glacier Bay ◆

DRAKE ISLAND

Geikie Inlet

1966

1892

WILLOUGHBY ISLAND

Beartrack Cove

BEARDSLEE ISLANDS

**Visitor Center/
Glacier Bay Lodge**

Brady Icefield

Wood Lake

Berg Bay

Dundas River

Bartlett Cove

1794

Bartlett Cove

Airport ✝

Brady Glacier

1794

1961

Gustavus

PLEASANT ISLAND

1750-80

Palma Bay

Dixon Harbor

Dundas Bay

Taylor Bay

North Passage

LEMESURIER ISLAND

Icy Strait

Graves Bay

INIAN ISLANDS

South Passage

0 — 10 mile

0 — 10 kilometer

Cross Sound

CHICHAGOF ISLAND

Don your jacket and head to the outside deck for spectacular views of Glacier Bay.

continuing on to Lamplugh Glacier—one of the bluest in the park—at the mouth of Johns Hopkins Inlet. Next, at the end of the inlet, is the massive Johns Hopkins Glacier, where you're likely to see a continuous shower of calving ice. (Sometimes there are so many icebergs in the inlet that ships must avoid the area. And access isn't allowed early in the season because it's where sea lions give birth to their babies.) Farther north, near the end of the western arm, is Margerie Glacier, which is also quite active. Adjacent is Grand Pacific Glacier, the largest glacier in the park.

Competition for entry permits into Glacier Bay is fierce. To protect the humpback whale, which feeds here in summer, the Park Service limits the number of ships that can call. Check your cruise brochure to make sure Glacier Bay is included in your sailing. Most ships that do visit spend at least one full day exploring the park. There are no shore excursions or landings in the bay—the steep-sided and heavily forested fjords aren't conducive to pedestrian exploration—but a Park Service naturalist boards every cruise ship.

HAINES

Haines encompasses an area that has been occupied by Tlingit peoples for centuries on the collar of the Chilkat Peninsula, a narrow strip of land that divides the Chilkat and Chilkoot inlets. Missionary S. Hall Young and famed naturalist John Muir were intent on establishing a Presbyterian mission in the area, and, with the blessing of local chiefs, they chose the site that later became Haines. It's hard to imagine a more beautiful setting—a heavily wooded peninsula with magnificent views of Portage Cove and the snowy Coast Range.

The downtown area feels as small as a postage stamp, and the town exudes a down-home friendliness. Haines's popularity as a stop for cruise ships both large and small is growing, especially as travelers look for an alternative to the crowds in Skagway. Visitors should be prepared for a relative lack of souvenir and T-shirt shops compared to other ports. Local weather is drier than in much of Southeast Alaska.

COMING ASHORE

SHORE EXCURSIONS

Chilkat Bald Eagle Preserve Float Trip. A raft trip through the Chilkat Bald Eagle Preserve introduces you to some eagles and—if you're lucky—a moose or a bear. The trip starts with a 30-minute guided van tour through Chilkat Valley to the heart of the preserve. Then you board rafts for a gentle, scenic float trip down the Chilkat River (no children under age seven). In October the trees are filled with some 3,000 bald eagles. ⊙ *4 hrs* 🚐 *$199.*

Chilkoot Bicycle Adventure. This easy half-day drive-and-bike tour starts with a van ride to Lutak Inlet. From there you can hop on a mountain bike for a 7- to 8-mi jaunt along this picturesque bay, which boasts a backdrop of mountains and glaciers. Eagles are a common sight, and brown bears an occasional one. ⊙ *3 hrs* 🚐 *$90.*

Chilkat Rain Forest Nature Hike. Explore a lush Alaskan rain forest on this 3-mi guided hike along Chilkoot Inlet, which focuses on the area's plant, animal, and bird life. The path is easy and well maintained, and spotting scopes are provided to watch for bald eagles, mountain goats, and other wildlife along the way. ⊙ *3½–4 hrs* 🚐 *$69–$84.*

Deluxe Haines Highlights. This bus tour includes a visit to Ft. Seward and the Sheldon Museum or American Bald Eagle Foundation wildlife educational center before venturing out to Letnikof Cove (on the Chilkat Peninsula) for a view across the mighty Chilkat River to Rainbow Glacier and a tour of a working fish-processing facility and smokery. ⊙ *3 hrs* 🚐 *$69.*

Offbeat Haines. Embark on a small-group adventure to visit three of Haines's most unusual and out-of-the-way attractions. The trip includes time at the delightfully eclectic Hammer Museum (the only museum in the world devoted to

HAINES BEST BETS

■ **Float the Chilkat River.** Running through one of Alaska's most stunning mountain ranges, the mellow Chilkat caters more to sightseers than to thrill-seekers.

■ **Pound the pavement.** Haines has a delightfully funky vibe welcoming to visitors; Mountain Market, Sheldon Bookstore, and the public library are favorite local hangouts.

■ **Hit the road.** The Haines Highway is one of the nation's most beautiful roads. Whether you enlist a local tour operator or rent a car, a drive up this highway is an unforgettable experience.

rabilia, such as Jack Dalton's sawed-off shotgun, in the 1880s, and started an exhibit of his finds in 1925. Today, his collection is the core of the museum's impressive array of artifacts, including Chilkat Blankets, a model of a Tlingit tribal house, and the original lens from the Eldred Rock lighthouse just south of Haines on the Lynn Canal. Repatriated Bear Clan items such as an 18th-century carved ceremonial Murrelet Hat are on display thanks to loans to the museum. ⊠ *11 Main St.* ☎ *907/766–2366* ⊕ *www.sheldonmuseum.org* 🎫 *$3* 🕙 *Mid-May–mid-Sept., weekdays 10–4, weekends 1–4; mid-Sept.–mid-May, Mon.–Sat. 1–4.*

OUTDOOR ACTIVITIES

FodorsChoice **Alaska Nature Tours** (☎ *907/766–2876* ⊕ *www.alaskanaturetours.net*)
★ conducts bird-watching and natural-history tours through the Alaska Chilkat Bald Eagle Preserve, operates brown bear watching excursions in July and August, and leads hiking treks in summer throughout the summer.

Battery Point Trail is a fairly level path that hugs the shoreline for 2 mi, providing fine views across Lynn Canal. The trail begins a mile east of town, and a campsite can be found at Kelgaya Point near the end. For other hikes, pick up a copy of "Haines Is for Hikers" at the Haines Convention and Visitors Bureau.

SHOPPING

Tresham Gregg's **Sea Wolf Gallery** (⊠ *Ft. Seward* ☎ *907/766–2540* ⊕ *www.tresham.com*) sells wood carvings, silver jewelry, prints, and T-shirts with his native-inspired designs. Haines's most charming gallery, the **Wild Iris Gallery** (⊠ *Portage St.* ☎ *907/766–2300*) displays attractive jewelry, prints, and fashion wear created by owner Fred Shields and his daughter Melina. Other local artists are also represented. It's just up from the cruise-ship dock, and its summer gardens alone are worth the visit.

WHERE TO EAT

$–$$ ✕ **Mosey's.** The fare at this Mexican restaurant just one block up from
MEXICAN the cruise-ship dock is on the spicy side—owner Martha Stewart (yes, that's her real name) travels to New Mexico each year and brings back bushels of roasted green chilies, the signature ingredient. If your taste buds can handle the kick, you'll be rewarded: the food is bursting with fresh flavors, and the atmosphere is a cheery south-of-the-border alternative to the rest of Haines's more mainstream offerings. Order lunch at the counter or sit down for table service in the evening. ⊠ *Soap Suds Alley, Ft. Seward* ☎ *907/766–2320* ▭ *MC, V.*

¢–$ ✕ **Mountain Market.** Meet the locals over espresso, brewed from fresh-
AMERICAN roasted beans, and a fresh-baked pastry at this busy corner natural-foods store, deli, café, wine-and-spirits shop, de facto meeting hall, and hitching post—the only thing missing is Wi-Fi connectivity. But

Mountain Market is great for lunchtime sandwiches, wraps, soups, and salads. Friday is pizza day, but come early, since it's often gone by early afternoon. ⊠ *3rd Ave. and Haines Hwy.* ☎ *907/766–3340* ▭ *AE, D, MC, V.*

WHERE TO DRINK

Locals might rule the pool tables at **Fogcutter Bar** (⊠ *122 Main St.* ☎ *907/ 766–2555*), but they always appreciate a little friendly competition. Like many bars in Southeast Alaska, the Fogcutter sells drink tokens that patrons often purchase for their friends; you'll notice folks sitting at the bar with a small stack of these tokens next to their beverage. The Fogcutter's embossed metal tokens are among the Southeast's most ornate. Purchase one for a keepsake—or for later use. **Haines Brewing Company** (⊠ *108 Whitefang Way* ☎ *907/766–3823*), a microbrewery among the Dalton City buildings at the fairgrounds, sells beer by the sample glass, pint glass, or liter growlers to go.

HOMER

It's a shame that of the hundreds of thousands of cruise passengers who visit Alaska each year only a very few get to see Homer. Its scenic setting on Kachemak Bay, surrounded by mountains, spruce forest, and glaciers, makes Homer unique even in Alaska. Homer lies at the base of a 4-mi-long sandy spit that juts into Kachemak Bay and provides beautiful bay views. Founded just before the turn of the 20th century as a gold-prospecting camp, this community was later used as a coal-mining headquarters. Today Homer is a funky fishing port famous for its halibut and salmon fishing, and serves as a base for bear-viewing flights. It's also one of the top arts communities in Alaska, with several first-rate galleries, a theater company, and an active music-and-dance scene.

COMING ASHORE

SHORE EXCURSIONS

Gull Island, Seldovia, or Halibut Fishing. Since Homer isn't a common port and the town itself offers so much to explore, shore-excursion offerings aren't as predictable here as in other ports of call. Your ship may offer boat charters to Gull Island (a nearby island chock-full of cacophonous seagulls and other seabirds) or Seldovia (a small, scenic town with quality art galleries across Katchemak Bay). Halibut fishing is also huge here, and if you take one fishing-charter excursion during your trip this would be the place to do it. ☉ *Durations vary* ▱ *Prices vary.*

TRANSPORTATION AND TOURS

FROM THE PIER

Ships and Alaska Marine Highway ferries dock at the end of the Homer Spit, where you can find charters, restaurants, and shops. The routine for cruise lines calling in Homer is to provide a shuttle from the Spit to downtown.

VISITOR INFORMATION

In the Homer Chamber of Commerce's **Visitor Information Center,** brochures from local businesses and attractions fill racks. ⊠ *201 Sterling Hwy.* ☎ *907/235–7740* ⊕ *www.homeralaska.org* ☉ *Memorial Day– Labor Day, weekdays 9–7, weekends 10–6.*

INTERNET   Check your e-mail for free at the **Homer Public Library** (⊠ *500 Hazel Ave.* ☎ *907/235–3180* ⊕ *library.ci.homer.ak.us*), or check out a list of additional Internet spots at the Visitor Information Center.

EXPLORING HOMER

Ⓒ   Protruding into Kachemak Bay, **Homer Spit** provides a sandy focal point
Fodor'sChoice   for visitors and locals. A paved path stretches most of the 4 mi and is
★   great for biking or walking. A commercial-fishing-boat harbor at the end of the path has restaurants, hotels, charter-fishing businesses, sea-kayaking outfitters, art galleries, and on-the-beach camping spots. Fly a kite, walk the beaches, drop a line in the Fishing Hole, or just wander through the shops looking for something interesting; this is one of Alaska's favorite summertime destinations.

Ⓒ   **Islands and Ocean Center** provides a wonderful introduction to the Alaska
★   Maritime National Wildlife Refuge. The refuge covers some 3.5 million acres spread across some 2,500 Alaskan islands, from Prince of Wales Island in the south to Barrow in the north. Opened in 2003, this 37,000-square-foot facility with towering windows facing Kachemak Bay is a must-see for anyone interested in wild places—and it's free! A film takes visitors along on a voyage of the Fish and Wildlife Service's research ship, the MV *Tiglax*. Interactive exhibits detail the birds and marine mammals of the refuge (the largest seabird refuge in America), and one room even re-creates the noisy sounds and pungent smells of a bird rookery. In summer, guided bird-watching treks and beach walks are offered. ⊠ *95 Sterling Hwy.* ☎ *907/235–6961* ⊕ *www. islandsandocean.org* ☑ *Free* ☉ *Memorial Day–Labor Day, daily 9–6; Labor Day–Sept. 30, Tues.–Sat. 10–5; Oct.–May 1, Tues.–Sat. noon–5; May 2–Memorial Day, daily 10–5.*

Kachemak Bay abounds in wildlife. Shore excursions or local tour operators take you to bird rookeries in the bay or to gravel beaches for clam digging. Most charter-fishing trips include an opportunity to view whales, seals, sea otters, porpoises, and seabirds close up. The bay supports a large population of bald eagles, gulls, murres, puffins, and other birds.

Directly across Kachemak Bay from the end of the Homer Spit, **Halibut Cove** is a small community of people who make their living on the bay or by selling handicrafts. There are

> **HOMER BEST BETS**
>
> ■ **Charter a fishing boat.** Nothing beats wrestling a monster halibut out of the icy depths.
>
> ■ **People-watch on the Spit.** Homer is home to a thriving arts community, and makes for an interesting cultural mix.
>
> ■ **Cruise to a waterfront restaurant.** Crossing the bay to the Saltry Restaurant for a meal is another favorite experience.

Continued on page 230

MADE IN ALASKA

Intricate Aleut baskets, Athabascan birch-bark wonders, Inupiaq ivory carvings, and towering Tlingit totems are just some of the eye-opening crafts you'll encounter as you explore the 49th state. Alaska's native peoples—who live across 570,000 square miles of tundra, boreal forest, arctic plains, and coastal rain forest—are undeniably hardy, and their unique artistic traditions are just as resilient and enduring.

TIPS ON FINDING AN AUTHENTIC ITEM

1 The Federal Trade Commission has enacted strict regulations to combat the sale of falsely marketed goods; it's illegal for anything made by non-native Alaskans to be labeled as INDIAN, NATIVE AMERICAN, or ALASKA NATIVE.

2 Some authentic goods are marked by a silver hand symbol or are labeled as an AUTHENTIC NATIVE HANDICRAFT FROM ALASKA.

3 The Alaska State Council on the Arts, in Anchorage, is a great resource if you have additional questions or want to confirm a permit number. Call 907/269–6610 or 888/278–7424 in Alaska.

4 The MADE IN ALASKA label, often accompanied by an image of a polar bear with cub, simply denotes that the handicraft was made in the state.

5 Be sure to ask for written proof of authenticity with your purchase, as well as the artist's name. You can also request the artist's permit number, which may be available.

6 Materials should be legal. For example, only some feathers, such as ptarmigan and pheasant feathers, comply with the Migratory Bird Act. Only native artisans are permitted to carve new walrus ivory. The seller should be able to answer your questions about material and technique.

THE NATIVE PEOPLE OF ALASKA

There are many opportunities to see the making of traditional crafts in native environments, including the Southeast Alaska Indian Cultural Center in Sitka and Anchorage's Alaska Native Heritage Center.

After chatting with the artisans, pop into the gift shops to peruse the handmade items. Also check out prominent galleries and museum shops.

RUSSIA

Inupiaq

Athabascan

CANADA

Yup'ik, Cup'ik

Eyak, Tlingit, Haida, Tsimshian

Aleut, Alutiiq

NORTHWEST COAST INDIANS: TLINGIT, HAIDA & TSIMSHIAN

Scattered throughout Southeast Alaska's rain forests, these highly social tribes traditionally benefited from the region's mild climate and abundant salmon, which afforded them a rare luxury: leisure time. They put this time to good use by cultivating highly detailed crafts, including ceremonial masks, elaborate woven robes, and, most famously, totem poles.

(left) A wagging tongue at the Juneau-Douglas City Museum (right) A Tlingit totem reaches for the skies in Ketchikan

TOWERING TOTEM POLES

Throughout the Inside Passage's braided channels and forested islands, Native peoples use the wood of the abundant cedar trees to carve totem poles, which illustrate history, pay reverence, commemorate

a potlatch, or cast shame on a misbehaving person.

Every totem pole tells a story with a series of animal and human figures arranged vertically. Traditionally the totem poles of this area feature ravens, eagles, killer whales, wolves, bears, frogs, the mythic thunderbird, and the likenesses of ancestors.

K'alyaan Totem Pole

Carved in 1999, the K'alyaan totem pole is a tribute to the Tlingits who lost their lives in the 1804 Battle of Sitka between invading Russians and Tlingit warriors. Tommy Joseph, a venerated Tlingit artist from Sitka, and an apprentice spent three months carving the pole from a 35-ft western red cedar. It now stands at the very site of the skirmish, in Sitka National Historical Park.

Raven: Atop the pole sits the striking raven, the emblem of one of the two moieties (large multi-clan groups) of Tlingit culture.

Woodworm: The woodworm—a Tlingit clan symbol—is a wood-boring beetle that leaves a distinctive mark on timber.

Sockeye Salmon (above) and Dog/ Chum Salmon (below): These two symbols signify the contributions of the Sockeye and Dog Salmon Clans to the 1804 battle. They also illustrate the symbolic connection to the tribe's traditional food sources.

Beaver: Sporting a fearsome pair of front teeth, this beaver symbol cradles a child in its arms, signifying the strength of Tlingit family bonds.

Frog: This animal represents the Kik.-sádi Clan, which was very instrumental in organizing the Tlingit's revolt against the Russian trespassers. Here, the frog holds a raven helmet—a tribute to the Kik.sádi warrior who wore a similar headpiece into battle.

Tools and Materials

As do most modern carvers, Joseph used a steel adz to carve the cedar. Prior to European contact—and the accompanying introduction of metal tools—Tlingit artists carved with jade adzes. Totem poles are traditionally decorated with paint made from salmon-liver oil, charcoal, and iron and copper oxides.

ALEUT & ALUTIIQ

The Aleut inhabit the Alaska Peninsula and the windswept Aleutian Islands. Historically they lived and died by the sea, surviving on a diet of seals, sea lions, whales, and walruses, which they hunted in the tumultuous waters of the Gulf of Alaska and the Bering Sea. Hunters pursued their prey in *Sugpiaq*, kayaklike boats made of seal skin stretched over a driftwood frame.

WATERPROOF *KAMLEIKAS*
The Aleut prize seal intestine for its remarkable waterproof properties; they use it to create sturdy cloaks, shelter walls, and boat hulls. To make their famous cloaks, called *kamleikas*, intestine is washed, soaked in salt water, and arduously scraped clean. It is then stretched and dried before being stitched into hooded, waterproof pullovers.

FINE BASKETRY
Owing to the region's profusion of wild rye grass, Aleutian women are some of the planet's most skilled weavers, capable of creating baskets with more than 2,500 fibers per square inch. They also create hats, socks, mittens, and multipurpose mats. A long, sharpened thumbnail is their only tool.

ATHABASCANS

Inhabiting Alaska's rugged interior for 8,000 to 20,000 years, Athabascans followed a seasonally nomadic hunter-gatherer lifestyle, subsisting off of caribou, moose, bear, and snowshoe hare. They populate areas from the Brooks Range to Cook Inlet, a vast expanse that encompasses five significant rivers: the Tanana, the Kuskwin, the Copper, the Susitna, and the Yukon.

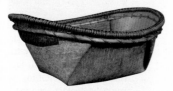

BIRCH BARK: WATERPROOF WONDER
Aside from annual salmon runs, the Athabascans had no access to marine mammals—or to the intestines that made for such effective boat hulls and garments. They turned to the region's birch, the bark of which was used to create canoes. Also common were birch-bark baskets and baby carriers.

FUNCTIONAL & ORNAMENTED PIECES
Much like that of the neighboring Eskimos, Athabascan craftwork traditionally served functional purposes. But tools, weapons, and clothing were often highly decorated with colorful embroidery and shells. Athabascans are especially well known for ornamenting their caribou-skin clothing with porcupine quills and animal hair—both of which were later replaced by imported western beads.

INUPIAQ, YUP'IK & CUP'IK

Residing in Alaska's remote northern and northwestern regions, these groups are often collectively known as Eskimos or Inupiaq. They winter in coastal villages, relying on migrating marine mammals for sustenance, and spend summers at inland fish amps. Ongoing artistic traditions include ceremonial mask carving, ivory carving (not to be confused with scrimshaw), sewn skin garments, basket weaving, and soapstone carvings.

Thanks to the sheer volume of ivory art in Alaska's marketplace, you're bound to find a piece of ivory that fits your fancy—regardless of whether you prefer traditional ivory carvings, scrimshaw, or a piece that blends both artistic traditions.

IVORY CARVING
While in Alaska, you'll likely see carved ivory pieces, scrimshaw, and some fake ivory carvings (generally plastic). Ivory carving has been an Eskimo art form for thousands of years. After harvesting ivory from migrating walrus herds in the Bering Sea, artisans age tusks for up to one year before shaping it with adzes and bow drills.

KEEP IN MIND
The Marine Mammal Protection Act states that only native peoples are allowed to harvest fresh walrus ivory, which is legal to buy after it's been carved by a native person. How can you tell if a piece is real and made by a native artisan? Real ivory is likely to be pricey; be suspect of anything too cheaply priced. It should also be hard (plastic will be softer) and cool to the touch. Keep an eye out for mastery of carving technique, and be sure to ask questions when you've found a piece you're interested in buying.

WHAT IS SCRIMSHAW?
The invention of scrimshaw is attributed to 18th-century American whalers who etched the surfaces of whale bone and scrap ivory. The etchings were filled with ink, bringing the designs into stark relief.

More recently the line between traditional Eskimo ivory carving and scrimshaw has become somewhat blurred, with many native artisans incorporating both techniques.

TIPS
Ivory carving is a highly specialized native craft that is closely regulated. As it is a by-product of subsistence hunting, all meat and skin from a walrus hunt is used.

Ivory from extinct mammoths and mastodons (usually found buried underground or washed up on beaches) is also legal to buy in Alaska; many native groups keep large stores of it, as well as antique walrus tusk, for craft purposes. Many of the older pieces have a caramelized color.

several art galleries and a restaurant that serves local seafood. The cove itself is lovely, especially during salmon runs, when fish leap and splash in the clear water.

Central Charter Booking Agency (☎ *907/235–7847 or 800/478–7847* ⊕ *www.centralcharter.com*) runs frequent boats to the cove from Homer.

☺ For an outstanding introduction to Homer's history—both human and
★ natural—visit the **Pratt Museum**, where you can see a saltwater aquarium and exhibits on pioneers, flora and fauna, Native Alaskans, and the 1989 *Exxon Valdez* oil spill. Spy on wildlife with robotic video cameras set up on a seabird rookery and at the McNeil River Bear Sanctuary. In 2005 the Pratt was presented with the National Award for Museum Service, the highest national honor for museums. Outside are a wild-flower garden and a short nature trail. The museum also leads 1½-hour walking tours of the harbor for $5 per person several times a week. ⊠ *Bartlett St. off Pioneer Ave.* ☎ *907/235–8635* ⊕ *www.prattmuseum. org* 🖙 *$6* ⊙ *Mid-May–mid-Sept., daily 10–6.*

Seldovia, isolated across the bay from Homer, retains the charm of an earlier Alaska. The town's Russian heritage is evident in its onion-dome church and its name, derived from a Russian place-name meaning "herring bay." You can find excellent fishing, whether you drop your line into the deep waters of Kachemak Bay or cast into the surf for silver salmon on the shore of Outside Beach, near town. Self-guided hiking and berry picking in late July are other options.

OUTDOOR ACTIVITIES

BEAR-WATCHING
Homer is a favorite departure point for viewing Alaska's famous brown bears in Katmai National Park. **Emerald Air Service** (☎ *907/235–4160* or 877/235–9600 ⊕ *www.emeraldairservice.com*) is one of several companies offering all-day and custom photography trips starting around $625 per person. **Hallo Bay Wilderness** (☎ *907/235–2237 or 888/535–2237* ⊕ *www.hallobay.com*) offers guided close-range viewing without the crowds. Day trips are offered, but it's the two- to seven-day stays at this comfortable coastal location that provide the ultimate in world-class bear- and wildlife-viewing.

FISHING
Homer is both a major commercial fishing port (especially for halibut) and a very popular destination for sport anglers in search of giant halibut or feisty king and silver salmon. Quite a few companies offer charter fishing in summer, for around $225 per person per day (including bait and tackle). **Central Charters** (⊠ *4241 Homer Spit Rd.* ☎ *907/235–7847* ⊕ *www.centralcharter.com*) arranges fishing and bay tours.

Homer Ocean Charters (☎ *800/426–6212* ⊕ *www.homerocean.com*) on the spit sets up fishing and sightseeing trips, as well as sea-kayaking and water-taxi services and remote-cabin rentals. Some of its most popular cruises go to the **Rookery Restaurant** at Otter Cove Resort. Also try

Inlet Charters (☎ *800/770–6216* ⊕ *www.halibutcharters.com*) for fishing charters, water-taxi services, sea-kayaking, and wildlife cruises.

★ **SEA KAYAKING**

Several local companies offer guided sea-kayaking trips to protected coves within Kachemak Bay State Park and nearby islands. **True North Kayak Adventures** (☎ *907/235–0708* ⊕ *www.truenorthkayak.com*) has a range of such adventures, including a six-hour paddle to Elephant Rock for $130 and an all-day boat and kayak trip to Yukon Island for $150 (both trips include round-trip water taxi to the island base camp, guide, all kayak equipment, and bakery lunch).

SHOPPING

4

The **Bunnell Street Gallery** (⊠ *106 W. Bunnell St. on corner of Main St.* ☎ *907/235–2662* ⊕ *www.bunnellstreetgallery.org*) displays innovative contemporary art, all of it produced in Alaska. The gallery, which occupies the first floor of a historic trading post, also hosts workshops, lectures, musical performances, and other community events. **Ptarmigan Arts** (⊠ *471 E. Pioneer Ave.* ☎ *907/235–5345*) is a cooperative gallery with photographs, paintings, pottery, jewelry, woodworking, and other pieces by local artisans.

WHERE TO EAT

$$$–$$$$ ✕ **Homestead Restaurant.** This former log roadhouse 8 mi from town
CONTINENTAL is a favorite of locals who appreciate artfully presented food served
Fodor'sChoice amid contemporary art. The Homestead specializes in seasonal fish
★ and shellfish prepared with garlic, citrus fruits, or spicy ethnic sauces, as well as steak, rack of lamb, and prime rib. Epic views of the bay, mountains, and hanging glaciers are yours for the looking. Homestead has an extensive wine list and locally brewed beer on tap. ⊠ *Mi 8.2, E. End Rd.* ☎ *Box 3041, Homer 99603* ☎ *907/235–8723* ⊕ *www. homesteadrestaurant.net* ⊟ *AE, MC, V* ☉ *Closed Nov.–Mar. 8.*

¢ ✕ **Two Sisters Bakery.** This very popular café is just a short walk from
CAFÉ both Bishops Beach and the Islands and Ocean Center. In addition to fresh breads and pastries, Two Sisters specializes in deliciously healthful lunches, such as vegetarian focaccia sandwiches, homemade soups, quiche, and salads. Sit on the wraparound porch on a summer afternoon, or take your espresso and scone down to the beach to watch the waves roll in. ⊠ *233 E. Bunnell Ave.* ☎ *907/235–2280* ⊕ *www. twosistersbakery.net* ⊟ *MC, V.*

WHERE TO DRINK

★ Dance to lively bands on weekends at **Alice's Champagne Palace** (⊠ *195 E. Pioneer Ave.* ☎ *907/235–6909*). The bar attracts nationally known singer-songwriters on a regular basis.

The spit's infamous **Salty Dawg Saloon** (⊠ *4380 Homer Spit Rd.* ☎ *907/ 235–6718*) is a tumbledown lighthouse of sorts, sure to be frequented by a carousing fisherman or two, along with half the tourists in town.

HUBBARD GLACIER

The 24-million-acre international wilderness that embraces Hubbard can only be described with superlatives. For example, the massive St. Elias and Fairweather ranges form the largest nonpolar glaciated mountain system in the world. British Columbia's only winter range for Dall sheep is here, and the region supports a population of both grizzlies and rare, silver-blue "glacier" bears.

This glacier is famous for "surging"—moving forward quickly. Most glaciers slide an inch or two a day. However, in 1986, the Hubbard Glacier made headlines around the world by advancing to the mouth of Russell Fjord, damming it, and creating a huge lake that lasted five months. By September it was advancing 30 meters a day. This was an event without precedent in recent geologic history, and it was mapped by the Landsat 5 satellite from 6 mi above Earth. Seals, sea lions, and porpoises were trapped behind the dam, and efforts were mounted to relocate them. "Russell Lake" eventually reached a level almost 90 feet higher than the level of Disenchantment Bay. When the dam broke on October 8, it produced an enormous rush of fresh water—something like a tidal wave in reverse.

The glacier surged again in summer 2002, creating another dam in the space of a month—by coincidence, just about the time glaciologists convened in Yakutat for an international symposium on fast glacier flow. Nervous Yakutat residents continue to lobby the government to build a channel to make sure the glacier cannot form "Russell Lake" again. They fear this would change river courses, endanger important fisheries, and inundate the Yakutat Airport, the chief transportation link with the rest of Alaska.

EXPLORING HUBBARD GLACIER

The Hubbard Glacier is an icy tongue with its root on Mt. Logan in Yukon Territory. The vast Hubbard ice field originates near 15,300-foot Mt. Hubbard and flows 76 mi to lick the sea at Yakutat and Disenchantment bays. With its 400-foot snout, Hubbard Glacier is also a prime pausing point for cruise ships. Hubbard calves great numbers of icebergs, making it difficult to get close. There are no roads to the glacier. Unless you are a seasoned mountaineer with ice experience, Hubbard Glacier is no shore excursion.

JUNEAU

Juneau, Alaska's capital and third-largest city, is on the North American mainland but can't be reached by road. The city owes its origins to two colorful sourdoughs (Alaskan pioneers)—Joe Juneau and Richard Harris—and to a Tlingit chief named Kowee, who led the two men to rich reserves of gold at Snow Slide Gulch, the drainage of Gold Creek around which the town was eventually built. That was in 1880, and shortly thereafter a modest stampede resulted in the formation of a mining camp, which quickly grew to become the Alaska district government capital in 1906. The city may well have continued under its original appellation—Harrisburg, after Richard Harris—were it not for Joe Juneau's political jockeying at a miner's meeting in 1881.

For some 60 years after Juneau's founding gold was the mainstay of the economy. In its heyday the AJ (for Alaska Juneau) Gold Mine was the biggest low-grade ore mine in the world. It was not until World War II, when the government decided it needed Juneau's manpower for the war effort, that the AJ and other mines in the area ceased operations. After the war, mining failed to start up again, and government became the city's principal employer. Juneau's mines leave a rich legacy, though; the AJ Gold Mine alone produced more than $80 million in gold.

Perhaps because of its colorful history, Juneau is full of contrasts. Its dramatic hillside location and historic downtown buildings provide a frontier feeling, but the city's cosmopolitan nature comes through in fine museums, noteworthy restaurants, and a literate and outdoorsy populace. Here you can enjoy the Mt. Roberts Tramway, plenty of densely forested wilderness areas, quiet bays for sea kayaking, and even the famous drive-up Mendenhall Glacier.

COMING ASHORE

SHORE EXCURSIONS
ADVENTURE
Alpine Zipline & Rain-forest Eco-Tour. Get set to fly through the trees of a scenic alpine rain forest on this accredited eco-adventure. Guides lead you from tree to tree until you reach a platform where you are greeted with spruce tea and a local snack. On the final zip, your landing spot is a uniquely designed tree house. Your guides will point out interesting sights in the rain forest during the walk back to the lodge. ⊙ 3½ hrs 🖃 $140.

Dog Sled Summer Camp. Learn about Alaska's official state sport, dog mushing, and see an exact replica of an Iditarod Race checkpoint. Then, climb aboard a wheeled sled and relax as your highly trained husky team whisks you along the 1.5-mi trail through the scenic landscape. Kids love meeting and petting the adorable camp puppies. Minimum age is five. ⊙ 2½ hrs 🖃 $159.

Exploring Glaciers by Helicopter and Dog Sled. Fly deep into the Juneau Icefield by helicopter on this high-adventure excursion. A guide greets you when you land, explains dogsledding, then takes you on a sled ride across the snow-covered glacier. Return to Juneau by helicopter, with additional flightseeing en route. ⊙ 3 hrs 🖃 $549–$579.

Mendenhall River Rafting. Suit up in rubber rain boots, protective clothing, and life jackets at Mendenhall Lake before your professional guide takes you down the Mendenhall River through alternating stretches of calm water and gentle rapids. Children love this one (the minimum age is six). ⊙ 3½ hrs 🖃 $129.

Photo Safari by Land and Sea. A professional photographer guides you to Juneau "photo hot spots," while sharing picture-taking tips and techniques. The first part of the tour takes place on land, and includes Mendenhall Glacier and the colorful downtown area. Next you board a covered exploration vessel for a journey through the waterways of Stephen's Passage to photograph marine wildlife. Your photographer guide will help you take full advantage of the conditions and opportunities of the day. ☉ 4½–5 hrs ▦ $199.

Pilot's Choice Helicopter Flightseeing. One of Alaska's most popular helicopter tours includes a landing on the Juneau Icefield for a walk on a glacier. Boots and rain gear are provided. ☉ 3–4 hrs ▦ $429.

Tram and Guided Alpine Walk. You start with a short tour of downtown Juneau, then ride up the Mt. Roberts Tramway on this very popular trip. Once you reach the top—1,800 feet over the city—a guide takes you through pristine rain forest and alpine meadows. The hike is ½ mi over gravel and boardwalk trails, and is conducted in all weather conditions. Sturdy, comfortable walking shoes and warm, waterproof clothing are advised. If you'd rather relax than hike, the tram complex has lots of shops and a restaurant called the Timberline Bar & Grill. You can return via the tram at any time. ☉ 2½ hrs ▦ $74.

Whale Watching & Wildlife Quest. After a short motor-coach ride to scenic Auke Bay, board a catamaran specially designed for wildlife-viewing. An onboard naturalist explains the habits and habitat of the wildlife you may encounter, which include humpback and killer whales, sea lions, harbor seals, porpoises, bald eagles, blacktail deer and, occasionally, bears. Wildlife is so abundant in this area that you're guaranteed to see a whale—and if you don't, you'll receive a $100 cash refund as you disembark. Don't anticipate a refund, though. Whales have been sighted on every tour for the past 14 years. ☉ 3 hrs ▦ $149.

SCENIC

Gold Mine Tour and Gold Panning. Don a hard hat and follow a former miner underground for a three-hour tour of the historic A.J. Gold Mine south of Juneau. You're guaranteed to "strike it rich" during the gold-panning demonstration. Approximately 45 minutes of the tour is spent inside the old tunnels. Tours depart from downtown by bus. This trip is highly recommended for an authentic look into Juneau's rich mining history. ☉ 1½ hrs ▦ $55.

Grand Tour of Juneau. Take this bus excursion to see Mendenhall Glacier, spawning salmon at the Macaulay Salmon Hatchery, and the Glacier Gardens rain forest. ☉ 5 hrs ▦ $99.

JUNEAU BEST BETS

■ **Walk South Franklin Street.** Juneau's historic downtown still retains much of its hardscrabble mining feel. While away hours in the saloons and shops of this charming district.

■ **Ride the Mt. Roberts Tram.** On Juneau's favorite attraction, enjoy panoramic views of the area's stunning scenery from 1,800 feet above town.

■ **Marvel at the Mendenhall Glacier.** With an otherworldly blue hue and a visitor center that answers all your glacier questions, Alaska's most accessible—and most popular—glacier is a must-see.

Best Shore Excursions for Kids

Juneau: For a day of family together-ness, the Gold Creek Salmon Bake hits the spot. After an all-you-can-eat buffet lunch of barbecued fresh Alaska salmon (there's chicken and ribs for picky eaters), baked beans, corn bread, and blueberry cake, the kids can roast marshmallows over the open fire and explore the abandoned Wagner Mine. If you're lucky, you'll spot salmon spawning in the clear water beneath the Salmon Creek waterfall.

Ketchikan: One of the cheesiest, yet most kid-pleasing tastes of old-time woodsman skills is the Great Alaskan Lumberjack Show. All summer long this hour-long contest demonstrates

such authentic "sports" as sawing, ax throwing, chopping, and a log-rolling duel. There's even a speed climb up a 50-foot tree. At 50 Main Street, all the fun's within walking distance of the cruise-ship pier.

Skagway: Spend the day in real Alaskan wilderness. Get a map at the Convention and Visitors Bureau and take the entire family on the inexpensive city bus to 23rd Avenue, where a 10-minute walk on a dirt road leads to the Gold Rush Cemetery. Let the kids discover where the town's villain Soapy Smith and its hero Frank Reid are buried, and then continue along the trail a quarter mile to Reid Falls.

4

TASTES OF ALASKA
Floatplane Ride and Taku Glacier Lodge Salmon Bake. Fly over the Juneau Icefield to rustic Taku Glacier Lodge, where you can dine on outstanding barbecued salmon. Hole-in-the-Wall Glacier is directly across the inlet from the lodge. Nature trails wind through the surrounding country, where black bears and bald eagles are frequently sighted. Afterward, explore the virgin rain forest or relax in the lodge. This tour consistently gets rave reviews. ⊙ *3½ hrs* ▭ *$299.*

Gold Creek Salmon Bake. Alaska wild salmon barbecued over an open fire is included at this all-you-can-eat outdoor meal. After dining you can walk in the woods, explore the abandoned Wagner mine, and return to your ship at your leisure. ⊙ *1½–2 hrs* ▭ *$44.*

TRANSPORTATION AND TOURS
FROM THE PIER
Most cruise ships dock on the south edge of town between the **Marine Park** and the **A.J. Dock.** Several ships can tie up at once; others occasionally anchor in the harbor. Juneau's downtown shops are a pleasant walk from the docks. A shuttle bus ($2 all day) runs from the A.J. Dock to town whenever ships are in port.

CITY TOURS
Juneau Trolley Car Company (☎ *907/586–7433 or 877/774–8687 ⊕ www. juneautrolley.com*) conducts narrated tours, stopping at 13 of Juneau's historic and shopping attractions. An all-day pass is $19. **Mighty Great Trips** (☎ *907/789–5460 ⊕ www.mightygreattrips.com*) leads bus tours that include a visit to Mendenhall Glacier. The **Juneau Steamboat Company** (☎ *907/723–0372 ⊕ www.juneausteamboat.com*) offers one-hour scenic tours of Gastineau Channel aboard an authentic wood-fired

steam launch, similar to those used around Juneau in the late 1800s and early 1900s. Tours come with entertaining narration that focuses on the historic mines of the Juneau area.

VISITOR INFORMATION

Pick up maps, bus schedules, charter-fishing information, and tour brochures at the small kiosks on the pier at Marine Park and in the cruise-ship terminal on South Franklin Street. Both are staffed when ships are in port.

The **Centennial Hall Visitor Center** has details on local attractions and nature trails. ⊠ *101 Egan Dr.* ☎ *907/586–2201 or 888/581–2201* ⊕ *www. traveljuneau.com* ☉ *May–Sept., weekdays 8:30–5, weekends 9–5.*

INTERNET Check your e-mail at **Universe Cyber Lounge** (⊠ *109 S. Franklin St.* ☎ *907/463–4330).*

EXPLORING JUNEAU

Downtown Juneau is compact enough that most of its main attractions are within walking distance of one another. Note, however, that the city is very hilly, so your legs will get a real workout. Look for the 20 signs around downtown that detail Juneau's fascinating history.

TOP ATTRACTIONS

❷ **Alaska State Museum.** This is one of Alaska's finest museums. Those interested in native cultures will enjoy examining the 38-foot walrus-hide *umiak* (an open, skin-covered Inupiaq boat). Natural-history exhibits include preserved brown bears and a two-story-high eagle nesting tree. Russian-American and gold-rush displays and contemporary art complete the collection. ■TIP➔ Be sure to visit the cramped gift shop with its extraordinary selection of native art, including baskets, carvings, and masks. ⊠ *395 Whittier St.* ☎ *907/465–2901* ⊕ *www.museums.state. ak.us* ⊠ *$5* ☉ *Mid-May–mid-Sept., daily 8:30–5:30; mid-Sept.–mid-May, Tues.–Sat. 10–4.*

❽ **Mt. Roberts Tramway.** One of Southeast Alaska's most popular tourist attractions, this tram whisks you from the cruise terminal 1,800 feet up the side of Mt. Roberts. After the six-minute ride you can take in a film on the history and legends of the Tlingits, visit the nature center, go for an alpine walk on hiking trails (including the 5-mi round-trip hike to Mt. Roberts's 3,819-foot summit), purchase native crafts, or enjoy a meal while savoring mountain views. A local company leads guided wilderness hikes from the summit, and the bar serves locally brewed beers. ☎ *907/463–3412 or 888/461–8726* ⊕ *www.goldbelttours.com* ⊠ *$27* ☉ *May–Sept., hrs vary; closed in winter.*

❻ **South Franklin Street.** The buildings on South Franklin Street (and neighboring Front Street), among the oldest and most inviting structures in the city, house curio and crafts shops, snack shops, and two salmon shops. Many reflect the architecture of the 1920s and 1930s. When the small **Alaskan Hotel** opened in 1913, Juneau was home to 30 saloons; the Alaskan gives today's visitors the most authentic glimpse of the town's whiskey-rich history. The barroom's massive, mirrored, oak

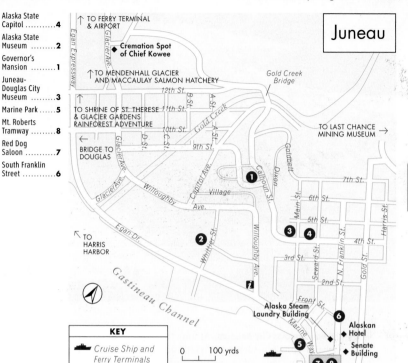

4

back bar is accented by Tiffany lights and panels. Topped by a wood-shingled turret, the 1901 **Alaska Steam Laundry Building** now houses a coffeehouse and other stores. The **Senate Building,** another of South Franklin's treasured landmarks, is across the street.

WORTH NOTING

❹ Alaska State Capitol. Completed in 1931 and remodeled in 2006, this rather unassuming building houses the governor's office and hosts state legislature meetings in winter, placing it at the epicenter of Alaska's increasingly animated political discourse. Historical photos line the upstairs walls. Feel free to stroll right in. ■**TIP→** You can pick up a self-guided tour brochure as you enter. ⊠ *Corner of Seward and 4th Sts.* ☎ *907/465–4648* ⊗ *Weekdays 8–5.*

❶ Governor's Mansion. Completed in 1912, this stately colonial-style home overlooks downtown Juneau. With 14,400 square feet, six bedrooms, and 10 bathrooms, it's no miner's cabin. Out front is a totem pole that tells three tales: the history of man, the cause of ocean tides, and the origin of Alaska's ubiquitous mosquitoes. Alaska's famous ex-governor, Sarah Palin, lived here with her husband ("First Dude" Todd Palin) and their children. Unfortunately, tours of the residence are not permitted. ⊠ *716 Calhoun Ave.*

"We hiked to the tongue of the Mendenhall Glacier to find this roaring waterfall crashing into the bay. It gave us a perspective on man's insignificance next to mother nature." —Chris Marlow, Photo Contest Winner

3 Juneau-Douglas City Museum. Among the exhibits interpreting local mining and Tlingit history is an Assay Lab diorama, a reconstructed Tlingit fish trap and video of excavation, historic photos, and pioneer artifacts, including a century-old store and kitchen. Digital story kiosks highlight Alaska's government, civil rights in Alaska, Alaska's quest for statehood, and cultures of Juneau. Youngsters will appreciate the hands-on room, where they can try on clothes similar to ones worn by the miners or look at gold-rush stereoscopes. Guided historic walking tours are offered May to September. ⊠ *114 4th St.* ☎ *907/586–3572* ⊕ *www. juneau.org/parksrec/museum* ⊠ *$4* ☉ *May–Sept., weekdays 9–5, weekends 10–5; Oct.–Apr., Tues.–Sat. 10–4.*

7 Red Dog Saloon. The frontierish quarters of the Red Dog have housed an infamous Juneau watering hole since 1890. Nearly every conceivable surface in this two-story bar is cluttered with graffiti, business cards, and memorabilia, including a pistol that reputedly belonged to Wyatt Earp, who failed to reclaim the piece after checking it in at the U.S. Marshall's office on June 27, 1900. The saloon's food menu includes halibut, reindeer sausage, potato skins, burgers and locally brewed Alaskan beers. A little atmospheric sawdust covers the floor as well. Musicians pump out ragtime piano tunes when cruise ships are docked. ⊠ *278 S. Franklin St.* ☎ *907/463–3658* ⊕ *www.reddogsaloon.com.*

OUTSIDE TOWN

Glacier Gardens Rainforest Adventure. Spread over 50 acres of rain forest, Glacier Gardens has ponds, waterfalls, hiking paths, a large atrium, and gardens. The roots of fallen trees, turned upside down and buried in the ground, act as bowls to hold planters that overflow with begonias, fuchsias, and petunias. Guided tours in covered golf carts lead you along the 4 mi of paved paths, and a 580-foot-high overlook provides dramatic views of the Mendenhall wetlands wildlife refuge, Chilkat mountains, and downtown Juneau. A café and gift shop are here, and the conservatory is a popular wedding spot. ■TIP→ The Juneau city bus, which departs from multiple locations in downtown Juneau, stops right in front of Glacier Gardens. ⊠ *7600 Glacier Hwy.* ☎ *907/790–3377* ⊕ *www. glaciergardens.com* ✉ *$22 including guided tour* ⊙ *May–Sept., daily 9–6; closed in winter.*

Macaulay Salmon Hatchery. Watch through an underwater window as salmon fight their way up a fish ladder from mid-June to mid-October. Inside the busy hatchery, which produces almost 125 million young salmon annually, you will learn about the environmental considerations of commercial fishermen and the lives of salmon. A retail shop sells gifts and salmon products. ⊠ *2697 Channel Dr.* ☎ *907/463–4810 or 877/463–2486* ⊕ *www.dipac.net* ✉ *$3.25 including short tour* ⊙ *Mid-May–mid-Sept., weekdays 10–6, weekends 10–5; Oct.–mid-May by appointment.*

Fodor'sChoice
★

Alaska's most visited drive-up glacier spans 12 mi and is fed by the massive Juneau Icefield. Like many other Alaska glaciers, it is retreating up the valley, losing more than 100 feet a year as massive chunks of ice calve into the small lake separating Mendenhall from the **Mendenhall Visitor Center.** The center has highly interactive exhibits on the glacier, a theater and bookstore, educational exhibits, and panoramic views. It's a great place for children to learn the basics of glacier dynamics. Nature trails lead along Mendenhall Lake and into the mountains overlooking Mendenhall Glacier; the trails are marked by posts and paint stripes delineating the historic location of the glacier, providing a sharp reminder of the Mendenhall's hasty retreat. An elevated viewing platform allows visitors to look for spawning sockeye and coho salmon—and the bears that eat them—at Steep Creek, 0.5 mi south of the visitor center along the Moraine Ecology Trail. Several companies lead bus tours to the glacier. A glacier express bus leaves from the cruise-ship terminal and heads right out to Mendenhall Glacier; ask at the visitor information center there. ⊠ *End of Glacier Spur Rd. off Mendenhall Loop Rd.* ☎ *907/789–0097* ⊕ *www.fs.fed.us/r10/tongass/districts/ mendenhall* ✉ *Visitor center $3 in summer, free in winter* ⊙ *May–Sept., daily 8–7:30; Oct.–Apr., Thurs.–Sun. 10–4.*

OUTDOOR ACTIVITIES

BIKING

Drop by the Centennial Hall Visitor Center for details on local trails open to bikes. Nearby is **Driftwood Lodge** (⊠ *435 Willoughby Ave.* ☎ *907/586–2280* ⊕ *www.driftwoodalaska.com*), which has basic bikes for rent.

BOATING, CANOEING, AND KAYAKING

Above & Beyond Alaska (☎ *907/364–2333* ⊕ *www.beyondak.com*) guides day and overnight camping, ice climbing, Mendenhall Glacier trips, and sea-kayaking trips in the Juneau area.

★ **Adventure Bound Alaska** (☎ *907/463–2509 or 800/228–3875* ⊕ *www. adventureboundalaska.com*) offers all-day trips to Sawyer Glacier within Tracy Arm in summer.

HIKING

Gastineau Guiding (☎ *907/586–8231* ⊕ *www.stepintoalaska.com*) leads a variety of hikes in the Juneau area. Especially popular are the walks from the top of the tram on Mt. Roberts.

WHALE-WATCHING

Alaska Whale Watching (☎ *907/321–5859 or 888/432–6722* ⊕ *www. akwhalewatching.com*) offers small-group excursions (up to 12 guests) aboard a luxury yacht with an onboard naturalist. The company also offers a whale-watching/fishing combination tour, which is popular with multigenerational groups. Several companies lead whale-watching trips from Juneau. **Juneau Sportfishing & Sightseeing** (☎ *907/586–1887* ⊕ *www. juneausportfishing.com*) has been around for many years, and its boats carry a maximum of six passengers, providing a personalized trip.

★ **Orca Enterprises (with Captain Larry)** (☎ *907/789–6801 or 888/733–6722* ⊕ *www.alaskawhalewatching.com*) offers whale-watching tours via jet boats designed for comfort and speed. The operator boasts a whale-sighting success rate of 99.9% between May 1 and October 15.

SHOPPING

Rie Muñoz, of the **Rie Muñoz Gallery** (✉ *2101 N. Jordan Ave.* ☎ *907/789–7449 or 800/247–3151* ⊕ *www.riemunoz.com*) is one of Alaska's best-known artists. She's the creator of a stylized, simple, and colorful design technique that is much copied but rarely equaled. The gallery is in Mendenhall Valley, a 10-minute walk from the airport. In downtown Juneau, see Rie Muñoz's paintings and tapestries at **Decker Gallery** (✉ *233 S. Franklin St.* ☎ *907/463–5536 or 800/463–5536*). Located upstairs through a separate entrance next to Heritage Coffee, **Wm. Spear Design** (✉ *172 S. Franklin St.* ☎ *907/586–2209* ⊕ *www.wmspear.com*) is an interesting store where this lawyer-turned-artist produces a fun and colorful collection of enameled pins and zipper pulls.

Taku Store (✉ *550 S. Franklin St.* ☎ *907/463–5319 or 800/582–5122* ⊕ *www.takustore.com*), at the south end of town near the cruise-ship docks and Mt. Roberts Tramway, processes nearly 6 million pounds of fish a year, mostly salmon. ■TIP→ The smoked sockeye fillets make excellent gifts. You can view the smoking procedure through large windows and then purchase the packaged fish in the deli-style gift shop or have some shipped back home.

WHERE TO EAT

$$$$ ✕ **Gold Creek Salmon Bake.** Trees, mountains, and the rushing water of
SEAFOOD   Salmon Creek surround the comfortable, canopy-covered benches and tables at this authentic salmon bake. Fresh-caught salmon is cooked over an alder fire and served with a succulent sauce. For $39 there are all-you-can-eat salmon, pasta, and chicken along with baked beans, rice pilaf, salad bar, corn bread, and blueberry cake. Wine and beer are

extra. After dinner you can pan for gold in the stream, wander up the hill to explore the remains of the Wagner gold mine, or roast marshmallows over the fire. A round-trip bus ride from downtown is included. ⊠ *1061 Salmon Lane Rd.* ☎ *907/789–0052 or 800/323–5757* ⊕ *www. bestofalaskatravel.com* ▤ *AE, MC, V* ☾ *Closed Oct.–Apr.*

$$–$$$
ECLECTIC

✕ **Hangar on the Wharf.** Crowded with locals and travelers, the Hangar occupies the building where Alaska Airlines started business. Flight-theme puns dominate the menu (i.e., "Pre-flight Snacks" and the "Plane Caesar"), but the comfortably worn wood and vintage airplane photos create a casual dining experience that outweighs the kitsch. Every seat has views of the Gastineau Channel and Douglas Island. On warm days, outdoor seating is offered. This Juneau hot spot makes a wide selection of entrées, including locally caught halibut and salmon, filet mignon, great burgers, and daily specials. Two dozen beers are on tap. On Friday and Saturday nights jazz or rock bands take the stage, and prime rib arrives on the menu. ⊠ *2 Marine Way, Merchants Wharf Mall* ☎ *907/586–5018* ⊕ *www.hangaronthewharf.com* ▤ *AE, D, MC, V.*

¢
CAFÉ

✕ **Heritage Coffee Company.** Juneau's favorite coffee shop is a downtown institution, with locally roasted coffees, gelato, fresh pastries, and all sorts of specialty drinks. ■ TIP➔ The window-front bar is good for people-watching while you sip a chai latte. ⊠ *174 S. Franklin St.* ☎ *907/586–1087* ☎ *907/789–0692* ⊕ *www.heritagecoffee.com* ▤ *AE, D, MC, V* ☾ *No dinner.*

¢
VEGETARIAN

✕ **Rainbow Foods.** Housed upstairs in a building that began life as an Assembly of God church, this crunchy natural foods market is a popular lunch-break destination for downtown workers. Organic produce, coconut milk ice cream, and vitamin supplements fill the shelves, but the real attraction is the weekday buffet, with various hot entrées, salads, soups, and deep-dish pizzas. Arrive before 11 AM for the best choices. Self-serve coffee and freshly baked breads are available, along with a few inside tables. ⊠ *224 4th St.* ☎ *907/586–6476* ⊕ *www.rainbow-foods.org* ▤ *MC, V.*

WHERE TO DRINK

If you're a beer fan, look for **Alaskan Brewing Company** (⊠ *5429 Shaune Dr.* ☎ *907/780–5866* ⊕ *www.alaskanbeer.com*). These tasty brews, including Alaskan Amber, Pale Ale, IPA, Stout, Alaskan Summer Ale, and Smoked Porter, are brewed and bottled in Juneau. You can visit the brewery (and get free samples of the goods) 11 to 6 daily May through September, with 20-minute tours every half hour. Between October and April tours take place Thursday through Sunday 11 to 4. ■ TIP➔ This is no designer brewery—it's in Juneau's industrial area, and there is no upscale café/bar attached—but the gift shop sells T-shirts and beer paraphernalia.

The **Alaskan Hotel Bar** (⊠ *167 S. Franklin St.* ☎ *907/586–1000*) is Juneau's most historically authentic watering hole, with flocked-velvet walls, antique chandeliers, and vintage Alaska frontier-brothel decor. The atmosphere, however, is anything but dated, and the bar's live music and open-mike night draw high-spirited crowds.

KETCHIKAN

Ketchikan is famous for its colorful totem poles, rainy skies, steep–as–San Francisco streets, and lush island setting. Some 13,000 people call the town home, and, in summer cruise ships crowd the shoreline, floatplanes depart noisily for Misty Fiords National Monument, and salmon-laden commercial fishing boats motor through Tongass Narrows. In the last decade Ketchikan's rowdy, blue-collar heritage of logging and fishing has been softened by the loss of many timber-industry jobs and the dramatic rise of cruise-ship tourism. With some effort, though, visitors can still glimpse the rugged frontier spirit that once permeated this hardscrabble cannery town.

This town is the first bite of Alaska that many travelers taste. Despite its imposing backdrop, hillside homes, and many staircases, Ketchikan is relatively easy to walk through. Downtown's favorite stops include the Spruce Mill Development shops and Creek Street. A bit farther away you'll find the Totem Heritage Center and Deer Mountain Hatchery. Out of town (but included on most bus tours) are two longtime favorites: Totem Bight State Historical Park and Saxman Totem Pole Park.

COMING ASHORE

SHORE EXCURSIONS
ADVENTURE
Alaska Canopy Adventures. Featuring a series of zip lines, nature trails, and suspension bridges, canopy tours provide an up-close view of the coastal forests. A course at the Alaska Rainforest Sanctuary, 16 mi south of town (⊕ *www.alaskacanopy.com*), has the longest of the tour's eight zip lines, stretching 850 feet and whisking you along some 135 feet off the ground. (This is an excursion you might find better prices for by booking independently.) ⊙ *3¼ hrs* ☎ *907/225–5503* 🕮 *$179.*

Misty Fiords by Floatplane. Aerial views of granite cliffs that rise 4,000 feet from the sea, waterfalls, rain forests, and wildlife are topped off with a landing on a high wilderness lake. ⊙ *2 hrs* 🕮 *$ 259.*

Misty Fiords Wilderness Cruise and Flight. See this beautiful area from the air and sea on a 20-minute floatplane trip and a 2¾-hour cruise. The plane lands in the heart of the wilderness, where you climb onboard a small boat for the narrated voyage back to Ketchikan. ⊙ *4 hrs* 🕮 *$359.*

Mountain Point Snorkeling Adventure. Stay warm as you immerse yourself in Mountain Point's waters in a state-of-the-art 7-millimeter wet suit complete with hood, boots, and gloves. Water temperatures reach a surprising 65°F. Observe and handle a variety of multicolor invertebrates and fish while snorkeling over the kelp forest. After PADI-certified professional guides lead you on the marine-life tour, hot beverages are provided before you return to your ship. ⊙ *3 hrs* 🕮 *$99.*

Sportfishing. Cast your line for Alaska king and silver salmon or halibut along the Inside Passage. All equipment is provided, and you can buy your license on board. Group size is limited. Fish will be cleaned, and arrangements can be made to have your catch frozen or smoked and shipped home. ⏱ *5 hrs* 🎫 *$190–$199*.

Tatoosh Islands Sea Kayaking. A scenic drive to Knudson Cove is followed by a boat ride to Tatoosh Islands, where you board an easy-to-paddle sea kayak for a whale's-eye view of a remote part of Tongass National Forest. The minimum age is seven. ⏱ *4½ hrs* 🎫 *$144–$149*.

CULTURAL

Saxman Native Village. Learn about Tlingit culture in this native village with more than 20 totem poles. You can watch totem-pole carvers and a theatrical production in the Beaver Clan House. ⏱ *2½ hrs* 🎫 *$59–$65*.

Totem Bight and Ketchikan City Tour. Visit the bustling center of Ketchikan and Totem Bight State Park to the north, where totem poles and a native clan house face the saltwater. ⏱ *2½ hrs* 🎫 *$40–$45*.

KETCHIKAN BEST BETS

■ **Exploring Creek Street.** No visit to Ketchikan would be complete without a stroll along this elevated wooden boulevard, once the site of the town's rip-roaring bordellos.

■ **Totem gazing at Saxman Totem Pole Park.** View one of the best totem collections in all of Southeast Alaska at this must-see stop.

■ **Rain-forest Canopy Tours.** Zip through the towering trees of Ketchikan's coastal rain forest, experiencing the majesty of this unique ecosystem from a bird's-eye view.

TRANSPORTATION AND TOURS

FROM THE PIER

Most ships dock or tender passengers ashore directly across from the Ketchikan Visitors Bureau on Front and Mission streets, in the center of downtown. A new dock, several blocks north on the other side of the tunnel, is still within easy walking distance of most of the town's sights. Walking-tour signs lead you around the city. For panoramic vistas of the surrounding area—and a wee bit of exercise—climb the stairs leading up several steep hillsides.

To reach sights farther from downtown, rent a car, hire a cab, or ride the local buses. Metered taxis meet the ships right on the docks and also wait across the street. Rates are $3.70 for pickup and $3.50 per mi. Up to six passengers can hire a taxi to tour for $75 per hour. Local buses run along the main route through town and south to Saxman. The fare is $1.

VISITOR INFORMATION

Ketchikan Visitors Bureau. The helpful visitors bureau is right next to the cruise-ship docks. Half the space is occupied by day-tour, flight-seeing, and boat-tour operators. ✉ *131 Front St.* ☎ *907/225–6166 or 800/770–3300* ⊕ *www.visit-ketchikan.com* ⏱ *May–Sept., 6–6 when cruise ships are docked.*

INTERNET Check your e-mail ($6 per hour) right near the dock at **SeaPort Cyber** (✉ *5 Salmon Landing, Suite 216* ☎ *907/247–4615* ⊕ *www.seaportel.com*).

EXPLORING KETCHIKAN

TOP ATTRACTIONS

③ ★ **Creek Street.** This was once Ketchikan's infamous red-light district. During Prohibition, Creek Street was home to numerous speakeasies, and, in the early 1900s more than 30 houses of prostitution operated here. Today the small, colorful houses, built on stilts over the creek waters, have been restored as trendy shops.

⑦ **The Falls at Salmon Falls Resort.** Get out your camera and set it for high speed at the fish ladder, a series of pools arranged like steps that allow fish to travel upstream around a dam or falls. When the salmon start running from June onward, thousands of fish leap the falls (or take the easier fish-ladder route). They spawn in Ketchikan Creek's waters farther upstream. Many can also be seen in the creek's eddies above and below the falls. The falls, fish ladder, and a large carving of a jumping salmon are just off Park Avenue on Married Man's Trail. The trail was once used by married men for discreet access to the red-light district on Creek Street. ⊠ *Married Man's Trail off Park Ave.*

① **☯** **★** **Southeast Alaska Discovery Center.** This impressive public lands interpretive center features exhibits—including one on the rain forest—that focus on the resources, native cultures, and ecosystems of Southeast Alaska. The U.S. Forest Service and other federal agencies provide information on Alaska's public lands, and a large gift shop sells natural-history books, maps, and videos about the sights in Ketchikan and the Southeast. America the Beautiful–National Park and Federal Recreational Land Passes are accepted and sold. ⊠ *50 Main St.* ☎ *907/228–6220* ⊕ *www.fs.fed.us/r10/tongass/districts/discoverycenter* ⊠ *$5 May–Sept., free Oct.–Apr.* ☉ *May–Sept., weekdays 8–5, weekends 8–4; Oct.–Apr., Thurs.–Sun. 10–4.*

⑩ **★** **Totem Heritage Center.** Gathered from uninhabited Tlingit and Haida village sites, many of the authentic native totems in this rare collection are well over a century old—a rare age for cedar carvings, which are frequently lost to decay in the Southeast's exceedingly wet climate. The center also features guided tours and displays crafts of the Tlingit, Haida, and Tsimshian cultures. Outside are several more poles carved in the three decades since this center opened. The center offers an annual series of classes, workshops, and seminars related to Northwest Coastal Native art and culture. ⊠ *601 Deermount St.* ☎ *907/225–5900* ⊠ *$5* ☉ *May–Sept., daily 8–5; Oct.–Apr., weekdays 1–5.*

WORTH NOTING

⑤ **Cape Fox Lodge.** For the town's best harbor views and one of Southeast Alaska's most luxurious lobbies, walk to the top of steep Venetia Avenue or take the funicular ($2) up from Creek Street. ⊠ *800 Venetia Way* ☎ *907/225–8001 or 800/225–8001* ⊕ *www.capefoxlodge.com.*

③ **Creek Street Footbridge.** Stand over Ketchikan Creek for good salmon-viewing when the fish are running. In summer you can see impressive runs of coho, king, pink, and chum salmon, along with smaller numbers of steelhead and rainbow trout heading upstream to spawn. ■ TIP➔ Keep your eyes peeled for sea lions snacking on the incoming fish.

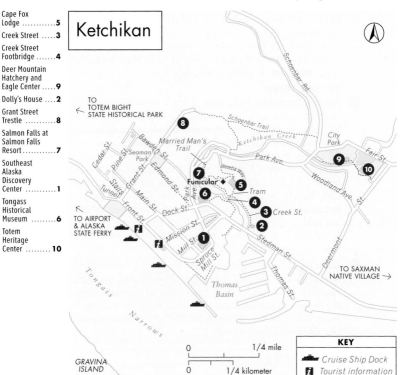

4

9 **Deer Mountain Hatchery and Eagle Center.** Owned by the Ketchikan Indian
Community, tens of thousands of king and coho salmon are raised at
this hatchery on Ketchikan Creek. Midsummer visitors can view natural spawning in the creek by pink salmon and steelhead trout as well
as workers collecting and fertilizing the salmon eggs for the hatchery.
Also here is a nesting pair of injured bald eagles. Other resident birds
are used in educational programs in the interpretive theaters. ⊠ *1158
Salmon Rd.* ☎ *907/228–5530 or 800/252–5158* ⊕ *www.kictribe.org*
🎟 *$12 for hatchery admission, additional $3 for bird program* ☉ *Early
May–Sept., daily 8–4:30.*

2 **Dolly's House.** Formerly owned by the inimitable Dolly Arthur, this steep-
roofed home once housed Creek Street's most famous brothel. The
house has been preserved as a museum, complete with furnishings,
beds, and a short history of the life and times of Ketchikan's best-known
madam. ⊠ *Creek St.* ☎ *907/225–6329 (summer only)* 🎟 *$5* ☉ *Daily
8–4, when cruise ships are in port; closed in winter.*

8 **Grant Street Trestle.** At one time virtually all of Ketchikan's walkways
and streets were made from wooden trestles, but now only one of these
handsome wooden streets remains, constructed in 1908.

6 **Tongass Historical Museum.** Native artifacts and pioneer relics revisit the
mining and fishing eras at this museum in the same building as the

library. Exhibits include a big, brilliantly polished lens from Tree Point Lighthouse, well-presented native tools and artwork, and photography collections. Other exhibits rotate, but always include Tlingit items. ✉ *629 Dock St.* ☎ *907/225–5600* 💲 *$2* 🕙 *May–Sept., daily 8–5; Oct.– Apr., Wed.–Fri. 1–5, Sat. 10–4, Sun. 1–4.*

OUTSIDE TOWN

⑮ Saxman Totem Pole Park. named for a missionary who helped native Alaskans settle here before 1900. A totem park dominates the center of Saxman, with poles that represent a wide range of human and animal-inspired figures, including bears, ravens, whales, and eagles. There is a $3 charge to enter. Saxman's Beaver Clan tribal house is said to be the largest in Alaska. Carvers create totem poles and totemic art objects in the adjacent carver's shed. You can get to the park on foot or by taxi, bicycle, or city bus. You can visit the totem park on your own, but to visit the tribal house and theater you must take a tour. Tickets are sold at the gift shop across from the totems. Call ahead for tour schedules. ✉ *S. Tongass Hwy., 2 mi south of town* ☎ *907/225–4421* ⊕ *www.capefoxtours.com.*

❾ Totem Bight. Totem Bight has many totem poles and a hand-hewn native tribal house; it sits on a scenic spit of land facing the waters of Tongass Narrows. The clan house is open daily in summer. About a quarter of the Ketchikan bus tours include Totem Bight. ✉ *N. Tongass Hwy.* ✛ *Approx. 10 mi north of town* ☎ *907/247–8574* ⊕ *www.alaskastateparks. org* 💲 *Free* 🕙 *Dawn–dusk.*

OUTDOOR ACTIVITIES

The **Great Alaskan Lumberjack Show** is a 60-minute lumberjack competition providing a Disney-esque taste of old-time woodsman skills, including ax throwing, bucksawing, springboard chopping, log-rolling duels, and a 50-foot speed climb. Shows take place in a covered, heated grandstand directly behind the Salmon Landing Marketplace and go on rain or shine all summer. ✉ *420 Spruce Mill Way* ☎ *907/225–9050 or 888/320–9049* ⊕ *www.lumberjacksports.com* 💲 *$35* 🕙 *May–Sept., 2–4 times daily; hrs vary.*

FISHING

Sportfishing for salmon and trout is excellent in the Ketchikan area, in both saltwater and freshwater lakes and streams. As a result, a plethora of local boat owners offer charter and guide services. Contact the **Ketchikan Visitors Bureau** (☎ *907/225–6166 or 800/770–3300* ⊕ *www.visitketchikan.com*) for information on guide services and locations.

FLIGHTSEEING

Alaska Travel Adventures (☎ *800/323–5757, 907/247–5295 outside Alaska* ⊕ *www.bestofalaskatravel.com*) runs a speedy catamaran and catamaran-floatplane combo excursions to Misty Fiords National Monument. There is also a rain forest island adventure tour in Ketchikan.

Ketchikan. "On a cool spring day, after walking on glaciers and seeing so much wildlife in the Tundra and sea coast, Ketchikan is comfortable and warm." —Sandy Cook, Fodors.com photo contest participant.

HIKING

Get details on hiking around Ketchikan from the Southeast Alaska Discovery Center and Ketchikan Visitors Bureau *(⇨ Exploring, above)*. The 3-mi trail from downtown to the 3,000-foot summit of **Deer Mountain** will repay your efforts with a spectacular panorama of the city below and the wilderness behind. The trail officially begins at the corner of Nordstrom Drive and Ketchikan Lake Road, but consider starting on the paved, 1.5 mi scenic walk on the corner of Fair and Deermount streets. Pass through dense forests before emerging into the alpine country. A shelter cabin near the summit provides a place to warm up.

SEA KAYAKING

Southeast Exposure (☎ *907/225–8829* ⊕ *www.southeastexposure.com*) offers a 3½-hour self-guided Eagle Islands sea kayak tour and a 4½-hour Tatoosh Islands sea-kayak tour in Behm Canal.

Southeast Sea Kayaks (☎ *907/225–1258 or 800/287–1607* ⊕ *www. kayakketchikan.com*) leads kayak tours of Ketchikan and Misty Fiords, and offers kayak lessons and rentals. It specializes in remote day trips and guided multinight trips to Misty Fiords.

SHOPPING

■ TIP→ Because artists are local, prices for Native Alaskan crafts are sometimes lower in Ketchikan than at other ports. The **Saxman Village** gift shop has some Tlingit wares.

In business since 1972, **Scanlon Gallery** (✉ *318 Mission St.* ☎ *907/247–4730 or 888/228–4730* ⊕ *www.scanlongallery.com*) carries prints from a number of well-known Alaska artists, including Byron Birdsall, Rie Muñoz, John Fehringer, Barbara Lavallee, and Jon Van Zyle.

Design, art, clothing, and collectibles converge in the stylish **Soho Coho Contemporary Art and Craft Gallery** (⊠ *5 Creek St.* ☎ *907/225–5954 or 800/888–4070* ⊕ *www.trollart.com*), where you'll find an eclectic collection of art and T-shirts featuring the work of owner Ray Troll—best known for his wacky fish art—and other Southeast Alaska artists.

WHERE TO EAT

$$$–$$$$
AMERICAN

╳ **Annabelle's Famous Keg and Chowder House.** Nestled into the ground floor of the historic Gilmore Hotel, this unpretentious Victorian-style restaurant serves a hearty array of seafood and pastas, including several kinds of chowder and steamer clams. Prime rib on Friday and Saturday evenings is a favorite, and the lounge with a jukebox adds a friendly vibe. ⊠ *326 Front St.* ☎ *907/225–6009* ⊕ *www.gilmorehotel. com* ▭ *AE, D, MC, V.*

$–$$
MEXICAN

╳ **Ocean View Restaurant.** This locals' favorite eatery has burgers, steaks, pasta, pizzas, and seafood. They're all fine, but the main draws are authentic and very filling south-of-the-border dishes prepared under the direction of the Mexican-American owners. Three tables in the back have nice views of the Tongass Narrows. ⊠ *1831 Tongass Ave.* ☎ *907/225–7566* ⊕ *www.oceanviewmex.com* ▭ *MC, V.*

WHERE TO DRINK

Ketchikan has quieted down in recent years as the economy shifted from logging to tourism, but it remains something of a party town, especially when crews stumble off fishing boats with cash in hand. You won't have any trouble finding something going on at several downtown bars. **First City Saloon** (⊠ *830 Water St.* ☎ *907/225–1494*) is the main dance spot, with live music throughout the summer. The **Potlatch Bar** (⊠ *126 Thomas Basin* ☎ *907/225–4855*) delivers up music on weekends as well.

KODIAK ISLAND

On the second-largest island in the United States (Hawaii's Big Island is the largest), the town of Kodiak is the least touristy of all the Alaska port towns. It's an out-of-the-way destination for smaller cruise ships and Alaska state ferries, and despite its small population (just over 6,000 people), there's a lot of "big" stuff here: Kodiak is home to a very large commercial fishing fleet, and is almost always one of the top two or three in the country for tonnage of fish brought in. It's also home to the country's largest Coast Guard base, and the world-famous Kodiak brown bear, billed as the largest land carnivore in the world.

Today commercial fishing is king in Kodiak. A clearinghouse for fish caught by islanders throughout the Kodiak archipelago—about 15,000 people are scattered among the islands—the city is among the busiest fishing ports in the United States. The harbor is also an important supply point for small communities on the Aleutian Islands and the Alaska Peninsula.

CLOSE UP

Common Nautical Terms

Before acquainting yourself with your ship, you should add a few nautical terms to your vocabulary:

Berth. Sleeping space on a ship (literally refers to your bed).

Bow. The pointy end of the ship, also known as forward. Yes, it's also the front of the ship.

Bridge. The navigational control center (where the captain drives the ship).

Bulkhead. A wall or upright partition separating a ship's compartments.

Cabin. Your accommodation on a ship (used interchangeably with *stateroom*).

Course. Measured in degrees, the direction in which a ship is headed.

Debark. To leave a ship (also known as disembarkation).

Draft. The depth of water needed to float a ship; the measurement from a ship's waterline to the lowest point of its keel.

Embark. To go on board a ship.

Galley. The ship's kitchen.

Gangway. The stairway or ramp used to access the ship from the dock.

Hatch. An opening or door on a ship, either vertical or horizontal.

Head. A bathroom aboard a ship.

Helm. The apparatus for steering a ship.

Muster. To assemble the passengers and/or crew on a ship.

Pitch. Plunging in a longitudinal direction; the up-and-down motion of a ship. (A major cause of seasickness.)

Port. The left side of the ship when you're facing forward.

Promenade. Usually outside, a deck that fully or partially encircles the ship, popular for walking and jogging.

Roll. Side-to-side movement of the ship. (Another seasickness culprit.)

Stabilizers. Operated by gyroscopes, these retractable finlike devices below the waterline extend from a ship's hull to reduce roll and provide stability. (Your best friend if you're prone to motion sickness.)

Starboard. The right side of the ship when you're facing forward.

Stern. The rounded end of the ship, also called aft. It's the back end.

Tender. A boat carried on a ship that's used to take passengers ashore when it's not possible to tie up at a dock.

Thrusters. Fanlike propulsion devices under the waterline that move a ship sideways.

Wake. The ripples left on the water's surface by a moving ship.

COMING ASHORE

SHORE EXCURSIONS
ADVENTURE

Kodiak Bear Viewing by Floatplane. Weather permitting, you can fly over Kodiak's lush green hills and remote backcountry waterways, then spend at least two hours on the ground watching the world's largest carnivores in their natural habitat. During the flight out and back the pilot will also point out marine and terrestrial mammals and other points of interest. ⊙ *1½–4½ hrs* ☜ *$250–$490.*

Halibut fishing. From picturesque St. Paul Harbor you can thread your way through the commercial fishing fleet and into the icy waters of the Gulf of Alaska in pursuit of the wily and tasty Pacific halibut. Be prepared to work for your food, though—the state record halibut weighed 459 pounds, and 100- to 200-pound fish are common. Along the way you can spot marine mammals such as seals, sea lions, and sea otters, and numerous seabirds as well. All bait and tackle is supplied, and local fish processors can arrange to clean, package, and ship your catch for you. ⊙ *6 hrs* ☜ *$275–$325.*

SCENIC

Waterfront and Wildlife Cruise. Take a cruise along the waterfront and view the fishing fleet, canneries, the Russian Orthodox church and seminary, and the abandoned World War II defense installation. Chances of seeing seabirds and marine mammals such as sea lions and sea otters are excellent. ⊙ *3 hrs* ☜ *$239.*

TRANSPORTATION AND TOURS

FROM THE PIER

Most cruise ships dock at Pier 2, ½ mi south of downtown Kodiak. Most ships offer shuttles into town (about $7 round-trip), but if yours doesn't, it's a 15-minute walk. You can catch a cab ride from **A&B Taxi** (☎ *907/486–4343*).

AREA TOURS

Kodiak Island Charters (☎ *907/486–5380 or 800/575–5380* ⊕ *www. ptialaska.net/~urascal*) operates boat tours for fishing, hunting, and sightseeing aboard the 43-foot *U-Rascal.* They'll take you on a combined halibut and salmon trip, with sightseeing and whale-watching thrown in as well.

VISITOR INFORMATION

Pick up maps, details on kayaking trips, bear-viewing flights, marine tours, and more from the **Kodiak Island Convention & Visitors' Bureau** (✉ *100 E. Marine Way, Suite 200* ☎ *907/486–4782* ⊕ *www.kodiak.org*).

INTERNET   Visitors can check e-mail at various private businesses with wireless communication (check with the Visitors' Bureau); alternatively, head to the **A. Holmes Johnson Memorial Library** (✉ *319 Lower Mill Bay Rd.* ☎ *907/486–8680* ⊕ *www.city.kodiak.ak.us/library*).

EXPLORING KODIAK

★   The **Alutiiq Museum and Archaeological Repository** is home to one of the largest collections of Alaska Native materials in the world, and contains archaeological and ethnographic items dating back 7,500 years. The museum displays only a fraction of its more than 150,000 artifacts, including harpoons, masks, dolls, stone tools, seal-gut parkas, grass baskets, and pottery fragments. The museum store sells native arts and educational materials. ✉ *215 Mission Rd., Suite 101* ☎ *907/486–7004* ⊕ *www.alutiiqmuseum.org* ☜ *$5* ⊙ *June–Aug., weekdays 9–5, Sat. 10–5, Sun. by appointment; Sept.–May, Tues.–Fri. 9–5, Sat. noon–4.*

The **Baranov Museum** presents artifacts from the area's Russian past. On the National Register of Historic Places, the building was built in 1808 by Alexander Baranov to warehouse precious sea-otter pelts. W.J. Erskine made it his home in 1911. On display are samovars, a collection of intricate native basketry, and other relics from the early native Koniags and the later Russian settlers. ✉ *101 Marine Way* ☎ *907/486–5920* ⊕ *www. baranovmuseum.org* ☞ *$3* ☉ *May–Sept., Mon.–Sat. 10–4, Sun. noon–4; Oct.–Apr., Tues.–Sat. 10–3.*

☾ As part of America's North Pacific defense in World War II, Kodiak was the site of an important naval station, now occupied by the Coast Guard fleet that patrols the surrounding fishing grounds. Part of the old military installation has been incorporated into **Fort Abercrombie State Historical Park**, 3½ mi north of Kodiak on Rezanof Drive. Self-guided tours take you past concrete bunkers and gun emplacements. There's a spectacular scenic overlook, great for bird- and whale-watching, and there are 13 campsites suitable for tents or RVs (no hookups), with pit toilets, drinking water, fire grates, and picnic tables. ✉ *Mi 3.7, Rezanof Dr.* ☝ *Alaska State Parks, Kodiak District Office, 1400 Abercrombie Dr., 99615* ☎ *907/486–6339* ⊕ *www.dnr.alaska.gov/parks/units/kodiak/ftaber.htm* ☞ *Park free, campsites $10* ▭ *No credit cards.*

The ornate **Holy Resurrection Russian Orthodox Church** is a visual feast, both inside and out. The cross-shaped building is topped by two onion-shape blue domes, and the interior contains brass candelabra, distinctive chandeliers, and numerous icons representing Orthodox saints. Three different churches have stood on this site since 1794. Built in 1945, the present structure is on the National Register of Historic Places. ✉ *Mission Rd. and Kashevaroff Rd.* ☎ *907/486–3854 parish priest* ☞ *Donations accepted* ☉ *By appointment.*

Floatplane and boat charters are available from Kodiak to numerous remote attractions. Chief among these areas is the 1.6-million-acre **Kodiak National Wildlife Refuge**, lying partly on Kodiak Island and partly on Afognak Island to the north, where spotting the enormous Kodiak brown bears is the main goal of a trip. Seeing the bears, which weigh a pound at birth but up to 1,500 pounds when fully grown, is worth the trip to this rugged country. The bears are spotted easily in July and August, feeding along salmon-spawning streams. ✉ *1390 Buskin River Rd.* ☎ *907/487–2600* ⊕ *kodiak.fws.gov.*

KODIAK BEST BETS

■ **Visit the world's largest bears.** Join one of the local flight operators and spend the day watching these animals devour amazing quantities of salmon.

■ **Relax, have a brew.** Stop by the local brewery for a tasting session and tour, and stock up on fresh local beer for your stay.

■ **Walk off those calories.** Pick up a map of the Kodiak hiking trails at the Visitors' Bureau and head for the hills. Chances are you won't be eaten by a bear.

4

OUTDOOR ACTIVITIES

BEAR-WATCHING

Kodiak Adventures Unlimited (☎ 907/486–8766 ⊕ *www.kodiakadventure sunlimited.com*) books charter and tour operators for all of Kodiak. Find it in St. Paul Harbor across from Wells Fargo.

SHOPPING

The Alutiiq Museum store sells native arts and educational materials.

WHERE TO EAT

$$–$$$ ✕ **Henry's Great Alaskan Restaurant.** Henry's is a big, boisterous, friendly
AMERICAN place at the mall near the small-boat harbor. The menu is equally big, ranging from fresh local seafood and barbecue to pastas and even some Cajun dishes. Dinner specials, a long list of appetizers, salads, rack of lamb, and a tasty dessert list round out the choices. ✉ *512 Marine Way* ☎ *907/486–8844* ⊕ *www.henryskodiak.com* ▬ *AE, MC, V.*

¢–$ ✕ **Mill Bay Coffee & Pastries.** Serving lunches and fabulous pastries, this
CAFÉ charming little shop is well worth a visit. The coffee is freshly roasted on-site every other day. Inside, elegant antique furnishings are complemented by local artwork and handicrafts. ✉ *3833 Rezanof Dr. E* ☎ *907/486–4411* ⊕ *www.millbaycoffee.com* ▬ *MC, V* ⊗ *No dinner.*

$$–$$$ ✕ **Old Powerhouse Restaurant.** This converted powerhouse facility allows
SEAFOOD a close-up view of Near Island and the channel connecting the boat harbors with the Gulf of Alaska. Enjoy fresh sushi and sashimi while watching the procession of fishing boats gliding past on their way to catch or deliver your next meal. Keep your eyes peeled for sea otters, seals, sea lions, and eagles, too. The menu also features tempura, *yakisoba* (fried noodles), and rice specials; there's live music on occasion. ✉ *516 E. Marine Way* ☎ *907/481–1088* ▬ *MC, V.*

WHERE TO DRINK

The **Kodiak Island Brewing Co.** (✉ *338 Shelikof Ave.* ☎ *907/486–2537* ⊕ *www.kodiakbrewery.com*) sells fresh-brewed, unfiltered beer in a variety of styles and sizes of containers, from 20-ounce bottles up to full kegs, so you can stock up for your wilderness expedition and avoid beer withdrawal. Brewer Ben Millstein will also give you a tour of the facility on request. It's open noon–7 daily in summer. Due to a change in state liquor laws, some on-premise sales and consumption are now allowed.

METLAKATLA

The village of Metlakatla—the name translates roughly as "saltwater passage"—is on Annette Island, just a dozen miles by sea from busy Ketchikan but a world away culturally. A visit to this quiet community offers visitors a chance to learn about life in a small Inside Passage native community.

In most Southeast native villages the people are Tlingit or Haida in heritage. Metlakatla is the exception, as most folks are Tsimshian. They moved to the island from British Columbia in 1887, led by William Duncan, an Anglican missionary from England. The town grew rapidly and soon contained dozens of buildings on a grid of streets, including a cannery, a sawmill, and a church that could seat 1,000 people. Congress declared Annette Island a federal Indian reservation in 1891, and it remains the only reservation in Alaska today. Father Duncan continued to control life in Metlakatla for decades, until the government finally stepped in shortly before his death in 1918.

COMING ASHORE

Cruise ships dock at the Metlakatla dock adjacent to town. Buses from **Metlakatla Tours** (☎ 907/886–8687 ⊕ *www.metlakatlatours.net/*) meet all ships and provide a standard shore excursion that includes a bus tour of town taking in most of the beautifully carved totem poles and a dance performance at the longhouse.

INTERNET   If you can supply your own laptop or Wi-Fi–enabled handheld device, check your e-mail at **Metlakatla Artists' Village** (⊠ *Airport Rd.* ☎ *907/ 886–4437*).

EXPLORING METLAKATLA

Metlakatla's religious heritage still shows today. The clapboard **William Duncan Memorial Church,** topped with two steeples, burned in 1948 but was rebuilt several years later. It is one of nine churches in tiny Metlakatla. **Father Duncan's Cottage** is maintained to appear exactly as it would have in 1891, and includes original furnishings, personal items, and a collection of turn-of-the-20th-century music boxes. ⊠ *Corner of 4th Ave. and Church St.* ☎ *907/886–8687* ⊕ *www.metlakatlatours.com* 🖃 *$2* ☉ *Weekdays 8:30–12:30, or when cruise ships are in port.*

Father Duncan worked hard to eliminate traditional Tsimshian beliefs and dances, but today the people of Metlakatla have resurrected their past; they perform old dances in traditional regalia. The best place to catch these performances is at the traditional **longhouse** (known as *Le Sha'as* in the Tsimshian dialect), which faces Metlakatla's boat harbor. Three totem poles stand on the back side of the building, and the front is covered with a Tsimshian design. Inside are displays of native crafts and a model of the fish traps that were once common throughout the Inside Passage. Native dance groups perform here on Wednesday and Friday in summer. Just next to the longhouse is an **Artists' Village,** where booths display locally made arts and crafts. The village and longhouse open when groups and tours are present.

MISTY FIORDS NATIONAL MONUMENT

Fodor's Choice
★

In the past, cruise ships bypassed Misty Fiords on their way up and down the Inside Passage. But today more and more cruise passengers are discovering its unspoiled beauty as ships big and small feature a day of scenic cruising through this protected wilderness. At the southern end of the Inside Passage, Misty Fiords is usually visited just before or after a call at Ketchikan. The attraction here is the wilderness—3,500 square mi of it—highlighted by waterfalls and cliffs that rise 3,000 feet. Small boats enable views of breathtaking vistas. Traveling on these waters can be an almost mystical experience, with the greens of the forest reflected in waters as still as black mirrors. You may find yourself in the company of a whale, see bears fishing along the shore, or even pull in your own salmon for an evening meal. Park rangers may kayak out to your cruise ship to help point out wildlife and explain the geology of the area. ■TIP→ Keep in mind that the name Misty refers to the weather you're likely to encounter in this rainy part of Alaska.

4

GETTING HERE ON YOUR OWN

The dramatic fjords and isolated alpine lakes of the 2.3-million-acre Misty Fiords National Monument don't exactly lend themselves to pedestrian exploration. But thanks to flightseeing services like **Island Wings Air Service** (☎ *907/225–2444 or 888/854–2444 ⊕ www.islandwings.com*) and **Southeast Aviation** (☎ *907/225–2900 or 888/359–6478 ⊕ www. southeastaviation.com*), the sublime splendor of this region doesn't go unseen. Based in Ketchikan, Island Wings offers a popular two-hour tour that includes a 35-minute stopover at one of the Monument's many lakes or fjords. Southeast Aviation offers transportation from the cruise-ship pier and a two-and-a-half-hour tour that includes a water landing for photos.

NOME

Nome is visited by Cruise West as part of its Bering Sea voyages, which include Homer, Kodiak, Dutch Harbor, the Pribilofs, Russia's Chukotka Peninsula, and sailing into the upper reaches of the Bering Sea far enough to cross the Arctic Circle where it intersects with the International Date Line. More than a century has passed since a great stampede for gold put a speck of wilderness now called Nome on the Alaska map, but gold mining and noisy saloons are still mainstays here. This frontier community on the icy Bering Sea once boasted 20,000 during the gold stampede in the 1890s but now only has 3,500 year-round residents. At first glance, the town may come off as a collection of ramshackle houses and low-slung commercial buildings—like a vintage gold-mining camp or, because of the spooky abandoned monolithic microwave towers from World War II that sit atop Anvil Mountain, the movie set for an Arctic horror movie—but only a couple of streets back you'll find tidy, modern homes and charming, hospitable shopkeepers.

A network of 250 mi or so of gravel roads around the town leads to creeks and rivers for gold panning or fishing for trout, salmon, and arctic grayling. You may also see reindeer, bears, foxes, and moose on the back roads that once connected early mining camps and hamlets.

COMING ASHORE

TRANSPORTATION AND TOURS
FROM THE PIER
Cruise ships dock a mile south of Nome at the city dock. Taxis are available to downtown for $5.

AREA TOURS
Most travelers take a tour of the area through **Nome Discovery Tours** (*Box 2024, Nome 99762 ☎ 907/443–2814 ⊕ www.nomechamber. org/discoverytours*), in which former Broadway showman Richard Beneville emphasizes Nome's gold rush and the region's Inupiat history.

VISITOR INFORMATION
To explore downtown, stop at the **Nome Convention and Visitors Bureau** (⊠ *301 Front St.* ☎ *907/443–6624* ⊕ *www.visitnomealaska.com*) for a historic-walking-tour map, a city map, and information on local activities from flightseeing to bird-watching.

INTERNET   Check your e-mail for free at the **Kegoayah Kozga Library** (⊠ *223 Front St.* ☎ *907/443–6628* ⊕ *www.nomealaska.org/library*). If you have a laptop, you can also access free wireless at several hotels and the local restaurant, **Airport Pizza** (⊠ *406 Bering St.*).

EXPLORING NOME

Since the sun stays up late in the summer months, get a ride to the top of **Anvil Mountain**, near Nome, for a panoramic view of the old gold town and the Bering Sea. Be sure to carry mosquito repellent.

Nome's **Carrie M. McClain Memorial Museum** showcases the history of the Nome gold rush, from the "Lucky Swedes" discovery in 1898 to Wyatt Earp's arrival in 1899 and the stampede of thousands of people into Nome in 1900. The museum also has exhibits about the Bering Strait Inupiat Eskimos, plus displays on the Nome Kennel Club and its All-Alaska Sweepstakes. However, the highlight of the museum is the historical photo collection: thousands of pictures from the early days make it a perfect place to lose yourself on a rainy day. ⊠ *223 Front St.* ☎ *907/443–6630* ⊠ *Free* ☉ *June–early Sept., daily 10–5:30; early Sept.–May, weekdays noon–5:30.*

WHERE TO EAT

$$–$$$ ✕ **Airport Pizza.** This family-friendly pizza joint isn't like any other. Not
PIZZA   only does it make some of the best food in town with a menu boasting
☺   great pizza and toppings, but it also features Tex-Mex, sandwiches, and
Fodor'sChoice   a full breakfast menu. What's given this restaurant national attention is
★   its delivery service: not only in town, but also to the surrounding Bush villages. Call up, order a pizza, and for $30 it'll be put on the next plane out. There are 15 beers on tap (many of which are microbrews), an extensive wine selection, and nightly music and games year-round.

DID YOU KNOW?

Lakes like this one in the
Rousseau Range in Misty
Fiords National Monument
make attractive places to
contemplate how an area
that was covered in glaciers
17,000 years ago is now
filled with saltwater fjords,
tidewater estuaries, 3,000-
foot mist-shrouded moun-
tains, and miles and miles of
pristine solitude.

It also has a drive-thru coffee shop. ✉ *406 Bering St.* ☎ *907/443–7992* ⊟ *MC, V.*

SHOPPING

Nome is one of the best places to buy ivory, because many of the Eskimo carvers from outlying villages come to Nome first to sell their wares to dealers. The **Arctic Trading Post** (✉ *Bering and Front Sts.* ☎ *907/443–2686*) has an extensive stock of authentic Eskimo ivory carvings and other Alaskan artwork, jewelry, and books.

PETERSBURG

Getting to Petersburg is an experience, whether you take the "high road" by air or the "low road" by sea. Alaska Airlines claims the shortest jet flight in the world, from takeoff at Wrangell to landing at Petersburg. The schedule calls for 20 minutes of flying, but it's usually more like 15. At sea level only ferries and smaller cruisers can squeak through Wrangell Narrows with the aid of more than 50 buoys and range markers along the 22-mi waterway, which takes almost four hours. But the inaccessibility of Petersburg is also part of its charm: you'll never be overwhelmed here by hordes of other cruise passengers; only smaller ships can reach the town.

Although Petersburg is nice to explore, commercial fishing is more important than tourism—in other words, you'll find more hardware stores than jewel merchants. The main attractions are the town's Norwegian heritage, its vibrant community, and its magnificent mountain-backed setting. The country around Petersburg provides an array of outdoor fun, from whale-watching and glacier-gazing to hiking and fishing.

COMING ASHORE

SHORE EXCURSIONS

LeConte Glacier Flightseeing. One of the best flightseeing tours in Alaska takes you to the southernmost calving glacier in North America, which is backed by one of the Southeast's most beautiful collections of mountain peaks, including the Devil's Thumb. ⊙ *50 mins* 🖃 *$215.*

The Town That Fish Built. Here's a chance to explore all the landmarks of this pretty fishing town by bus, and see the largest salmon ever landed at the Clausen Museum. You'll travel 3 mi from town to stop at Sandy Beach, where ancient natives built fish traps, before returning to your ship. ⊙ *2 hrs* 🖃 *$39.*

Waterfront Walking Tour. A guide will relate the history and fishing heritage of Petersburg as you explore the old part of town on foot. ⊙ *1½ hrs* 🖃 *$20.*

TRANSPORTATION AND TOURS

FROM THE PIER

Cruise companies with stops at Petersburg include: American Safari Cruises, Cruise West, and Lindblad Expeditions. All of these are smaller, adventure-oriented ships. The ships dock in the South Harbor, which is about a ½-mi walk from downtown.

CITY TOURS

If you want to learn about local history, the commercial fishing industry, and the Tongass National Forest, you can take a guided tour with Viking Travel (⇨ *see Outdoor Activities, below*).

VISITOR INFORMATION

The **Petersburg Visitor Information Center,** within walking distance of the harbor, is a good source for local information, including details on tours, charters, and nearby outdoor recreation opportunities. ⊠ *1st and Fram Sts.* ☎ *907/772–4636* ⊕ *www.petersburg.org.*

INTERNET Check your e-mail for free at **Petersburg Public Library** (⊠ *12 Nordic Dr.* ☎ *907/772–3349* ⊕ *www.psglib.org*).

EXPLORING PETERSBURG

One of the most pleasant things to do in Petersburg is to roam among the fishing vessels tied up dockside in the town's expanding harbor. This is one of Alaska's busiest, most prosperous fishing communities, with an enormous variety of seacraft. You'll see small trollers, big halibut vessels, and sleek pleasure craft. By watching shrimp, salmon, or halibut catches being brought ashore (though be prepared for the pungent aroma), you can get a real appreciation for this industry.

❸ **Clausen Memorial Museum.** The museum's exhibits explore commercial fishing and the cannery industry, the era of fish traps, the social life of Petersburg, and Tlingit culture. Don't miss the museum shop; the 126.5-pound king salmon—the largest ever caught commercially— as well as the Tlingit dugout canoe; the Cape Decision lighthouse station lens; and *Earth, Sea and Sky,* a 3-D wall mural outside. ⊠ *203 Fram St.* ☎ *907/772–3598* ⊕ *www. clausenmuseum.net* ⊠ *$3* ☺ *May– early Sept., Mon.–Sat. 10–5; mid-Sept.–Apr. by appointment.*

❶ **Eagle's Roost Park.** Just north of the Petersburg Fisheries cannery, this

PETERSBURG BEST BETS

■ **Soak up the Scandinavian heritage.** Little Norway's cultural history is readily accessible at landmarks like the Clausen Memorial Museum and the Sons of Norway Hall.

■ **Cycle to Sandy Beach.** Rent a bike and pedal up to Sandy Beach, where you can find killer views of Frederick Sound and the Coast Mountains beyond.

■ **Stroll the harbor docks.** Petersburg is one of Alaska's most prosperous fishing communities, and the variety of seacraft is enormous. You can see small trollers, big halibut vessels, and sleek pleasure craft.

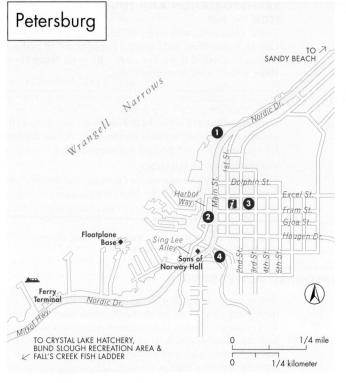

small roadside park is a great place to spot eagles, especially at low tide. On a clear day you will also discover dramatic views of the sharp-edged Coast Range, including the 9,077-foot summit of Devil's Thumb.

❹ **Hammer Slough.** Houses on high stilts and the historic Sons of Norway Hall border this creek that floods with each high tide, creating a photogenic reflecting pool.

LeConte Glacier. Petersburg's biggest draw lies at the foot of the ice cap, about 25 mi east of town. Accessible only by water or air, the LeConte is the continent's southernmost tidewater glacier and one of its most active, often calving off so many icebergs that the tidewater bay at its face is carpeted shore to shore with floating bergs. LeConte Glacier is accessible only by water or air, but if you're cruising to Petersburg, you'll almost definitely stop to see LeConte.

❷ **Petersburg Marine Mammal Center.** Visitors to this nonprofit research and learning center can share and gather information on marine mammal sightings, pick up reference material, and have fun with the interactive educational kiosk. ⊠ *Gjoa St. and Sing Lee Alley, behind Viking Travel* ☎ *907/772–4170 summer only* ⊕ *www.psgmmc.org* ⊠ *Free* ☉ *Mid-June–Aug., Mon.–Sat. 9–5.*

OUTDOOR ACTIVITIES

HIKING

For an enjoyable loop hike from town, follow Dolphin Street uphill from the center of town. At the intersection with 5th Street, a board-walk path leads 900 feet through forested wetlands to the baseball fields, where a second boardwalk takes you to 12th Street and Haugen Drive. Turn left on Haugen and follow it past the airport to **Sandy Beach Park,** where picnickers can sit under log shelters and low tide reveals remnants of ancient fish traps and a number of petroglyphs. From here you can return to town via Sandy Beach Road, or hike the beach when the tide is out. Along the way is the charming **Outlook Park,** a covered observatory with binoculars to scan for marine life. A pullout at Hungry Point provides views to the Coast Range and Frederick Sound. Across the road the half-mile **Hungry Point Trail** takes you back to the baseball fields—a great spot for panoramic views of the mountains—where you can return downtown on the nature boardwalk. Plan on an hour and a half for this walk.

For something more strenuous, a 4-mi trail begins at the airport and climbs 1,600 feet in elevation to **Raven's Roost Cabin.** Along the way you take in a panorama that reaches from the ice-bound Coast Range to the protected waters and forested islands of the Inside Passage far below. The two-story Forest Service cabin is available for rent ($35 per night); contact the **National Recreation Reservation Service** (☎ 518/885–3639 or 877/444–6777 ⊕ www.recreation.gov). Get details on these and other hikes from the Petersburg Visitor Information Center or from the **Petersburg Ranger District** (✉ 12 N. Nordic Dr. ☎ 907/772–3871 ⊕ www.fs.fed.us/r10/tongass).

SHOPPING

At **Tonka Seafoods,** across the street from the Sons of Norway Hall, you can tour the small custom seafood plant, check out the gift shop, and sample smoked or canned halibut and salmon. Be sure to taste the white king salmon—an especially flavorful type of Chinook that the locals swear by. Tonka will also ship. ✉ 22 Sing Lee Alley ☎ 907/772–3662 or 888/560–3662 ⊕ www.tonkaseafoods.com ⚃ Free, tours $15 ☉ June–Aug., daily 8–5; Sept.–May, Mon.–Sat. 8–5; tours at 1 PM (minimum 5 people).

WHERE TO EAT

¢–$ ✕ **Coastal Cold Storage.** This busy little seafood deli in the heart of Peters-
SEAFOOD   burg serves daily lunch specials, including fish chowders and halibut beer bits (a local favorite), along with grilled-chicken wraps, steak sand-wiches, breakfast omelets, and waffles. It's a great place for a quick bite en route to your next adventure; there isn't much seating in the shop's cramped interior. Live or cooked crab is available for takeout, and the shop can process your sport-caught fish. ✉ 306 N. Nordic Dr. ☎ 907/772–4177 or 877/257–4746 ⚌ AE, D, DC, MC, V.

¢ ✕ **Helse Restaurant.** Locals flock to this modest mom-and-pop place for
AMERICAN lunch. It's the closest thing to home cooking Petersburg has to offer,
and most days it's open from 8 to 5, even in winter. A couple of dozen
sandwiches grace the menu, as do rotating soups and homemade bread.
The daily specials are a good bet, and the gyros are decent as well. Helse
also doubles as an ice cream and espresso stand. ⌧ *13 Sing Lee Alley*
☎ *907/772–3444* ▭ *MC, V.*

WHERE TO DRINK

The **Harbor Bar** (⌧ *310 N. Nordic Dr.* ☎ *907/772–4526*), with ships'
wheels, nautical pictures, and a mounted red snapper, is true to the
town's seafaring spirit. A separate outside entrance leads to the bar's
liquor store. Sample the brew and blasting music at the smoky **Kito's
Kave** (⌧ *Sing Lee Alley* ☎ *907/772–3207*), a popular hangout among
rowdy local fishermen. La Fonda, a Mexican restaurant, leases space
inside the bar.

PRINCE RUPERT, BRITISH COLUMBIA

Just 40 mi (66 km) south of the Alaskan border, Prince Rupert is the
largest community on British Columbia's north coast. Set on Kaien
Island at the mouth of the Skeena River and surrounded by deep green
fjords and coastal rain forest, Prince Rupert is rich in the culture of the
Tsimshian, people who have been in the area for thousands of years.

As the western terminus of Canada's second transcontinental railroad
and blessed with a deep natural harbor, Prince Rupert was, at the time
of its incorporation in 1910, poised to rival Vancouver as a center
for trans-Pacific trade. This didn't happen, partly because the main
visionary behind the scheme, Grand Trunk Pacific Railroad president
Charles Hays, went down with the *Titanic* on his way back from a
financing trip to England. Prince Rupert turned instead to fishing and
forestry. A port of call for both British Columbia and Alaska ferries,
but relatively new to cruise ships, this community of 15,000 retains a
laid-back, small-town air.

COMING ASHORE

SHORE EXCURSIONS

Khutzeymateen Grizzly Bear Viewing. Travel by boat to see one of North
America's highest concentrations of grizzly bears, passing stunning
scenery and two First Nations villages en route. Eagles, porpoises, and
whales may also be spotted. Since boats are not permitted to land at the
sanctuary, you'll watch the bears from a safe distance offshore. Viewing is best between mid-May and late July; trips may not be offered in
August and September. ☉ *5½ hrs* ⬟ *$199.*

Marine Life & Whales Discovery. Meet your guide on the dock and walk
a short distance to your waiting boat that features both indoor and
outdoor seating. A 30-minute cruise takes you to the established
whale-watching grounds. You may also see porpoises, seals, Steller
sea lions, puffins, eagles, and other wildlife in the natural beauty of

northern British Columbia. ⏱ *4 hrs* 🎫 *$119.*

Prince Rupert Deluxe Highlights. This three-in-one excursion includes a city tour, a trip to the North Pacific Cannery—a Canadian National Historic Site and the oldest salmon cannery on the coast—and a visit to the renowned Museum of Northern British Columbia. ⏱ *3½ hrs* 🎫 *$75.*

Skeena Kayaking. After a short transfer from the pier, experienced and fully trained guides outfit you and give you a brief introduction to your kayak and safety gear for this half-day eco-adventure. Follow your guide through the rain forest as eagles soar high above and seals survey the kayaks that have entered their domain. ⏱ *4 hrs* 🎫 *$89.*

PRINCE RUPERT BEST BETS

■ **Looking for wildlife?** The Khutzeymateen Grizzly Bear Sanctuary is home to North America's largest concentration of humpbacks and a strong population of orcas.

■ **Short on time?** Pay a visit to the excellent Museum of Northern British Columbia, followed by a stroll around the funky **Cow Bay** neighborhood.

■ **Want something different?** If you have a little extra time, hit the North Pacific Historic Fishing Village.

TRANSPORTATION

FROM THE PIER

Large cruise ships calling at Prince Rupert dock at the **Northland Cruise Terminal,** while smaller ships tie up at **Atlin Terminal** next door. Both terminals are in the city's historic Cow Bay district, steps from the Museum of Northern British Columbia and about five blocks from the central business district. The terminals for both British Columbia and Alaska ferries as well as the VIA Rail station are grouped together about 2 km (1 mi) from town.

Most points of interest are within walking distance of the cruise-ship terminals. **Far West Bus Lines** (☎ *250/624–6400*) offers service around town. For a taxi, contact **Skeena Taxi** (☎ *250/624–2185*).

VISITOR INFORMATION

Prince Rupert's **Visitor Information Centre** (✉ *100 Cow Bay Rd.* ☎ *250/624–5637 or 800/667–1994*) is at the Atlin Terminal. **Tourism Prince Rupert** (🌐 *www.tourismprincerupert.com*) has a useful Web site.

TIME

■TIP➔ If you're coming from Alaska, remember to adjust your watch. British Columbia is on Pacific Time, one hour ahead of Alaska Time.

EXPLORING PRINCE RUPERT

Home to both of Prince Rupert's cruise-ship terminals, **Cow Bay** is a historic waterfront area of shops, galleries, seafood restaurants, yachts, canneries, and fishing boats. Cow Bay takes its name seriously; lampposts, benches, and anything else stationary is painted Holstein-style. While here, you can stop for a coffee or seafood lunch, shop for local crafts, or watch fishermen bring in their catch.

★ The **Museum of Northern British Columbia**, in a longhouse-style facility overlooking the waterfront, has one of the province's finest collections of coastal First Nations art, with artifacts portraying 10,000 years of Northwest Coast history. You may also have a chance to see artisans working in a nearby carving shed. Between June and August, museum staff also operate the **Kwinitsa Railway Museum**, a five-minute walk away on the waterfront. ⊠ *100 1st Ave.* W ☎ *250/624–3207* ⊕ *www. museumofnorthernbc.com* ☑ *C$5* ⊙ *June–Aug., Mon.–Sat. 9–8, Sun. 9–5; Sept.–May, Mon.–Sat. 9–5.*

SHOPPING

Prince Rupert has a great selection of locally made crafts and First Nations artwork. Look for items carved in argillite, a kind of slate unique to this region. The **Cow Bay Gift Galley** (⊠ *24 Cow Bay Rd.* ☎ *250/627–1808*) has gifts, souvenirs, and local art. The **North Coast Artists' Cooperative Ice House Gallery** (⊠ *At Atlin Cruise Ship Terminal* ☎ *250/624–4546*) has paintings, jewelry, weaving, pottery and more, all by local artists.

WHERE TO EAT

$–$$ ✕**Cow Bay Café.** Local seafood and creative vegetarian dishes shine at
CONTEMPORARY this tiny waterfront café, where the friendly chef-owner makes almost everything (including breads and desserts) from scratch. What's on the chalkboard menu depends on what's fresh that day, but could include curries, Mexican dishes, or the popular crab cakes. The solariumlike room with floor-to-ceiling ocean-view windows only seats 35, so reservations are highly recommended. ⊠ *205 Cow Bay Rd., Cow Bay* ☎ *250/627–1212* ⊟ *AE, MC, V* ⊙ *Closed Sun. and Mon. No dinner Tues.*

$ ✕**Cowpuccino's Coffee House.** When Rupertites want to while away a
CAFÉ wet afternoon, they flock to this cozy meeting place in Cow Bay. You can curl up on the sofa with an espresso and a magazine or pull up a chair for homemade soup, sandwiches, panini, and luscious house-made desserts (try the cow patty: a chocolate-macaroon concoction). Hearty breakfasts are served here, too. Outdoor tables are a great place to watch eagles gathering across the street. ⊠ *25 Cow Bay Rd., Cow Bay* ☎ *250/627–1395* ⊟ *MC, V.*

PRINCE WILLIAM SOUND

Tucked into the east side of the Kenai Peninsula, the sound is a peaceful escape from the throngs of people congesting the towns and highways. Enhanced with steep fjords, green enshrouded waterfalls, and calving tidewater glaciers, Prince William Sound is a stunning arena. It has a convoluted coastline, in that it is riddled with islands, which makes it hard to discern just how vast the area is. The sound covers almost 15,000 square mi—more than 12 times the size of Rhode Island—and is home to more than 150 glaciers. The sound is vibrantly alive with all manner of marine life, including salmon, halibut, humpback and orca whales, sea otters, sea lions, and porpoises. Bald eagles are easily seen soaring above, and often brown and black bears, Sitka black-tailed deer, and gray wolves can be spotted on the shore.

Unfortunately, the *Exxon Valdez* oil spill in 1989 heavily damaged parts of the sound, and oil still washes up on shore after high tides and storms. The original spill had a devastating effect on both animal and human lives. What lasting effect this lurking oil will have on the area is still being studied and remains a topic of much debate.

■ TIP➜ Bring your rain gear—Prince William Sound receives more than 150 inches of rain per year.

EXPLORING PRINCE WILLIAM SOUND

The major attraction in Prince William Sound on most Gulf of Alaska cruises is the day spent in **College Fjord.** This deep finger of water boasts the largest collection of tidewater glaciers in the world, and is ringed by 16 glaciers, each named after one of the colleges that sponsored early exploration of the fjord.

A visit to **Columbia Glacier,** which flows from the surrounding Chugach Mountains, is included on many Gulf of Alaska cruises (often via Valdez). Its deep aquamarine face is 5 mi across, and it calves new icebergs with resounding cannonades. This glacier is one of the largest and most readily accessible of Alaska's coastal glaciers.

The three largest Prince William Sound communities—Valdez, Whittier, and Cordova—are all visited by cruise ships, but none is a major destination. Valdez (pronounced val-*deez*) and Cordova are visited only by the smaller, expedition-style cruise ships. Whittier has replaced Seward as a terminus for many sailings by Princess Cruises and some from Cruise West (although passengers actually fly into Anchorage and take transportation provided by the cruise line to Whittier). Cruise West has a special transfer tour from Anchorage to its ships that passes through Whittier village and is included in the fare. Unless you book a shore expedition such as sea kayaking, fishing, or a sound cruise, you won't see much of Whittier (not that you'll be missing anything).

SEWARD

It seems hard to believe that such beauty exists as in Seward. Surrounded on all sides by Kenai Fjords National Park, Chugach National Forest, and Resurrection Bay, Seward offers all the quaint realities of a small railroad town with the bonus of jaw-dropping scenery. This little town of fewer than 3,000 citizens was founded in 1903, when survey crews arrived at the ice-free port and began planning a railroad to the Interior. Since its inception, Seward has relied heavily on tourism and commercial fishing. It is also the launching point for excursions into Kenai Fjords National Park, where it is quite common to see marine life and calving glaciers.

Seward is an important embarkation and disembarkation port for cruise-ship travelers. Many large cruise ships terminate (or start) their seven-day Alaskan voyages in Seward. Although many cruise ships stop in Seward, travelers are often shunted off to Anchorage on waiting buses or train cars with no time to explore this lovely town.

COMING ASHORE

SHORE EXCURSIONS
ADVENTURE
Godwin Glacier Dog Sled Tour. These outstanding tours begin with a 15-minute helicopter flight to remote Godwin Glacier. Here you step onto the ice and learn about mushing from an Iditarod veteran, meet the dogs, and head out across the glacier by dog sled. ⏱ *2 hrs* ✉ *$559.*

SCENIC
Resurrection Bay Cruise. Boats depart from the Seward harbor and cruise near Bear Glacier and past playful sea otters, a sea-lion rookery, and nesting seabirds (including puffins). Whales are commonly sighted, too. ⏱ *3–5 hrs* ✉ *$99.*

TRANSPORTATION AND TOURS
FROM THE PIER
Cruises officially start or end in Seward, but transportation from (or to) Anchorage is either included in your cruise fare or available as an add-on. Cruise ships dock approximately ½ mi from downtown.

AREA TOURS
Kenai Fjords Tours (☎ *907/224–8068 or 877/777–4051* ⊕ *www. kenaifjords.com*) has a good half-day cruise of Resurrection Bay with a stop for a salmon bake on Fox Island ($89 including taxes for a five-hour cruise).

Major Marine Tours (☎ *907/274–7300 or 800/764–7300* ⊕ *www. majormarine.com*) conducts half-day and full-day cruises of Resurrection Bay and Kenai Fjords National Park. Park cruises are narrated by a national park ranger, and buffet meals featuring salmon and prime rib are an option.

Renown Charters and Tours (☎ *907/224–3806 or 888/514–8687* ⊕ *www.renowntours.com*) is the only outfit that operates tours into Resurrection Bay. Cruises include a four-hour whale-watching tour (March 31 through May 18) and a six-hour Kenai Fjords trip, which runs from May 19 through September 16. The latter trip is on a speedy and stable custom-built catamaran.

SEWARD BEST BETS

■ **Get your sea legs.** Seward's main claims to fame and most notable draws are Resurrection Bay and Kenai Fjords National Park.

■ **Landlubber?** Visit the park at Exit Glacier north of town, any of the numerous trails in the area, or shop at one of the stores near the small-boat harbor or in the downtown business district.

■ **Rainy day?** The Sealife Center is not to be missed. It's a combination aquarium, rescue facility for marine animals, and research center. If the seas are too rough or the rain too bothersome, there's interesting stuff here for all ages.

VISITOR INFORMATION

The **Seward Chamber of Commerce** (☏ 907/224–8051 ⊕ *www.sewardak.org*) has a visitor information center at the cruise-ship dock that is staffed when ships are in port. The **Kenai Fjords National Park visitor center** (☏ *907/224–7500* ⊕ *www.nps.gov/kefj* ⊙ *Daily 8:30–7*) is within walking distance: turn left as you leave the pier, then left again onto 4th Avenue; the center is two blocks ahead. Ask here about visiting scenic Exit Glacier, which is 13 mi northwest of Seward. The Alaska National Historical Society operates a book and gift store in the Park Service center. The Chugach National Forest Ranger District office is at 334 4th Avenue. It has maps and information on local trails, cabins, and wildlife.

MARITIME EXPLORATIONS

The protected waters of the bay provide the perfect environment for sailing, fishing, sea kayaking, and marine wildlife–watching. There are numerous tours to choose from—just check out the boardwalk area adjacent to the docks. Half-day tours include Resurrection Bay, while all-day tours also allow you to view parts of spectacular Kenai Fjords National Park. The more adventurous trips venture out of the bay and into the Gulf of Alaska when the notoriously fickle weather permits visits to the more distant glaciers and attractions.

INTERNET   Check your e-mail at the **Sea Bean** (✉ *225 4th Ave.* ☏ *907/224–6623* ✉ *seabeancafe@gmail.com*), or **Rainy Days Internet Cafe** (✉ *1406 4th Ave., Suite D* ☏ *907/224–5774*). The **Seward Memorial Library** has free computer access as well (✉ *238 5th Ave.* ☏ *907/224–4082* ⊕ *www.cityofseward.net/library*).

EXPLORING SEWARD

Ⓒ   Spend an afternoon at the **Alaska SeaLife Center,** with massive cold-
Fodor's Choice   water tanks and outdoor viewing decks, as well as interactive displays
★   of cold-water fish, seabirds, and marine mammals, including harbor seals and a 2,000-pound sea lion. A research center as well as visitor center, it also rehabilitates injured marine wildlife and provides educational experiences for the general public. Appropriately, the center was partially funded with reparations money from the *Exxon Valdez* oil spill. Films, hands-on activities, a gift shop, and behind-the-scenes tours ($12 and up) complete the offerings. ✉ *301 Railway Ave.* ☏ *907/224–6300 or 888/378–2525* ⊕ *www.alaskasealife.org* 💲 *$20* ⊙ *Mid-May–mid-Sept., Mon.–Thurs. 9–6:30, Fri.–Sun. 8–6:30; mid-Sept.–mid-May, daily 10–5.*

The first mile of the historic original **Iditarod Trail** runs along the beach and makes for a nice, easy stroll. There is also a great walking tour designed by the city—maps are available at the visitor bureau, the converted railcar at the corner of 3rd Avenue and Jefferson Street, or the Seward Chamber of Commerce Visitor Center at Mile 2 on the Seward Highway.

Fishing is an important industry and popular recreational activity in Seward.

★ A short walk from the parking lot along a paved path will bring you face to face with **Exit Glacier** (part of **Kenai Fjords National Park**), just outside Seward. Look for the marked turnoff at Mile 3.7 as you enter town or ask locals for directions. There's a small walk-in campground here, a ranger station, and access to the glacier. Exit Glacier is the most accessible part of the **Harding Icefield.** This mass of ice caps the Kenai Mountains, covering more than 1,100 square mi, and it oozes more than 40 glaciers from its edges and down the mountainsides. Reach it from Mile 3.7. The hike to the ice field from the parking lot is a 9-mi round-trip that gains 3,000 feet in elevation, so it's not for the timid or out of shape. But if you're feeling up to the task, the hike and views are breathtaking. Local wildlife includes mountain goats and bears both black and brown, so keep a sharp eye out for them. Once you reach the ice, don't travel across it unless you have the gear and experience with glacier travel. Glacier ice is notoriously deceptive—the surface can look solid and unbroken, while underneath a thin crust of snow crevasses lie in wait for the unwary.

Seward Museum. The Seward Museum displays photographs of the 1964 quake's damage, model rooms and artifacts from the early pioneers, and historical and current information on the Seward area. ⊠ *336 3rd Ave., at Jefferson St.* ☎ *907/224–3902* ✉ *$3* ⊘ *Mid-May–Sept., daily 9–5; Oct.–mid-May, weekends noon–4. Hrs may vary seasonally; call for recorded information.*

Continued on page 274

DID YOU KNOW?

The blue glow of a glacier is caused by the light-absorbing properties of glacial ice. Ice readily absorbs long-wavelength frequencies of light (associated with the color red) but reflects short-wavelength frequencies, which, you guessed it, are blue.

ALASKA'S GLACIERS
NOTORIOUS LANDSCAPE ARCHITECTS

(opposite) Facing the Taku Glacier challenge outside of Juneau. (top) River of ice

Glaciers—those massive, blue-hued tongues of ice that issue forth from Alaska's mountain ranges—perfectly embody the harsh climate, unforgiving terrain, and haunting beauty that make this state one of the world's wildest places. Alaska is home to roughly 100,000 glaciers, which cover almost 5% of the state's land.

FROZEN GIANTS

A glacier occurs where annual snowfall exceeds annual snowmelt. Snow accumulates over thousands of years, forming massive sheets of compacted ice. (Southeast Alaska's **Taku Glacier,** popular with flightseeing devotees, is one of Earth's meatiest: some sections measure over 4,500 feet thick.) Under the pressure of its own weight, the glacier succumbs to gravity and begins to flow downhill. This movement results in sprawling masses of rippled ice (Alaska's **Bering Glacier,** at 127 miles, is North America's longest). When glaciers reach the tidewaters of the coast, icebergs calve, or break off from the glacier's face, plunging dramatically into the sea.

THE RAPIDLY RETREATING GLACIERS IN KENAI FJORDS NATIONAL PARK

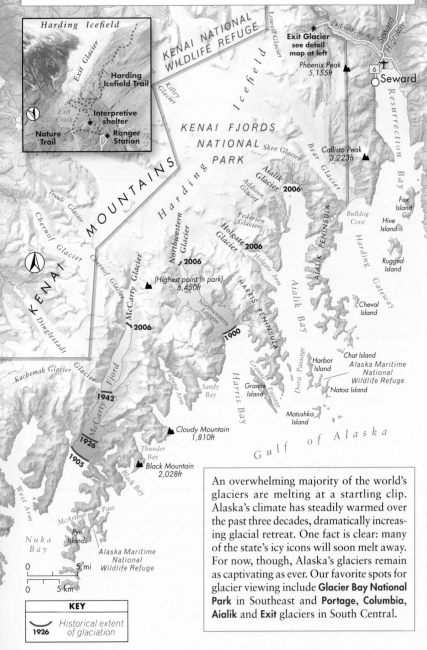

Harding Icefield

Exit Glacier

Harding Icefield Trail

Interpretive shelter

Nature Trail

Ranger Station

Exit Creek

KENAI NATIONAL WILDLIFE REFUGE

Lowell Glacier

Exit Glacier Rd

Exit Glacier see detail map at left

Phoenix Peak 5,155ft

Seward

6

Resurrection Bay

Seward Highway

Icefield

KENAI FJORDS NATIONAL PARK

Skee Glacier

Bear Glacier

Callisto Peak 3,223ft

Aialik Glacier 2006

Addison Glacier

Pedersen Glacier

Holgate Glacier 2006

Holgate Arm

Killey Glacier

Harding Mountains

Northwestern Glacier

2006

(Highest point in park) 6,450ft

Northwestern Lagoon

HARRIS PENINSULA

1900

AIALIK PENINSULA

Bulldog Cove

Aialik Bay

Harding Gateway

Fox Island

Hive Island

Rugged Island

Cheval Island

Trauli Glacier

Chernof Glacier

McCarty Glacier

Chernof Glacier

McCarty Glacier

2006

McCarty Fjord

Paguna Arm

Harris Bay

Granite Passage

Dora Passage

Harbor Island

Chat Island

Alaska Maritime National Wildlife Refuge

Natoa Island

KENAI MOUNTAINS

Dinglestadt Glacier

Kachemak Glacier

Glacier

1942

1926

1905

Sandy Bay

Granite Island

Matushka Island

Cloudy Mountain 1,810ft

Gulf of Alaska

West Arm

Black Bay

Thunder Bay

Black Mountain 2,028ft

Nuka Bay

McArthur Pass

Pye Islands

Alaska Maritime National Wildlife Refuge

0   5 mi
0   5 km

An overwhelming majority of the world's glaciers are melting at a startling clip. Alaska's climate has steadily warmed over the past three decades, dramatically increasing glacial retreat. One fact is clear: many of the state's icy icons will soon melt away. For now, though, Alaska's glaciers remain as captivating as ever. Our favorite spots for glacier viewing include **Glacier Bay National Park** in Southeast and **Portage, Columbia, Aialik** and **Exit** glaciers in South Central.

KEY

1926 *Historical extent of glaciation*

ICY BLUE HIKES & THUNDEROUS BOATING EXCURSIONS

Glaciers enchant us with their size and astonishing power to shape the landscape. But let's face it: nothing rivals the sheer excitement of watching a bus-size block of ice burst from a glacier's face, creating an unholy thunderclap that resounds across an isolated Alaskan bay.

Most frequently undertaken with a seasoned guide, **glacier trekking** is becoming increasingly popular. Many guides transport visitors to and from glaciers (in some cases by helicopter or small plane), and provide ski excursions, dogsled tours, or guided hikes on the glacier's surface. Striding through the surreal landscape of a glacier, ice crunching underfoot, can be an otherworldly experience. Whether you're whooping it up on a dogsled tour, learning the fundamentals of glacier travel, or simply poking about on a massive field of ice, you're sure to gain an acute appreciation for the massive scale of the state's natural environment.

You can also experience glaciers **via boat**, such as the Alaska Marine Highway, a cruise ship, a small chartered boat, or even your own bobbing kayak. Our favorite out of Seward is the ride with Kenai Fjords Tours. Don't be discouraged by rainy weather. Glaciers often appear even bluer on overcast days. When piloting your own vessel, be sure to keep your distance from the glacier's face.

■ TIP→ For more information about viewing Alaska's glaciers, see Chapter 1: Sports & Wilderness Adventures.

Taking in the sights at Mendenhall Glacier

DID YOU KNOW?

What do glaciers and cows have in common? They both *calve*. While bovine calving refers to actual calf-birth, the word is also used to describe a tidewater glacier's stunning habit of rupturing icebergs from its terminus. When glacier ice meets the sea, steady tidal movement and warmer temperatures cause these frequent, booming deposits.

GLACIER-VIEWING TIPS

- The most important rule of thumb is never to venture onto a glacier without proper training or the help of a guide.

- Not surprisingly, glaciers have a cooling effect on their surroundings, so wear layers and bring gloves and rain gear.

- Glaciers can powerfully reflect sunlight, even on cloudy days. Sunscreen, sunglasses, and a brimmed hat are essential.

- Warm, thick-soled waterproof footwear is a must.

- Don't forget to bring a camera and binoculars (preferably waterproof).

OUTDOOR ACTIVITIES

FISHING

For several weeks in August the **Seward Silver Salmon Derby** attracts hundreds of competitors for the $10,000 top prize. Get details from the **Fish House** (✉ *Small-boat harbor* ☎ *907/224–3674 or 800/257–7760* ⊕ *www. thefishhouse.net*), Seward's oldest booking agency for deep-sea fishing.

HIKING

The strenuous **Mt. Marathon** trail starts at the west end of Lowell Canyon Road and runs practically straight uphill. An easier and more convenient hike is the **Two Lakes Trail,** a loop of footpaths and bridges on the edge of town. A map is available from the **Seward Chamber of Commerce** (✉ *2001 Seward Hwy.* ☎ *907/224–8051* ⊕ *www.sewardak.org*).

Exit Glacier Guides (✉ *Small-boat harbor* ☎ *907/224–5569 or 907/491– 0552 [Sept.–May]* ⊕ *www.exitglacierguides.com*) offers guided tours to Exit Glacier—and not just to the moraine, where most tourists stop, but to the glacier itself and Harding Icefield. For those going it alone, catch their hourly shuttle from downtown to the glacier for $10 round-trip.

SHOPPING

The **Ranting Raven** (✉ *228 4th Ave.* ☎ *907/224–2228*) is a combination gift shop, bakery, and lunch spot, adorned with raven murals on the side of the building. **Resurrect Art Coffeehouse** (✉ *320 3rd Ave.* ☎ *907/224– 7161* ⊕ *www.resurrectart.com*) is a darling coffeehouse and gallery-gift shop. It is housed in a 1932 church, and the ambience and views from the old choir loft are reason enough to stop by. Art tends toward the local rather than mass-produced.

WHERE TO EAT

$$$$
SEAFOOD
✕ **Chinooks Waterfront Restaurant.** On the waterfront in the small-boat harbor, Chinooks has a dazzling selection of fresh seafood dishes, brews on tap, a great wine selection, and a stunning view from the upstairs window seats. Pasta dishes and a few beef specialties round out the menu. ✉ *1404 4th Ave.* ☎ *907/224–2207* ⊕ *www.chinookswaterfront. com* ☰ *MC, V* ☉ *Closed mid-Oct.–May.*

¢–$
MEXICAN
✕ **Railway Cantina.** This little hole-in-the-wall in the harbor area is a local favorite. A wide selection of burritos, quesadillas, and great fish tacos incorporates local seafood and is supplemented by an array of hot sauces, many contributed by customers who brought them from their travels. ✉ *1401 4th Ave.* ☎ *907/224–8226* ☰ *MC, V.*

SITKA

Sitka was home to the Kiksádi clan of the Tlingit people for centuries prior to the 18th-century arrival of the Russians under the direction of territorial governor Alexander Baranof. The Tlingits attacked Baranof's people and burned his buildings in 1802, but Baranof returned in 1804 with formidable strength, including shipboard cannons. He attacked the

Tlingits at their fort near Indian River (site of the present-day, 105-acre Sitka National Historical Park) and drove them to Chichagof Island, 70 mi northwest of Sitka. The Tlingits and Russians made peace in 1821, and eventually the capital of Russian America was shifted from Kodiak to Sitka.

Today Sitka is known for its beautiful setting and some of Southeast Alaska's most famous landmarks: the onion-dome St. Michael's Cathedral; the Alaska Raptor Center, where you can come up close to ailing and recovering birds of prey; and Sitka National Historical Park, where you can see some of the oldest and most skillfully carved totem poles in the state.

COMING ASHORE

SHORE EXCURSIONS
ADVENTURE
***Sea Life Discovery* Semi-Submersible.** Large underwater windows on this vessel let you see Sitka Sound's kelp forests, fish, and crab. Just outside the boat, divers capture underwater camera images that are then displayed on the boat's video monitor. ⊘ *2 hrs* ◻ *$89.*

Sitka Bike and Hike Tour. This guided, three-hour hike-and-bike excursion takes you out of town for a 5-mi ride over gently rolling terrain. Stop at Thimbleberry Creek for a short hike that crosses a picturesque waterfall and resume your bike ride to Whale Park. End at Theobroma Chocolate Factory, where you can enjoy a locally made chocolate bar before taking the bus back to town. ⊘ *3 hrs* ◻ *$89.*

Sportfishing. Try for the abundant salmon and halibut in these waters. All equipment is provided; you buy your license on board. Your catch can be frozen and shipped. ⊘ *4 hrs* ◻ *$230.*

Wilderness Sea Kayaking Adventure. Kayak Sitka's coves and tranquil waterways against the backdrop of the Mt. Edgecumbe volcano. Warm up with a hot beverage and snack at the base camp before returning to your ship. ⊘ *3 hrs* ◻ *$95–$116.*

CULTURAL
History and Nature Walking Tour. A guided walk through Sitka details its political and natural history. This tour includes all the major sites plus a visit to the Sitka National Historic Park for a stroll through the rain forest, and time at the Alaska Raptor Center. Return downtown by van. ⊘ *3 hrs* ◻ *$56.*

Russian-America Tour. Stops at Castle Hill, the Russian Cemetery, St. Michael's Cathedral, and Sitka National Historic Park are included in this bus-and-walking tour of Sitka's rich Russian heritage. The finale is a Russian-style folk-dance performance by the New Archangel Dancers, local women who have mastered the timing and athletic feats required for this traditional style of dance. ⊘ *2½ hrs* ◻ *$46.*

SCENIC
Sea Otter Quest. This search for the sea otter and other Sitka wildlife is a cruise passenger favorite. Creatures that you're likely to see from the boat include whales, eagles, puffins, and more. ⊘ *3 hrs* ◻ *$120.*

Tongass Forest Nature Hike. This 4-mi hike provides an excellent introduction to the rain forests that surround Sitka. The hike covers a mix of boardwalk and gravel trails through tall spruce forests and open muskeg, and then loops back via the shore. ⏱ *3 hrs* 🚌 *$82.*

TRANSPORTATION AND TOURS

FROM THE PIER
Only the smallest excursion vessels can dock at Sitka. Medium to large cruise ships must drop anchor in the harbor and tender passengers ashore near **Harrigan Centennial Hall.** You can recognize the hall by the big Tlingit war canoe to the side of the building. Sitka is an extremely walkable town, and the waterfront attractions are all fairly close to the tender landing.

SITKA BEST BETS

■ **Take in the Totems.** Just east of downtown, Sitka National Historical Park features a workshop, interpretive center, and 15 topnotch totem poles spread along a meandering waterfront wooded trail.

■ **Visit the Alaska Raptor Center.** Alaska's only full-service avian hospital lets you get face-to-beak with more than 100 injured and rehabilitating bald eagles, hawks, owls, and other raptors.

■ **Stroll Around.** Sitka's oceanfront setting, picturesque streets, and rich, varied history make it one of the Southeast's best walking towns.

VISITOR INFORMATION
Housed in Harrigan Centennial Hall is an information desk for the **Sitka Convention and Visitors Bureau** (✉ *303 Lincoln St.* ☎ *907/747–5940* ⊕ *www.sitka.org*), where you can get a list of local charter-fishing operators.

INTERNET Check your e-mail via Wi-Fi on your own device for free (with coffee purchase) at **Highliner Coffee** (✉ *327 Seward St.* ☎ *907/747–4924*).

EXPLORING SITKA

It's hard not to like Sitka, with its eclectic blend of Native, Russian, and American history and its dramatic and beautiful setting. ■TIP→ This is one of the best Inside Passage towns to explore on foot.

❾ **Alaska Raptor Center.** The only full-service avian hospital in Alaska, the
Ⓒ Raptor Center rehabilitates 100 to 200 birds each year. Situated just
★ above Indian Creek, the center is a 20-minute walk from downtown. Well-versed guides provide an introduction to the rehabilitation center (including a short video), and guests are able to visit with one of these majestic birds. The Raptor Center's primary attraction is an enclosed 20,000-square-foot flight training center, built to replicate the rain forest, where injured eagles relearn survival skills, including flying and catching salmon. Visitors watch through one-way glass windows. A large deck out back faces an open-air enclosure for eagles and other raptors whose injuries prevent them from returning to the wild. Additional mews with hawks, owls, and other birds are along a rain-forest path. The gift shop sells all sorts of eagle paraphernalia, the proceeds from which fund the center's programs. ✉ *1000 Raptor Way, off Sawmill*

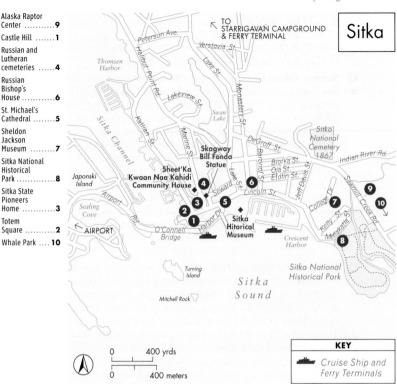

Creek Rd. ☎ 907/747–8662 or 800/643–9425 ⊕ www.alaskaraptor. org ⊠ $12 ☉ Mid-May–Sept., daily 8–4.

⑥ Russian Bishop's House. A registered historic landmark, this house facing the harbor was constructed by the Russian-American Company for Bishop Innocent Veniaminov in 1842 and completed in 1843. Inside the house, one of the few remaining Russian-built log structures in Alaska, are exhibits on the history of Russian America, including several places where portions of the house's structure are peeled away to expose Russian building techniques. The ground level is a free museum, and Park Service rangers lead guided tours of the second floor, which houses the residential quarters and a chapel. ⊠ 501 Lincoln St. ☎ 907/747–6281 ⊕ www.nps.gov/sitk ⊠ Tours $5 ☉ May–Sept., 9–5; Oct.–Apr. by appointment.

⑤ St. Michael's Cathedral. This cathedral, one of Southeast Alaska's best-★ known national landmarks, is treasured by visitors and locals alike—so treasured that in 1966, as a fire engulfed the building, townspeople risked their lives and rushed inside to rescue the cathedral's precious Russian icons, religious objects, and vestments. Using original blueprints, an almost exact replica of onion-dome St. Michael's was completed in 1976. Today you can see what could possibly be the largest collection of Russian icons in the United States, among them the much-prized *Our Lady of Sitka* (also known as the *Sitka Madonna*) and the *Christ Pantocrator* (*Christ the World Judge*), displayed on the altar screen. ⊠ *240 Lincoln St.* ☎ *907/747–8120* ⊡ *$2 requested donation* ⊙ *May–Sept., daily 8:30–4; Oct.–Apr., hrs vary.*

❼ Sheldon Jackson Museum. Near the campus of the former **Sheldon Jack-**
★ **son College,** this octagonal museum, which dates from 1895, contains priceless Native Alaskan items collected by Dr. Sheldon Jackson (1834–1909), who traveled the remote regions of Alaska as an educator and missionary. This state-run museum features artifacts from every native Alaska culture; on display are carved masks, Chilkat blankets, dogsleds, kayaks, and even the impressive helmet worn by Chief Katlean during the 1804 battle against the Russians. The museum's gift shop, operated by the Friends of the Sheldon Jackson Museum, carries books, paper goods, and handicrafts created by Alaska native artists. ■ **TIP➔ Native artisans are here all summer, creating baskets, carvings, or masks.** ⊠ *104 College Dr.* ☎ *907/747–8981* ⊕ *www.museums.state.ak.us* ⊡ *$4 mid-May–mid-Sept., $3 mid-Sept.–mid-May* ⊙ *Mid-May–mid-Sept., daily 9–5; mid-Sept.–mid-May, Tues.–Sat. 10–4.*

❽ Sitka National Historical Park. The main building at this 113-acre park
Fodor's Choice houses a small museum with fascinating historical exhibits and photos
★ of Tlingit native culture. Highlights include a brass peace hat given to the Sitka Kiksádi by Russian traders in the early 1800s and Chilkat robes. Head to the theater to watch a 12-minute video about Russian-Tlingit conflict in the 19th century. Also here is the **Southeast Alaska Indian Cultural Center,** where native artisans demonstrate silversmith-ing, weaving, wood carving, and basketry. Don't be afraid to strike up a conversation; the artisans are happy to talk about their work and Tlingit cultural traditions. At the far end of the building are seven totems (some more than a century old) that have been brought indoors to protect them from decay. Behind the center, a wide, 2-mi path takes you through the forest and along the shore of Sitka Sound. Scattered along the way are some of the most skillfully carved native totem poles in Alaska. Keep going on the trail to see spawning salmon from the footbridge over Indian River. Park Service rangers lead themed walks in summer, which focus on the Russian-Tlingit conflict, the area's natural history, and the park's totem poles. ⊠ *106 Metlakatla St.* ☎ *907/747–6281, 907/747–8061 gift shop* ⊕ *www.nps.gov/sitk* ⊡ *$4* ⊙ *Daily 8–5.*

❸ Sitka State Pioneers Home. Known locally as just the Pioneers Home, this large, red-roof home for elder Alaskans has an imposing 14-foot statue in front symbolizing Alaska's frontier sourdough spirit ("sourdough" generally refers to Alaska's American pioneers and prospectors); it was modeled by an authentic prospector, William "Skagway Bill" Fonda. Adjacent to the Pioneers Home is **Sheet'ka Kwaan Naa Kahidi** commu-nity house, where you can watch native dance performances throughout the summer. ⊠ *Lincoln and Katlian Sts.* ☎ *907/747–3213.*

❷ Totem Square. On this grassy square directly across the street from the Pioneers Home are three anchors discovered in local waters and believed to be of 19th-century British origin. Look for the double-headed eagle of czarist Russia carved into the cedar of the totem pole in the park.

DID YOU KNOW?

Individual elements of totem poles can be interpreted with some specificity—the two bottom faces on this Heida house post in Sitka, for example, represent the passing of information between generations—but traditionally, it's thought that no one can fully interpret a single totem's interconnected stories except the carver.

Sitka in wintry late-morning dawn light.

⑩ Whale Park. This small waterside park sits in the trees 4 mi east of Sitka
right off Sawmill Creek Road. Boardwalk paths lead to five viewing
platforms and steps take you down to the rocky shoreline. A gazebo
next to the parking area contains signs describing the whales that visit
Silver Bay, and you can listen to their sounds from recordings and an
offshore hydrophone here. ■TIP→ Tune your radio to FM 88.1 anywhere
in Sitka to hear a broadcast of humpback whale sounds picked up by the
hydrophone.

SPORTS AND THE OUTDOORS

Allen Marine Tours (☎907/747–8100 or 888/747–8101 ⊕ *www.
allenmarinetours.com*), one of the Southeast's largest and best-known
tour operators, leads different boat-based Sitka Sound tours throughout
the summer. The Wildlife Quest tours are a fine opportunity to view
humpback whales, sea otters, puffins, eagles, and brown bears in a
spectacular setting. When seas are calm enough, it offers a tour to the
bird sanctuary at **St. Lazaria Islands National Wildlife Refuge.**

Sea Life Tours (☎907/966–2301 or 877/966–2301 ⊕ *www.sealife
discoverytours.com*) operates a semisubmersible tour vessel with large
underwater windows that provide views of kelp forests, fish, crab, sea
urchins, anemones, and starfish. Divers with underwater cameras zoom
in for close-up views via the video monitor.

SHOPPING

Fishermen's Eye Fine Art Gallery (⊠ *239 Lincoln St.* ☎ *907/747–6080* ⊕ *www.fishermenseye.com*) is a tasteful downtown gallery that prides itself on its vibrant collection of made-in-Sitka art including silver jewelry, native masks, and carved bowls.

Fresh Fish Company (⊠ *411 DeGroff St.* ☎ *907/747–5565, 888/747–5565 outside Alaska*) sells and ships fresh locally caught salmon, halibut, and shrimp.

WHERE TO EAT

$$$–$$$$
MEDITERRANEAN
Fodor'sChoice
★
✕ **Ludvig's Bistro.** This remarkably creative eatery used to escape detection by most tourists (much to the pleasure of Sitkans). It's now almost always packed with food lovers from all corners of the globe, so be prepared for a wait—but rest assured that Ludvig's is worth it. The interior evokes an Italian bistro, with rich yellow walls and copper-topped tables. Seafood (particularly king salmon and scallops) is the specialty, and organic ingredients are used whenever possible. You'll also find Caesar salads, vegetarian specials, Angus filet mignon, and one of the state's best wine lists. From 2 to 5 the café serves Spanish-style tapas with house wine for $13–$17. ⊠ *256 Katlian St.* ☎ *907/966–3663* ▭ *AE, MC, V* ☉ *Closed mid-Feb.–Apr.*

$–$$
AMERICAN
✕ **Nugget Restaurant.** Travelers flying out from Sitka head here while hoping their jet will make it through the pea-soup fog outside. The setting is standard, and the menu encompasses burgers (15 kinds), sandwiches, tuna melts, salads, steaks, pasta, seafood, and Friday-night prime rib. There's a big breakfast menu, too, but the real attraction is the range of homemade pies, which are known throughout Southeast Alaska. ■ **TIP➜** Get a slice à la mode, or buy a whole pie to take with you. The lemon custard is a local favorite. Reservations are recommended. ⊠ *Sitka Airport Terminal* ☎ *907/966–2480* ▭ *AE, D, DC, MC, V.*

WHERE TO DRINK

As far as the locals are concerned, a spot in one of the limited green-and-white-vinyl booths at **Pioneer Bar** (⊠ *212 Katlian St.* ☎ *907/747–3456*), across from the harbor, is a fine destination. It's vintage Alaska, with hundreds of pictures of local fishing boats, rough-hewn locals clad in Carhartts and Xtra-Tuff boots, occasional live music, and pool tables. Regulars, mostly local fishermen, swear by the submarine sandwiches and hot dogs.

SKAGWAY

Located at the northern terminus of the Inside Passage, Skagway is a one-hour boat ride from Haines. You'll find the town to be an amazingly preserved artifact from North America's biggest, most storied gold rush. Most of the downtown district forms part of the Klondike Gold Rush National Historical Park, a unit of the national park system dedicated to commemorating and interpreting the frenzied stampede of 1897 that extended to Dawson City in Canada's Yukon.

Nearly all the historic sights are within a few blocks of the cruise-ship and ferry dock, allowing visitors to meander through the town's attractions at whatever pace they choose. You'll quickly discover that tourism is the lifeblood of this town; you aren't likely to find a quiet Alaska experience around Skagway.

COMING ASHORE

SHORE EXCURSIONS

ADVENTURE

Heli-Hike Glacier Trek. The helicopter flight that begins this popular trip is followed by a 4-mi hike to Laughton Glacier. Return to Skagway on the famous White Pass & Yukon Route Railway. Participants must be in strong physical condition. ⊙ 5½ hrs 🔁 $374.

Hike and Float the Chilkoot Trail. This trip opens with a guided van tour to the historic gold-rush townsite of Dyea, start of the historic Chilkoot Trail. From here you hike 2 mi along the Taiya River, then board rafts for an easy 40-minute float back to Dyea. No children under seven are allowed. ⊙ 4¼ hrs 🔁 $100–$105.

Klondike Bicycle Tour. Ride a van to the top of the Klondike Pass and then bike 15 mi downhill, taking in the spectacular views of White Pass and Alaska's scenery along the way. Stops are made to take photographs of the area's glaciers, coastal mountains, and waterfalls. ⊙ 2½ hrs 🔁 $85.

CULTURAL/SCENIC

Klondike Summit, Yukon Suspension Bridge & Gold. Travel by motor coach for a narrated trip 3,290 feet above sea level to the White Pass Summit, then visit the Yukon Suspension Bridge to learn how early settler's survived in this harsh environment. Complete the tour by panning for gold in warm-water troughs at The Klondike Gold Fields. Gold is guaranteed and there's a special treasure hunt available for kids. Passport required. ⊙ 4½ hrs 🔁 $84 (adult), $43 (children).

Skagway Streetcar. Ride in the Skagway Streetcar Company's vintage 1930s cars through town to the Gold Rush Cemetery and Reid Falls, accompanied by a knowledgeable tour guide dressed in Victorian-style costume. ⊙ 2 hrs 🔁 $40.

White Pass & Yukon Railroad. The 20-mi trip in vintage railroad cars skims along the edge of granite cliffs, climbs to 2,865 feet at White Pass Summit, and zigzags through dramatic scenery—including the actual Trail of '98, worn into the mountainside a century ago. Alternate routes take you as far as Fraser, British Columbia (where bus connections are available for the trip back to Skagway), or Carcross, Yukon. ⊙ 3½ hrs 🔁 $125.

TRANSPORTATION AND TOURS

FROM THE PIER

Skagway is a major stop for cruise ships in Alaska, and this little town sometimes has four large ships in port at once. Some dock a short stroll from downtown, others ½ mi away at the Railroad Dock, where city buses are waiting to provide transportation to the center of town. The charge is $2 one-way, or $5 for a day pass.

Virtually all the shops and gold-rush sights are along Broadway, the main strip that leads from the visitor center through the middle of town. It's a nice walk from the docks up through Broadway, but you can also take tours in horse-drawn surreys, antique limousines, and modern vans.

AREA TOURS

Fodor'sChoice ★ Visitors to Skagway can travel at least part of the way along the gold-rush route aboard the **White Pass & Yukon Route** (WP & YR) narrow-gauge railroad. The historic diesel locomotives tow vintage viewing cars up the route's steep inclines, hugging the walls of precipitous

cliff sides and providing views of craggy peaks, plummeting waterfalls, lakes, and forests. Two or three times daily the WP & YR leaves Skagway for a three-hour, round-trip excursion to the White Pass summit. Sights along the way include Bridal Veil Falls, Inspiration Point, and Dead Horse Gulch. Longer trips into the Yukon, special steam excursions, and a Chilkoot Trail hikers' service are also offered. For dockside boarding, cruise passengers must purchase their train tickets aboard their ships. ✉ *231 2nd Ave.* ☎ *800/343–7373* ⊕ *www.whitepassrailroad.com* ☯ *Mid-May–late Sept., daily.*

VISITOR INFORMATION

You can't help but notice the Arctic Brotherhood Hall—just up Broadway between 2nd and 3rd avenues—with its curious driftwood-mosaic facade. Inside is the **Skagway Convention and Visitors Bureau** (☎ *907/983–2854* ⊕ *www.skagway.com*), along with public restrooms. From the pier you can see the large maroon-and-yellow building that houses the museum and visitor center of **Klondike Gold Rush National Historical Park** (☎ *907/983–2921* ⊕ *www.nps.gov/klgo*), which presents historical photographs, artifacts, and films. Rangers lead guided walks through town, and can provide details on nearby hiking trails (including the famous Chilkoot Trail). Next door to the visitor center is the White Pass & Yukon Route Depot, the departure point for Skagway's most popular shore excursion.

INTERNET Check your e-mail at **Glacial Smoothies** (✉ *336-B 3rd Ave.* ☎ *907/983–3223*).

EXPLORING SKAGWAY

Skagway is one of the easiest ports in Alaska to explore on foot. The town is flat, and nearly all the historic sights are within a few blocks of the cruise-ship and ferry dock, so you can take all the time you want. Just walk up and down Broadway, detouring here and there into the side streets. Keep an eye out for the humorous architectural details and advertising irreverence that mark the Skagway spirit.

❷ ★ Arctic Brotherhood Hall. The Arctic Brotherhood was a fraternal organization of Alaska and Yukon pioneers. Local members of the Brotherhood built the building's (now renovated) false front out of 8,833 pieces of driftwood and flotsam gathered from local beaches. The result: one of the most unusual buildings in all of Alaska. The AB Hall now houses the **Skagway Convention and Visitors Bureau,** along with public restrooms. ⊠ *Broadway between 2nd and 3rd Aves., Box 1029* ☎ *907/983–2854, 888/762–1898 message only* ⊕ *www.skagway.com* ☉ *May–Sept., daily 8–6; Oct.–Apr., weekdays 8–noon and 1–5.*

❹ Corrington's Museum of Alaskan History. Inside a gift shop, this impressive (and free) scrimshaw museum highlights more than 40 exquisitely carved walrus tusks and other exhibits that detail Alaska's history. Dennis Corrington, a one-time Iditarod Race runner, and the founder of the Museum, is often present. A bright flower garden decorates the exterior. ⊠ *5th Ave. and Broadway* ☎ *907/983–2579* ⊠ *Free* ☉ *Open when cruise ships are in port.*

❸ ★ Since 1927 locals have performed a show called *The Days of '98 with Soapy Smith* at **Eagles Hall.** You'll see cancan dancers (including Molly Fewclothes, Belle Davenport, and Squirrel Tooth Alice), learn a little local history, and watch desperado Soapy Smith being sent to his reward. At the evening show you can enjoy a few warm-up rounds of mock gambling with Soapy's money. Performances of Robert Service poetry start a half hour before showtime. ⊠ *Broadway and 6th Ave.* ☎ *907/983–2545 May–mid-Sept., 808/328–9132 mid-Sept.–Apr.* ⊠ *$20* ☉ *Mid-May–mid-Sept., daily at 10:30, 2:30, and 8.*

❶ ★ Klondike Gold Rush National Historical Park. Housed in the former White Pass and Yukon Route Depot, this wonderful museum contains exhibits, photos, and artifacts from the White Pass and Chilkoot trails. It's a must-see for anyone planning on taking a White Pass train ride, driving the nearby Klondike Highway, or hiking the Chilkoot Trail. Films, ranger talks, and walking tours are offered. Special free Robert Service poetry performances by Buckwheat Donahue—a beloved local character and head of the Skagway Convention and Visitors Bureau—occasionally take place at the visitor center. ⊠ *2nd Ave. at Broadway* ☎ *907/983–2921 or 907/983–9224* ⊕ *www.nps.gov/klgo* ⊠ *Free* ☉ *May–Sept., daily 8–6; Oct.–Apr., weekdays 8–5.*

❺ Moore Cabin. Built in 1887 by Captain William Moore and his son Ben Moore, the tiny cabin was the first structure built in Skagway. An early homesteader, Captain Moore prospered from the flood of miners, constructing a dock, warehouse, and sawmill to supply them, and selling land for other ventures. Next door, the larger **Moore House** (1897–98) contains interesting exhibits on the Moore family. Both structures are

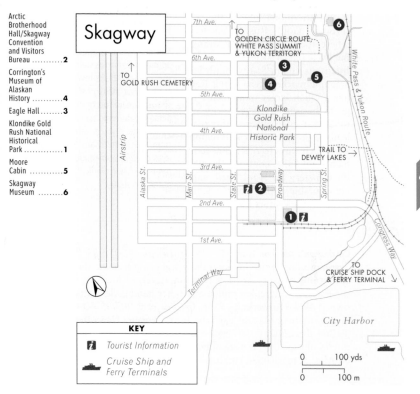

KEY

🛈 *Tourist Information*

⛴ *Cruise Ship and Ferry Terminals*

maintained by the Park Service, and the main house is open daily in summer. ⊠ *5th Ave. between Broadway and Spring St.* ☎ *907/983–2921* ⊙ *Memorial Day–Labor Day, daily 10–5.*

6 Skagway Museum. This nicely designed museum occupies the ground floor of the beautiful building that also houses Skagway City Hall. Inside, you'll find a 19th-century Tlingit canoe (one of only two like it on the West Coast), historic photos, a red-and-black sleigh, and other gold rush–era artifacts, along with a healthy collection of contemporary local art and post–gold rush history exhibits. ⊠ *7th Ave. and Spring St.* ☎ *907/983–2420* 💲*$2* ⊙ *Mid-May–Sept., weekdays 9–5, weekends 10–4; Oct.–mid-May, hrs vary.*

OUTDOOR ACTIVITIES

HIKING

Real wilderness is within a stone's throw of the docks, which makes this an excellent hiking port. Try the short jaunt to beautiful Lower Dewey Lake. Start at the corner of 4th Avenue and Spring Street, go toward the mountain, cross the footbridge over Pullen Creek, and follow the trail uphill. It's a 20-minute climb to the lake.

A less strenuous hike is the trip through Gold Rush Cemetery, where the epitaphs offer strange but lively bits of social commentary. Infamous villain Soapy Smith has a simple marker; hero Frank Reid has a much larger monument. To get to the cemetery, take the city bus to 23rd Avenue, where a dirt road leads to the graves; it's a 10-minute walk each way. To reach 300-foot-high Reid Falls, continue through the cemetery for ¼ mi. Trail maps are available at the Skagway Convention and Visitors Bureau.

> **DID YOU KNOW?**
>
> You may find it strange to see so many diamonds being sold in these small Alaska towns. The truth is that many of the jewelry shops in major ports of call are actually international chain-store operations. If you'd rather buy from a local merchant, keep your eyes peeled; year-round residents often post signs indicating their authentic status.

SHOPPING

Corrington's Alaskan Ivory (⊠ *525 Broadway* ☎ *907/983–2579*) is the destination of choice for scrimshaw seekers; it has one the state's best collections of ivory art. For those in search of locally produced silver jewelry, watercolor prints, and other handmade crafts, the artist-owned **Alaska Artworks** (⊠ *555C Broadway* ☎ *907/983–3443* ⊕ *www.skagwayartworks.com*) can't be beat. **Skaguay News Depot & Books** (⊠ *264 Broadway* ☎ *907/983–3354*), its moniker a throwback to the town's old spelling, is a small but quaint bookstore that carries books on Alaska, magazines, children's books, maps, and gifts.

WHERE TO EAT

¢ ✕ **Glacial Smoothies and Espresso.** This local hangout is the place to go
CAFÉ for a breakfast bagel or a lunchtime soup-and-sandwich combo. Prices are steeper than at some coffee shops—a 12-ounce mocha goes for $4—but the ingredients are fresh and local, and nearly everything on the menu is made on-site. Customers can cool down with a Mango Madness or Blueberry Blues smoothie, and soft-serve ice cream in summer. ⊠ *3rd Ave. between Main and State Sts.* ☎ *907/983–3223* ☰ *MC, V* ☺ *No dinner.*

$–$$ ✕ **Skagway Pizza Station.** Housed in a former gas station, this year-round
PIZZA restaurant is known for its comfort-food specials, such as meat loaf or stuffed pork chops with mashed potatoes and gravy. (Friday is prime-rib day.) The huge calzones are stuffed and served piping hot with sides of house marinara and ranch dressing—build your own or choose one of the chef's creations, like the Chicken Hawk Squawk with pineapple and jalapeños. ⊠ *4th Ave. between Main and State Sts.* ☎ *907/983–2200* ☰ *MC, V.*

$$–$$$ ✕ **Stowaway Cafe.** Always crowded, this noisy little harborside café is
CAFÉ just a few steps from the cruise-ship dock. Seafood is the attraction—including wasabi salmon and glacé de poisson—but you can also eat steaks, chicken, or smoked ribs. The café is open daily for dinner

Travel the White Pass and Yukon route via train out of Skagway.

only. ⊠ *205 Congress Way* ☎ *907/983–3463* ▭ *AE, MC, V* ⊘ *Closed Oct.–Apr. No lunch.*

WHERE TO DRINK

Whereas Skagway was once host to dozens upon dozens of watering holes in its gold-rush days, the **Red Onion Saloon** (⊠ *Broadway at 2nd Ave.* ☎ *907/983–2222* ⊕ *www.redonion1898.com*) is pretty much the sole survivor among them. The upstairs was Skagway's first bordello, and you'll find a convivial crowd of Skagway locals and visitors among the scantily clad mannequins who represent the building's former illustrious tenants. A ragtime pianist tickles the keys in the afternoons, and local musicians strut their stuff on Thursday nights. The saloon closes up shop for winter.

TRACY ARM

Tracy Arm and its sister fjord, Endicott Arm, have become staples on many Inside Passage cruises. Ships sail into the arm just before or after a visit to Juneau, 50 mi to the north. A day of scenic cruising in Tracy Arm is a lesson in geology and the forces that shape Alaska. The fjord was carved by a glacier eons ago, leaving behind sheer granite cliffs. Waterfalls continue the process of erosion that the glaciers began. Very small ships may nudge their bows under the waterfalls so crew members can fill pitchers full of glacial runoff. It's a unique Alaska refreshment. Tracy Arm's glaciers haven't disappeared, though; they've just receded, and at the very end of Tracy Arm you'll come to two of them, known as the twin Sawyer Glaciers. Because the glaciers constantly shed enormous blocks of ice, navigating the passage is sometimes difficult, which can prevent ships from reaching the glacier's face.

VALDEZ

Valdez (pronounced val-*deez*) is the largest of the Prince William Sound communities. This year-round ice-free port was the entry point for people and goods going to the Interior during the gold rush. Today that flow has been reversed, as Valdez Harbor is the southern terminus of the Trans-Alaska Pipeline, which carries crude oil from Prudhoe Bay and surrounding oil fields nearly 800 mi to the north. This region, with its dependence on commercial fishing, is still feeling the aftereffects of the massive oil spill in 1989. Much of Valdez looks modern, because the business area was relocated and rebuilt after its destruction by the 1964 Good Friday earthquake. Even though the town is younger than the rest of developed Alaska, it's acquiring a lived-in look.

COMING ASHORE

SHORE EXCURSIONS

Columbia Glacier Cruise. A 30-minute drive takes you to the Valdez Small Boat Harbor where you board your tour vessel for a 6½ hour journey through Prince William Sound to Columbia Glacier. On the way, you will have a chance to view the Sounds' wildlife that includes sea otters, sea lions, puffins, eagles, porpoises, humpback whales, and orcas while your guide relates the mining, oil, earthquake, and fishing history of the area and tells stories about the first people to explore and live in the Sound. ⊙ 7½ hrs ≊ $249.

Duck Flats Sea Kayaking. Guides present a basic kayaking and safety demonstration before participants board a two- or three-person kayak. The group makes its way along the coastline and through a chain of islands known for nesting birds and wildflowers; this area is also a popular hangout for harbor seals. ⊙ 4 hrs ≊ $119.

Fishing Charters. Step off the cruise boat for full- or half-day fishing excursions for halibut, salmon, ling cod, and more. Various outfitters can be found on the Convention and Visitors Bureau's Web site (*see below*). ⊙ Varies ≊ Varies.

Thompson Pass and Worthington Glacier. Travel via motor coach through Keystone Canyon, a narrow break in the Chugach Mountains. Bridal Veil Falls and Horsetail Falls cascade from the canyon walls high above as you make the ascent to Thompson Pass, through which the Trans-Alaska pipeline passes. Just over Thompson Pass lies Worthington

> **COMPETE!**
>
> Many Alaskan communities have summer fishing derbies, but Valdez may hold the record for the number of such contests, stretching from late May into September. The Valdez Silver Salmon Derby begins in late July and runs the entire month of August. Fishing charters abound in this area of Prince William Sound for a good reason: the fertile waters provide some of the best saltwater sportfishing in all of Alaska.

Glacier, which descends from Girls Mountain, passing within a few feet of the parking area and viewing shelter. This incredible hanging glacier is located near the snowiest place in Alaska. High alpine tundra, a glacial landscape, and sweeping views of the valley make this an excellent place to hone your photographic skills. ☾ *3 hrs* ✈ *$99.*

Worthington Glacier Hike. A scenic, 45-minute drive through Keystone Canyon and over Thompson Pass to Worthington Glacier State Park, with a stop along the way to view Bridal Veil Falls, delivers you to the park. After a short walk to the toe of the glacier you will don crampons to ensure your safety when traveling on the ice. After providing a detailed explanation of the glacier walk, your guide will then lead you on your 1½ hour trek across this vast glacier, while explaining the glacier environment. During a rest stop, a light snack is served. ☾ *4 hrs* ✈ *$179.*

> ### VALDEZ BEST BETS
>
> ■ **Tour the Sound.** Take a tour of Prince William Sound with Stan Stephens Tours, and get a seaside view of the Alyeska Pipeline terminal, where the 800-mi-long Trans-Alaska Pipeline loads oil into huge tanker ships.
>
> ■ **Visit a sea otter.** Several local companies offer sea-kayaking tours of varying lengths and degrees of difficulty.
>
> ■ **Hike on a glacier.** Worthington Glacier State Park at Thompson Pass is a roadside attraction. If you want to learn glacier travel or ice climbing, H2O Guides can hook you up.

TRANSPORTATION AND TOURS
FROM THE PIER
Ships tie up at the world's largest floating container dock. About 3 mi from the heart of town, the dock is used not only for cruise ships but also for cargo ships loading with timber and other products bound for markets "outside" (that's what Alaskans call the rest of the world). Ship-organized motor coaches meet you on the pier and provide transportation into town. Cabs and car-rental services will also provide transportation from the pier, and individualized tours of the area can be arranged with the cab dispatcher. Several local ground- and adventure-tour operators meet passengers as well.

VISITOR INFORMATION
Once in town, you find that Valdez is a very compact community. Almost everything is within easy walking distance of the **Valdez Convention and Visitors Bureau** (✉ *200 Chenega St.* ☎ *907/835–2984* ⊕ *www. valdezalaska.org*) in the heart of town. Motor coaches drop passengers at the Visitors Bureau.

INTERNET If you bring a laptop or handheld device, ask at the VCVB for any of the free local wireless spots town, but if not, check your e-mail for free on a public computer at the **Consortium Library** (✉ *212 Fairbanks St.* ☎ *907/835–4623* ⊕ *www.ci.valdez.ak.us/library*).

EXPLORING VALDEZ

The **Valdez Museum** explores the lives, livelihoods, and events significant to Valdez and surrounding regions. Exhibits include a restored 1880s Gleason & Baily hand-pump fire engine, a 1907 Ahrens steam fire engine, a 19th-century saloon, information on the local native peoples, and an exhibit on the 1989 oil spill. Every summer the museum hosts an exhibit of quilts and fiber arts made by local and regional artisans. At a separate site a 35- by 40-foot model of **Historical Old Town Valdez** (⊠ *436 S. Hazlet Ave.*) depicts the original town, which was devastated by the 1964 earthquake. There's also an operating seismograph and an exhibit on local seismic activity. A Valdez History Exhibits Pass includes admission to both the museum and the annex. ⊠ *217 Egan Dr.* ☎ *907/835-2764* ⊕ *www.valdezmuseum.org* ⊡ *$6* ◯ *May–Sept. (through Labor Day), daily 9–5.*

OFF THE BEATEN PATH

A visit to **Columbia Glacier,** which flows from the surrounding Chugach Mountains, will likely be on a Prince William Sound cruising agenda even if you're not stopping in Valdez. Its deep aquamarine face is 5 mi across, and it calves icebergs with resounding cannonades. This glacier is one of the largest and most readily accessible of Alaska's coastal glaciers.

OUTDOOR ACTIVITIES

Anadyr Adventures (☎ *907/835-2814 or 800/865-2925* ⊕ *www. anadyradventures.com*) offers sea-kayaking trips into Prince William Sound. Whether you're looking for a full-on winter backcountry heli-ski excursion or a shorter glacier experience, **H2O Guides** can hook you up. The guides can set up any level of icy adventure you desire, from a half-day walk on Worthington Glacier to full-day or multiday ice-climbing trips. They can also arrange fishing, flightseeing, multiday, and multisport trips. (☎ *907/835-8418 or 800/578-4354* ⊕ *www. h2oguides.com*).

WHERE TO EAT

$

SEAFOOD

✕ **MacMurray's Alaska Halibut House.** At this very casual family-owned establishment you order at the counter, sit at the Formica-covered tables, and check out the photos of local fishing boats. The battered halibut is excellent—light and not greasy. Other menu items include homemade clam chowder, but if you're eating at the Halibut House, why try anything else? ⊠ *208 Meals Ave.* ☎ *907/835-2788* ▭ *MC, V.*

$$

AMERICAN

✕ **Mike's Palace Ristorante.** Across from the scenic boat harbor, Mike's is a local favorite. The menu offers the world: from the standard American hamburger and Greek gyros to Mexican dishes and Italian pastas, there's a little bit of everything for every type of palate. There is an excellent selection of salads (a rarity throughout Alaska), steaks, and seafood. ⊠ *201 N. Harbor Dr.* ☎ *907/835-2365* ▭ *AE, D, MC, V.*

VICTORIA, BRITISH COLUMBIA

Although Victoria isn't in Alaska, it's a port of call for many ships cruising the Inside Passage. Victoria is the oldest city (founded 1843) on Canada's west coast and the first European settlement on Vancouver Island. It was chosen to be the westernmost trading outpost of the British-owned Hudson Bay Company in 1843, and became the capital of British Columbia in 1868. Just like the communities of Southeast Alaska, Victoria had its own gold-rush stampede in the 1800s, when 25,000 miners flocked to British Columbia's Cariboo country. Victoria has since evolved into a walkable, livable seaside town of gardens, waterfront pathways, and restored 19th-century architecture. Often described as the country's most British city, Victoria is these days—except for the odd red phone box, good beer, and well-mannered drivers—working to change that image, preferring to celebrate its combined native, Asian, and European heritage. Though it's quite touristy in summer, it's also at its prettiest then, with flowers hanging from 19th-century lampposts and strollers enjoying the beauty of its natural harbor.

COMING ASHORE

SHORE EXCURSIONS

Butchart Gardens. More than 700 varieties of flowers grow in these spectacular gardens north of town. If you're there in the evening you can witness the romantic nighttime illumination. Some excursions include a narrated tour of Victoria en route, while others offer such add-ons as an English Tea, or a wine and chocolate tasting at a local winery. ⊗ *3½–4 hrs* ▧ *Gardens only: $70; with English Tea: $119; with wine and chocolate tasting: $139.*

Grand City Drive and Empress High Tea. Travel by bus through Victoria's downtown, past its historic residential neighborhoods, and along a scenic ocean drive. Some tours include a stop at a viewpoint atop Mount Tolmie. The tour finishes with an elaborate afternoon tea at the historic Fairmont Empress Hotel. ⊗ *2½–3 hrs* ▧ *$119–$149.*

Whale-Watching. Orcas (killer whales), seals, sea lions, and porpoises are abundant in the waters off Victoria. Some of the covered jet boats are equipped with hydrophones so you can hear the whales communicate. ⊗ *3½ hrs* ▧ *$120–$127.*

> ### VICTORIA BEST BETS
>
> ■ Most cruise ships visit Victoria in the late afternoon and evening, which is an ideal time for a stroll around the city's compact downtown or a visit to the splendid 55-acre Butchart Gardens.
>
> ■ Victoria's other main attraction is the city center itself, with its street entertainers, yachts at harbor, cafés, funky little shops, intriguing museums, and illuminated Victorian architecture.
>
> ■ A promenade around the Inner Harbour with, perhaps, a carriage ride for two (available at the corner of Belleville and Menzies streets, next to the Parliament Buildings) is a romantic option.

TRANSPORTATION AND TOURS

FROM THE PIER

Only the smallest excursion vessels dock downtown in Victoria's Inner Harbour. Cruise ships tie up at the Ogden Point cruise-ship terminal (⊕ *www.victoriaharbour.org*), 2.4 km (1½ mi) from the Inner Harbour, and a few pocket cruise ships moor at Sidney, 29 km (18 mi) north of Victoria. When ships are in port a shuttle bus makes trips between Ogden Point and downtown Victoria at least every 20 minutes. The C$7 (US$6.50) fare allows you to make as many return trips as you like. The walk downtown is pleasant and will take 20 to 30 minutes.

Taxis also meet each ship, and fares run about C$1 per minute; the meter starts at $3. A cab from Ogden Point to the downtown core will cost about C$10–C$12. **Bluebird Taxi** (☎ *250/384–1155 or 800/665–7055*) serves the Victoria area.

GETTING AROUND

Most points of interest are within walking distance of the Inner Harbour. For those that aren't, public and private transportation is readily available. The public bus system is excellent; pick up route maps and schedules at the Tourism Victoria Visitor InfoCentre. City tours by horse-drawn carriage, pedicab, and double-decker bus, as well as limousine service, are available at the cruise-ship terminal.

■ **TIP→ If you're coming from Alaska, remember to adjust your watch.** British Columbia is on Pacific Time, one hour ahead of Alaska Time.

VISITOR INFORMATION

The **Tourism Victoria Visitor InfoCentre** (✉ *812 Wharf St.* ☎ *250/953–2033 or 800/663–3883* ☉ *Daily 9–5* ⊕ *www.tourismvictoria.com*) is across the street from the Empress Hotel, on the Inner Harbour.

EXPLORING VICTORIA

❹ Victoria's heart is the **Inner Harbour,** always bustling with ferries, sea-planes, and yachts. In summer the waterfront comes alive with strollers and street entertainers.

❶ **Chinatown.** Chinese immigrants built much of the Canadian Pacific Railway in the 19th century, and their influence still marks the region. Victoria's Chinatown, founded in 1858, is the oldest and most intact such district in Canada. If you enter Chinatown from Government Street, you'll pass under the elaborate **Gate of Harmonious Interest.** Along Fisgard Street, merchants display paper lanterns, wicker baskets, and exotic produce. Mah-jongg, fan-tan, and dominoes were among the games of chance played along **Fan Tan Alley,** said to be the narrowest street in Canada. Once the gambling and opium center of Chinatown, it's now lined with offbeat shops, few of which sell authentic Chinese goods. ✉ *Fisgard St. between Government and Store Sts., Chinatown.*

❻ **Fairmont Empress.** Opened in 1908 by the Canadian Pacific Railway, the Empress is one of the grand château-style railroad hotels that grace many Canadian cities. Designed by Francis Rattenbury, who also designed the Parliament Buildings across the way, the Empress, with its solid Edwardian grandeur, has become a symbol of the city. **Miniature**

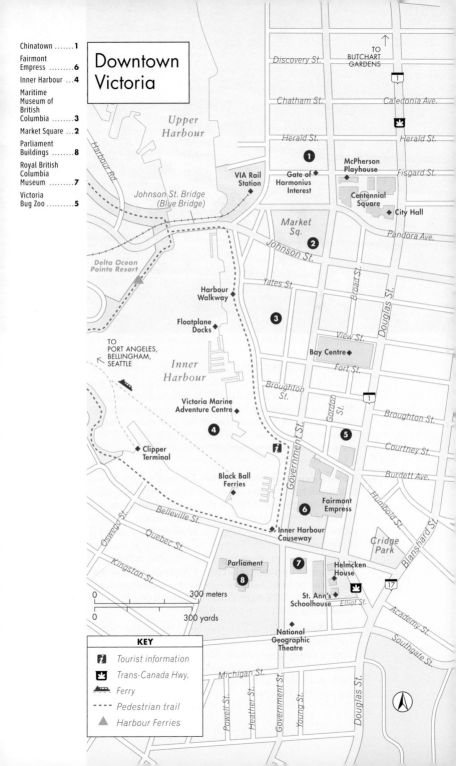

Downtown Victoria

Discovery St.

TO
BUTCHART
GARDENS

Chatham St.

Caledonia Ave.

*Upper
Harbour*

Herald St.

Herald St.

Fisgard St.

1

Gate of
Harmonious
Interest

McPherson
Playhouse

VIA Rail
Station

Centennial
Square

City Hall

*Market
Sq.*

2

Pandora Ave.

Johnson St.

*Johnson St. Bridge
(Blue Bridge)*

*Harbour
Rd.*

Yates St.

Broad St.

Douglas St.

Delta Ocean
Pointe Resort

Harbour
Walkway

View St.

Floatplane
Docks

3

Bay Centre

Fort St.

*Inner
Harbour*

TO
PORT ANGELES,
BELLINGHAM,
SEATTLE

Broughton
St.

Victoria Marine
Adventure Centre

Gordon St.

Broughton St.

4

5

Courtney St.

Clipper
Terminal

Government St.

Burdett Ave.

Black Ball
Ferries

6

Fairmont
Empress

Humbold St.

Belleville St.

Inner Harbour
Causeway

*Cridge
Park*

Blanshard St.

Oswego St.

Quebec St.

Parliament

7

Helmcken
House

Kingston St.

8

St. Ann's
Schoolhouse

Elliot St.

Academy St.

0   300 meters

0   300 yards

National
Geographic
Theatre

Southgate St.

Michigan St.

Pawell St.

Heather St.

Government St.

Young St.

Douglas St.

The Butchart Gardens, Victoria, British Columbia

World (☎ 250/385–9731 ⊕ *www.miniatureworld.com* ✉ C$13.05 ⊗ *Daily; May–Sept. 9–9, shorter hrs or closed during noncruising seasons*), a display of more than 80 miniature dioramas, including one of the world's largest model railways, is on the Humboldt Street side of the complex. ⊠ *721 Government St., entrance at Belleville and Government, Downtown* ☎ 250/384–8111, 250/389–2727 *tea reservations* ⊕ *www.fairmont.com/empress* ✉ *Free; afternoon tea C$55 May–Sept., C$44 Oct.–Apr.*

❸ Maritime Museum of British Columbia. The model ships, Royal Navy charts, photographs, uniforms, and ship bells at this museum in Victoria's original courthouse chronicle the province's seafaring history. Among the hand-built boats on display is the *Tilikum*, a dugout canoe that sailed from Victoria to England between 1901 and 1904. Kids can climb a crow's nest and learn some scary tales about the pirates of the coast. An 1899 hand-operated cage elevator, believed to be the oldest continuously operating lift in North America, ascends to the third floor, where the original 1888 vice-admiralty courtroom looks ready for a court-martial. ⊠ *28 Bastion Sq., Downtown* ☎ 250/385–4222 ⊕ *www. mmbc.bc.ca* ✉ C$10 ⊗ *Daily 9:30–4:30.*

❷ Market Square. During Victoria's late-19th-century heyday, this three-level square, originally the courtyard of an old inn, provided everything a sailor, miner, or up-country lumberjack could want. Now beautifully restored to its original architectural, if not commercial, character, it's a traffic-free café- and boutique-lined hangout. ⊠ *560 Johnson St., Old Town* ☎ 250/386–2441.

4

8 **Parliament Buildings.** Officially the British Columbia Provincial Legislative Assembly Buildings, these massive stone structures are more popularly referred to as the Parliament Buildings. Designed by Francis Rattenbury (who also designed the Fairmont Empress Hotel) when he was just 25 years old and completed in 1898, they dominate the Inner Harbour. Atop the central dome is a gilded statue of Captain George Vancouver (1757–98), the first European to sail around Vancouver Island. Free 30- to 60-minute tours run several times an hour during the summer, and several times a day in the off-season. ⊠ *501 Belleville St., Downtown* ☎ *250/387–3046* ⊕ *www.leg.bc.ca* ⊡ *Free* ☉ *Mid-May–early Sept., Mon.–Thurs. 9–5, Fri.–Sun. 9–7; early Sept.– mid-May, weekdays 9–4.*

7 **Royal British Columbia Museum.** This excellent museum, one of Victoria's
☺ leading attractions, traces several thousand years of British Columbian
★ history. Its First Peoples Gallery, home to a genuine Kwakwaka'wakw big house and a dramatically displayed collection of masks and other artifacts, is especially strong. The Environmental History Gallery traces British Columbia's natural heritage, from prehistory to modern-day climate change, in realistic dioramas. An Ocean Station exhibit gets kids involved in running a Jules Verne–style submarine. In the Modern History Gallery a replica of Captain Vancouver's ship, the HMS *Discovery,* creaks convincingly, and a re-created frontier town comes to life with cobbled streets, silent movies, and the rumble of an arriving train. Also on-site is an IMAX theater showing *National Geographic* films on a six-story-tall screen. ⊠ *675 Belleville St., Downtown* ☎ *250/356–7226 or 888/447–7977* ⊕ *www.royalbcmuseum.bc.ca* ⊡ *C$15, IMAX theater C$11, combination ticket C$23. Rates may be higher during special-exhibit periods* ☉ *Museum: daily 9–5 (open until 10 PM most Fri. and Sat. early June–late Sept. Theater: daily 10–8; call for showtimes.*

5 **Victoria Bug Zoo.** Local kids clamor to visit this offbeat mini-zoo, home
☺ to the largest live tropical insect collection in North America. You can even hold many of the 70 or so varieties, which include walking sticks, scorpions, millipedes, and a pharnacia—at 22 inches the world's longest insect. The staff members know their bug lore, and are happy to dispense scientific information. ⊠ *631 Courtney St., Downtown* ☎ *250/384–2847* ⊕ *www.bugzoo.bc.ca* ⊡ *C$8* ☉ *Mid-June–early Sept., daily 10–6; early Sept.–mid-June, Mon.–Sat. 10–5, Sun. 11–5.*

OUTSIDE TOWN

Fodor'sChoice **The Butchart Gardens.** This stunning 55-acre garden and National Historic
★ Site has been drawing visitors since it was planted in a limestone quarry in 1904. Seven hundred varieties of flowers grow in the site's Japanese, Italian, rose, and sunken gardens. Highlights include the view over the ivy-draped and flower-filled former quarry, the dramatic 70-foot-high Ross Fountain, and the formal and intricate Italian garden, complete with a gelato stand. In July and August kids' entertainers perform Sunday through Friday afternoons, and jazz, blues, and classical musicians play at an outdoor stage each evening. The wheelchair- and stroller-accessible site is also home to a seed-and-gift shop, a plant identification center, two restaurants (one offering traditional afternoon tea), and a coffee shop; you can even call ahead for a picnic basket. Some

transportation options to compare to your cruise line's shore excursion (which will most likely be well narrated): the Butchart Gardens Express Shuttle, run by Grey Line West, runs hourly service between downtown Victoria (leaving from the bus depot at 700 Douglas Street, behind the Empress Hotel) and Butchart Gardens during peak season. The C$45 round-trip fare includes admission to the gardens. Alternatively, take Bus 75 from Douglas Street downtown. ⊠ *800 Benvenuto Ave., Brentwood Bay* ☎ *250/652–5256 or 866/652–4422* ⊕ *www.butchartgardens. com* ⊠ *Mid-June–late Sept. C$28, discounted rates rest of yr* ⊗ *Mid-June–Labor Day, daily 9* AM*–10* PM*; Sept.–mid-June, daily 9* AM*–dusk; call for exact times.*

SHOPPING

Shopping in Victoria is easy: virtually everything is in the downtown area on or near Government Street stretching north from the Fairmont Empress hotel. Victoria stores specializing in English imports are plentiful, though Canadian-made goods are usually a better buy. If your time is limited, head straight to Lower Johnson Street.

Fort Street between Blanshard and Cook streets is known as **Antique Row,** home to dozens of antiques, curio, and collectibles shops.

Stock at **Hill's Native Art** ranges from affordable souvenirs to original West Coast First Nations art. ⊠ *1008 Government St., Downtown* ☎ *250/385–3911.*

Fodor's Choice ★ **Lower Johnson Street,** a row of candy-color Victorian shopfronts between Government and Store streets, is Victoria's hub for independent fashion-designer boutiques. Storefronts—some closet size—are filled with local designers' wares, funky boutiques, and no fewer than three shops selling ecologically friendly clothes of hemp and organic cotton. ⊠ *Johnson St. between Government and Store Sts., Downtown.*

★ **Munro's Books,** one of Canada's prettiest bookstores, is in a beautifully restored 1909 building. ⊠ *1108 Government St., Downtown* ☎ *250/382–2464.*

Fodor's Choice ★ **Silk Road Aromatherapy & Tea Company & Spa** is a chic and multifaceted shop that stocks exotic teas (which you can sample at the tasting bar), aromatherapy remedies, and spa treatments (think green-tea facials). ⊠ *1624 Government St., Downtown* ☎ *250/704–2688.*

WHERE TO EAT

$$$
CANADIAN
Fodor's Choice ★ ✕ **Aura.** One of Canada's top young chefs (Culinary Olympics star Brad Horen) meets the city's best waterfront patio at this chic eatery on the Inner Harbour's south shore. The seasonal-changing fare is locally sourced with Asian leanings: think wild local halibut and salmon; a "surf-and-turf" done with a sukiyaki-braised short rib, smoked scallops, and a maki roll; and a cellar full of hard-to-find Vancouver Island farm-gate wines. Sleek lines, warm colors, and water-view windows create a room that's both stylish and cozy. Live jazz plays Sundays. ⊠ *680*

Montreal St., at the Inn at Laurel Point, James Bay ☎ *250/414–6739* ⊕ *www.aurarestaurant.ca* ▭ *AE, D, DC, MC, V* ✢ *C4.*

$$$
CANADIAN
Fodor's Choice
★

✕ **Cafe Brio.** "Charming, comfortable, and hip with walls of art—all backed by city's best chef and kitchen," is how one fodors.com user describes this bustling Italian villa–style room. The frequently changing menu highlights regional, organic fare; favorites include roast veal strip loin with crispy sweetbreads, butter-poached pheasant breast, local sablefish, albacore tuna, Cowichan Bay duck breast, and house-made charcuterie. Virtually everything, including the bread, pasta, and desserts, is made in-house—even the butter is hand churned. The 400-label wine list has a top selection of B.C. choices. ⊠ *944 Fort St., Downtown* ☎ *250/383–0009 or 866/270–5461* ▭ *AE, MC, V* ☽ *No lunch* ✢ *H4.*

$–$$
ASIAN
★

✕ **The Noodle Box.** Noodles, whether Indonesian style with peanut sauce, thick Japanese udon in teriyaki, or Thai-style chow mein, are piled straight from steaming woks in the open kitchen to bowls or cardboard take-out boxes at this local answer to fast food. Malaysian, Singapore, and Cambodian-style curries tempt those who like it hot. The brick, rose, and lime walls keep things modern and high energy at the Douglas Street location near the Inner Harbour. The Fisgard Street outlet is a tiny hole-in-the-wall near Chinatown. ⊠ *818 Douglas St., Downtown* ☎ *250/384–1314* ⌦ *Reservations not accepted* ▭ *AE, MC, V* ✢ *F4* ⊠ *626 Fisgard St., Downtown* ☎ *250/360–1312* ⌦ *Reservations not accepted* ▭ *AE, MC, V* ✢ *F2.*

WHERE TO DRINK

Pub culture is an important part of life in Victoria, providing a casual, convivial atmosphere for lunch, a casual dinner, or an afternoon pint. The pubs listed here all serve food, and many brew their own beer. Patrons must be 19 or older to enter the pub itself, but many pubs have a restaurant section where kids are welcome, too. Smoking is banned indoors and on patios in all Victoria pubs.

Bengal Lounge. Deep leather sofas and a Bengal tiger skin help to recreate the days of the British Raj at this iconic lounge in the Fairmont Empress Hotel. Martinis and a curry buffet are the draws through the week. On Friday and Saturday nights a jazz combo takes the stage. ⊠ *721 Government St., Downtown* ☎ *250/384–8111* ⊕ *www.fairmont.com/empress.*

Canoe Brewpub. One of Victoria's biggest and best pub patios overlooks the Gorge, the waterway just north of the Inner Harbour. Inside, the former power station has been stylishly redone, with high ceilings, exposed brick and beams, a wide range of in-house brews, top-notch bar snacks, and an all-ages restaurant. ⊠ *450 Swift St., Downtown* ☎ *250/361–1940.*

WRANGELL

A small, unassuming timber and fishing community, Wrangell sits on the northern tip of Wrangell Island, near the mouth of the fast-flowing Stikine River—North America's largest undammed river. Like much of the Southeast, the town has suffered in recent years from a declining resource-based economy. The rough-around-the-edges town is off the track of the larger cruise ships, so it does not get the same seasonal traffic that Ketchikan and Juneau do. Hence, it is nearly devoid of the souvenir shops that dominate so many other nearby downtown areas, but gift shops and art galleries do sell locally created work.

COMING ASHORE

TRANSPORTATION AND TOURS
FROM THE PIER
Cruise ships calling in to Wrangell dock downtown, within walking distance of the museum and gift stores. Greeters welcome you and are available to answer questions. Wrangell's few attractions—the most notable being totem-filled Chief Shakes Island—are within walking distance of the pier. The Nolan Center houses an excellent museum, and Petroglyph Beach, where rocks are imprinted with mysterious prehistoric symbols, is 1 mi from the pier. Most cruise-ship visitors see it on guided shore excursions or by taxi. Call **Northern Lights Taxi** (☎ 907/874–4646) or **Star Cab** (☎ 907/874–3622).

AREA TOURS
Breakaway Adventures (☎ 907/874–2488 or 888/385–2488 ⊕ www. breakawayadventures.com) leads day trips up the majestic Stikine River by jet boat, including a visit to Chief Shakes Glacier, along with time to take a dip at Chief Shakes Hot Springs. **Sunrise Aviation** (☎ 907/874–2319 or 800/874–2311 ⊕ www.sunriseflights.com) is a charter-only air carrier that offers trips to the Anan Creek Wildlife Observatory, LeConte Glacier, or Forest Service cabins.

VISITOR INFORMATION
The **Wrangell Visitor Center** (☎ 907/874–2829 or 800/367–9745 ⊕ www. wrangellalaska.org ☉ During museum hrs) is housed in the Nolan Center. Stop by for details on local adventure options and for free Internet access.

INTERNET   Check your e-mail for free at the **Irene Ingle Public Library** (⊠ 124 2nd Ave. ☎ 907/874–3535).

EXPLORING WRANGELL

❹ **Chief Shakes Island.** This small island sits in the center of Wrangell's
★ protected harbor and is accessible by a footbridge from the bottom of Shakes Street. Seven totem poles surround a traditionally styled tribal house, built in the 1930s as a replica of one that was home to many of the various Shakes and their peoples. ⊠ Off Shakes St. ☎ 907/874–3481 ☜ $3.50 ☉ Daily when cruise ships are in port (ask at Wrangell Visitor Center) or by appointment.

❷ **Mt. Dewey.** Despite the name, this landmark is more of a hill than a peak. Still, it's a steep 15-minute climb from town to the top through a second-growth forest. The trail begins from 3rd Street behind the high school, and an observation platform on top provides a viewpoint for protected waterways and islands named from its Russian history, including Zarembo, Vank, and Woronkofski.

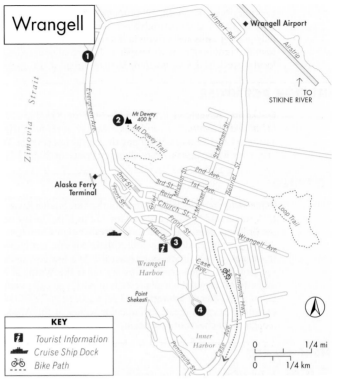

❸ **Nolan Center.** Wrangell's museum moved into a building that acts as a centerpiece for cultural life in Wrangell. Exhibits provide a window on the region's rich history. Featured pieces include the oldest known Tlingit house posts dating from the late 18th century, decorative posts from Chief Shakes's clan house, petroglyphs, century-old spruce-root and cedar-bark baskets, masks, gold-rush memorabilia, and a fascinating photo collection. If you're spending any time in town, don't pass this up. Also in the building are the town's **Civic Center** (☎ *907/874–2829 or 800/367–9745 ⊕ www.wrangell.com*), a 200-seat movie theater/performance space/convention center, and the **Wrangell Visitor Center.** The latter is staffed when the museum is open, and has details on local adventure options. ⊠ *296 Outer Dr.* ☎ *907/874–3770* 🎟 *$5* ⊙ *May–Sept., Tues.–Sat. 10–5, and when ferry or cruise ships are in port; Oct.–Apr., Tues.–Sat. 1–5.*

❶ **Petroglyph Beach State Historic Park.** Scattered among other rocks at this public beach are three dozen or more large stones bearing designs and pictures chiseled by unknown, ancient artists. No one knows why the rocks at this curious site were etched the way they were, or even exactly how old these etchings are. You can access the beach via a boardwalk, where you'll find signs describing the site along with carved replicas of the petroglyphs. Most of the petroglyphs are to the right between the viewing deck and a large outcropping of rock in the tidal beach area. Because the original petroglyphs can be damaged by physical contact, only photographs are permitted. But you are welcome to use the replicas to make a rubbing from rice paper and charcoal or crayons (available in local stores). ⊠ *0.6 mi north of ferry terminal off Evergreen Ave.*

OUTDOOR ACTIVITIES

Breakaway Adventures (☎ *907/874–2488 or 888/385–2488* ⊕ *www. breakawayadventures.com*) leads a variety of jet-boat trips, including a tour to Chief Shakes Glacier and the nearby hot springs. You can catch one of its water taxis to Petersburg or Prince of Wales Island.

SHOPPING

Garnet Ledge, a rocky ledge at the mouth of the Stikine River, is the source for garnets sold by local children for 25¢ to $50. The site was deeded to the Boy Scouts in 1962 and to the Presbyterian Church in Wrangell in 2006, so only children can collect these colorful but imperfect stones, the largest of which are an inch across. At a few covered shelters near the city dock when cruise ships are in, at the Wrangell Museum, or at the ferry terminal when a ferry is in port, you can purchase garnets. Local artist **Brenda Schwartz** (⊠ *7 Front St.* ☎ *907/874–3508* ⊕ *www. marineartist.com*) creates watercolor scenes of the Alaskan coast on navigational charts of the region.

WHERE TO EAT

$$–$$$ ✕ **Zak's Cafe.** Despite its simple, no-nonsense atmosphere, Zak's is a
AMERICAN standout among Wrangell's limited dining choices, with good food and reasonable prices. Check out the day's specials or try the steaks, chicken, seafood, and salads. At lunch the menu includes burgers, sandwiches, fish-and-chips, and wraps. ⊠ *314 Front St.* ☎ *907/874–3355* ▭ *MC, V.*

Sports and Wilderness Adventures

WORD OF MOUTH

"I saw this particular bear around the camp. . . . On this particular evening I took a boat ride and saw him fighting with another bear. I stopped the boat to take some photos of them and he stood up and stared us down, then gave us a slight bluff charge. We were safe because we were in a boat, but it was still exciting."

—Brian Embacher, Photo Contest Winner

Updated by Jessica Bowman

Alaska's landscape is big enough to hold every traveler's dream: hidden in range after range of mountains are canyons and waterfalls, alpine valleys, salmon-rich rivers, clear lakes, blue glaciers, temperate rain forests, and sweeping, spongy tundra plains. Add in more than 5,000 mi of coast, and it's obvious: Alaska's the place for unforgettable outdoor adventuring!

Flip through this chapter to find in-depth descriptions of sports, from kayaking to skiing to biking; our favorite regions for each sport; and, finally, our best wildlife-viewing advice. In Chapter 4, sports and outdoor excursions are included in our coverage for each port; in this chapter, you can flip to the activity that interests you and read about which regions you might want to cruise to or arrange excursions to accordingly. We also include information about activities in Alaska's Interior where it's applicable, just in case your travels pre- or postcruise take you beyond Denali.

Alaska has more parks, wilderness areas, and wildlife refuges than all the other states combined. About one-third of Alaska's 375 million acres is set aside in protected public lands, and they are as varied as they are magnificent. Recreational activities include wildlife-viewing, hiking, mountain biking, kayaking, rafting, canoeing, fishing, hunting, mountaineering, skiing, and snowboarding. Limited road access (Alaska averages only 1 mi of road for every 42 square mi of land; the U.S. average ratio is 1 to 1) means that many destinations can only be reached via small airplane, boat, all-terrain vehicle, or what might be a really long walk. Dog sleds are frequently an option, too, in winter months.

Even the most visited parks—Denali National Park and Preserve, Glacier Bay National Park and Preserve, and Kenai Fjords National Park—allow backpackers and kayakers abundant opportunities for remote wilderness experiences. Parks closer to roads and cities, like the massive Chugach State Park near Anchorage and Chena River State Recreation Area outside Fairbanks, draw more visitors, but it's still possible to be

BEST WILDLIFE VIEWING		Bears	Birds	Caribou	Dall Sheep	Whales or Marine Animals
SOUTHEAST	Alaska Chilkat Bald Eagle Preserve & Chilkat River	◗	●	○	○	○
	Alaska Marine Highway	◗	●	○	○	●
	Glacier Bay National Park & Preserve	◗	●	○	○	●
	Mendenhall Wetlands State Game Refuge	◗	●	○	○	◗
	Pack Creek	●	●	○	○	●
SOUTH CENTRAL	Chugach State Park	●	●	○	●	●
	Kenai Fjords National Park	◗	●	○	○	●
INTERIOR	Creamer's Field Migratory Waterfowl Refuge	◗	●	○	○	○
	Denali National Park & Preserve	●	●	◗	●	○
BUSH	Arctic National Wildlife Refuge	◗	●	●	○	○
	Katmai National Park	●	●	◗	○	◗
	Kodiak National Wildlife Refuge	●	●	○	○	○
	Pribilof Islands	○	●	○	○	●
	Round Island (Walrus Islands State Game Sanctuary)	○	●	○	○	●

KEY: ● = likely ◗ = somewhat ○ = not likely

10 minutes outside a city and be all alone with the wilderness. Particularly remote and solitary experiences await in the state's least visited places, such as Wood-Tikchik State Park, where only two rangers patrol 1.6 million acres, or Aniakchak National Monument and Preserve, south of Katmai, where trekkers can go days or weeks without seeing another human.

SPORTS AND TOP REGIONS

Alaska! It's a gigantic, vibrant state teeming with fish-packed rivers, snow-dusted mountaintops, and massive glaciers. Who has a travel wish list that *doesn't* include this enormous frontier? Thrill-seekers might check out helicopter skiing in the Chugach Mountains out of Girdwood, Valdez, or Cordova, or rafting in Denali National Park and Preserve. Sea kayakers will find solitude and abundant marine wildlife in the Southeast's Glacier Bay or South Central's Kenai Fjords.

Backcountry adventurers can escape civilization with a sled-dog team in Gates of the Arctic National Park far above the Arctic Circle, or in the Susitna Valley less than a two-hour drive north of Anchorage. The Aleutian and Pribilof islands are bird-watching meccas, while Katmai National Park and Kodiak National Wildlife Refuge are hot spots for bear viewing. An increasing number of trips and tours now make it possible to spend a week or two (or more) learning—and performing—feats from horse packing within sight of Mt. McKinley to hiking or mountain biking through some of the state's most challenging landscapes. Below you'll find some of our favorite sports, along with recommended trips and experiences, questions to consider, and suggestions to help you choose the right program.

BIKING

There's just nothing like pedaling through weaving stalks of fireweed and feeling a light breeze on your face as you take in the lush, intimidating, and all-encompassing landscape of Alaska. Biking is an excellent way to see the state, whether it's on a prearranged tour or an afternoon jaunt on some rented wheels. There are bike-rental shops in larger communities such as Anchorage and Fairbanks; they frequently offer street maps and can tell you their favorite routes. Alaska's dirt trails, including many within city parks, promise biking opportunities for cyclists of all abilities, while hundreds of miles of paved trails and highways provide choice touring routes. Whether you plan to grind your way up a dusty mountain path or cruise swiftly along a well-traveled highway, come prepared to handle emergencies. Always carry a basic bicycle repair kit including chain tool, Allen wrenches, spare inner tubes, and tube-repair materials, along with a compact bicycle-tire pump. Bring plenty of fluids (either in water bottles or camel packs),

BIKING TO CRESCENT

The ascent is gradual, but the trek over Crescent Creek Trail, 100 highway mi south of Anchorage, can feel steeper and longer under a hot July sun. In places the trail goes almost vertical, and hairpin switchbacks broken by spruce roots require caution. None of that seems to matter, though, once Crescent Lake appears through the cottonwoods. On a windless afternoon the lake resembles an ice-blue gem surrounded by rocky ridgelines and an endless sky.

enough food to sustain your energy, and a light jacket or rain shell. And remember to take all proper animal-related precautions if you're peddling remote stretches of road.

TOP REGIONS AND EXPERIENCES

Biking is especially popular within the larger cities and along the road systems of South Central and the Interior. Favored touring routes include the unpaved Denali and Taylor highways and McCarthy Road. The Copper River Highway outside Cordova and some of the less traveled roads north of Fairbanks also beckon cyclists seeking several-speed adventures. Biking is a fantastic way to explore the Southeast's coastal towns.

CANOEING

The art of canoeing is peaceful, invigorating, and unsurpassed in Alaska, as the state boasts 3 million lakes and 3,000 rivers. Although it's possible to launch at any of hundreds of lakes and streams crossing Alaska's road system, the most easily accessed canoe trail systems with well-marked, maintained portages are found in South Central. Canoes, paddles, and life vests can be rented for $20 to $30 a day from area rental outfits.

Lakes and rivers around sea level in South Central are usually ice-free from mid-May through September, while those at higher elevations and in the Interior and northern regions are more likely ice-free from early June to mid-September. Many paddlers find the first couple of weeks after breakup and the final two weeks before freeze-up the most pleasant, for their cool temperatures and absence of mosquitoes and black flies.

TOP REGIONS AND EXPERIENCES

Three spectacular canoe trail systems are located in South Central, including the **Swan Lake Canoe Trail** and **Swanson River Canoe Trail**, both set in the 1.3-million-acre Kenai National Wildlife Refuge on the Kenai Peninsula, and the **Nancy Lake Canoe Trail** in the Susitna Valley.

FLIGHTSEEING

Amelia Earhart said, "You haven't seen a tree until you've seen its shadow from the sky." Alaska is full of trees and, luckily, full of flightseeing opportunities as well. Air-taxi services in all major cities and many smaller communities offer flightseeing tours. Most offer a variety of packages, allowing clients to design their own tours if discussed in advance. The smaller companies are often more flexible, while the multiplane companies can better match plane size to your needs. Prices usually depend on the size of the plane, number of clients, and the route and length of the tour. As with taxicabs, passengers can often split costs for charters. Generally, a half-hour flightseeing trip runs each person around $75 per person, depending on the kind of plane and the destination; some areas, planes, and routes can be a lot more expensive. Hourly rates, depending on the plane's size and the competition, can run from $85 to more than $300 per person. If there's a drop-off and pick-up

involved, you pay for all the time the plane is operating, in both directions. ■TIP→ Shop around before committing to any one service; some
very good flightseeing bargains are available.

Flights in smaller planes and helicopters are particularly dependent
on weather. In some cases, clouds may simply obscure certain sites,
while bad weather often grounds pilots altogether, forcing tours to be
canceled. This is an especially important point to remember if you're
waiting for a pick-up from a remote cabin or campsite. Be prepared
for weather delays. Ask about cancellation policies if you've paid in
advance. Alaska's pilots are the best in the world. Trust their knowledge
and skill to get you where you're going in safety.

TOP REGIONS AND EXPERIENCES
SOUTHEAST

In the Southeast, flightseeing services based in communities surrounding **Misty Fiords National Monument,** the **Tongass National Forest, Mendenhall Glacier,** and **Glacier Bay National Park and Preserve** offer aerial views
of coastal mountain ranges, remote shorelines, glaciers, ice fields, and
wildlife. Some even include opportunities to land and fish or view local
wildlife, such as brown bears, black bears, sea otters, seals, and whales.
Visitors passing through the Southeast on cruise lines or via the Alaska
Marine Highway System will find flightseeing options in all ports.

ANCHORAGE AND SOUTH CENTRAL

This area is the state's air-travel hub. Plenty of flightseeing services
operating out of city airports and floatplane bases can take you on
spectacular tours of **Mt. McKinley,** the **Chugach Range, Prince William Sound,
Kenai Fjords National Park,** and the **Harding Icefield.** Flightseeing services
are available in Seward, Homer, Talkeetna, and other South Central
communities. Anchorage hosts the greatest number and variety of services, including companies operating fixed-wing aircraft, floatplanes,
and helicopters.

THE BUSH Why not head to the state's most remote parts in a small plane? Check
out scenic **Katmai National Park and Preserve** and the **Valley of 10,000
Smokes,** a volcanic region of steaming calderas and hardened lava moon-
scapes. Most services are based in the communities of King Salmon or
Naknek, which are served by a common airport with jet service from
Anchorage.

GLACIER TREKKING

Roughly 100,000 glaciers flow out of Alaska's mountains, covering 5%
of the state. These slow-moving "rivers of ice" concentrate in the Alaska
Range, Wrangell Mountains, and the state's major coastal mountain
chains: the Chugach, St. Elias, Coast, and Kenai ranges. The Juneau Ice
Fields are the biggest non-polar chunk of ice on the continent. Alaska's
largest glacier, the Bering, covers 2,250 square mi. If you're an adventurous backcountry traveler, glaciers present icy avenues into the remote
corners of premier mountain wilderness areas. And every traveler enjoys
the opportunity to walk on water. ⇨ *For information about glaciers, flip
to Glaciers: Notorious Landscape Architects in Chapter 4.*

Don't forget your crampons: hikers make their way across glacial ice.

Glacier terrain includes a mix of ice, rock debris, and often-deep surface snow; sometimes frigid pools of meltwater collect on the surface. Watch out for glacier crevasses. Sometimes hidden by snow, especially in spring and early summer (a popular time for glacier trekking), these cracks in the ice may present life-threatening traps. Though some are only inches wide, others may be several yards across and hundreds of feet deep. ■TIP→ Glacier travel should be attempted only after you've been properly trained. If you haven't been taught proper glacial travel and crevasse-rescue techniques, hire a backcountry guide to provide the necessary gear and expertise. Some companies offer day or half-day hikes onto glaciers that don't have the same physical demands as longer treks but that still require proper equipment and training. For instance, St. Elias Alpine Guides takes hikers of all ages and abilities on one of its glacier walks.

TOP REGIONS AND EXPERIENCES
SOUTHEAST
In the Southeast, visitors to the capital city of Juneau can drive or take the bus to **Mendenhall Glacier,** on the outskirts of town. This 85-mi-long, 45-mi-wide sheet of ice, just the tiniest finger of the 1,500-square-mi Juneau Icefields, provides awesome glacier-trekking opportunities. Guided tour packages are a very good idea for beginners.

SOUTH CENTRAL AND THE INTERIOR
The mountains outside the state's largest city have their share of glaciers. Among the most popular for trekkers of all abilities is **Matanuska Glacier,** at Mile 103 off the Glenn Highway (about a 90-minute drive northeast of Anchorage). Anchorage-based guides often use the Matanuska as a training ground for those new to navigating glaciers.

Talkeetna, a two-hour drive north of Anchorage, is a small community famous as the jumping-off point to some of the world's greatest and most challenging glacier treks. The town rests a short bush-plane hop from the foot of the Alaska Range and the base of Mt. McKinley. Miles of ice await the most intrepid and experienced trekkers. Local and Anchorage-based guide services offer training and tours into the region.

HIKING AND BACKPACKING

From the Southeast's coastal rain forests and the Interior's historic Yukon River country to the high Arctic tundra, Alaska presents some of the continent's finest landscape for wilderness hiking and backpacking. Or if remote backcountry is not your preference, it's possible to travel well-maintained and well-marked trails on the edges of Alaska's largest cities and still get a taste of the wild—in some places just a few steps take you into the heart of a forest or to the base of a mountain pass. Many of the trails in road-accessible parklands, refuges, and forests are well maintained, and cross terrain that is easy for novice hikers, seniors, and families.

> ### BLISS IN BOOTS
>
> In late June and early July, when the sun barely sets in much of Alaska, it's tempting to shoulder your pack and keep on hiking. Around 10 PM the light grows mellow and golden. The birds seem prepared to call all night long. Your boots crunch softly over gravel bars and hillocks. During this time of year Alaska rarely sleeps; there will be time for rest when summer is over.

Most of Alaska is pristine wilderness, with few or no trails. In such areas it's best to be accompanied by an experienced backcountry traveler who understands the challenges of trail-less wilderness: how to behave in bear country, how to navigate using map and compass techniques, and how to cross glacial streams. Below we've listed some notable exceptions—trails where you can experience Alaska's wilderness on slightly beaten paths.

TOP REGIONS AND EXPERIENCES

SOUTHEAST Virtually all Southeast hiking is in the 17-million-acre Tongass National Forest, administered by the U.S. Forest Service. It can be wet and steep here, but you also will be walking through temperate rain forest—lush and gorgeous!

FROM ANCHORAGE TO DENALI **Chugach State Park,** along Anchorage's eastern edge, has dozens of trails, many of them suited for day hikes or overnight camping. Across Turnagain Arm, near Hope, hikers can step onto the **Resurrection Pass Trail,** which traverses the forests, streams, and mountains of the Chugach National Forest. And though it is best known for its trail-less wilderness, **Denali National Park and Preserve** has some easy-to-hike trails near the park entrance, not to mention miles of taiga and tundra waiting to be explored. Nearby "Little Denali"—**Denali State Park**—has the 36-mi-long Kesugi Ridge Trail, within easy reach of the Parks Highway.

RIVER RAFTING

So much of Alaska is roadless wilderness that rivers often serve as the best avenues for exploring the landscape. This is especially true in several of Alaska's premier parklands and refuges. Here, as elsewhere, rivers are ranked according to their degrees of difficulty. ■TIP➜ Class I rivers are considered easy floats with minimal rapids; at the other extreme, Class VI rivers are extremely dangerous and nearly impossible to navigate.

HIKING TERRAINS

RIVERS

Crossing Alaska's rivers requires care. Many are hard-to-read, swift, silty streams. They often flow over impermeable bottoms (either rock or permafrost), which means a good rain can raise water levels a matter of feet, not inches, in a surprisingly short time. For this very reason, avoid pitching tents near streams, particularly on gravel or sandbars. Warm days can also dramatically increase the meltwater from glaciers. Be aware of weather changes that might affect river crossings. Look for the widest, shallowest place you can find, with many channels. This may entail traveling up- or downstream. A guide who knows the region is invaluable at such times.

A sturdy staff, your own or made from a handy branch, is useful to help you keep your balance and measure the depths of silty water. Make sure one foot is firmly planted before you lift the next. Do not hurry, no matter how cold the water feels. You should unbuckle your pack when crossing a swift stream. Avoid wearing a long rain poncho; it can catch the water and tip you over. For added stability it helps for two or more people to link arms when crossing.

Hikers debate the best footwear for crossing Alaska's rivers. Some take along sneakers and wear them through the water; others take off their socks so they will remain dry and can comfort cold feet on the opposite shore. But bear in mind that Alaska waters are generally frigid, and the bottom is often rocky and rough; bare feet are not advised.

TUNDRA

Tundra hiking, especially in higher alpine country, can be a great pleasure. In places the ground is so springy you feel like you're walking on a trampoline. In the Arctic, however, where the ground is underlaid with permafrost, you will probably find the going as wet as it is in the Southeast forests. Summer sunshine melts the top, leaving puddles and marshy spots behind. Comfortable waterproof footgear can help when traversing such landscapes. Tundra travel can require the skill and stamina of a ballet dancer if the ground is tufted with tussocks.

FORESTS

Forest trails are hard to maintain and often wet, especially in coastal lowlands, and they may be potholed or blocked with beaver dams. The ground stays soggy much of the time, and brush grows back quickly after it is cut. Especially nasty is devil's club, a large, broad-leaved plant with greenish flowers that eventually become clusters of bright red berries; it's also thickly armored with stinging, needle-sharp thorns.

Generally, only very experienced river runners should attempt anything above Class II on their own. Also be aware that river conditions change considerably from season to season and sometimes from day to day, so always check on a river's current condition. The National Weather Service Alaska–Pacific River Forecast Center keeps tabs on Alaska's most popular streams. The center's Web site (⊕ *aprfc.arh.noaa.gov/ ak_ahps2.php*) provides the latest data on water levels and flow rates, including important flood-stage alerts.

Do-it-yourselfers would be wise to consult two books on Alaska's rivers: *Fast & Cold: A Guide to Alaska Whitewater* (Skyhouse), by Andrew Embick (though intended primarily for white-water kayakers, it has good information for rafters as well), and *The Alaska River Guide: Canoeing, Kayaking, and Rafting in the Last Frontier* (Alaska Northwest Books), by Karen Jettmar.

Fortunately you don't have to be an expert river runner to explore many of Alaska's premier waterways. Experienced rafting companies operate throughout the state. Some outfits emphasize extended

> **RIOTOUS RIVERS**
>
> From the Southeast Panhandle to the far reaches of the Arctic, Alaska is blessed with an abundance of wild, pristine rivers. The federal government has officially designated more than two dozen Alaska streams as "Wild and Scenic Rivers," but hundreds more would easily qualify. Some meander gently through forests or tundra. Others, fed by glacier run-off, rush wildly through mountains and canyons.

wilderness trips and natural-history observations, whereas others specialize in thrilling one-day (or shorter) runs down Class III and IV white-water rapids that will get your adrenaline—and possibly your arms—pumping. And some combine a little of both.

TOP REGIONS AND EXPERIENCES

Never has the phrase "it's all good" been truer than in the context of river rafting in Alaska. Be it a Class I or Class VI, it's an experience that, with the right preparation and safety considerations, can make you feel like a class-act adventurer. With thousands of rivers to choose from, virtually every region of the state promises prime rafting. Which region and river you float depends largely upon the impetus of your trip. White-water thrill-seekers will find challenging streams tumbling from the mountainous areas of South Central, while rafters interested in sportfishing may choose extended float trips on the gentler salmon- and trout-rich rivers of the Southwest. Birders and campers may consider the pristine rivers draining the North Slope of the Brooks Range or Northwest Alaska, or the Stikine River, which ends near Wrangell, in Southeast. Beyond your agenda, though, which river you choose to float should depend upon your rafting and backcountry skills. If there's any question at all, go with an experienced river guide.

SEA KAYAKING

Sea kayaking can be as thrilling or as peaceful as you want. More stable than a white-water kayak and more comfortable than a canoe, a sea kayak, even one loaded with a week's worth of gear, is maneuverable enough to poke into hidden crevices, explore side bays, and beach on deserted spits of sand. Don't assume, though, that if you've kayaked 10 minutes without tipping over you'll be adequately prepared to circumnavigate Glacier Bay National Park and Preserve. There's a lot to learn, and until you know your way around tides, currents, and nautical charts, you should go with an experienced guide who also knows what and how to pack and where to pitch a tent.

Cruisers enjoy a whitewater rafting excursion on the Nenana River.

It's important to honestly evaluate your tolerance for cold, dampness, and high winds. Nothing can ruin a trip faster than pervasive discomfort, and it's worse once you're out on the water with no choice but to keep going.

TOP REGIONS AND EXPERIENCES

SOUTHEAST This largely roadless coastal region is the setting of North America's last great temperate wilderness. Sometimes called Alaska's Panhandle, this appendage of islands, mainland, and fjords is a sparsely populated, scenic paradise for sea kayaking. In Southeast, Ketchikan is a popular starting point for many sea kayakers. Set in the heart of the **Tongass National Forest** and an easy boat or floatplane ride from **Misty Fiords National Monument,** this former logging town is home to several sea-kayaking guides and rental businesses. Ketchikan is also a stop on the Alaska Marine Highway, making it convenient for travelers to simply drive or walk off the state ferry and spend a couple of days exploring local bays and fjords before boarding another ferry.

An equally popular destination for Southeast saltwater paddlers is **Glacier Bay National Park and Preserve.** The hub for this region is Juneau, where kayakers can hop a plane or ferry to the small community of Gustavus, located next to the park.

SOUTH CENTRAL **Prince William Sound,** with its miles of bays, islands, forests, and glaciers, is a big draw for sea kayakers. Popular ports include Whittier, Cordova, and Valdez. Of the three, Whittier and Valdez are on the state highway system, making them most accessible (Whittier is a one-hour drive south from Anchorage). Guides catering to ocean paddlers are found in all three ports.

Two Kenai Peninsula venues also lure sea kayakers. About a two-hour drive south of Anchorage, at the terminus of the Seward Highway, **Resurrection Bay** serves up awesome scenery and marine wildlife. Homer, perched over **Kachemak Bay,** at the terminus of the Sterling Highway (a five-hour drive south of Anchorage), is also an excellent spot.

SPORTFISHING

Alaska's biggest hobby in the warmer months is sportfishing; the *Anchorage Daily News* even has a special section with articles, inside tips, and videos online for those seeking the perfect catch (⊕ *www.adn.com/outdoors/fishing*). Six species of Pacific salmon (king, silver, sockeye, pink, steelhead—most people don't know steelhead was taxonomically promoted from trout to salmon a few years back—and chum) spawn in Alaska's innumerable rivers and creeks, alongside rainbow trout, cutthroat trout, arctic char, sheefish, Dolly Varden char, arctic grayling, northern pike, and lake trout, among other freshwater species. Salmon are also caught in saltwater, along with halibut, lingcod, and many varieties of rockfish (locally called snapper or sea bass).

> ### THE STROKES
>
> Anyone who doesn't mind getting a little wet and has an average degree of fitness can be a sea kayaker. The basic stroke is performed in a circular motion with a double-bladed paddle: you pull one blade through the water while pushing forward with the other through the air. Most people pick it up with a minimal amount of instruction.

Even though the world-record king salmon, weighing 97¼ pounds, was caught in the Kenai River, and many halibut exceeding 300 pounds are caught annually, some anglers will tell you that bigger isn't necessarily better. Sockeyes, salmon averaging 6 to 8 pounds, are considered by many to be the best tasting and best fighting of any fish, and most locals won't bother to eat a halibut that weighs over 30 pounds or so. And though the sail-finned arctic grayling commonly weighs a pound or less, its willingness to rise for dry flies makes it a favorite among fly fishermen.

■TIP➜ Sportfishing regulations vary widely from area to area. Licenses are required for both fresh- and saltwater fishing. To learn more about regulations, contact the **Alaska Department of Fish and Game** (☏ *907/465–4180 sportfishing seasons and regulations, 907/465–2376 licenses ⊕ www. adfg.state.ak.us*). To purchase a fishing license online, visit the State of Alaska Web site (⊕ *www.admin.adfg.state.ak.us/license*).

TOP REGIONS AND EXPERIENCES

Roadside fishing for salmon, trout, char, pike, and grayling is best in **South Central** and **Interior Alaska.** In fact, Alaska's best-known salmon stream, the **Kenai River,** parallels the Sterling Highway. But in most of the state, prime fishing waters can be reached only by boat or by air. Not surprisingly, hundreds of fishing charters and dozens of sportfishing lodges operate statewide, attracting anglers from around the world. **Southwest Alaska,** in particular, is known for its fine salmon, trout, and char fishing; many of its best spots are remote and expensive to reach, but fishing opportunities here are unparalleled.

SOUTHEAST This huge coastal region is renowned for its outstanding sportfishing for salmon, rockfish, and halibut. Charters operate out of all main ports, and the action is frequently so good that catching your limit is almost a given. Splendid scenery is guaranteed—even when shrouded in misty rains, which are common. Streams offer fine angling for steelhead, cutthroat, rainbow, and Dolly Varden trout. The waters of **Prince of Wales Island** are especially popular among steelhead, salmon, and trout anglers, with the Karta and Thorne rivers among the favorites.

SOUTH CENTRAL AND THE INTERIOR Alaska lives up to its reputation for angling excellence in South Central. From the hub of Anchorage, the Seward and Sterling highways provide access to the world-famous spots on the Kenai Peninsula. Anglers

Fishing excursions can also double as wildlife-viewing bonanzas.

seeking rainbow trout, Dolly Varden, and salmon will do no better than the **Kenai River.** This dream stream—tinted an opaque emerald from glacial runoff—serves up fine fishing from ice-out in spring to freeze-up in late fall. The **Russian River,** a tributary that joins the upper Kenai River near Cooper Landing, is a dashing mountain stream that runs crystal-clear—except when it's chock-full of red salmon from mid-June through August. Other fine Kenai Peninsula streams include **Quartz Creek, Deep Creek,** and **Anchor River.** When the salmon are running, most of the better-known streams can be shoulder-to-shoulder fishermen, angling for a spot to stand as much as for fish. Luckily, for those looking to avoid combat fishing, a few miles' drive can make a considerable difference in conditions. Many excellent trout and salmon guides are based in the Kenai River towns of Cooper Landing, Sterling, Soldotna, and Kenai, and their experience can get you to places you'd never find on your own.

Saltwater angling out of the ports of **Whittier, Seward,** and **Homer** is legendary for king, pink, and silver salmon as well as huge halibut. Charter operators are in all three ports, offering half-day and full-day fishing trips.

North of Anchorage, the Parks Highway courses through the **Mat-Su Valley,** a scenic piece of wilderness backed by Mt. McKinley and veined with fine streams. Six species of salmon, rainbow trout, Dolly Varden, grayling, northern pike, and lake trout are among the draws here. Some of the most popular Parks Highway streams include **Willow, Sheep, Montana,** and **Clear** creeks. Fishing guides based in Wasilla, Houston, Willow, and Talkeetna offer riverboat and fly-in trips. Remember that salmon runs are seasonal. Kings run late May through mid-July, and silvers run from mid-July through August. And don't forget the lakes; scores of them brim with trout, landlocked salmon, arctic char, and grayling. Cast for them from canoes or float tubes on calm summer afternoons.

ENJOYING ALASKA'S WILDLIFE

Here are a couple of facts you might learn, watching Alaska's animals: up close, bears smell like very large, very wet dogs. And try to avoid ever having a whale breathe on you; that smell makes bears seem like roses.

Yes, it is possible to get that close to Alaska's wildlife—actually, it gets that close to you. But even if it remains in the distance, the possibilities—

ALASKA'S TOP FISH & THEIR SOURCES

SPECIES	COMMON NAME	WHERE FOUND
Arctic Char (F, S)	Char	SC, SW, NW, I, A
Arctic Grayling (F)	Grayling	SE, SC, SW, NW, I, A
Brook Trout (F)	Brookie	SE
Burbot (F)	Lingcod	SC, I, SW, NW, A
Chinook Salmon (F, S)	King	SE, SC, SW, I
Chum Salmon (F, S)	Dog	SE, SC, SW, NW, I
Coho Salmon (F, S)	Silver	SE, SC, SW, NW, I
Cutthroat Trout (F, S)	Cutt	SE, SC
Dolly Varden (F, S)	Dolly	SE, SC, SW, NW, I, A
Lake Trout (F)	Laker	SC, SW, NW, I, A
Northern Pike (F)	Northern	SC, SW, NW, I
Pacific Halibut (S)	'But	SE, SC, SW, NW
Pink Salmon (F, S)	Humpy	SE, SC, SW, NW
Rainbow Trout (F)	'Bow	SE, SC, SW, I
Sheefish (F)	Shee, Inconnu	NW, I
Smelt (F, S)	Hooligan	SE, SC, SW, NW, I, A
Sockeye Salmon (F, S)	Red	SE, SC, SW, NW, I
Steelhead (F, S)	Steelie	SE, SC, SW

(F) = Freshwater, (S) = Saltwater, (F, S) = Freshwater and Saltwater, A = Arctic,
SC = South Central, I = Interior, SE = Southeast, NW = Northwest, SW = Southwest

5

brown bears, black bears, moose with racks of antlers six feet across, the slow rise of a humpback whale breaching into full sunshine—are Alaska's truest, greatest glory.

And it isn't just the big things. Alaska's 375 million acres support more than 800 species of mammals, birds, and fish. The 105 different mammals range from fin whales the size of yachts to shrews the size of bottle caps (Alaska's shrews are the smallest of North America's land mammals, weighing 1/10 ounce). Up in the skies are 485 species of birds, ranging from hummingbirds to bald eagles, which are so common it's hard not to see them. Migrant birds come to Alaska from every continent (clearly understanding the best place to take a vacation) to take advantage of Alaska's rich breeding and rearing grounds in its wetlands, rivers, shores, and tundra. Toss in the vagrants from Sedge warblers to Russian fish eagles that might show,it's possible to hit the 500-species mark on the life list, just in the borders of Alaska.

And if that weren't enough, sharing the waters with whales, seals, sea lions, dolphins, and porpoises are at least 430 different kinds of fish—including six kinds of salmon. In late summer Alaska's rivers can seem so thick with spawning salmon that it looks like you could walk across them without getting wet—although the bears who come down to feed might object.

Both black and brown (grizzly) bears live in virtually every part of the state, and it's not all that unusual for them to walk into towns from time to time. Across the state, bear-viewing areas let visitors get up close (but not too close) and personal with the wonder that is a bear. Watching a grizzly swat a salmon out of a stream and rip it open (with winter coming on, they'll eat only the fattiest parts of the fish, leaving the rest for eagles, ravens, crows, and more) is reason enough to come to Alaska.

But bears aren't the only big things running around Alaska's forests and plains. Anchorage has a moose problem, and almost anywhere in South Central and the Interior you might come across one of these beauties. Moose look slow and ungainly, but they can run close to 30 MPH and kick both forward and backward. Still, they're happiest standing in a pond eating grasses. It's not at all uncommon to see moose from almost any road in the state.

Caribou can be a little harder to find, even though the state has more than 100,000 of them. The massive Porcupine herd travels in the sub-arctic, moving across the Arctic National Wildlife Refuge and into Vuntut National Park in Canada. Denali National Park has a good-sized caribou population as well.

The coastal mountains of the Southeast and South Central harbor mountain goats, and the mountains of the South Central, Interior, and Arctic regions are home to white Dall sheep. Wolves and lynx, though more rarely seen, live in many parts of the Southeast, South Central, Interior, and Arctic regions; if you're lucky, a wolf may dash across the road in front of you, or a smaller mammal, such as a red fox or snowshoe hare, may watch you when you're rafting or even when you're traveling on wheels.

STRATEGIES FOR SPOTTING WILDLIFE

Know what you're looking for. Season and time of day are critical. Many animals are nocturnal and best viewed during twilight, which in summer in Alaska's northern regions can last all night. In winter, large creatures such as moose and caribou can be spotted from far away, as their dark bodies stand out against the snow. It is also possible to track animals after a fresh snowfall. You have only a few hours of sunlight each day during which you can look for wildlife in winter, and in northern Alaska there won't be any direct sunlight at all in winter months. But the simple truth is, animals will be where they want, when they want. It's not at all unusual for travelers to have ticked off every item of the Alaskan safari—moose, black bear, grizzly bear, caribou, wolf—without ever leaving the state's roads.

Be careful. Keep a good distance, especially with animals that can be dangerous. Whether you're on foot or in a vehicle, don't get too close. A pair of good binoculars or a spotting scope is well worth the expense and extra weight. Don't get too close to or even think about trying to touch wildlife (and, if you're traveling with pets, keep them leashed—dogs get very stupid when they smell bears, and that never goes anywhere good). **Move slowly,** stop often, look, and listen. The exception is when you see a bear; let the animal know you're there by making noise. Avoid startling an animal and risking a dangerous confrontation, especially with a mama bear with cubs or a cow moose with a calf. Moose injure far more people in Alaska than bears do.

Keep your hat on if you are in territory where arctic terns, gulls, or pomarine jaegers nest, often around open alpine or tundra lakes and tarns. These species are highly protective of their nests and young and are skillful dive-bombers. Occasionally, they connect with human heads, and the results can be painful.

Be prepared to wait; patience often pays off. And if you're an enthusiastic birder or animal watcher, **be prepared to hike over some rough terrain** to reach the best viewing vantage. **Respect and protect** the animal you're watching and its habitat—you, after all, are a visitor in its territory. Don't chase or harass the animals. The willful act of harassing an animal is punishable in Alaska by a $1,000 fine. This includes flushing birds from their nests and purposely frightening animals with loud noises. The basic rule is never get closer than a hundred yards to any animal. If they want to come up to you—not uncommon at many of the bear observatories, or on whale-watching trips—that's their business. But you are to keep your distance.

Don't disturb or surprise the animals, which also applies to birds' eggs, the young, the nests, and such habitats as beaver dams. It's best to let the animal discover your presence quietly, if at all, by keeping still or moving slowly (except when viewing bears or moose). If you accidentally disturb an animal, limit your viewing time and leave as quietly as possible. Never watch a single animal for longer than a half hour, at the very most. Even if they are ignoring you, your presence is still a cause of stress, and the animals need every bit of energy they have for getting through the upcoming winter. **Don't use a tape recorder or any device** to call a bird or to attract other animals if you're in bear country, as you might call a hungry bear. And **don't feed animals,** as any creature that comes to depend on humans for food almost always comes to a sorry end. Both state and federal laws prohibit the feeding of wild animals. For campers and hikers, it's a bad idea to smell like food anyway.

The **Alaska Marine Highway,** the route plied by Alaska's state ferries, passes through waters rich with fish, sea mammals, and birds. Throughout the Southeast, a ticket on the ferry almost always comes with sightings of whales, porpoises, and sea otters. Bald eagles are about as common as sparrows back home. Other great water expeditions for animal-watching include boat trips in **Kenai Fjords National Park,** and **Glacier Bay National Park and Preserve;** both are especially good places to spot humpback whales, puffins, seals, shorebirds, and perhaps a black or brown bear, as well as the occasional orca. **Denali National Park and Preserve** is known worldwide for its wildlife; you are likely to see grizzlies, moose, Dall sheep, caribou, foxes, golden eagles, and maybe even some of the park's rare wolves. The **Alaska Chilkat Bald Eagle Preserve** hosts the world's largest gathering of bald eagles each fall and winter. And just a few miles down the highway south of Anchorage, on the fringes of **Chugach State Park,** are well-marked spots where Dall sheep like to hang out on the land side of the road, and beluga whales swim by in the waters of the inlet.

TOP REGIONS AND EXPERIENCES

BEARS   You can't be absolutely sure you'll spot a grizzly bear in **Denali National Park and Preserve** (☎ 907/683–2294 ⊕ *www.nps.gov/dena*), but chances are better than 50–50, especially in the early morning, that you'll see grizzlies digging in the tundra or eating berries. Sometimes females even nurse their cubs within sight of the park road. Denali's grizzlies are Toklats, a subspecies that's much smaller and usually more cinnamon-colored than their more famous relatives in Kodiak and other parts of Alaska. For the most recent sightings, talk with the staff at the visitor center near the park entrance when you arrive, and the bus drivers who will take you into the park are seriously skilled at spotting wildlife.

Katmai National Park (☎ 907/246–3305 ⊕ *www.nps.gov/katm*), on the Alaska Peninsula, has an abundance of bears, on average more than one brown bear per square mile, among the highest densities of any region in North America. In July, when the salmon are running up Brooks River, bears concentrate around Brooks River falls, resulting in a great view of these animals as they fish, and the spectacle of hundreds of salmon leaping the falls. Many operators in Homer and Anchorage run day-trips to the edges of Katmai, where you can fly in, watch bears for a few hours, and return to your hotel in time for dinner. It's not cheap, but it *is* unforgettable.

Kodiak National Wildlife Refuge (☎ 907/487–2600 or 888/408–3514 ⊕ *kodiak.fws.gov*), on Kodiak Island, is an excellent place to see brown bears, particularly along salmon-spawning streams.

The **McNeil River State Game Sanctuary,** on the Alaska Peninsula, hosts the world's largest gathering of brown bears. As many as 70 have been counted at one time at McNeil Falls, affording unsurpassed photographic opportunities. Peak season, when the local salmon are running, is early June through mid-August. Much-sought-after reservations are by a lottery conducted in March by the **Alaska Department of Fish and Game** (☎ 907/267–2253 ⊕ *www.wc.adfg.state.ak.us*).

At **Pack Creek,** on Admiralty Island in Southeast, brown bears fish for spawning salmon—pink, chum, and silver. To get here, you can fly by air charter or take a boat from Juneau. If you time your visit to coincide with the salmon runs in July and August, you will almost surely see bald eagles. Permits are required to visit during the peak bear-viewing period; contact **Admiralty Island National Monument** (☎ 907/586–8800 ⊕ *www.fs.fed.us/r10/tongass/districts/admiralty/packcreek/index.shtml*).

In Southeast, near the town of Wrangell, **Anan Bear Reserve** is at one of the few streams where black and brown bears share the waters, fishing at the same time (although the black bears usually hide when the browns show up). More than a quarter-million salmon run Anan in July and August, making it a feast for as many as a hundred bears that fish the stream at different times during high season. Book trips through

Wilderness Safety Tips

PREPARATION

You need to be in good physical shape to venture into the backcountry. Avoid traveling alone. If your outdoor experience is limited, travel with a guide. Bring a tide book when traveling by boat along the coast. If backpacking, know in advance whether you'll have to cross large glacial rivers.

MAPS

Use maps (preferably 1 inch : 1 mi maps published by the U.S. Geological Survey) and a compass at the minimum. Other options for emergency use are electronic locator devices, global positioning systems, and handheld aviation radios. Know how to use all your navigation equipment before you leave home.

WEATHER

Always be prepared for storms and wintry conditions and for unexpected delays. One of the most common phrases used by Alaska's pilots is "weather permitting." Never "push" the weather; every year people die in aviation, boating, and overland accidents trying get home despite dangerously stormy conditions.

STAY FOUND

Leave a detailed itinerary and list of emergency contacts with family and park rangers. Be specific about your destination and return date. Do not expect to be able to make a cellphone call for help—most of Alaska's wilderness is cell-free. If you do get lost, those you've notified in town will know when and where to start looking. It's also smart to carry a whistle.

HYPOTHERMIA

Hypothermia, the lowering of the body's core temperature, is an everpresent threat in Alaska's wilderness.

Wear layers of warm clothing when the weather is cool and/or wet; this includes a good wind- and waterproof parka or shell, warm head- and hand gear, and waterproof or water-resistant boots. Heed the advice of locals who will tell you, "cotton kills." It does nothing to move moisture away from your skin, and can speed the onset of hypothermia. Any time you're in the wilderness, eat regularly to maintain energy, and stay hydrated.

Early symptoms of hypothermia are shivering, accelerated heartbeat, and goose bumps; this may be followed by clumsiness, slurred speech, disorientation, and unconsciousness. In the extreme, hypothermia can result in death. If you notice any of these symptoms in yourself or your group, stop, add layers of clothing, light a fire or camp stove, and warm up; a cup of tea or any hot fluid also helps. Avoid alcohol, which speeds hypothermia and impairs judgment. If your clothes are wet, change immediately. Be sure to put on a warm hat (most of the body's heat is lost through the head) and gloves. If there are only two of you, stay together: a person with hypothermia should never be left alone. Keep an eye on your traveling companions; frequently people won't recognize the symptoms in themselves until it's too late.

WATER SAFETY

Alaska's waters often carry Giardia (locally called "beaver fever"), a parasite that can cause diarrhea and sap your strength. In the backcountry, boil water, treat it with iodine tablets, or use a filter (available at camping stores).

5

permitted outfitters in Wrangell. ⊕ *www.fs.fed.us/r10/ro/naturewatch/ southeast/anan/anan.htm*.

The **Silver Salmon Creek Lodge** (☏ *888/872–5666* ⊕ *www.silversalmon creek.com*) conducts a bear-viewing program along the shores of western Cook Inlet, near Lake Clark National Park, with lodging, meals, and guide services for both bear-viewing and sportfishing. There are also photo tours.

BIRDS If you come on your own, try the following sure and easily accessed bets for bird spotting. In **Anchorage,** walk around Potter Marsh or Westchester Lagoon or along the Tony Knowles Coastal Trail and keep your eye out for shorebirds, waterfowl, and the occasional bald eagle. Songbird enthusiasts are likely to see many species in town or neighboring Chugach State Park. The **Anchorage Audubon Society** (☏ *907/338–2473* ⊕ *www.anchorageaudubon.org*) has a bird-report recording and offers various trips, such as the Owl Prowl and Hawk Watch.

In **Juneau,** visit the Mendenhall Wetlands State Game Refuge, next to the airport, for ducks, geese, and swans. There are trails and interpretive signs. In **Fairbanks,** head for the Creamer's Field Migratory Waterfowl Refuge on College Road. In summer the field is so full of sandhill cranes, ducks, and geese that almost no one can take off or land without bumping into other birds. The woods behind the main field are full of songbirds and smaller species.

Homer, at the end of the Kenai Peninsula, has an annual shorebird festival (⊕ *www.homeralaska.org/events/kachemakBayShorebirdFestival/ index.htm*) and maintains one of the state's most active birding groups. Those interested in feathers should check the Birder's Guide to Kachemak Bay Web site (⊕ *www.birdinghomeralaska.org*) to get an idea of what Kenai offers. On the eastern side of the peninsula, boat trips into Resurrection Bay are a great chance to see puffins, as well as murres, murrelets, and more.

As for the national bird, more bald eagles gather on the Chilkat River, near **Haines** in Southeast Alaska, each November and December than live in the continental United States. In summer, rafting on almost any Alaska river brings the near certainty of sighting nesting shorebirds, arctic terns, and merganser mothers trailed by chicks. Approximately 200 species of birds have been sighted on the **Pribilof Islands,** but you will almost certainly need to be part of a guided tour to get there. The Aleutians—particularly Dutch Harbor—are also spots for adding to the life list, since many vagrants appear.

The folks at **Alaska Birding & Wildlife** (☏ *877/424–5637* ⊕ *www. alaskabirding.com*) can take you to St. Paul Island in the Pribilofs to see the huge range of birds and get to know local Aleut culture and customs.

Alaska Discovery (☏ *800/831–7526* ⊕ *www.mtsobek.com*) offers trips to Pack Creek, including a floatplane trip, sea kayaking, and bear viewing.

With **Mariah Tours** (☏ *877/777–2805* ⊕ *www.alaskaheritagetours.com*), the Kenai Fjords National Park comes to life on tailor-made birding and

Continued on page 325

KEEPERS OF THE DEEP:
A LOOK AT ALASKA'S WHALES

(top) A breaching humpback (left) An Orca whale

It's unforgettable: a massive, barnacle-encrusted humpback breaches skyward from the placid waters of an Alaskan inlet, shattering the silence with a thundering display of grace, power, and beauty. Welcome to Alaska's coastline.

Alaska's cold, nutrient-rich waters offer a bounty of marine life that's matched by few regions on earth. Eight species of whales frequent the state's near-shore waters, some migrating thousands of miles each year to partake of Alaska's marine buffet. The state's most famous cetaceans (the scientific classification of marine mammals that includes whales, dolphins, and porpoises) are the humpback whale, the gray whale, and the Orca (a.k.a. the killer whale).

BEST REGIONS TO VIEW WHALES

Whales can be viewed throughout the world; after all, they are migratory animals. But thanks to its pristine environment, diversity of cetacean species, and jaw-dropping beauty, Alaska is perhaps the planet's best whale-watching locale.

From April through October, humpbacks visit many of Alaska's coastal regions, including the Bering Sea, the Aleutian Islands, and Prince William Sound. The **Inside Passage**, though, is the best place to see them: it's home to a migratory population of up to 600 humpbacks. Good bets for whale-viewing include taking a trip on the **Alaska Marine Highway**, spending time in **Glacier Bay National Park**, or taking a day cruise out of any of Southeast's main towns. While most humpbacks return to

Mutually curious!

Hawaiian waters in the winter, some spend the whole year in Southeast Alaska.

Gray whales favor the coastal waters of the Pacific, which terminate in the Bering Sea. Their healthy population—some studies estimate that 30,000 gray whales populate the west coast of North America—make

---

THE HUMPBACK: Musical, Breaching Giant

Humpbacks' flukes allow them to breach so effectively that they can propel two-thirds of their massive bodies out of the water.

Known for their spectacular breaching and unique whale songs, humpbacks are captivating. Most spend their winters in the balmy waters off the Hawaiian Islands, where females, or sows, give birth. Come springtime, humpbacks set off on a 3,000-mile swim to their Alaskan feeding grounds.

Southeast Alaska is home to one of the world's only groups of bubble-net feeding humpbacks. Bubble-netting is a cooperative hunting technique in which one humpback circles below a school of baitfish while exhaling a "net" of bubbles, causing the fish to gather. Other humpbacks then feed at will from the deliciously dense group of fish.

The Song of the Humpback

All whale species communicate sonically, but the humpback is the most musical. During mating season, males emit haunting, songlike calls that can last for up to 30 minutes at a time. Most scientists attribute the songs to flirtatious, territorial, or competitive behaviors.

QUICK FACTS:

Scientific name:
Megaptera novaeangliae

Length: Up to 50 ft.

Weight: Up to 90,000 pounds (45 tons)

Coloring: Dark blue to black, with barnacles and knobby, lighter-colored flippers

Life span: 30 to 40 years

Reproduction: One calf every 2 to 3 years; calves are generally 12 feet long at birth, weighing up to 2,000 pounds (1 ton)

them relatively easy to spot in the spring and early summer months, especially around **Sitka** and **Kodiak Island** and south of the **Kenai Peninsula**, where numerous whale-watching cruises depart from Seward into **Resurrection Bay.**

Orcas populate nearly all of Alaska's coastal regions. They're most commonly viewed in the **Inside Passage** and **Prince William Sound**, where they reside year-round. A jaunt on the Alaska Marine Highway is one option, but so is a kayaking or day-cruising trip out of **Whittier** to Prince William Sound.

When embarking on a whale-watching excursion, don't forget rain gear, a camera, and binoculars!

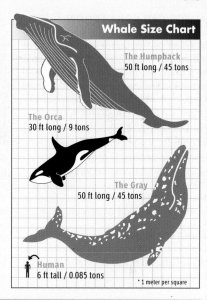

Whale Size Chart

The Humpback
50 ft long / 45 tons

The Orca
30 ft long / 9 tons

The Gray
50 ft long / 45 tons

Human
6 ft tall / 0.085 tons

* 1 meter per square

5

IN FOCUS KEEPERS OF THE DEEP

THE GRAY WHALE: Migrating Leviathan

Though the average lifespan of a gray whale is 50 years, one individual was reported to reach 77 years of age—a real old-timer.

While frequenting Alaska during the long days of summer, gray whales tend to stay close to the coastline. They endure the longest migration of any mammal on earth—some travel 14,000 mi each way between Alaska's Bering Sea and their mating grounds in sunny Baja California.

Gray whales are bottom-feeders that stir up sediment on sea floor, then use their baleen—a comb-like collection of long, stiff hairs inside their mouths—to filter out sediment and trap small crustaceans and tube worms.

Their predilection for near-shore regions, coupled with their easygoing demeanor—some "friendly" gray whales have even been known to approach small tour boats—cements their spot on the short list of Alaska's favorite cetacean celebrities. (Gray whales aren't always in such amicable spirits: whalers dubbed mother gray whales "devilfish" for the fierce manner in which they protected their young.)

QUICK FACTS:

Scientific name: *Eschrichtius robustus*

Length: Up to 50 ft.

Weight: Up to 90,000 pounds (45 tons)

Coloring: Gray and white, usually splotched with lighter growths and barnacles

Life span: 50 years

Reproduction: One calf every 2 years; calves are generally 15 feet long at birth, weighing up to 1,500 pounds (3/4 ton)

AN AGE-OLD CONNECTION

Nearly every major native group in Alaska has relied on whales for some portion of its diet. The Inupiaq and Yup'ik counted on whales for blubber, oil, meat, and intestines to survive. Aleuts used whale bones to build their semisubterranean homes. Even the Tlingit, for whom food was perennially abundant, considered a beached whale a bounty.

Subsistence whaling lives on in Alaska: although gray-whale hunting was banned in 1996, the Eskimo Whaling Commission permits the state's native populations to harvest 50 bowhead whales every year.

Other Alaskan whale species:
Bowhead, northern right, minke, fin, and beluga whales also inhabit Alaskan waters.

barnacles

BARNACLES These ragged squatters of the sea live on several species of whales, including humpbacks and gray whales. They're conspicuously absent from smaller marine mammals, such as Orcas, dolphins, and porpoises. The reason? Speed. Scientists theorize that barnacles are only able to colonize the slowest-swimming cetacean species, leaving the faster swimmers free from their unwanted drag.

THE ORCA: Conspicuous, Curious Cetacean

Why the name killer whale? Perhaps for this animal's skilled and fearsome hunting techniques, which are sometimes used on other, often larger, cetaceans.

Perhaps the most recognizable of all the region's marine mammals, Orcas (also called killer whales) are playful, inquisitive, and intelligent whales that reside in Alaskan waters year-round. Orcas travel in multigenerational family groups known as pods, which practice cooperative hunting techniques.

Orcas are smaller than grays and humpbacks, and their 17-month gestation period is the longest of any cetacean. They are identified by their white-and-black markings, as well as by the knifelike shape of their dorsal fins, which, in the case of mature males, can reach 6 feet in height.

Pods generally adhere to one of three common classifications: **residents,** which occupy inshore waters and feed primarily on fish; **transients,** which occupy larger ranges and hunt sea lions, squid, sharks, fish, and whales; and **offshores,** about which little is known.

QUICK FACTS:

Scientific name: *Orcinus orca*

Length: Up to 30 ft.

Weight: Up to 18,000 pounds (9 tons)

Coloring: Smooth, shiny black skin with white eye patches and chin and white belly markings

Life span: 30 to 50 years

Reproduction: One calf every 3 to 5 years; calves are generally 6 feet long at birth, weighing up to 400 pounds (0.2 ton)

photography boat tours, as well as on daily tours that take in the best of the park: whale-watching, glacier-viewing, and more. This is one of the best-run trips in the Fjords, and is part of Alaska Heritage Tours, which also runs a beautiful lodge in Seward.

The Web site of the **University of Alaska Fairbanks** (⊕ *www.uaf.edu/ museum/bird/products/checklist.pdf*) has a checklist of Alaska's 485 bird species.

★ The owners of **Wilderness Birding Adventures** (☎ *907/694–7442* ⊕ *www. wildernessbirding.com*) are both experienced river runners and expert birders. Among their trips is a rafting, hiking, and birding expedition through one of the world's last great wilderness areas, the Arctic National Wildlife Refuge.

CARIBOU The migrations of caribou across Alaska's Arctic regions are wonderful to watch, but they are not always easy to time because of annual variations in weather and routes that the herds follow. The U.S. Fish and Wildlife Service and Alaska Department of Fish and Game will have the best guess as to where you should be and when, but the migrations move through very remote parts of the state that are difficult and expensive to get to. For caribou on a budget, Denali National Park and Preserve is the place to go.

MARINE ANIMALS Keep in mind that many of the tours listed as whale-watching—for example, anything in Kenai Fjords—are also likely to turn up porpoises, dolphins, seals, sea lions, and more. But if you're after something specific, here are a few places to consider.

⇨ *Skip ahead to the next section in this chapter for in-depth information about whale-watching cruises. For more on whales, go to Keepers of the Deep: A Look at Alaska's Whales.*

At **Round Island**, outside Dillingham in the Southwest, bull walruses by the thousands haul out in summer. Part of the Walrus Islands State Game Sanctuary, Round Island can be visited by permit only. For details, contact the **Alaska Department of Fish and Game** (☎ *907/842–2334* ⊕ *www.wildlife.alaska.gov/index.cfm?adfg=refuge.rnd_is*). Access is by floatplane or, more commonly, by boat. Expect rain, winds, and the possibility of being weathered in. Rubber boots are essential, as are a four-season tent, high-quality rain gear, and plenty of food.

It's easier, but expensive (more than $1,000 for travel and tour), to visit the remote **Pribilof Islands**, where about 80% of the world's northern fur seals and 200 species of birds can be seen, but you may also encounter fog and Bering Sea storms. Tours to the Pribilofs leave from Anchorage. Contact the **Alaska Maritime National Wildlife Refuge** (☎ *907/235–6546* ⊕ *alaskamaritime.fws.gov*) for information about wildlife viewing.

WHALE-WATCHING CRUISES

Whales are hard to describe to someone who hasn't seen them. "An animal 45 feet long and weighing 30 tons" is pretty simple to understand, but seeing that translated into a living, breathing creature, moving almost silently through the water, is another matter entirely. Seeing whales is, plain and simple, an encounter with grace.

Alaska has many species of whale—fin, beluga, minke, gray—but the humpbacks are the main show. Humpbacks—named after the distinctive bend in their back that looks almost like a right angle as they swim—are common throughout Southeast, South Central, and into the Aleutians.

And there is no experience quite like watching humpbacks. They breach—their entire bodies coming out of the water in what seems like impossible slow motion; they bubble-net feed, when a group of them will get together, swim around a school of fish, exhaling the whole time, and then swim up, mouths wide open, through the center, to get as many fish as possible. And sometimes they just swim along, every now and then diving down deeper, the wide arc of their tails the last thing you'll see.

Whales migrate along much of Alaska's coast from March through September: from the Southeast region's Inside Passage to South Central's Prince William Sound, Kodiak Archipelago, and Kenai Fjords National Park, and then north through the Bering, Chukchi, and Beaufort seas in Arctic waters. Whale-watching is not the average spectator sport. It's more like a seagoing game of hide-and-seek. Whales are unpredictable, so be prepared to wait patiently, scanning the water for signs. Sometimes the whales can seem elusive; other times they might rub up against the boat. Also unpredictable are the weather and sea conditions. Bring along a jacket or fleece outerwear and rain gear to keep from getting wet and chilled, and consider using Dramamine or scopolamine patches if you're prone to seasickness.

Since you'll be traveling via cruise ship already, your chances of seeing whales at some point are likely great. However, taking a separate whale-watching excursion through your ship or on your own might be for you if whale-watching is one of the main reasons for travelling here, and if the ship you're on is large. Most cruises travel in or through waters that attract several species, although some focus on a particular type of whale. ■ TIP➔ Ask when the best time to take a specific trip is; the whale-sighting record is likely better during some months than others. You have to weigh the pros and cons of traveling on small versus "large" (but still likely much smaller than your cruise ship) boats. A trip with 15 people will be quite different from one with 150. Larger boats can handle stormy seas much better than smaller boats and offer much better indoor accommodations when the weather turns nasty. Smaller boats will appeal to those who want to steer clear of crowds and those who like to feel closer to the surrounding seascape. More flexible itineraries are another benefit of small boats.

INDEX

PHOTO CREDITS

NOTES

NOTES

NOTES

NOTES

NOTES